easy entertaining
darina allen

WITHDRAW

darina allen

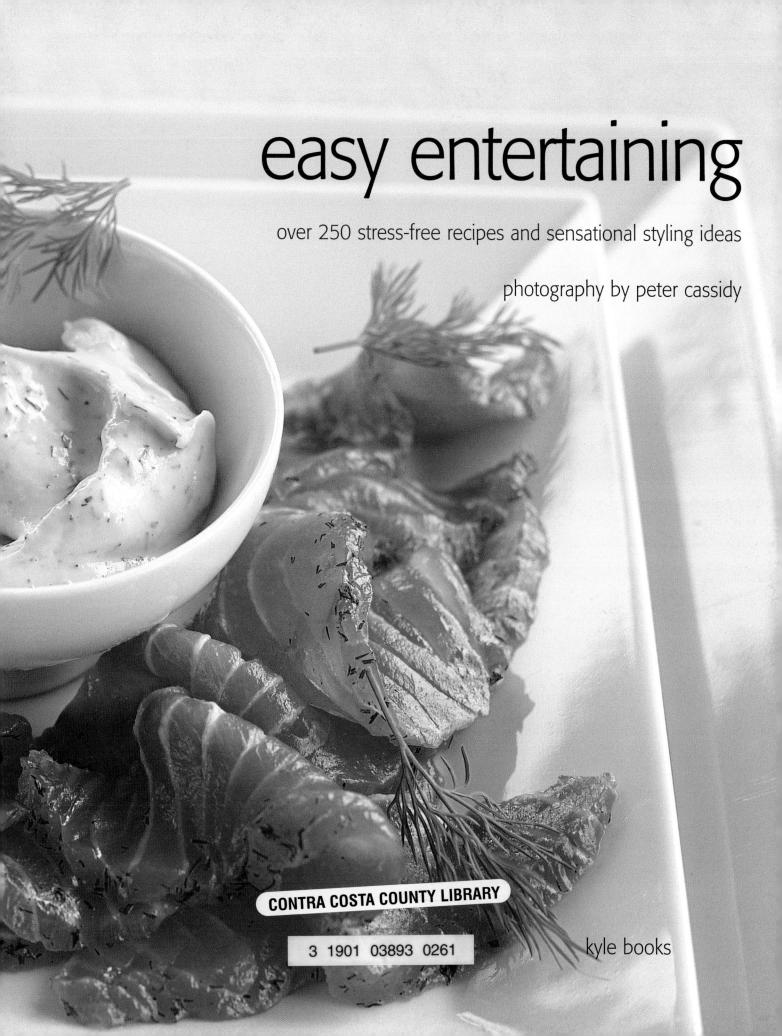

easy entertaining

over 250 stress-free recipes and sensational styling ideas

photography by peter cassidy

kyle books

For Rosalie, who has helped to make my life EASY for the past 21 years.

No book is ever the work of just one person but this book has had input from more than most. Twenty years later I still can't type or use a word processor so every syllable is written in long hand and then has to be typed by a team of long-suffering keen-sighted people who struggle to read my scrawl. So for this I am deeply grateful to Truus Boelhouwer, Robin Bryant, Patrick Treacy, Adrienne Forbes, Sharon Hogan, and Dorothee Krien.

Emer Fitzgerald and her team at the Ballymaloe Cookery School helped to test recipes in the midst of a hectic work schedule.

I would also like to acknowledge my friend, Mary Dowey, whose idea it originally was to do an easy entertaining book. We planned to do this book together but I was so slow and hopeless about meeting my deadlines that Mary understandably had to honor her other engagements.

A huge thank you also to the many guest chefs and friends who have shared their recipes with me over the years which has greatly enhanced our repertoire.

Tom Doorley's inspired wine and food pairings have added a wonderful extra dimension to this book—thank you Tom.

I especially asked for Peter Cassidy to do the photos for this book and his gorgeous images have not disappointed.

Thank you also to Linda Tubby for her wonderful food styling, Charis White and Roisin Nield for their stylish props, and Geoff Hayes for his inspired design.

My editor Muna Reyal is some kind of saint, a brilliant strategist who manages to extract manuscripts from busy authors by a myriad of clever subtle devices. Thank you Muna for your brilliant editing, and most of all, for your patience.

My agent Jacqueline Korn and my publisher Kyle Cathie have been unflinching in their encouragement and support as have my truly wonderful family and staff—for this I am ever grateful.

This edition published in 2006 by Kyle Books, an imprint of Kyle Cathie Limited.
general.enquiries@kyle-cathie.com   www.kylecathie.com

Distributed by National Book Network
4501 Forbes Blvd., Suite 200, Lanham, MD 20706
Phone: (301) 459 3366   Fax: (301) 429 5746

ISBN-13: 978 1 90492 036 6   ISBN-10: 1 90492 036 5

Text © 2005 by Darina Allen, except for pp.10–11 and wine notes © Tom Doorley
Photography © 2005 by Peter Cassidy

Senior editor **Muna Reyal**
Designer **Geoff Hayes**
Photographer **Peter Cassidy**
Food stylist **Linda Tubby**
Props stylists **Charis White** (pp. 24–27, 32, 36, 46–49, 52, 60, 102–105, 107, 190–195, 260–263, 274, 291) and **Roisin Nield**
Copyeditor **Marion Moisy**
Editorial assistant **Cecilia Desmond**
Production **Sha Huxtable and Alice Holloway**
US edition Americanized by Delora Jones

Darina Allen is hereby identified as the author of this work in accordance with Section 77 of the Copyright, Designs and Patents Act 1988.

The Library of Congress Cataloguing-in-Publication Data is available on file

Printed in Singapore

contents

introduction

Entertaining is one of the easiest and most pleasurable things in the world. All it means is that you and some friends or family gather together, share some food, and generally enjoy yourselves. But somehow the word seems to invoke more fear than fun. So what I want to do is to show you that that pleasure can come without pain.

The first place to start is with the thought that you are probably more experienced in it than you think you are. If you have friends around for a coffee or a quick drink with a bite to eat, then you are entertaining. Inviting friends to lunch, having an impromptu barbecue on a sunny day, or an evening in watching films are all types of entertaining and they don't differ in principle from the more ceremonious social events such as parties or formal dinners.

So whatever the occasion, the *raison d'etre* is to get everyone together and have lots of fun and good conversation. And whether it is a multi-course meal or, in the words of the legendary Elizabeth David "an omelette and a glass of wine," you need only follow a few key guidelines.

● Firstly, keep it simple, keep it simple, keep it simple.

● Secondly, and I can't stress this enough, be prepared. Make shopping lists, plan the preparation and cooking time, and check that you have enough cutlery and glasses.

● And finally, relax. This is not just so that you can have fun—it's crucial that the hosts are not tense or stressed, as the tension will easily transmit itself to the guests.

So this is my mantra, and while I readily admit that I don't always practice what I preach, I have written this book because I firmly believe that with a little forethought, some good food, and a few special touches, anybody can entertain effortlessly and memorably.

choosing food

Because there are as many ways to entertain as there are ways to eat, I have divided this book into styles of party, so that you can choose the food to match your event.

The first chapter is devoted to brunch, because I think this is a brilliant way to entertain a large group of people, particularly families—and it takes care of breakfast and lunch. The chapter on Finger Food will be helpful for cocktail parties or buffet meals, but you should also take a look in Appetizers for more ideas. The recipes in Soups and Salads complement the Appetizers chapter, but they also make great light meals by themselves.

Then come lots of Quick and Easy Meals, perfect for when you are short of time or need to prepare something with little notice. The recipes in Prepare-ahead Suppers, on the other hand, will help when you have more time to plan but less on the day. Then there are chapters on Slow Food and Festive Meals for special occasions, as well as some fantastic recipes for Formal Suppers, not to forget yummy ideas for a children's party. Portable Food will be useful for barbecues and picnics; this and Foraging are two of my favorite ways to entertain, so you'll find many of my best-loved recipes here. Another chapter is devoted to irresistible Sweet Things, to finish a meal and perfect for a tea party: and there are many lovely options to encourage you to serve A Cheese Course.

Tom Doorley, an inspired wine writer and a good friend, has suggested delicious wines to serve with some tempting menus for each chapter, and I've also included a Drinks chapter with a few suggestions for aperitifs.

I hope you will find all you need in these chapters, but please remember that nothing is carved in stone. You can enjoy experimenting, but the most important thing of all is to pick up the phone, invite people over, and have fun.

feel free to mix and match

When you flick through this book you will discover that it includes an eclectic mix of recipes—everything from Irish stew to Moroccan Tagine, from sushi to fajitas, so pick and choose what appeals to you. Having said that, don't throw caution to the wind altogether, be careful not to be too random or your guests will end up with serious indigestion! In general, stick to a particular style, be it Indian, Mexican, Moroccan, or European. Fajitas followed by Irish stew followed by Tira Misu would clash quite strongly, but you would be safe to mix Thai and Japanese or French with Italian. Or be a bit more adventurous and plan an Indian appetizer and main course, to be followed by Western dessert.

achieving the "wow" factor!

Taste at the beginning, taste in the middle, and taste at the end—that's the secret of really good food. That and starting off with the finest-quality ingredients. I personally seek out as much organic and free-range

produce as I can get my hands on. Freshness is of paramount importance. Locally produced is also a priority with me—it makes no kind of sense to use jet-lagged food which has traveled halfway across the world, arriving on our shelves days, weeks, or in some cases months after it was produced or harvested and therefore containing less flavor and fewer nutrients. When you begin with mass-produced, denatured food you need to be a magician to get it to taste good—and that's when life gets complicated and you have to add twiddles, bows, and M & Ms on top to compensate for the fact that the flavor wasn't there in the first place.

So why not make your job easier and spend a little time locating really good, fresh, naturally produced, local food in season? Then it's easy to achieve the "wow" factor. When you start off with a piece of spanking fresh fish or freshly picked vegetables you have only to cook them simply and they will taste sublime.

how many people?

If you are not planning to use outside help (which is the premise behind this book), six to eight people is the optimum number for a dinner party. Once the numbers go to 12 or 14, it is almost essential to have help with the serving and clearing, otherwise the food will be cold and service too slow. You don't have to hire professional help—a local teenager may be thrilled to earn some pocket money and learn some extra skills, or you can rope in your own children. The size of your dining room and table will also dictate the numbers you invite. Don't ask more people than you can seat easily. Alternatively, a buffet or fork supper will remove the problems of service as well as reducing the amount of crockery and cutlery needed.

Choose a menu that can be served easily whatever the circumstances. A mezze or selection of bruschetta can double as finger food and appetizer, with maybe a little pâté or salmon rillettes. Soup can be served in coffee mugs or cappuccino cups, so—with a bit of strategic washing up between courses—the cups could be used for appetizer and then for coffee.

cooking for large numbers

Recipes like Tagine of Lamb (see p.112) and Spiced Chicken and Red Peppers (p.113) are easy to serve for big numbers with rice, couscous or orzo followed by a big green salad. To finish, it's nice to serve a selection of locally-made cheese and a dessert buffet. Choose desserts that complement each other so that your guests can try them all .

Lots of other recipes in this book are suitable for big numbers, just multiply up the quantities (but note the guidelines under **How much food?** on p.9).

cutting corners

Here are a few tips to make entertaining easier.

● Numero uno is to keep your fridge and cupboards well stocked, so that you always have something in reserve in case someone turns up unexpectedly. A number of my recipes can be made using such ingredients; others need only the addition of a few fresh vegetables or herbs. See p.299 for my suggestions on standby ingredients.

● My big breakthrough came on the day I started to freeze soups, stews, curries, and various vegetables, and bean stews in small containers. Previously I froze everything in large quantities, but spontaneous entertaining is out of the question if you are faced with a solid iceberg to defrost—stress free it is not. If you know you have a selection of little containers of this and that, it doesn't matter who breezes into your kitchen—you won't be fazed. Simply fill the sink with hot water and pop the sealed containers in to defrost for 8–10 minutes. The contents will slip out of the containers and you can then pop them into a saucepan on a gentle heat—Thai green or red curry, Italian beef stew, spicy chicken with almonds, mild madras curry are all favorites. By the time the rice is cooked, the stew will be bubbling. Scatter with freshly chopped herbs, and presto, instant meal.

● Put your most frequently used recipes in a ring binder—divide into appetizers, mains, desserts, and make notes as necessary. In the same folder keep a list of useful contacts—where to get ice or rent glasses as well as carpet cleaners!

● Write quantities for mayonnaise, soda bread, French dressing, frittata, chocolate mousse on the inside of cupboards for when you want to whizz up something in a hurry.

● An herb garden or at least a window box brimming with fresh herbs is a must for easy entertaining. Snip and scatter freshly chopped herbs to transform basic grub instantly into posh nosh.

● Keep a few hens in your garden. Friends will be so enchanted by collecting the eggs that they will be happy to have boiled eggs and sticks of toast for supper.

● A visit to your local Farmers' Market can yield a variety of delicious foods. You don't have to cook everything from scratch—smoked fish, cured meat, pâtés, locally-made cheese, crusty bread, homemade cakes, and tarts are perfect for easy entertaining.

● If you are entertaining with someone, agree responsibilities ahead of time—who is getting the fish or buying the flowers. On the day, decide who will take coats and offer drinks. Knowing who is supposed to clear the table avoids glaring across the table or kicking under it! If you are entertaining single-handedly, ask a friend if they would mind arriving early to take charge of pouring wine. It is also ok to ask for help in chopping garnishes or bringing plates through.

planning a menu

A good menu is about well-chosen food, but part of that is based on careful thought and preparation.

First decide what sort of event you are hosting. Hopefully the chapters of this book will simplify the process, but here is a summary of the most likely scenarios:

● A formal affair, where you have plenty of time to plan and plenty to prepare.
● A meal where some or all can be prepared in advance, good for after-work dinners.
● An impromptu meal that you can whizz up in minutes using ingredients on hand.
● Slow-cooked dishes—these cook long and slowly (in your absence if necessary) to produce a robust, comforting, and trouble-free meal.
● A meal specific to an occasion, be it Christmas Day, a children's party, or picnic.

Next you need to consider whether you want to serve three courses, all on individual plates, or begin with, say, a mezze where people can help themselves. At the end of many of the chapters I have put together a selection of menu plans in the hope that they will form a good base for you.

With each recipe, I have also given guideline timings for preparation (P) and cooking (C), as well as time required for chilling or marinating. These should help you plan your schedule, but bear in mind that it is difficult to prepare all three courses at the same time. However, if one dish needs to go into the oven for an hour, this will give space to prepare another.

If you have small children, it can be a huge effort to get the house ship-shape. If you've got a long list of "must haves," why not entertain two nights in a row—the flowers will last, the house is looking good, and you can prepare twice the amount of food ahead of time and serve the same menu.

menu considerations

The words "menu planning" strike terror in many people. It sounds complicated and mysterious, but in lots of ways it is just common sense. Here are a few guiding principles to save you from potential pitfalls. In general, it is easiest to decide on a main course first, then choose an appetizer and dessert to complement it.

The Occasion

This is an important factor when choosing a menu and laying the table. For anniversaries or romantic evenings, you might incorporate a heart-shaped tart or a dish to share. Foreign guests will be intrigued if you cook them a traditional meal. It can also be fun to plan a meal on a particular color scheme—for example, the colors of your favorite sports team at a victory dinner.

Pleasing Your Guests

For formal or large dinners you may have to do a little subtle research to avoid dishes that your guests are unable to eat, whether for religious, moral, or health reasons. As our understanding of food allergies and intolerances grows, it's good to have a repertoire of gluten-free or dairy-free dishes ready to go. Keep a few cartons of beans or vegetable stews in your freezer for emergencies. If you are sending formal invites or emails, ask guests to let you know if they have any dietary restrictions when they R.S.V.P.

Similarly, it is not usually wise to present anything too challenging or unusual to first-time guests. The golden rule is to be considerate: if you are unsure of your guests' tastes, or think that they might be unfamiliar with certain foods, avoid those foods. Many people find variety meats off-putting; others don't appreciate very hot curries and other spicy foods. Corn on the cob might present problems for older people and some of my favorite dishes like squid, sea urchins, shrimp in the shell, and artichokes can all be a challenge to tackle.

Pot-luck Parties

New York hostesses have become so frustrated by trying to cater for their guests' specific requirements that they now ask each guest to bring a dish—brilliant idea! This works particularly well for buffet meals, barbecues, or participation parties (see pp.102–107). Among close friends, you could ask each guest to bring a separate course, which not only makes entertaining easy, but also, depending upon how tightly it is planned, can produce a completely unexpected menu.

Season and Weather

People need and can digest much heartier meals in winter than in summer, so keep rich soups, stews, and cassoulets for chilly days. Cold soups and sunny Mediterranean salads will delight in the summer. I let the seasons choose the ingredients and use locally produced food. In addition to having a better flavor, it helps to narrow the choice and it is usually cheaper than imported food.

Don't forget about simple, everyday foods that are seldom found on restaurant menus, but which lots of people love, e.g., rhubarb, carrigeen moss, rutabaga, and turnips.

Budget

Given a bit of imagination it is perfectly possible to prepare exciting meals on a small budget. There is no need to splash out on all three courses—lots of posh nosh can be created with ingredients you have on hand. Cheaper cuts of meat make succulent braises and slow-cooked dishes. Egg-based dishes such as frittatas are inexpensive and amazingly versatile.

Consider the Number of Dishes

The number of dishes you choose will depend on various factors. The first is the skill of the cook: don't be over-ambitious and don't cook anything new and complicated for guests. Make sure the menu is realistic. I know it sounds very "back to school" but it's a terrific idea to jot down an order of work. Think through the menu to see whether you need any special equipment. If you are entertaining single-handed or with very little help, plan the menu so that you can prepare as much as possible in advance, particularly any complex dishes. The number of dishes you need will also depend upon how you plan to serve the meal, whether formal or informal plate service or a buffet.

Balance

This is often the most perplexing element of planning a menu. Try to provide a contrast of ingredients, texture, and flavor. This sounds obvious but it's surprisingly easy to unwittingly repeat foods in your menu, particularly common ingredients such as eggs. On the face of it, this menu below looks balanced enough:
Cheese Souffle
French Onion Tart
Tomato and Mint Salad, Green Salad
Crème Caramel with Caramel Shards
but each guest will be consuming about five eggs in the course of the meal!

The idea of an appetizer is to whet the appetite with something light and delicious. It sets the mood for the rest of the meal, but it ought not to be so substantial as to fill people up before the main course.

It's also easier on the cook and more practical to use different cooking methods, so, for example, avoid grilling everything. Another easy pitfall is serving sauces which seem to be different but have the same basis, such as an appetizer containing mayonnaise followed by fish and tartar sauce.

Serve a green salad with lunch and dinner. It has magical properties and makes people feel less full—leaving room for dessert! If the first two courses are rich or creamy, consider a lighter dessert, perhaps something citrus-based to wake things up.

Color and Contrast

In addition to the "balance" factors mentioned above, don't overlook the question of color. Try not to repeat colors unless you are deliberately working to a color scheme. In particular, guard against an all-white plate, e.g., Haddock with Dijon Mustard Sauce, Buttered Cucumber, and Scallion Champ—sounds delicious but it will look bland. A little Tomato Fondue or at least a sprig of chervil, fennel, or watercress would make all the difference.

It also makes for more interesting eating if there is a juxtaposition of texture in the food—crisp with creamy, e.g., buttered crumbs on fish pie, or croûtons with creamy soup.

Contrasts of flavor are also important, e.g., mild with spicy—Cucumber raita with curry. Sharp with bland—Blue cheese sauce on pasta or salad. Sweet with sour—Carrot and apple cruditées with sweet-sour dressing.

Seasonings

Try not to get carried away with chiles and spices unless you feel like a hot fest! You may want to confine strong flavoring or spices to one dish in the menu unless you are cooking a specifically Indian or Chinese meal, in which case make sure not to repeat the same spices in each course.

Garnishing

We "eat" with our eyes, so it is crucial to present a meal well. An herb garden will mean edible herb flowers, but remember the maxim—flavor is of paramount importance and any garnish should be relevant and edible.

cheat

As I said earlier, don't feel you have to cook everything from scratch. A plate of good charcuterie with olives with piquillo pepper and country bread followed by a tart or chocolate confection, bought from your local deli, will look and taste great!

how much food?

All the recipes indicate the number of servings. For large numbers, just multiply up. If you're doing four or five times a recipe, for soup for example, you can usually cut down on the butter or olive oil for sweating the vegetables; otherwise calculate carefully, stick to the recipe, and don't forget to taste.

timing

Planning is everything and lists are crucial. Think about when you need to buy your ingredients, particularly the ones that need to be fresh. Fish, herbs, and flowers should always be bought on the day if possible.

Little Touches

● Look out for tiny containers for butter, salt, and pepper—little tea-light holders, tiny ramekins, even teeny terracotta flower pots. Oyster shells also look great.

● Serve tiny tapenade or pesto bread strips or square sandwiches as an accompaniment with each bowl of soup.

● Offer a wedge of nougat, halva, or fudge with an espresso at the end of the meal.

9

choosing wine and drinks

by Tom Doorley

"Red with carpet, white with lino," was the wine advice given in Katherine Whitehorn's *Cooking in a Bedsit*, and it remains sound. A great deal of nonsense is spouted about matching food and wine, while most normal human beings tend to resort to the time-honored formula of using whatever happens to be in the house.

That is not to say that our enjoyment of food and of wine will not be enhanced by using a bit of logic. It stands to reason, for example, that if you serve a dish with a wine from the same region, it has a good chance of being a pleasant combination; in Europe, regional food and regional wines have grown up together over centuries.

It also stands to reason that rich food will respond well to a crisp, acidic wine, just as mackerel, say, goes with gooseberries. And big, hearty, spicy stews and casseroles taste good with wines that are...well, big and hearty and spicy. Nobody is going to win the Nobel prize for pointing this out.

Having said that, in most cases, matching food and wine is a rather hit and miss affair, or, at best a question of getting it as right as possible. Marriages made in heaven are few, but there are some worth bearing in mind. Sauvignon blanc wines work brilliantly with very ripe goat cheese, and sweet dessert wines are superb with Roquefort. The Thai flavors of ginger, galangal, and cilantro seem to be even more vibrant with a dry Australian Riesling.

Roast lamb or beef, especially if cooked rare, takes the edge off red Bordeaux and Burgundy, while pork needs something crispier and juicier like a good Beaujolais or a Chianti. Roast chicken and turkey often work better with a ripe chardonnay (either from the New World or from the more expensive bits of Burgundy) than with many reds.

And while I might prefer salmon with a Chablis or a dry Alsace wine, there's no doubt that some light red wines go well with it (especially Chinon and others from the Loire); so let's just forget all the old "rules."

For white wines that are crisp enough to cut richness—say in oysters—it's probably best to look to Europe because New World examples tend to be riper; that's part of their appeal. A good Muscadet or Chablis will go down well but so will any dry, zesty white wine from Verdicchio to Albarinho.

what of the new world?

New World whites, especially the new wave ones made from Viognier, Verdelho, Marsanne, and other off-beat grape varieties are often bigger on fruit than acidity but while they might not cut rich dishes, they seem very much at home with fusion and Pacific Rim cooking.

New World reds, generally speaking, are rich, robust, and packed with fruit, a style that suits them to equally robust food. In addition to the more familiar cabernets and Syrahs, Malbec from Argentina, Carmanere from Chile, and Pinotage from South Africa all seem expressly made for a steaming stew. Many of them not only go well with rare roast beef but can also tackle a spoonful of horseradish head-on.

organic wines

While organic meat, vegetables, and fruit are becoming almost commonplace, the wine world is lagging behind. In fact, organic wines are much the same as conventionally produced wines: there are some good ones and some bad ones. The world's largest producer of (very good) organic wines is Bonterra of Medocino, California, which is owned by Fetzer. Bonterra wines are widely available. If you are concerned about sustainability, concentrate on small producers.

champagne vs. sparkling

Non-vintage champagne, especially the famous brands, is generally over-priced (although Darina has a fondness for Veuve Clicquot). Sparkling wines, often made in exactly the same way, can offer more for less. Prosecco, from Italy, is possibly the best value of all—and if you add a dash of peach juice, you have a Bellini! Cava from Spain can be great too, but if you want something made from the same grapes as champagne, try Australia, New Zealand, or California. Names to watch include Green Point, Lindauer, Deutz, Jansz, and Mumm. Champagne from individual growers is often half the price of the grandes marques and most traditional wine merchants will stock at least one.

but does it have to be wine?

We are gradually waking up to the fact that beer and alcoholic cider can be worthy accompaniments to food. Steak and kidney pie could not have a better companion than traditional English beer or other dark ales, and these go well with roast meats, too. Lager beers—not the bland, big brand ones—can tackle hot spices but will also work with seafood, especially crab. Guinness, the doyen of stouts, is as good with oysters as the best Chablis. And it's a great deal cheaper. A fresh, citrus-scented beer like Hoegaarden is excellent with simply cooked fish.

Alcoholic cider has a well-known affinity with pork, both in the pot and on the table, but its refreshing sharpness (especially if it's a dry version) can often have an almost wine-like quality. Again, seafood is a good companion, especially if the dish features cilantro, lime, or ginger.

calculating quantities

Choosing wine, beer, or cider for entertaining will always be an art rather than a science. The same could be said of judging how much you are going to need, but it is a little simpler.

It is always best to err on the side of generosity, so although you don't want to assume that all your guests are dipsomaniacs, have too much rather than just enough. As a rough guide, allow a half bottle of wine per head for the main course (a bottle equates to five glasses) and a single glass of whatever is being served with the appetizer. Dessert wines are a different matter; some guests simply don't like them and those who do usually have a small glass and perhaps a modest top-up. This means that a bottle will serve five or six people comfortably. However, one of the secrets of stress-free entertaining is to calculate as outlined above but to buy more as a precaution.

what about budget?

As to budget, this will depend on the occasion, but broadly speaking I think we can divide entertaining with food and wine into three categories. For the informal supper around the kitchen table, there is no need to go above $10 a bottle, although a dessert wine might merit a dollar or two extra. The rather more formal lunch or dinner, provided you don't feel the need to show off, weighs in at around $18 to $20 a bottle, while the very special occasion will merit as much as you want to spend. However, as a guide, I would suggest pushing the boat out to around $40 to $50. Although wine does indeed often taste better the more you spend (simply because the winemaker is getting a bigger cut), there are limits. Above this kind of price, wine can simply get silly.

standby wines

If you want to be prepared for all eventualities, consider putting together a mini-cellar. You will need a bottle of fizz

(champagne, if you wish, but a good sparkler such as Lindauer or Green Point will do fine). Then a couple of dependable whites which will cover most of the bases: Macon, Chablis, or a dry Riesling perhaps. Then a couple (or more) of red: a really good Côtes du Rhone is suitably flexible. Or you may want a contrast of styles: some fleshy young Beaujolais cru such as Brouilly or Moulin-à-Vent on the one hand, and maybe a Chilean Carmanere Reserva or Oz Grenache/Syrah blend on the other. Bear in mind, incidentally, that a good, fruity, dry rosé will go with just about anything. Cover the dessert wine possibilities with a Late Harvest Riesling or Semillon and a bottle of good tawny port that won't need decanting (Taylor or Fonseca 20 Year Old are superb and will keep).

bear in mind

Entertaining with wine is pretty simple. Take some care in choosing and don't talk much about it. Wine, for most people, is great to drink but mind-numbingly boring to discuss. If someone asks about a wine, they want to know where to buy it, not the details of the vineyard.

There are some things that most wine cannot take: horseradish, cranberries, excessive sweetness, and the vindaloo end of the curry scale are all beyond the ability of most wines to cope.

Remember to chill the white in good time, but don't over-chill; you want to be able to taste the wine. Room temperature is fine for red.

Decanting is only necessary for aged wines with sediment, but it can make other wines taste better simply because it aerates them. Odd as it may seem, this applies to whites as well as reds, so if you have both the time and the decanters, it may be worth doing.

Pulling corks in advance is a good idea from the point of view of convenience but, contrary to common belief, it won't make the wine taste any different.

Provide lots of bottled water (sparkling and still) and have something, such as an elderflower drink or homemade lemonade, for the drivers and teetotallers. Almost everyone enjoys food but wine is a different matter.

notes on wine

Wine is a very personal thing so do please bear in mind that the suggestions I make in this book are just that: suggestions. I think they are worth trying, and they certainly work for me. If you cannot easily get hold of the suggested wine, try something in a similar style. Wine merchants can appear a little daunting but most of them will respond very well to a request for advice and some of them really do enjoy discussing menus. You may end up with something quite different from what you were looking for but a good wine merchant will want you to come back and their suggestions may well be very sensible. Needless to say, if you have time for a dry run (not, perhaps, the most appropriate phrase in the circumstances) there is no substitute for trying out wine and food matches before springing them on your guests.

tom's top tips

● Don't be a perfectionist. There's no need to strive for the perfect match. Good food and good wine is what it's all about.

● Be bountiful. Err on the side of generosity. Buy too much wine rather than too little. It will keep.

● Get in the pink. A good dry rosé makes a perfect aperitif and goes well with virtually anything savory.

creating atmosphere

Once you have chosen the food, it's time to think about creating an atmosphere. This is another mysterious subject, but actually is nothing more than a few simple touches. The individual chapters of this book have suggestions specific to each occasion, but here are some general tips.

ornamentation

Make an effort to dress up a room or table. Look around for inspiration—lots of tea-lights surrounded by pretty shells or pebbles collected from the beach are adorable. Take inspiration from the seasons—dried autumn leaves, nuts, berries, and fruit are easy to arrange expressively; Spanish chestnuts in their shells look wonderfully dramatic. Spices such as star anise and cinnamon also smell delicious in the winter months. Use the natural beauty of artichokes, pomegranates (whole or halved), and figs. For a party, hang twists of ribbon along a picture rail or around window frames.

If you collect knick-knacks from trips abroad, you could use them to recreate a holiday dinner—tin figures from Mexico, pottery chickens from Guatemala, pewter and bamboo from Southeast Asia.

Flowers

To me, flowers are the simplest way to add color, scent, and glamour to an evening. There is so much to choose from, and the right flower can instantly change the mood of a room. Be creative about what you use as vases—try empty jam jars, glass bottles, or recycled cans—and where you place them. Tie posies with raffia for a table centerpiece or use single stems as place settings.

In summer, a bowl of gorgeous fragrant old roses in full bloom is irresistible but petals floating in a bowl or scattered on the table also create a sensuous and slightly decadent effect. Float a few flower heads or blossoms in a low dish; hellebores are particularly lovely and last much longer this way.

Check out florists' websites for inspiration. For formal arrangements, your local florist should be able to create something spectacular for your table.

Lighting

Flickery candles create a magical atmosphere in a way that no other lighting can. A tall candelabra on a long table looks wonderfully elegant but even cheap and cheerful tea-lights arranged in a line, circle, or diamond draw gasps of admiration and you can get funky holders in different shapes and formations. Resist the temptation to have scented candles—most are overpoweringly fragrant.

Look out for candleholders—tin, enamel, pottery, glass, or edible containers such as pumpkins or squashes. Outdoor lighting along an avenue or path creates excitement and anticipation—at its simplest just tea-lights in jam jars or thick candles in brown paper bags with some sand in the bottom look great. Fairy lanterns slung from trees are pretty in any season. Make your own by piercing holes in tin cans to form a pattern.

Remember never to leave candles unattended either indoors or outdoors.

Strings of Christmas lights now come in a range of shapes and colors—flowers, chiles, stars, bulbs—and you can drape them around tables, chairs, walls, trees, and plants.

If your indoor lighting is a bit harsh, try bringing in lamps from your bedroom or simply replacing the bulb with a softer light.

Table Cloths

One of the funkiest table settings I've ever seen consisted of a "cloth" of newspapers with flowers arranged in a line of fruit cans down the center. Lots of colored glasses, tin plates, and mismatched cutlery gave a cool look.

Plain white or colored sheets can solve the problem of an oversized table, while overlays of pretty materials, scarves, shawls, sari fabric, or sarongs make attractive "camouflage."

place settings

These can be as formal or subversive as you like. Fabric, paper, glass, and slate all make excellent table mats and if they are home-made, you can scribble or elegantly calligraph each guest's name or a witty, or rude, message. Some friends of mine made round place mats from cardboard and drew wonderful cartoon pics of each of the guests, which have now become collector's items. Bake cupcakes or shortbread cookies and ice the guest's name on each. And simplest of all, tie a luggage label with the guest's name on it around wine glasses.

crockery and cutlery

In this day and age you certainly don't need to have matching crockery and cutlery to have fun. Hunt out antiques, or pieces from around the world. Pile them into a funky container or terracotta pot so that your

getting the party going

when the guests arrive

What if, despite your best intentions, the guests arrive before you are fully prepared or even dressed? If you are running late it's a smart idea to get dressed and lay out some glasses, drinks, and nibbles in plenty of time. Then, when the doorbell rings, take a slow, deep breath, welcome your guests into the kitchen, pour some drinks (don't forget yourself), and drink a toast to the yummy dinner which is underway!

Spend money on the aperitifs. Something bubbly always gets the evening going—Champagne, sparkling wine, or Prosecco are divine. For a really special occasion, why not splash out and hire a portable bar, complete with bartenders, to create a range of cocktails especially for you? Or send your partner to a cocktail class the weekend before.

Passing around some nibbles helps guests to relax and feel comfortable. If the nibbles are reasonably substantial, they can double up as a first course.

If you need to introduce your guests to each other, give them a snippet of interesting info to get the conversation started: *"This is my accountant friend Ben who climbed Carrantwohill last week, meet Clarissa who is crazy about chickens, but is an airline pilot in real life…"*

Keep an eye out for people looking a little lonely and reintroduce as required. Asking them to top up glasses or pass around nibbles for you is a good way to get them talking to people.

Provide a room as a cloakroom and make sure it has a mirror. If children arrive unexpectedly, don't bat an eyelid. Dig out magic markers or crayons and paper. Better still, involve them—ask them to help you to pass around nibbles. If all else fails, pop them in front of the TV with a film or cartoon.

music

Try to find some time before the event to choose a stack of CDs so that you don't spend all evening hunting for the next one. If you have an MP3 player, set up some playlists for the occasion.

party games

Parties are the perfect opportunity to play some old-fashioned games. Charades and spin the bottle are always fun and there are lots of traditional games like Clue and poker. But how about a few more physical games to burn off some dinner.

The Cereal Box Game

For this test of agility you will need a light cardboard box, preferably taller than it is wide—an old cereal box is perfect. The box is placed on the floor and guests must pick the box up with their teeth, with the following limitations:

1 They must not touch the ground with any part of their body other than the soles of their feet.

2 They must not touch the box with any part of their body other than their mouth.
3 If they knock the box over, they're out!

Once all the guests have made their attempt, a strip is torn off the box—the depth of the strip depends upon how challenging the previous round was. The field is whittled down to the most elastic and persevering of your guests!

a theater supper

Some opera-buff friends invite us occasionally to what they call a "Theater Supper." It goes like this.

Guests are requested to arrive at 6:30 P.M., not before and certainly not after! Everyone dresses in black tie, theater hats, etc. We have an aperitif before curtain up, then we repair to the living room where we watch the first act of some wonderful opera on our hosts' large-screen TV, seated in comfortable sofas and armchairs. At the interval we go to the dining room for our first course. Another act, another course, and so on, four courses and coffee. The finale is at 11:30 P.M.—a fun way to entertain music-loving friends and a formula that could easily be adapted to show a film, play, or sporting event.

finishing touches

Make sure you have the number of a local, licensed cab firm at hand.

If a guest becomes tiresome, be polite but firm. Draw him or her away from the rest of the party to avoid drawing attention. A walk outside always helps to calm people down.

If you need to wrap up the party, the most subtle way is to stop filling people's glasses. Other more blatant tactics include turning off the music, turning up the lighting or simply asking if anyone wants to help with the dishes. Failing all else, yawn and pretend to fall asleep in an armchair.

a big brunch

Brunch is a great meal for family get-togethers and it combines two meals in one—the epitome of easy entertaining. It's also perfect for entertaining children—I feed them first and let them run off and play, before we adults settle down to our coffee and newspapers. The recipes in this chapter are a tempting mix of hearty dishes like kedgeree and eggs benedict as well as fruity compotes and sinful chocolate and orange muffins, and should see you through till dinner.

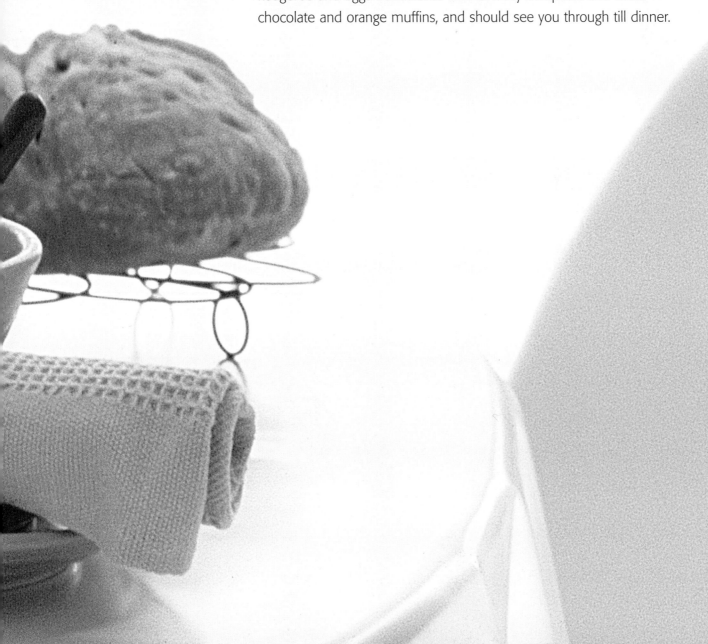

Crunchy Granola

MAKES 20 SERVINGS   (**P:** 5 mins./**C:** 30 mins.)

Preheat the oven to 350°F.

1 cup honey
1 cup sunflower oil
4 cups rolled oats
7 ounces barley flakes (about 1³/₄ cups)
7 ounces wheat flakes (about 1³/₄ cups)
4 ounces rye flakes (about 1 cup)
³/₄ cup raisins or golden raisins
1¹/₃ cups hazelnuts or cashews, split
   and roasted
¹/₄ cup sunflower seeds, toasted
¹/₃ cup dried apricots, chopped
¹/₄ cup dates, pitted and chopped (optional)
3 ounces wheat germ (about ²/₃ cup) and/or
millet flakes

In a pot, mix the honey and oil together and heat just enough to melt the honey. Mix the oats, barley, wheat, and rye flakes together and then add to the honey/oil mixture. Stir until the grains are coated. Spread thinly on two baking trays.

Bake for 20–30 minutes, turning frequently, until just golden and toasted, not roasted—ensure the edges don't burn. Let the mixture cool.

Mix in the raisins, nuts, seeds, apricots, dates (if using), and wheat germ and/or millet flakes.

The granola will keep for 1–2 weeks, stored in a screw-top jar or sealed plastic container.

Crunchy Granola Layered in a Glass

SERVES 2   (**P:** 5 mins.)

This is a cool way to serve breakfast in a glass—bursting with goodness and totally yummy.

1 cup homemade yogurt (see p.33)
2¹/₂ tablespoons honey
1 cup granola (see recipe above)
²/₃ cup blueberries, raspberries,
   strawberries, or even sliced banana
sprigs of mint (optional)

2 straight squat glasses, 5 inches tall

Mix the yogurt and honey together. Divide about half the granola between the two glasses, then top with half of the yogurt. Sprinkle the berries over the top, retaining a few for garnish, then add the remaining granola and finally add the rest of the yogurt.

Garnish with the reserved berries, and perhaps a sprig of mint. Provide long-handled spoons and tuck in.

Fruity Smoothies

Mix and match to your heart's content.

Banana and Yogurt Smoothie
SERVES 1–2   (**P:** 5 mins.)

1 ripe banana
1 cup plain yogurt (see p.33)
1 teaspoon honey (optional)

Peel the banana, chop coarsely, then blend with the other ingredients in a blender until smooth.

Pour into glasses and serve immediately.

Mango Smoothie
SERVES 1–2   (**P:** 5 mins.)

Follow the recipe above, but use mango instead of banana. You'll need about 5 ounces (1 cup or so). For a more Indian flavor, add ¹/₄ teaspoon freshly ground cardamom pods. Or add the seeds from 1 passionfruit for a marriage made in heaven.

Mango and Banana Smoothie
SERVES 2–3   (**P:** 10 mins.)

1¹/₂ cups freshly squeezed orange juice
1 chopped mango
1 banana
1 cup plain yogurt

Put all the ingredients in a blender and whizz until smooth. Taste and add a little honey if necessary.

Raspberry and Nectarine Smoothie

Another delicious combination—add ¹/₄-¹/₃ cup fresh raspberries and 1 ripe nectarine.

Glebe House Eggs Benedict

SERVES 4   (P: 5 mins./C: 20 mins.)

Jean Perry's cafe, Glebe House near Baltimore in West Cork, Ireland, is a gem. The spinach comes from the organic garden, the eggs from his happy, lazy hens.

8 cage-free, organic eggs
4 thick slices of homemade white yeast bread
  (see p.34)
butter

For the creamed spinach:
2 pounds fresh spinach
1–1 1/2 cups cream
salt and freshly ground pepper
freshly grated nutmeg

roux, optional (see p.139)

First make the creamed spinach. Put the leaves into a heavy pot on a very low heat and cover tightly. After a few minutes, stir and replace the lid. When the spinach is cooked, after about 5–8 minutes, strain off the copious amount of liquid that has been released and press the spinach between two plates until almost dry. Chop roughly and return it to the pot. Increase the heat, add the cream to the spinach, and bring to a boil, stir well, and thicken with a little roux if desired (see p.139); continue stirring until the spinach has absorbed most of the cream. Season with salt, pepper, and freshly grated nutmeg to taste. (If you wish, the creamed spinach may be cooked ahead of time and reheated.)

Next poach the eggs. Bring a small pan of water to a boil. Reduce the heat, swirl the water with a ladle, crack open an egg, and slip it gently into the center of the whirlpool. Cook for 3–4 minutes until the white is set and the yolk still soft and runny—the water should not boil again, but bubble very gently just below boiling point.

Toast and butter the bread and place on four warm plates. Spread the creamed spinach over the toast and top each portion with two poached eggs. Serve with freshly ground pepper and a few flakes of Maldon sea salt—divine.

Scrambled Eggs and Variations

SERVES 4   (P: 5 mins./C: 5 mins.)

Simple scrambled eggs are always an option for a stress-free brunch or supper, when one has unexpected guests, or when one feels like plain, comforting food. You can add a huge variety of ingredients—chopped and seasoned tomatoes, pieces of freshly cooked asparagus, and smoked bacon or prosciutto cooked in olive oil. Cold scrambled egg with chives makes the best egg sandwiches.

8 cage-free, organic eggs
1/3 cup creamy milk
salt and freshly ground pepper
generous pat of butter
For serving: warm buttered toast or fresh soda
  bread (see p.36)

Break the eggs into a bowl, add the milk, and season with salt and pepper. Whisk well until the whites and yolks are thoroughly mixed. Put a pat of butter into a cold saucepan, pour in the egg mixture, and cook over a low heat, stirring continuously with a flat-bottomed wooden spoon, until the egg has scrambled into soft, creamy curds. Serve immediately on warm plates, with lots of warm buttered toast or fresh soda bread.

Scrambled Eggs with Wild Smoked Salmon
A few seconds before the scrambled egg is fully cooked, add 4–6 tablespoons chopped smoked salmon, stir once or twice, and sprinkle with a little chopped parsley.

Scrambled Eggs with Tarragon and Basil or Chives
A few seconds before the scrambled egg is fully cooked, add 2 teaspoons chopped fresh tarragon and basil or 1–2 teaspoons chopped fresh chives and stir once or twice.

Scrambled Eggs with Chorizo
Cook 1/2 cup chopped-up chorizo in 1 tablespoon extra virgin olive oil until it begins to become crispy and the fat runs. Drain. A few seconds before the scrambled egg is fully cooked, add the chorizo and 2 teaspoons chopped fresh parsley and stir once or twice.

Indian Scrambled Eggs

SERVES 4   (P: 10 mins./C: 10 mins.)

2 tablespoons butter
1 small onion, finely chopped
1/2–1 teaspoon peeled and finely grated
  fresh ginger root
1 green chile, seeded and chopped
1/4 teaspoon ground turmeric
2 teaspoons ground cumin

2 very ripe tomatoes, chopped
8 large cage-free, organic eggs
salt and freshly ground black pepper
2 tablespoons chopped cilantro
For serving: paratha, nan bread, or toast

Melt the butter in a medium sauté or frying pan over medium heat. Add the onion and cook for 2 minutes or until soft. Add the

ginger, chile, turmeric, cumin, and tomatoes. Stir and cook for 3–4 minutes or until the tomatoes soften.

Meanwhile whisk the eggs and season. Add to the pan and stir gently until the eggs scramble, then add the cilantro. Serve immediately with paratha, nan bread, or toast.

Pinhead Oatmeal Porridge

SERVES 8   (P: OVERNIGHT/C: 10 mins.)

Pinhead oatmeal, or steel-cut oats, is quite simply a feast and a perfect G.I. (Glycemic Index) breakfast. We eat it with rich creamy organic milk from our Jersey cows, and some soft brown sugar.

2 cups steel-cut oats
1/2 teaspoon salt
For serving: light cream or rich milk, and soft
  brown sugar

The night before, soak the oatmeal in 1 cup of cold water in a large saucepan. On the day, bring 3 cups water to a boil, then add to the oatmeal. Cook over low heat, stirring continuously, until the water returns to a boil. Cover and simmer for 15–20 minutes, stirring occasionally. Stir in the salt. Cover again and set aside overnight; the oatmeal will absorb all the water.

The next morning, reheat over a low heat, adding a little more water if necessary to make it smooth. Serve with cream or rich milk, and some soft brown sugar.

Ballymaloe Strawberry Muesli

SERVES 8   (P: 20 mins.)

This is a huge favorite with all our family and friends—it's delicious, made in minutes, and will keep you going through the morning. We vary the fruit through the seasons—in the summer, strawberries, raspberries, loganberries, and blueberries, and grated Cox's Orange apples or Egremont Russet apples in the autumn.

8 heaping tablespoons rolled oats
2 cups fresh strawberries
2 teaspoons honey

For serving: light cream and soft brown sugar

Soak the oatmeal in 1/2 cup water for 10–15 minutes. Mash the strawberries roughly with a fork and mix with the oatmeal. Sweeten to taste with honey; a couple of teaspoons is usually enough but it depends upon how sweet the strawberries are.

Serve with light cream and some soft brown sugar.

Freshly Squeezed Juices

It goes without saying that fresh juices come from freshly squeezed fruit, not from freshly opened bottles or cans! Drink the juice soon after making it as the amount of vitamin C decreases after being exposed to air. If the juice has to be made ahead, pour it into dark bottles and fill right to the top.

Choose from:
orange juice
mandarin or tangerine juice
citrus orange juice: a mixture of grapefruit,
  orange, tangerine, blood orange, ugli fruit, etc.
apple* juice
ruby grapefruit juice
carrot* and orange juice
carrot,* apple, and ginger juice
pineapple** and orange juice
beet, orange, and ginger juice

Cut the citrus fruit around the equator and juice it by hand or in an electric citrus juicer. Many other types of fruit will need to be chopped and then juiced in an electric juice extractor.

Experiment with different combinations.

* Use an electric juice extractor
** Use a blender and strain

Breakfast Burrito with Tomato and Cilantro Salsa and Home Fries

MAKES 6   (**P:** 15 mins./**C:** 5 mins.)

6 large 10-inch diameter flour tortillas
2 cups shredded cheddar cheese
3–6 mushroom and chorizo omelets
  (see p.108 and add some mushrooms and
  chorizo that have been lightly cooked in
  extra virgin olive oil)
Frijoles de Olla, see below
1/2 cup Tomato and Cilantro Salsa
  (see p.294)
salt and freshly ground pepper
For serving: sour cream, tomato and cilantro
  salsa (see p.294), roughly chopped fresh
  cilantro, and home fries (see below)

Preheat the oven to 350°F. Wrap the tortillas in aluminum foil and warm them in the oven while you make the omelets. Alternatively, heat them for a few seconds on each side in a hot frying pan.

Just before you assemble the burrito, sprinkle a small handful of shredded cheese over the center of each warm tortilla. Top with half an omelet—if someone is really hungry, go for it and give them a whole omelet. Add a generous tablespoon of Mexican beans and some salsa. Season to taste. Fold over the sides and roll into a sausage-like wrap.

Transfer to a warm plate, spoon a generous portion of sour cream on top, scatter generously with tomato and cilantro salsa, and sprinkle with some fresh cilantro. Serve a portion of home fries on the side.

Frijoles de Olla (Mexican Beans)

SERVES 6–8   (**P:** OVERNIGHT/**C:** 2 HOURS)

Beans cooked simply like this and the Frijoles Refritos (Refried Beans) that are made from them are virtually a staple in Mexico, served at almost every meal including breakfast. They keep well and taste even better the next day or the day after.

2 1/3 cups dried black beans, red kidney beans, or pinto beans
1–2 1/2 tablespoons. good-quality lard or butter
1 small onion, chopped
1 teaspoon salt, approximately (may need
  more depending on the beans)

The day before, cover the beans generously with cold water and soak overnight. Alternatively if you are in a hurry, bring the beans to a boil for 3–4 minutes, then remove from the heat and set aside for 1 hour or so. Drain the beans, cover with fresh water, add the lard or butter, and onion. Bring to a boil and simmer gently for 1–2 hours depending upon the beans. About 30 minutes before the end of the cooking time, add the salt. Keep an eye on the beans while they cook, they should always be covered with liquid. When they are cooked, the beans should be completely soft and the liquid slightly thick and soupy.

Refried Beans

These can accompany many snacks including tacos and Mexican Scrambled Eggs. The texture can be soupy or a thickish purée.

1/4-1/3 cup best-quality pork lard or butter
1 medium onion, finely chopped
1 cup Mexican beans (see recipe to left)

Heat the lard or butter in a heavy frying pan and cook the onion until soft and brown. Increase the heat and add about a third of the beans and their broth to the pan and cook over a high heat, mashing them as you stir with a wooden spoon, or you could even use a potato masher. Gradually add the rest of the beans little by little until you have a soft or thick purée. Taste, and season with salt if necessary. Although this sounds as though it might be a lengthy business, it only takes about 5–6 minutes. Refried Beans keep well and may be reheated many times.

Home Fries

SERVES 6   (**P:** 5 mins./**C:** 10 mins.)

4 tablespoons sunflower oil
1 medium onion, coarsely chopped
1 1/2 pounds potatoes, chopped into 1/4-inch
  pieces–about 4-4 1/2 cups (no need to peel
  new potatoes)
salt and freshly ground pepper
1 teaspoon freshly roasted and ground cumin
  seeds (optional)

Heat the oil in a wide nonstick frying pan, add the onion, and cook over low heat until soft and slightly colored. Transfer to a plate.

Increase the heat, add the potatoes to the pan (add more oil if necessary to stop them sticking) and fry, turning frequently, for 10–15 minutes until cooked and slightly crispy.

Season well with salt, freshly ground pepper, and ground cumin seeds (if using). Return the onion to the pan and mix well through the potatoes.

Serve with the burrito or with other brunch dishes.

Breakfast Panini

SERVES 4   (**P**: 10 mins./**C**: 40 mins.)

1 frittata (see p.117) omelet or 4 fried eggs
4–8 strips of organic bacon
4–8 wide-capped mushrooms
salt and freshly ground pepper
4 very ripe tomatoes
pinch of sugar
4 panini rolls, focaccia, or ciabatta

Alternative fillings:
crispy bacon and British baked beans
sausage, mushrooms, and applesauce
kipper and scrambled egg or frittata
sharp cheddar cheese, smoky bacon, and
  sun-blush tomatoes
crispy bacon, blood sausage, and applesauce

First make the frittata or fry the eggs.

Cook the bacon until crisp and golden (I prefer to cook them in a frying pan rather than under the broiler), then transfer to a plate and keep warm.

Fry the mushrooms in the bacon fat and season with salt and freshly ground pepper.

Slice the tomatoes and season with salt, freshly ground pepper, and a pinch of sugar.

Preheat a sandwich toaster. Cut the panini in two, but do not slice all the way through—keep them attached at one side. Put a slice of frittata, omelet, or fried egg on the bottom of each one, top with a few slices of tomato, then some bacon, and finally 1–2 mushrooms. Close the panini and toast for 3–4 minutes.

Alternatively, warm the panini, then fill and eat immediately.

French Toast Strips with Citrus Marmalade Butter

SERVES 4–6   (**P:** 10 mins./**C:** 5 mins.)

4 cage-free, organic eggs
1 cup whole milk
2¹/₂ tablespoons sugar
1 teaspoon vanilla extract
12 thick slices of best-quality white yeast bread
clarified butter (see p.108), for frying
confectioners' sugar, for dusting

For the marmalade butter:
¹/₂ cup (1 stick) butter, slightly softened
3–4 tablespoons marmalade, chopped

First make the marmalade butter. Cream the butter and mix in the marmalade.

To make the French toast, whisk the eggs well in a bowl with the milk, sugar, and vanilla extract. Cut the bread into rectangular pieces and soak in batches in the eggy milk until well saturated but not falling apart.

Heat a large, preferably nonstick frying pan over medium heat and add a little clarified butter. Cook the soaked bread strips in batches until golden brown, about 1 minute per side. Serve immediately, or keep warm in the oven.

Serve the French toast on a warmed plate, sprinkled with a little sifted confectioners' sugar, and accompanied with the marmalade butter.

Other good things to serve with French toast
Summer berries and crème fraîche or sugared strawberries
Sliced bananas and chopped walnuts
Crispy bacon and maple syrup or honey

American Buttermilk Pancakes with Crispy Bacon and Maple Syrup

Makes 14 x 3-inch pancakes
          (**P:** 5 mins./**C:** 10 mins.)

These are incredibly addictive and it's so difficult to know when to stop!

1 cup buttermilk
1 cage-free, organic egg
1 tablespoon butter, melted
¹/₂ cup white flour
good pinch of salt
1 teaspoon baking soda
clarified butter (see p.108)

For serving: butter, 12–18 pieces of crispy bacon, maple syrup

Mix the buttermilk, egg, and butter in a large bowl until smooth and blended. Sift the flour, salt, and baking soda together, then stir into the buttermilk until the ingredients are just combined—don't worry about the lumps. Do not overmix or the pancakes will be heavy.

Heat a heavy iron or nonstick frying pan until medium hot. Grease with a little clarified butter. Spoon 2 generous tablespoons of batter onto the center of the pan and spread slightly with the back of the spoon to a circle about 3 inches across. Cook until bubbles rise and break on the top of the pancake (about a minute). Flip over gently and cook the other side until pale golden. Transfer to a plate, cover with a lint-free dish towel or aluminum foil and continue making pancakes in the same way until all the batter is used up.

Spread each pancake with butter. Serve a stack of three with crispy streaky bacon and maple syrup. Alternatively, serve the pancakes with loganberry jam, sour cream, and sausages.

Cornmeal Pancakes
Follow the above recipe, but substitute 2¹/₂ tablespoons cornmeal for 2¹/₂ tablespoons of the white flour.

a family brunch

I adore serving brunch. This is a leisurely meal for me and I like to have lots of food ready so we can munch our way through hot savory dishes, warm fresh bread, and flaky pastries, all the while catching up with the week's events.

Mid-morning I pop a couple of loaves of soda bread and a Spotted Dog into the Aga. I lay the table and fill little bowls with homemade jam, marmalade, and local honey. Then I arrange some strawberry muesli, toasted granola, maybe a breakfast fruit salad with a bowl of thick unctuous yogurt out on the old marble work top in the kitchen.

I like to present the muesli in a large glass bowl, showing off the lovely fruit colors and tempting those who might normally refuse such healthy fare—often I mash the strawberries into the oatmeal so it becomes lovely and juicy. Next I make lots of freshly squeezed juices, so when people arrive, they can begin the day with plenty of good vitamins.

Once everyone is tucking into muesli and juice, I start taking orders for a hot breakfast and cook bacon and eggs, American pancakes, waffles, or even a big pot of softly scrambled eggs.

Then some sweet pastries and muffins, with lots of bread warm from the oven, are always welcome and I like to have a selection of fresh seasonal fruit to finish off the meal.

relaxed and informal

Even a big brunch should be a relaxed affair, so there is no need for elaborate styling or table decoration. I like to set individual places, but you could simply lay out rows of plates and bowls for people to help themselves. Encourage your guests to raid your cupboards for sauces and condiments, but I do think that it is worth pouring the milk into a pretty pitcher and sculpting little pats of butter in a small saucer.

A posy of fresh flowers will bring some morning sunshine into the room. Pick some from your garden or pick up a bunch when you pop out for the papers, but do buy those that are in season rather than imported exotics.

For a bit of fun for the kids, comics and colorful papers make great napkin rings and can line a basket of bread or muffins.

Photographs are actually a fab way to decorate the table and will make a great talking point, especially if you have not seen each other for a while. Use photographic corners to hold them in place and then cover with protective plastic—which also wipes clean easily! With the advent of digital cameras and home printing, it is easy to create a personal touch for each guest—for example, if it is a birthday breakfast, make mini flags or placemats using photos of the guest of honor—they also make sweet keepsakes.

Mary Jo's Waffles

MAKES 6   (**P**: 10 mins./**C**: 25 mins.)

Mary Jo McMillan worked with us at the cooking school on several occasions—she was a passionate and perceptive cook. This is her recipe for waffles, which I enjoy much more than mine. They can be served in a variety of ways, both sweet and savory. You will need a waffle iron.

1 1/4 cups white flour
2 teaspoons sugar
pinch of salt
2 teaspoons baking powder
1 1/2 cups milk, slightly warmed
1/4 cup (1/2 stick) butter, melted
2 cage-free, organic eggs, separated
confectioners' sugar for dusting

Preheat a waffle iron. Sift all the dry ingredients into a deep bowl and make a well in the center.

Mix the warm milk and melted butter, then whisk in the egg yolks. Pour the milky mixture into the well in the flour and stir together to form a batter. With a clean beater, beat the egg whites until stiff peaks form and gently fold into the batter.

Pour a 1/3 cup ladle of batter onto the waffle iron and cook for 3–4 minutes until crisp and golden. Sprinkle with confectioners' sugar and serve hot.

Good things to serve with waffles
Crispy bacon and honey or maple syrup
Crispy bacon and slices of Gruyère or Emmental cheese
Crispy bacon with sliced banana
White peaches with raspberries

Waffles with Fresh Fruit and Berries
Ripe fruit and berries of all kinds are delicious with waffles: sliced peaches, nectarines, apricots and bananas, strawberries, raspberries, loganberries, boysenberries. Pile the fruit on top of hot waffles, or serve it on the side of the plate. A spoonful of softly whipped cream doesn't go amiss either!

Waffles with Bananas, Toffee Sauce, and Chopped Walnuts

SERVES 6   (**P**: 5 mins./**C**: 10 mins.)

2–3 bananas, sliced
6 waffles (see recipe above)
1 cup walnuts, coarsely chopped

For the toffee sauce:
1/2 cup (1 stick) butter
3/4 cup dark soft brown sugar
1/2 cup granulated sugar
1 cup golden syrup (if unavailable, use corn syrup)
1 cup heavy cream
1/2 teaspoon vanilla extract

To make the toffee sauce, put the butter, both sugars, and the golden syrup into a heavy saucepan and melt gently over low heat. Simmer for about 5 minutes, then remove from the heat and gradually stir in the cream and the vanilla extract. Return to the heat and stir for 2–3 minutes until the sauce is absolutely smooth.

Put some banana slices on top of the waffles, pour the toffee sauce over them, and sprinkle with the chopped walnuts.

Top Tip: Toffee sauce is also delicious with ice cream. It will keep for several weeks, stored in a screw-top jar in the fridge.

Breakfast Fruit and Berry Plate

A serving of seasonal fruit and berries provides a delectable vitamin-rich and totally guilt-free breakfast. Use a selection of ripe and juicy fruit and berries, such as melon or pineapple, strawberries, red or yellow raspberries, loganberries or tay-berries, boysenberries, black currants… All are divine, just mix and match according to availability.

All of the fruit listed in the introduction to this recipe benefit from a squeeze of lime or lemon juice.

Serve with a bowl of homemade yogurt (see p.33) and some local honey.
I sometimes sprinkle a little chopped mint, lemon balm, or sweet cicely over them.

Compote of Plums or Greengage Plums

SERVES 4   (P: 1 min./C: 10 mins.)

Poach the fruit whole—they'll taste better. Serve for breakfast or dessert.

2 cups sugar, or a bit less if the fruit are
   very sweet
2 cups cold water
2 pounds plums (e.g., Italian plums or
   greengage plums)

For serving: whipped cream

Put the sugar and water into a saucepan over medium heat and bring to a boil. Tip in the fruit, cover, and simmer until they begin to burst (about 4–5 minutes).

Turn into a bowl and serve warm, with a spoonful of lightly whipped cream. Exquisite!

Top Tip: Poached plums keep very well in the fridge for weeks and are delicious for breakfast without the cream!

Poached Apricots with Sweet Geranium Leaves

SERVES 4   (P: 5 mins./C: 30 mins.)

4–6 large leaves of lemon-scented geranium
   (*Pelargonium graveolens*)
1 cup sugar
1 cup cold water
1 pound fresh apricots, left whole or cut in
   half and pitted (about 2¹/₂ cups)

For serving: light cream or Sweet
   Geranium Cream (see recipe below)

Put the geranium leaves into a saucepan with the sugar and water and bring slowly to a boil over medium heat.

Meanwhile, add the whole apricots to the syrup, or, if you prefer, cut them in half and pit them first. Cover the saucepan and simmer until the apricots are soft (about 15–30 minutes, depending on ripeness). Turn into a bowl and let cool, then store in the fridge. Serve chilled, with cream or sweet geranium cream.

Variation: Try this with 4 pears, cut in half and cored, instead of the apricots.

Sweet Geranium Cream

                        (C: 30 mins.)

2¹/₂ cups cream
3–4 leaves of lemon-scented geranium
   (*Pelargonium graveolens*)

Pour the cream into a saucepan, add the geranium leaves, and heat gently until the surface begins to shiver. Let cool. Whip lightly and serve.

A Great Kedgeree

SERVES 6–8   (P: 5 mins./C: 30 mins.)

The word kedgeree immediately conjures up images of country-house breakfasts, which were often a veritable feast. Usually it would be served on a silver dish set on the polished sideboard, so that guests could help themselves. Easy as pie to make and delicious for brunch.

1 pound raw wild salmon or
   8 ounces raw salmon and 8 ounces
   cooked smoked haddock
salt and freshly ground pepper
1 heaping cup white long-grain basmati rice
3 cage-free, organic eggs
1 cup cream
3 tablespoons butter
1/2 teaspoon red pepper flakes
1/4 cup chopped fresh parsley
2 tablespoons chopped fresh chives
good pinch of cayenne pepper

For serving: freshly baked bread or warm
   buttered toast

Put the salmon in a pan just large enough to fit it and cover with boiling salted water—use 1 1/2 teaspoons salt for every 2 cups water.* Bring to a boil, cover, and simmer for 20 minutes. Remove the pan from the heat, leave covered, and let sit for a few minutes before removing the salmon from the water, then let cool.

Meanwhile, cook the rice in boiling salted water for about 8–10 minutes.

Hard-boil the eggs in boiling salted water for 10 minutes, then drain off the water and run under cold water to cool and stop the cooking. Peel and chop roughly.

Remove the skin and any bones from the salmon (and haddock, if using) and flake into small pieces.

Heat the cream and butter in a large pan and add the red pepper flakes, parsley, and chives. As soon as the mixture bubbles, add the cooked rice, flaked fish, and hard-boiled eggs. Season well with salt and freshly ground pepper and a pinch of cayenne pepper. Mix very gently. Taste, adjust the seasoning to taste, pile into a hot dish, and serve with freshly baked bread or warm buttered toast.

* Note: If using salmon fillet, use 3/4 teaspoon salt for every 2 cups water and cook for just 8-10 minutes.

Congee with Chicken, Shrimp, and Mushrooms

SERVES 4–6   (P: 15 mins./C: 45 mins.)

Congee is a rice porridge—a staple breakfast food in China and Hong Kong, often eaten with dough sticks to dunk. I also love it as a soup—increase the amount of water. Feel free to add some extra tasty tidbits at the table.

1 1/3 cups jasmine rice, washed and drained
9 cups water
4 ounces raw chicken, very finely sliced
   (about 1/2 cup)
4 ounces raw or cooked shrimp (about
   3/4 cup)
1 teaspoon peeled and grated fresh
   ginger root
a little vegetable oil, for frying
1 chile, thinly sliced (optional)
4 ounces mushrooms, thinly sliced (about
   1 cup)
salt and freshly ground pepper
2 1/2 tablespoons roughly chopped cilantro
1–2 1/2 tablespoons sesame oil
2 1/2 tablespoons thinly sliced scallion

Put the rice into a pot, add the water, and bring to a boil, then cover and simmer for 30–40 minutes until the rice is cooked and the consistency is slightly soupy. Add the chicken and shrimp, ginger, and chile (if using), and cook for another 4–5 minutes.

Meanwhile heat a pan, add a very little vegetable oil, and sauté the mushrooms. Season with salt and freshly ground pepper and add it to the congee along with the cilantro. Taste and adjust the seasoning if necessary, then drizzle with sesame oil and sprinkle with the scallions.

Dark Chocolate and Seville Orange Muffins

MAKES ABOUT 10   (**P:** 15 mins./**C:** 40 mins.)

vegetable oil, for greasing
1/2 cup (1 stick) butter
3/4 cup sugar
finely grated zest of 1 unwaxed lemon
2 cage-free, organic eggs
1 cup buttermilk
1/3 cup Seville orange marmalade
3 ounces dark chocolate, chopped (about
   1/2 cup)
2 cups white flour
pinch of salt
3/4 teaspoon baking soda

Preheat the oven to 400°F. Grease the insides of the muffin cups in a muffin tray or line the cups with non-stick paper muffin cups.

Cream the butter and mix in the sugar and lemon zest. Add the eggs one at a time, beating well between each addition.

Next add the buttermilk, marmalade, and chopped chocolate. Blend well. Finally stir in the flour, salt, and baking soda, until just mixed.

Fill the muffin cups with the batter and bake for 30–40 minutes until golden. Serve warm.

Mini-muffins are an adorable option and great for kids of all ages.

Breakfast Fruit Salad

SERVES 8   (**P:** OVERNIGHT/**C:** 20 mins.)

Breakfast fruit salads that can be made ahead and kept in the fridge are a terrific standby. We love this one and also often eat it as a winter dessert, with a few pistachio nuts or toasted almonds added.

7 ounces prunes (about 1 1/2 cups)
6 ounces dried apricots (about 1 cup)
handful of raisins
grated zest of 1/2 unwaxed lemon
1–2 1/2 tablespoons pure honey

For serving: 3–4 bananas, sliced
1 cup freshly squeezed orange juice,
   and light cream or plain yogurt

Soak the prunes and apricots in lots of cold water overnight.

Next day, drain the fruit and retain the soaking water. Put the prunes, apricots, raisins, and grated lemon zest into a heavy pan.

Mix the honey with 1/2 cup warm water, pour it over the fruit, and add enough of the fruit soaking water to cover. Bring to a boil and simmer for 20 minutes.

Let cool, transfer to a sealed glass jar or casserole dish and store in the fridge; it will keep for 1–2 weeks.

Just before serving, add some banana slices and a little freshly squeezed orange juice to each bowl. Serve with light cream or plain yogurt.

Divine Homemade Yogurt

MAKES 8 CUPS
       (**P:** 5 mins./**C:** 45 mins. + OVERNIGHT)

Making one's own yogurt is a very simple and satisfying thing to do. Don't try using low-fat milk as the result will have only a fraction of the flavor.

10 cups whole milk
2/3 cup heavy cream
1 cup live plain yogurt

Put the milk into a large saucepan and bring to a boil. Reduce the heat to low and simmer, stirring occasionally, until reduced by at least half—better still, two thirds. Remove the pan from the heat and pour the milk into a thick ceramic bowl. Add the cream and stir well. Let cool.

When the milk has cooled enough that you can hold your clean finger in it for a count of 10, add the yogurt and stir well. If the milk is too hot when the yogurt is added, it will kill the live bacteria.

Cover with a lint-free dishtowel or plastic wrap and let thicken in a warm, dark place—we leave it beside the Aga. Sometimes it takes days to thicken. Once the yogurt has thickened, it will keep in the fridge for 7–10 days.

We serve this with apple blossom honey and toasted hazelnuts.

Ballymaloe White Yeast Bread

MAKES 2 LOAVES   (**P**: 15 mins./**C**: 3 HOURS)

**Making white yeast bread from scratch may
not be your idea of easy entertaining, but
the mixing takes just a few minutes, the
kneading can be done in a food mixer, and
the rising takes no effort on your part
except a glance every now and then to
check its progress. When the dough is risen,
the fun begins: you can make one loaf or
several, simple shapes or elaborate braids,
or a variety of rolls in every shape and form
from simple knots, coils, and clover leaves
to snails, hedgehogs, and wiggly worms to
amuse the younger guests.**

1 3/5-ounce (17g) cake fresh non-GM
   yeast (also called compressed yeast)
2 cups lukewarm water
1 1/2 pounds (about 5 cups) white bread
   flour, plus extra for dusting (optional)
2 teaspoons salt
2 teaspoons sugar
2 tablespoons butter
beaten egg and poppy or sesame seeds, for
   topping (optional)

2 loaf pans 5 x 8 inches

Mix the yeast with 2/3 cup of the lukewarm water and leave in a warm place for about 5 minutes.

In a large, wide mixing bowl, sift the flour, salt, and sugar. Rub in the butter and make a well in the center. Pour in the soaked yeast and most of the remaining lukewarm water. Mix to a loose dough, adding the rest of the water or a little extra flour if needed.

Turn the dough onto a lightly floured counter, cover with a lint-free dishtowel and let it relax for about 5 minutes. Then knead in a food mixer with a dough hook for about 5 minutes or until smooth, springy, and elastic; if kneading by hand, knead for 10 minutes.

Put the dough in a large ceramic bowl. Cover the top tightly with plastic wrap and set aside in a warm place for about 1 1/2–2 hours, until the dough has more than doubled in size (yeast dough rises best in a warm, moist atmosphere).

Punch down the dough (force out all the air) by kneading again by hand for about 2–3 minutes. Let it relax for 10 minutes.

Shape the dough into loaves, braids (see below), or rolls, transfer to the loaf pans or a baking tray and cover with a lint-free dishtowel. Let it rise again in a warm place, until the shaped dough has again doubled in size (about 20–30 minutes). The dough is ready for baking when a small dent remains after it is pressed lightly with a finger.

Meanwhile, preheat the oven to 450ºF.

If you like, brush the dough with beaten egg and sprinkle with poppy or sesame seeds, or dust lightly with flour for a rustic-looking loaf. Bake for 25–35 minutes depending upon size. When it is cooked, the bread should sound hollow when tapped underneath. Cool on a wire rack.

To make a braided loaf:
After the dough has been punched down, take half the dough and divide into three pieces. With both hands, roll each one into a rope—the thickness depends upon how fat you want the braid. Pinch the three ropes together at one end, then bring each outside strand into the center alternately to form a braid. Pinch the ends together and tuck in neatly. Transfer to a baking tray, cover, and let it double in size. Brush with beaten egg or dredge with flour and bake.

Tear-and-share Bread

MAKES 1 LOAF (SEE PHOTOGRAPH ON P.210.)
                    (**P**: 15 mins./**C**: 3 HOURS)

**A fun bread for a dinner party or family
supper—just tear and share.**

1 pound (about a half-recipe) Ballymaloe
   White Yeast Bread dough (see recipe, above)
cornmeal or flour, for dusting
poppy seeds (optional)

Roll out the dough into a circle about 8 inches across. Sprinkle a baking tray with cornmeal or flour and lay the dough on it, then let it rest for about 5 minutes. Brush with water and sprinkle with cornmeal or flour.

Press a 3-inch diameter biscuit cutter or small glass into the center of the dough to make a circular indent, but do not cut through. Sprinkle the center with poppy seeds (if using). With a knife, divide the dough on the outside of the circle into half, then quarters, then eighths, and then into sixteenths, so you are left with "petals" around the center circle.

Give each "petal" a quarter turn so part of the cut side faces upwards. Cover with a lint-free dishtowel and let rise in a warm place until doubled in size (about 20–30 minutes). Meanwhile preheat the oven to 450ºF.

Bake for 10–15 minutes, then reduce the heat to 350ºF and continue baking until the bread is crusty and golden. Cool on a wire rack.

Brown Yeast Bread

MAKES 1 LOAF   (**P:** 20 mins./**C:** 1¹/² HOURS)

I know the word "yeast" conjures up thoughts of kneading, rising, and punching down, but don't be afraid—the Ballymaloe Brown Yeast Bread is a cinch to make. It takes time—about 1¹/² hours from start to finish—but only 10 minutes of preparation: the rest of the time is spent allowing the bread to rise or bake. The main ingredients—whole-wheat flour, treacle, and yeast—are highly nutritious.

3¹/³ cups whole-wheat flour, or 3 cups whole-wheat flour and ¹/³ cup white bread flour
1 teaspoon salt
1 teaspoon black treacle or molasses
2 cups lukewarm water
1 to 1¹/² (³/⁵-ounce/17g) cakes fresh non-GM yeast. (Dry yeast may be used instead of compressed (fresh) yeast: follow the same method but use 1 to 1¹/² envelopes dry yeast (2¹/⁴-3¹/³ teaspoons) and allow longer to rise. Fast-action yeast may also be used: follow instructions on envelope.
sunflower oil, for greasing
sesame seeds (optional)

1 loaf pan, about 5 x 8 inches

The ingredients should all be at room temperature. In a large bowl, mix the flour with the salt. In a small bowl or measuring cup, mix the treacle or molasses with ²/³ cup of the warm water and crumble in the yeast. Set the bowl in a warm place (such as close to the aga or oven or near a radiator) for 4–5 minutes to allow the yeast to start to work; it is ready when it looks creamy and slightly frothy. Meanwhile brush the pans with sunflower oil.

Preheat the oven to 450°F.

When the yeasty water is ready, stir and pour it, along with the remaining warm water, into the flour to make a loose wet dough. The mixture should be too wet to knead. Pour the dough into the greased pan and sprinkle the top with sesame seeds if you like. Cover with a lint-free dishtowel and let rise in a warm place (about 10–15 minutes). Just before the dough reaches the top of the pan, remove the towel and bake for 50–60 minutes, until the bread looks nicely browned and the bottom sounds hollow when tapped. During baking, the bread will rise a little further; this is called "oven spring." If the dough has reached the top of the pan before it goes into the oven it will continue to rise and flow over the edges.

We usually remove the loaf from the pan about 10 minutes before the end of baking and put it back into the oven to crisp all around, but if you like a softer crust there's no need to do this. Cool on a wire rack.

Variation: To make Russian Village Bread, use 3 cups whole-wheat flour, ¹/³ cup rye flour and ¹/³ cup white bread flour. When the dough is ready, brush the pan with sunflower oil, sprinkle a layer of coriander seeds onto the bottom of the pan and sprinkle another layer over the top of the bread. Bake as above.

Breadsticks

(**P:** 20 mins./**C:** 15 mins.)

These are great for cocktail parties and go well with dips, soups, and salads. Breadsticks wrapped in a slice of prosciutto or serrano ham make delicious nibbles, to serve with an aperitif. They don't need to be perfectly even in shape—you could form the dough into wriggly worms to great effect!

Ballymaloe White Yeast Bread dough (see recipes on p.34 and above)
selection of sprinkles: coarse sea salt or Kosher salt and/or ground black pepper, chopped rosemary, crushed cumin seeds, sesame seeds, poppy seeds, red pepper flakes, grated Parmesan cheese (optional)

When the dough has been "punched down," preheat the oven to 425°F.

Sprinkle the counter with coarse sea salt or Kosher salt and black pepper if you wish, and/or your chosen flavoring.

Pull off small pieces of dough, ¹/²–1 ounce in weight. Roll into very thin, medium, or fat breadsticks with your hands, but bear in mind that they will double in size.

Roll in the chosen "sprinkle" (you may need to brush the dough lightly with cold water first). Place on a baking sheet. Repeat this process until all the dough has been used.

Bake for 8–15 minutes, depending upon size, until golden brown and crisp. Cool on a wire rack.

Top Tip: Breadsticks are usually baked without a final rising, but for a slightly lighter result, let the shaped dough rise for about 10 minutes before baking.

White Soda or Buttermilk Bread

MAKES 1 LOAF   (**P:** 10 mins./**C:** 45 mins.)

Soda bread uses baking soda instead of yeast to leaven the bread as well as an acidic ingredient—buttermilk or sour milk. It also requires all-purpose flour, not bread flour. This soda or buttermilk bread takes only 2–3 minutes to make and 45 minutes to bake. You can also add olives, sun-dried tomatoes, or caramelized onions to suit your menu, which makes this an infinitely useful bread.

3 1/3 cups all-purpose white flour, preferably unbleached
1 teaspoon salt
1 teaspoon baking soda
1 3/4 cups buttermilk

Preheat the oven to 475°F.

Sift all the dry ingredients into a large, wide bowl and make a well in the center. Pour in the milk. Using the fingers of one hand, stiff and outstretched like a claw, stir from the center to the edge of the bowl in concentric circles. The dough should be softish, but not too wet and sticky. When it all comes together, turn out onto a well-floured counter.

Wash and dry your hands. Pat the dough into a tidy shape and flip over gently, then pat it into a circle about 1 1/2 inches thick. Gently transfer to a floured baking tray. Cut a deep cross into the loaf and prick the center of each quarter to "let the fairies out!"

Bake for 15 minutes, then reduce the heat to 400°F and bake for another 30 minutes or until cooked. If you are in doubt, tap the bottom of the bread: it should sound hollow. Cool on a wire rack. Soda bread is best eaten on the day it is made.

For spotted dog, add 1 tablespoon sugar, 1/2 cup golden raisins, and 1 cage-free, organic egg to the above recipe. Reduce the buttermilk to 1 1/2 cups.

West Cork Cheddar Cheese "Focaccia"

MAKES 1 LOAF   (**P**: 10 mins./**C**: 30 mins.)

Here we bake the buttermilk bread flat with a bubbly cheddar cheese topping.

1 quantity White Soda Bread dough (see recipe on p.36)
extra virgin olive oil, for greasing
1-1³/₄ cups aged cheddar cheese

1 jelly-roll pan 12 x 9 inches

Preheat the oven to 450°F.

Make the bread in the usual way. Flatten the dough into a rectangle approximately 12 x 9 inches. Brush the pan with extra virgin olive oil. Press the dough gently into the pan. Scatter the grated cheese evenly over the top.

Bake for 5 minutes, then turn down the oven to 400°F and bake for about 20–25 minutes more or until just cooked and the cheese is bubbly and golden. Transfer to a wire rack to cool. Cut into squares and serve with drinks or with a steaming bowl of soup.

Wheaten Bread

MAKES 1 LOAF   (**P**: 10 mins./**C**: 40 mins.)

1²/₃ cups white flour
1²/₃ cups whole-wheat flour, plus extra for dusting
1 teaspoon salt
1 barely rounded teaspoon baking soda
2 cups buttermilk

Preheat the oven to 400°F.

Mix the flours in a large bowl, add the salt, and sift in the baking soda. Lift the flour up with your fingers to distribute the salt and baking soda.

Make a well in the center and pour in the buttermilk. With your fingers stiff and outstretched, stir from the center to the edge of the bowl in ever-increasing concentric circles. When you reach the edge of the bowl, the dough should be made—it will be soft, but not too wet or sticky. Sprinkle a little flour on a counter and turn the dough out onto it. Wash and dry your hands.

Sprinkle a little flour on your hands and gently tidy the dough around the edges. Tuck the edges underneath with the inner edge of your hands and gently pat the dough with your fingers into a loaf about 1¹/₂ inches thick.

Cut a deep cross into the bread (this is called "blessing the bread") and then prick it in the center of each quarter to "let the fairies out."

Sprinkle some flour onto a baking tray and put the dough on it. Bake for 30 minutes, then turn the bread over and bake for another 5–10 minutes until cooked (the bottom should sound hollow when tapped). Cool on a wire rack.

Teeny Weeny Rolls

MAKES 40   (**P**: 15 mins./**C**: 20 mins.)

Three teeny weenies, with different toppings and threaded onto a satay stick, look great with a bowl of steaming soup.

1 quantity Wheaten Bread dough (see recipe above) or White Soda Bread dough (see recipe p.36)
flour, for dusting
buttermilk or beaten egg, for glazing (optional)
toppings: sesame seeds, rolled oats, cracked wheat, poppy seeds, pumpkin seeds, grated cheddar cheese (optional)

Preheat the oven to 450°F.

Make the dough as per your chosen recipe. Turn out onto a floured counter. Roll out into a circle or square, an inch thick. The quickest and least wasteful way to make teeny weenies is to cut the dough into 1-inch squares. Alternatively, stamp the dough into circles with a floured 1¹/₂-inch cookie cutter so there is a minimum of waste, then gently roll the scraps and stamp out more shapes.

If you like, brush the tops with buttermilk or beaten egg and dip the pieces into one or a selection of the suggested toppings. Transfer to a baking sheet.

Bake for 15–20 minutes—when cooked they should sound hollow when tapped. Transfer to a wire rack and let cool.

Whole-wheat Soda Bread

MAKES 1 LARGE LOAF OR 3 SMALL LOAVES
(**P**: 20 mins./**C**: 60 mins.)

This is a modern version of soda bread, and it couldn't be simpler. Just mix and pour into a well-greased pan. This bread keeps very well for several days and is also great toasted.

3 cups stone-ground whole-wheat flour
1/2 cup white flour, preferably unbleached
1 teaspoon salt
1 teaspoon baking soda, sifted
1 cage-free, organic egg
1 1/2 tablespoons peanut or sunflower oil, plus
　extra for greasing
1 teaspoon honey
2 cups buttermilk or sour milk,
　plus a little extra if necessary
sunflower or sesame seeds (optional)

loaf pan 9 x 5 x 2 inches

Preheat the oven to 400°F.

Put all the dry ingredients, including the baking soda, into a large bowl and mix well.

Whisk the egg, then add the oil and honey and the buttermilk or sour milk. Make a well in the center of the dry ingredients and pour in all the liquid; mix well and add more buttermilk if necessary. The mixture should be soft and slightly sloppy.

Pour into an oiled pan or pans. Sprinkle some sunflower or sesame seeds on the top, if using. Bake for about 60 minutes, or until the bread is nice and crusty and sounds hollow when tapped on the bottom. Remove from the pan and cool on a wire rack.

Top Tip: For a healthy seed bread, add to the dry ingredients 1 tablespoon each sunflower seeds, sesame seeds, pumpkin seeds, and cracked wheat. Keep a little aside to scatter over the top before baking.

Fougasse (Provençal Flat Bread)

MAKES 4–6　　　(**P**: 20 mins./**C**: 60 mins.)

This is wonderful-looking bread with its ragged holes and lovely crust.

1 quantity Ballymaloe White Yeast Bread dough
　(see p.34)
extra virgin olive oil, for brushing
sea salt or Kosher salt
chopped fresh rosemary (optional)

Make the dough and knead it. Oil a large bowl and put in the dough. Cover with a lint-free dishtowel and let it rise as described on p.34. Punch down the dough by kneading for 2–3 minutes and divide it into 4–6 pieces. Preheat the oven to 450°F.

Gently roll each piece of dough into an oval shape at least 7 inches long and 4 inches wide. Using a very sharp knife or a razor blade, make 3 or 5 angled cuts through the dough. Brush a baking tray with olive oil. Transfer the dough to the baking tray, pulling the cuts apart to open holes in the dough.

Let it rise in a warm place until doubled in size, about 30 minutes. Brush the surface with olive oil, then sprinkle with sea salt or Kosher salt and rosemary (if using). Bake for 5 minutes, then reduce the temperature to 400°F and continue baking for another 20–25 minutes until golden. Cool on a wire rack.

Heart-shaped Bread

MAKES SEVERAL　　(**P**: 20 mins./**C**: 20 mins.)

1 quantity Ballymaloe White Yeast Bread
　dough (see p.34) or White Soda Bread dough
　(see p.36)
whole Kalamata olives
fresh rosemary sprigs
extra virgin olive oil, for brushing

heart-shaped cutter

Make the dough as given in the recipe and roll out to a 3/4-inch thickness. Preheat the oven to 450°F.

Using a heart-shaped cutter, stamp out heart shapes from the dough. Press a whole olive into the center of each one and tuck in a tiny sprig of rosemary behind it.

Bake for 15–20 minutes depending upon size. Brush with a little extra virgin olive oil and serve.

Pita Bread

MAKES 8 LARGE OR ABOUT 48 MINI PITA
BREADS   (P: 15 mins./C: 30 mins.)

Pita bread is readily available to buy, but it's easier to make than you might imagine and once you have tasted homemade pita bread it's difficult to settle for less. It's terrifically versatile: you can stuff it with salad, cured meats, or cheese, or simply eat it on its own, and mini pita breads make a great base for hummus and dips.

3 cups white bread flour
1 teaspoon salt
1 tablespoon sugar
$^1/_3$ ounce (10g) fresh non-GM yeast
   (about $^1/_2$ cube)
$2^1/_2$ tablespoons extra virgin olive oil
1 cup hot water

8 x 7-inch pieces of aluminum foil

Put 1 cup of the flour into the bowl of an electric mixer, add the salt and sugar and crumble in the yeast. Mix the oil with the hot water. Using the paddle and with the mixer on a low speed, mix the liquid with the dry ingredients for 30 seconds. Now change to the dough hook and add the remaining flour 2 tablespoons at a time, keeping the motor running. When all the flour has been added, continue to knead for another 4–5 minutes. The dough will be a shaggy mass. Continue to knead until the dough comes easily away from the sides of the bowl.

Turn the dough out onto a lightly floured counter. Knead by hand for another few minutes. The dough will be slightly sticky. Divide the dough into eight 7-inch pieces or 48 small pieces. Roll into balls, cover, and let rest for 20 minutes.

Preheat the oven to 475°F.

With the palm of your hand, gently flatten each ball and roll out to an oval shape about 6 inches across (1 inch for mini pitas) and about $^1/_2$-inch thick. Don't worry too much about getting a perfect shape, but it is important to make the discs thin. Put each piece of dough onto a piece of aluminum foil and let it rest for another 5 minutes. Meanwhile, put a baking sheet to warm in the oven.

Carefully put 2 or 3 of the breads onto the hot baking sheet and bake for 8 minutes (6 minutes for mini pitas) or until they have puffed up and are slightly golden—if you allow them to get too dark they will have a hard crust. Remove the breads from the oven and wrap them in aluminum foil or a lint-free dishtowel; the tops will fall and there will be a pocket that you can fill. Bake and wrap the remaining breads in the same manner. Serve warm or cold.

Indian Paratha Bread

MAKES 16   (P: 20 mins./C: 40 mins.)

These roughly triangular flat breads are eaten all over India. They are easy to make at home—all you need is a cast-iron frying pan. In India, ghee (clarified butter) is used instead of vegetable oil. Parathas can be reheated in the oven: wrap 3 or 4 at a time in foil and warm through at 350°F for 5–10 minutes.

$1^1/_4$ cups sifted whole-wheat flour (return
   the bran to the flour after sifting)
generous $1^1/_3$ cups white flour, plus extra for
   dusting
$^1/_2$ teaspoon salt
$2^1/_2$ tablespoons vegetable oil or clarified
   butter (see p.108), plus extra for brushing
   and frying
scant cup water

Put the whole-wheat flour, white flour, and salt into a bowl and mix. Sprinkle the vegetable oil or clarified butter over the top and rub in with your fingertips. The mixture will resemble coarse bread crumbs. Add the water and gradually mix together with your fingers to form a softish ball of dough.

Knead the dough on a clean counter for about 10 minutes. Rub the ball of dough with a little oil, put it into a bowl, cover with plastic wrap and let it rest for 30 minutes.

Knead the dough again for 1–2 minutes, shape into a cylinder, and divide into 16 pieces. While you work with each piece, keep the remainder covered with a lint-free dishtowel.

Flatten a piece of dough and dust with a little white flour. Roll out to a circle 6 inches across. Brush a little oil over the top and fold in half. Brush with oil again, then fold again to form a triangle. Roll out this triangle towards the point into a larger triangle with 7-inch sides. Dust with flour if necessary to prevent it from sticking during rolling. Cover and set aside. Repeat with the remaining dough.

Heat a cast-iron frying pan until it is really hot, slap a paratha in it, and cook for a minute or so. Brush the top generously with oil, then turn the paratha over and cook the other side for a minute or so. Both sides should have brownish spots. Move the paratha around as you cook so all parts are exposed evenly to the heat. Transfer the cooked paratha to a plate and cover with a saucepan lid or a piece of aluminum foil. Cook the remaining parathas in the same way. Serve warm.

Grilled Fremantle Flat Bread

MAKES 5 OR 6
(**P:** 5 mins. + OVERNIGHT/**C:** 50 mins.)

This flat bread is great served with dips or simply with good-quality extra virgin olive oil.

3³/₄ cups white flour
1 cup and 2 tablespoons water
3 tablespoons butter
pinch of sugar
salt and freshly ground pepper
rice flour or cornmeal, for rolling
extra virgin olive oil, for brushing

Put the flour, water, and butter into the bowl of an electric mixer. Add the sugar and 1 teaspoon salt. Mix together at a slow speed with a dough hook for about 5 minutes until the dough is really smooth and shiny.

Turn out onto a lightly floured counter and knead lightly for a couple of minutes. Roll the dough into a cylinder and wrap in plastic wrap. Refrigerate overnight.

The following day, let the dough come back to room temperature for about 30 minutes. Divide into 5 or 6 pieces. Dust the counter with rice flour or cornmeal and roll out each portion into a very thin circle—don't worry too much about the shape as long as it is thin. Cover and let rest for about 20 minutes.

The breads can be either broiled or cooked in a frying pan: either preheat the broiler to its highest setting, or heat a heavy, wide frying pan over medium heat.

Brush the dough pieces with olive oil and sprinkle with freshly ground pepper. If using the broiler, broil 1 or 2 pieces at a time for 2–3 minutes on both sides. They will puff up almost immediately. Be careful not to overcook or they will become crisp and brittle. If you are using a frying pan, slap a round piece of dough directly onto the hot pan, cook for a few minutes on one side, then turn over and continue to cook for 2–3 minutes on the other side.

Wrap in a warm lint-free dishtowel until needed. Brush with extra virgin olive oil. Sprinkle with salt and serve.

Yufka (Turkish Flat Bread)

MAKES 12
(**P:** 15 mins./**C:** 50 mins.)

Bread is a staple in Turkey, as in so many cultures. According to the Koran, bread was sent to Earth by God's command, hence it is revered and not a crumb should be wasted. There are many delicious ways to use up stale bread but I rarely have any left over to experiment with.

1 cup white bread flour
²/₃ cup all-purpose white flour
¹/₃ cup whole-wheat flour
1 scant teaspoon salt
scant cup (or more) warm water

Mix all the flours and the salt together in a bowl. Add a scant cup of warm water, mix to a dough, and knead well for a couple of minutes. Add more water if necessary. Shape into a roll, divide into 12 pieces, cover with a lint-free dishtowel and let rest for at least 30 minutes, preferably 45 minutes.

Roll out each piece of dough into a thin circle no more than ³/₈-inch thick.

Heat a grill pan or large nonstick iron frying pan. Cook the yufka quickly on both sides until brown spots just start to appear. The bread can be eaten immediately; alternatively, it can be stacked in a box for several days, even weeks, in a dry place

Before eating, sprinkle a little warm water over the breads, fold them in half, wrap in a cloth, and let soften for about 30 minutes. Eat with cheese or butter and honey, or fill with your chosen filling of roasted vegetables, cured meat, or salad—they are then called *durum*, meaning roll.

throwing a good brunch

When planning a menu, make sure you have a good mix of bread, fruit, and hot dishes. If it is more breakfast than lunch, French toast, muffins, and a good porridge or crunchy granola go down well. For a mid-morning meal, provide a couple of hot dishes and you may even want to add a drop of champagne to the orange juice.

If you have time, a basket of breads (soda bread, a brown yeast loaf, tear and share, wheaten bread, and teeny-weeny rolls) is a wonderful thing and perfect for nibbling on through the morning. As brunch turns into lunch, bring out some local cheese, succulent ham, and pickle relish, and a good green salad. What could be easier?

Brunch is a meal to linger over, to make any plans for the rest of the day. Turn the radio on for some background news or music, provide a selection of newspapers, then sit down, relax, and let your guests help themselves to whatever they want.

A light breakfast (see p.24–27)
Ballymaloe Strawberry Muesli (see p.20)
French Toast Strips with Citrus Marmalade Butter (see p.23)
Dark Chocolate and Seville Orange Muffins (see p.33)
White Soda Bread with Olives or Spotted Dog (see p.36)
A selection of fresh fruit

To drink
Breakfast is not really the time for wine but some inexpensive sparkling Cava added to freshly squeezed orange juice will add just a little kick to all that healthy vitamin C. If you want something with more of a hit, then a Bloody Mary will do the trick, or a few drops of elderflower syrup added to champagne or sparkling wine. If breakfast is early, consider serving a Virgin Mary (just leave out the vodka) and your guests may not know the difference.

Healthy breakfast menu
Pinhead Oatmeal Porridge (see p.20)
Breakfast Fruit Salad with Divine Homemade Yogurt (see p.33)
Healthy Seed Bread (see Whole-wheat Soda Bread, p.38)

To drink
Mango and banana smoothie (see p.16) will provide an instant hit of vitamins and energy, as will freshly squeezed juice (see p.20). For a fizzy refresher, add some elderflower syrup to sparkling water.

A hearty brunch
A Great Kedgeree (see p.30)
Breakfast Panini (see p.22)
Compote of Plums and Greengage Plums (see p.28)

To drink
A simple and fairly inexpensive white Burgundy, such as a Macon-Villages, will partner the kedgeree very effectively, and tackle the panini. Good alternatives include pinot grigio and Verdicchio. The relatively low alcohol Moscatel de Valencia is ideal with the compote.

finger food

When I was little, a neighbor gave a cocktail party and I was so intrigued that I went around to help her prepare the food. I was amazed to find little chunks of cheese and grapes on toothpicks sticking out of a melon. I thought it was the most exciting and sophisticated thing I'd ever seen. Canapés have come a long way since then. Nowadays we can let our imaginations run riot and come up with delicious bites, from soup served in shot glasses to tapas, sushi, and spring rolls.

Isaac's Sushi Rice

(**P:** 20 mins./**C:** 1 HOUR, 15 mins.)

2¹/₃ cups sushi rice "No. 1 Extra Fancy"
2¹/₂ cups water

For the vinegar water:
¹/₂ cup rice wine vinegar
¹/₄ cup sugar
5 teaspoons salt

Rinse the rice in a strainer under cold running water for 10 minutes or until the water runs clear.

"Wake up" the rice by sitting it in 2¹/₂ cups cold water for 30–45 minutes. In the same water, bring it to a boil, cover, and cook for 10 minutes until all the water has been absorbed. Do not stir: do not even remove the lid. Turn up the heat for 10 seconds before turning the heat off. Remove the lid, place a lint-free dishtowel over the rice, replace the lid, and leave it for 20 minutes.

Mix the rice wine vinegar, sugar, and salt together in a bowl until dissolved. Turn the rice out onto a big flat plate (preferably wooden). While the rice is still hot, pour the vinegar solution over it and mix the rice and vinegar together in a slicing action with the aid of a wooden spoon. Don't stir. You must mix quickly, preferably fanning the rice with a fan at the same time. (This is much easier if you have a helper!) Let the rice cool on the plate, covering it meanwhile with paper towels or a lint-free dishtowel. (It will soak up the liquid as it cools.)

Norimaki

MAKES 7–8 ROLLS, 6–8 PIECES IN EACH
(**P:** 30 mins.)

one 10-sheet package of nori seaweed
vinegar water (see recipe above)
1 quantity Isaac's Sushi Rice (see recipe above)

For the filling:
3–4 basil leaves per roll
6–8 strips of raw wild or smoked salmon or
  tuna cut into 1/4-inch strips
2 avocado slices, of similar size to the fish
¹/₂ English cucumber, seeded and cut
  into ¹/₄-inch strips
1 ounce cheddar cheese, cut into ¹/₄-inch
  strips (about ¹/₄ cup)

For serving: wasabi paste, soy sauce, and
  pickled ginger

bamboo sudari mat for rolling

Place a bamboo sudari mat on the counter. Wave a sheet of nori seaweed over a gas flame to freshen up the flavor and make it more pliable. Lay it on a bamboo sudari mat, with the shiny side down and grain running horizontally. Dip your hand in the vinegar water.

Spread a layer of rice over the nori, keeping it an inch from the top of the sheet of nori. Make a shallow indentation in the rice and put in the filling. You can use whatever you like for the filling—smoked salmon and basil, avocado, cucumber, even strips of cheddar cheese. Roll the mat tightly and press to seal, then unroll the mat.

To serve, cut the norimaki with a razor-sharp knife into 6 pieces (dip the knife in the vinegar water each time). Arrange on a plate, together with a blob of wasabi paste about the size of a small pea, a little dish of soy sauce, and a few slivers of pickled ginger. For perfection, sushi should not be refrigerated.

Note: sudari mats are available from Japanese or other Oriental stores as well as many health food stores and now even some supermarkets. If you can't find one, just use a clean lint-free dishtowel as though you were making a jelly roll.

Nigiri Sushi

MAKES 48–50 (**P:** 30 mins.)

1 quantity Isaac's Sushi Rice (see recipe above)
vinegar water (see recipe above)
6–8 strips of raw wild or smoked salmon or tuna
  (raw fish must be spanking fresh)
fennel leaves or package of nori seaweed

For serving: wasabi paste, soy sauce, and
  pickled ginger

First dip your hand in the vinegar water. Make a little oblong ball from the rice, molding it gently in a lightly clenched hand.

Put a slice of salmon or tuna on top. Garnish with fennel leaves or a strip of nori. Serve with wasabi paste, soy sauce, and pickled ginger.

Shermin Mustafa's Californian Roll (Inside-out Sushi)

MAKES 7–8 ROLLS (6–8 PIECES IN EACH)
(P: 30 mins.)

one 10-sheet package of nori seaweed
1 quantity Isaac's Sushi Rice (see p.44)
4 ounces wild smoked salmon, cut into
  oblong pieces about 1/2-inch wide
  (about 2/3 cup)
1 firm but ripe avocado, cut into long pieces of
  a similar size to the salmon
1/2 cup sesame seeds, lightly toasted

For serving: wasabi paste, soy sauce, and
  pickled ginger

bamboo sudari mat for rolling

Wave a sheet of nori seaweed over a gas flame until soft and pliable, about 8–10 seconds. Place the seaweed on a bamboo sudari mat, shiny side down and with the grain running horizontally.

Wet your hands to prevent the rice from sticking to them. Using your fingertips, press enough rice onto the seaweed to cover it as evenly and as thinly as possible. Lift up the seaweed and the rice, turn the whole thing upside-down and place back onto the bamboo mat. Arrange the strips of salmon and pieces of avocado horizontally across the seaweed and rice, tucking the end in. Carefully roll up, pressing firmly on the bamboo mat, then remove the mat.

Sprinkle some sesame seeds on a clean counter and roll the sushi roll in the seeds until evenly covered. Wet a sharp knife and cut the roll into 6–8 even-sized pieces, using a sawing motion. Serve with wasabi paste, soy sauce, and pickled ginger.

Temari Sushi (Plastic Wrap Sushi)

MAKES 20–30 PIECES   (P: 20 mins.)

20–30 sprigs of dill
1/2 quantity Isaac's Sushi Rice (see p.44)

For the filling:
2 ounces smoked salmon (lox), cut into
  1-inch squares (about 1/3 cup) *or*
20–30 cooked shrimp *or*
1/2 English cucumber, sliced wafer-thin and
  cut into 1-inch squares *or*
2 ounces rare roast beef, thinly sliced and cut
  into 1-inch squares (about 1/3 cup)
For serving: wasabi paste and pickled ginger

Lay a piece of plastic wrap, about 4 inches square, on a clean counter and place a sprig of dill and then a piece of smoked salmon or other filling of your choice at the center of it. Mold a teaspoonful of sushi rice into a loose ball and place on top of the dill and salmon.

Pick up all four corners of the plastic and gather them in the middle. Twist the plastic to compact the rice and form a small ball. Repeat the process with the remaining salmon and other fillings.

Keep each piece of sushi wrapped in the plastic until just before serving and keep cool but not refrigerated. You may want to put a dab of wasabi under the rice if served as finger food. For an appetizer, arrange on a plate and serve with pickled ginger and a little wasabi.

a cocktail party

A cocktail party is a brilliant way to entertain lots of guests, especially if they don't know each other very well. Handing around food and sipping cocktails will help people to mingle and get the conversation flowing.

Start by serving savory canapés with your cocktails, wine, or champagne. Variety is essential, and there are so many exciting choices from mini poppadoms to Bloody Mary jellos to mussels served in their shells. Haphazard combinations can work really well, but give some thought to the order you bring them out. Balance is also crucial—you will need a combination of hot and cold canapés as well as a mix of meat, fish, and vegetarian. Choose the canapés carefully so you have a contrast of flavors and texture—some mild, some hot and spicy, some perennial favorites. You may also want to balance expensive canapés which include shrimp or lobster with favorites like cheddar cheese croquettes and mixed bruschetta.

Try to bring out a new dish every 20 minutes or so—timing is everything because you don't want to overwhelm your guests—they will only be able to manage one at a time, but you don't want too big a gap, especially if the wine is good!

About two thirds of the way through the evening, you may want to switch to a good dessert wine and replace your savory selection with delicious sweet canapés such as petit fours, little lemon tartlets, glazed strawberries or ice creams served in egg cups.

sleek and stylish

Be creative when choosing serving plates—they don't have to be conventional. Improvise using old glass mirrors, a large slate tile, brie boxes, and flat, wicker baskets. Sea shells and banana leaves can be a great way to present food, as are antique spoons, Moroccan tea glasses, lemongrass stalks, and small tin plates or espresso cups.

Arrange each item dramatically on its serving plate—long lines or a symmetrical pattern are striking, but random displays can be equally dramatic—the trays should turn people's heads as the trays circulate, whetting their appetite. Although you can prepare a lot of food in advance (see individual recipes for advice), always garnish at the last moment.

Strew surfaces with grass, flowers, petals, glass beads, or even candies. Keep the lighting bright enough so that guests can see what they are eating and move around confidently, but place tea lights on reflective surfaces for extra sparkle.

Provide lots of bright paper napkins and toothpicks, and make sure that whoever is handing around the food also has a small bag or bowl to collect them; otherwise you will find them in your flower pots for months afterwards. Take turns handing around food and working in the kitchen, so that you can enjoy the party. Turn your guests into waiters—it's a good trick for shy friends or those that don't know many people.

Tomato and Coconut Milk Soup in Espresso Cups with Tiny Breadsticks

SERVES 6   (P: 10 mins./C: 15 mins.)

Canned tomatoes and coconut milk are mandatory in-stock ingredients. This recipe can be put together in a few minutes or made well ahead and frozen. For a cocktail party, serve in espresso cups, accompanied by tiny breadsticks.

1 small onion, finely chopped
$^1/_2$ tablespoon butter
4 cups homemade tomato puree (see p.294) or 2 x 14$^1/_2$-ounce cans tomatoes, blended and strained
14-ounce can coconut milk
1 cup homemade chicken broth or vegetable broth (see p.295)
2$^1/_2$ tablespoons chopped cilantro
salt and freshly ground pepper
sugar

For serving: crème fraîche (if unavailable, use sour cream and/or heavy cream), fresh cilantro, and tiny breadsticks (see p.35)

6 espresso cups

Sweat the onion in the butter over a gentle heat until soft but not colored.

Add the tomato puree (or blended canned tomatoes plus juice), coconut milk, and broth. Add the chopped cilantro and season with salt, pepper, and sugar to taste. Bring to a boil and simmer for a few minutes.

Blend, taste, and dilute further with broth if necessary. Return to a boil and correct the seasoning. Taste carefully: the final result depends upon the quality and balance of the homemade ingredients.

Pour into espresso cups. Garnish with a tiny spoonful of crème fraîche and some cilantro leaves. Serve 1 or 2 tiny breadsticks on the saucer as an accompaniment.

Top Tip: Canned tomatoes need a surprising amount of sugar to counteract their acidity. Fresh milk cannot be added to the soup—the acidity in the tomatoes will cause it to curdle.

Thai Chicken on Chinese Spoons with a Leaf of Fresh Cilantro

MAKES 30   (P: 10 mins./C: 20 mins.)

This is also delicious as an appetizer or main course, served with Thai fragrant rice.

1 pound skinless and boneless free-range, organic chicken breasts
$^1/_4$ cup ($^1/_2$ stick) butter
1$^1/_2$ ounces fresh ginger, peeled and finely chopped (about 3 tablespoons)
2 garlic cloves, crushed
$^1/_4$ teaspoon green peppercorns
1 lemongrass stalk, finely chopped
2 red chiles, finely chopped
2 teaspoons lime juice
$^1/_2$ teaspoon ground coriander
14-ounce can coconut milk
2 teaspoons chopped cilantro
salt and freshly ground pepper
30 cilantro leaves, for garnishing

30 Chinese porcelain spoons

Cut the chicken into 30 evenly sized cubes. Heat half the butter in a large frying pan and sauté the chicken pieces until lightly browned on all sides.

Melt the remaining butter in the frying pan and sauté the ginger, garlic, peppercorns, lemongrass, and chiles. Add the lime juice and ground cilantro. Gradually stir in the coconut milk, bring to a boil, then reduce the heat and simmer for 8 minutes.

Add the chicken pieces and continue to simmer for 2–3 minutes. Stir in the chopped cilantro leaves and season to taste. The recipe can be prepared ahead up to this point.

Serve on porcelain Chinese spoons, each garnished with a cilantro leaf.

Top Tip: Also delicious as an appetizer with fresh cilantro leaves or as a main course with Thai fragrant rice.

Mixed Bruschetta Plate

(P: 20 mins./C: 65 mins.)

Great for a casual party. Ensure each topping is well seasoned. Good bread is essential—you'll need lots of sourdough bread and plenty of napkins.

Making the bruschetta

1 loaf of sourdough or country bread
whole garlic cloves, cut in half
extra virgin olive oil

First prepare the toppings (see below). Slice the bread 1/2-inch thick (cut in half if the slices are too large) and charbroil the bread. Alternatively cook on a preheated, ridged grill pan until nicely marked on both sides. Rub each piece with a cut clove of garlic, drizzle with extra virgin olive oil, and coat with the chosen topping. Arrange a selection of bruschettas on a large platter or pass around on separate plates.

Roast Sweet Pepper and Flat Parsley Topping

a generous 1/3 cup extra virgin olive oil
1–2 garlic cloves, crushed
Roasted red and yellow peppers (see p.298), peeled, seeded, and cut into strips
2-3 tablespoons coarsely chopped flat-leaf parsley or basil
salt and freshly ground pepper

Heat the olive oil in a pan over medium heat. Add the garlic and cook for a few seconds. Add the peppers, toss, and cook for 5–6 minutes. Add the parsley or basil and season to taste. Spoon this over the warm bruschettas and serve immediately.

Spicy Roast Pepper Topping

Add 1/2–1 teaspoon red pepper flakes to the garlic in the pan and proceed as above.

Olive, Chili, and Caper Topping

1 cup tapenade (see p.75)
1/4 teaspoon red pepper flakes
1 generous tablespoon capers, rinsed
1 generous tablespoon chopped flat-leaf parsley

Whizz all the ingredients together in a food processor. Taste—you may need to add a little salt. Spoon onto warm bruschettas and serve as soon as possible.

Kale and Parsley Pesto Topping

1 pound fresh kale
1 garlic clove, crushed
1/2 teaspoon sea salt or Kosher salt
1/3 cup extra virgin olive oil
2 1/2 tablespoons chopped parsley (optional)

Remove the stalks from the kale leaves and wash well, then dry. Put all the ingredients in a food processor and whizz to a thick paste. This can be made ahead and stored in a covered jar in the fridge for several days.

Tip: If you prefer a more mellow flavor, blanch the kale in boiling, salted water for 3–4 minutes, refresh, drain well, and proceed as above.

Fava Bean and Mint Topping

Best made with fresh young fava beans.

1 pound shelled fresh fava beans (about 3 1/2 cups)
leaves from 6–8 sprigs of mint, plus extra for garnishing
4-5 tablespoons extra virgin olive oil
2 1/2 tablespoons freshly squeezed lemon juice
salt and freshly ground pepper

Cook the fava beans in boiling water until tender (just a few minutes). Drain, reserving the cooking liquid. Rinse the beans under running cold water, then blend in a food processor. Add the mint, olive oil, and lemon juice and mix to a puree, adding enough of the reserved cooking liquid to give a soft consistency. Season to taste with salt and pepper. Taste and adjust the levels of lemon and oil, if necessary. Garnish with mint.

More Toppings for Bruschetta or Crostini (see p.74)

1   Arugula leaves, mozzarella cheese, roasted red and yellow peppers
2   Potato, olives, and Provençal herbs
3   Smashed fava beans, extra virgin olive oil, and freshly grated Pecorino cheese
4   Artichoke hearts with olive oil and Parmesan cheese
5   Poached pear, Gorgonzola cheese, and arugula leaves
6   Sautéed wild or wide-capped mushrooms with marjoram and shavings of Parmesan cheese
7   Spiced eggplant (see p.243)
8   Gravadlax with mustard and dill mayonnaise (see p.140)
9   Goat cheese with onion marmalade (see p.298) and watercress
10 Buffalo mozzarella cheese, vine-ripened tomatoes, and basil leaves
11 Warm cannellini beans with extra virgin olive oil and rosemary
12 Pata Negra, serrano ham, or prosciutto and arugula leaves
13 Goat cheese, home-roasted tomatoes, crispy prosciutto, and arugula leaves
14 Spiced eggplant (see p.243), goat cheese, and arugula leaves
15 Manchego cheese and membrillo (quince paste)
16 Soft goat cheese with tapenade oil (see p.75) or caramelized onion
17 Avocado, tomato, chile, and cilantro
18 Ruffles of fresh prosciutto and arugula leaves
19 Thinly sliced raw tuna with picked ginger and wasabi

Croustade with Goat Cheese, Chestnut Honey, and Thyme Leaves

SERVES 2   (P: 5 mins./C: 5 mins.)

A delicious speedy snack.

2 slices of good bread, cut into 1/4-inch slices
2–3 ounces fresh goat cheese (about 1/2-3/4 cup)
1/2 teaspoon thyme leaves
4 teaspoons chestnut honey (or another strongly flavored honey)

For serving: thyme flowers (optional)

Preheat the broiler. Toast or charbroil the slices of bread. Spread thickly with goat cheese. Sprinkle generously with fresh thyme leaves.

Pop under the hot broiler for 2–3 minutes. Drizzle with chestnut honey and serve immediately, sprinkled with thyme flowers if available.

Rory's Spicy Popcorn

SERVES 10   (P: 5 mins./C: 5 mins.)

An irresistible munchie to nibble with drinks.

1/4 cup (1/2 stick) butter
1 teaspoon salt
1/2 teaspoon red pepper flakes (optional)
1/2 teaspoon cracked black pepper
1/2 teaspoon ground cumin
1/2 teaspoon curry powder (hot)
1 tablespoon fresh ginger root, grated
1 garlic clove, finely chopped
1/4 cup sunflower oil
1/2 cup popcorn, still unpopped of course

In a small saucepan, melt the butter and add all the seasonings. Do not let this mixture fry but keep it very hot.

In a large heavy pot, heat the vegetable oil over very high heat until it is nearly smoking. Add the popcorn, cover, and shake. Wait until you hear the first few pops, then quickly toss in the spiced butter, cover, and shake. Shake the pot continuously in a front to back motion until the corn stops popping. Quickly tip into a funky serving bowl or better still serve in paper cups or cones.

Mini Poppadoms with Spicy Chicken, and Banana and Cardamom Raita

MAKES 30   (P: 10 mins. + 30 mins.
                 TO MARINATE/C: 15 mins.)

All of the prep for these yummy canapés can be done ahead, but they taste best if the chicken is warm.

3 chicken breasts, preferably free-range organic
30 mini poppadoms
sunflower oil, for frying and roasting

For the spice marinade:
2 teaspoons ground cumin
2 teaspoons paprika
$1/2$ teaspoon cayenne pepper
2 teaspoons ground turmeric
1 teaspoon sugar
$1/2$ teaspoon freshly ground black pepper
1 teaspoon salt
1 large garlic clove, crushed
$2^1/2$ tablespoons freshly squeezed lemon juice

For serving: Banana and Cardamom Raita
  (see p.294) and cilantro leaves

First make the spice marinade by mixing all the ingredients in a bowl.

Cut the chicken breasts into cubes or small slices, toss them in the marinade, and refrigerate for at least 30 minutes.

Next make the Banana and Cardamom Raita (see p.294).

Cook the poppadoms in batches in sunflower oil in a deep-fat fryer at 400°F or in a frying pan with oil to a depth of 1 inch. When the oil is almost smoking, cook for just a few seconds. Drain well and set aside.

Preheat the oven to 400°F.

Spread the chicken cubes on a baking tray just large enough to hold them in a single layer. Drizzle with sunflower oil. Cook for 10–15 minutes or until fully cooked but still succulent and juicy. Toss regularly while cooking.

Arrange the poppadoms on a plate—square or rectangular plates look particularly good, but round is fine, too. Place a teaspoonful of the spicy chicken on each poppadom. Top with a little Banana and Cardamom Raita, and garnish with a cilantro leaf. Serve as soon as possible.

Tiny Yorkshire Puddings with Pink Lamb, Tapenade Mayo, and Arugula Leaves

MAKES ABOUT 28   (P: 10 mins. + 1 HOUR
                       TO STAND/C: 15 mins.)

$1^3/4$ cups white flour
2 cage-free, organic eggs
$1^1/4$ cups milk
1 tablespoon butter, melted and cooled
sunflower oil, for greasing

Tapenade Mayo (see p.297)

6–8 ounces slightly pink roast lamb, cut into slivers—about $3/4$-1 cup (or charbroil a thick chump chop until medium rare, let it rest, and slice thinly as needed)

For serving: $1/4$ cup membrillo (quince paste; optional) and arugula, mint, or flat-leaf parsley

Sift the flour into a bowl. Make a well in the center of the flour and drop in the eggs. Using a small whisk or wooden spoon, stir continuously, gradually drawing the flour from the sides into the eggs, while adding the milk to the central well in a steady stream. When all the flour has been incorporated, whisk in the remaining milk and the butter. Alternatively put all the ingredients into a blender and whizz for a few seconds. Let stand for 1 hour.

Preheat the oven to 450°F.

Heat two mini-muffin pans in the oven, grease with sunflower oil, and half-fill with the batter. Return to the oven and bake for 15 minutes or until crisp, golden, and bubbly.

Remove from the pans. Fill each pudding with a tiny blob of tapenade mayo. Top with a thin sliver of lamb and a little cube of membrillo (if available). Garnish with an arugula leaf, sprig of fresh mint, or flat-leaf parsley. Serve as quickly as possible.

Other serving suggestions
Rare roast beef, horseradish sauce (see p.158), and wild arugula leaf
Rare roast beef, onion marmalade (see p.298), and watercress leaves
A ruffle of Lollo Rosso lettuce, pink trout, dill mayo (see p.297), and horseradish sauce (see p.158)

Bocconcini, Olives, Sun-blush Tomatoes, and Pesto on Skewers

MAKES 20
(P: 50 mins. + 10 mins. TO MARINATE)

Bocconcini are baby mozzarella cheeses— great for salads, finger food, and some pasta dishes. They do, however, need a little bit of help with flavor, which is where the pesto comes in.

20 bocconcini
extra virgin olive oil
pesto (see p.297)
20–40 basil leaves
20 Kalamata olives, pitted
20 sun-blush tomatoes

bamboo cocktail sticks or satay sticks

Drain the bocconcini and pop them into a bowl, drizzle with extra virgin olive oil, and add a generous tablespoon of homemade pesto. Toss to coat. Cover closely and let marinate for at least 10 minutes.

Thread a bocconcino, a basil leaf, an olive, and a piece of sun-blush tomato onto each of 20 bamboo cocktail sticks.

Dill Potato Cakes with Gravadlax and Sweet Mustard Mayo

SERVES 8   (P: 30 mins./C: 5 mins.)

2 pounds unpeeled floury potatoes
2-4 tablespoons butter
3 tablespoons flour
2 1/2 tablespoons chopped dill
creamy milk, as required
salt and freshly ground pepper
flour seasoned with salt and pepper
clarified butter (see p.108) or olive oil,
   for frying

For serving: Mustard and Dill Mayonnaise
   (see p.140), Gravadlax (see p.140), and
   sprigs of dill

Cook the potatoes whole in their skins, in well-salted boiling water to cover. Drain, pull off the skin, and mash right away with the butter, flour, and chopped dill, adding a few drops of creamy milk if the mixture is too stiff. Season with lots of salt and pepper. Taste and adjust the seasoning if needed, adding more dill if necessary.

Shape into potato cakes 3/4-inch thick. Coat the cakes in seasoned flour and fry in clarified butter or olive oil until golden on one side, then flip over and cook on the other side, about 4–5 minutes in total. They should be crusty and golden. Serve on very hot plates.

Put a spoonful of Mustard and Dill Mayonnaise on top of each potato cake. Top with slivers of gravadlax and tiny sprigs of dill. Serve immediately.

Other good things to serve with the potato cakes
Use smoked salmon (lox), or smoked mackerel or trout instead of gravadlax, and substitute crème fraîche (or sour cream) for the mustard mayo.
Use hot crispy bacon or chorizo instead of gravadlax, with crème fraîche or sour cream.
Top the dill potato cakes with smoked haddock, a fried quail egg and some flat parsley.

Cheddar Cheese and Thyme Leaf Croquettes

MAKES 25–30   (P: 10 mins./C: 20 mins.)

2 cups milk
1 sprig of thyme
3/4 cup plus 1 1/2 tablespoons roux (see p.139)
salt and freshly ground pepper
2 cage-free, organic egg yolks
2 cups sharp cheddar cheese, grated,
   and 1/4 cup Parmesan or Gabriel cheese,
   grated
1 tablespoon thyme leaves
olive oil, for deep-frying
For serving: Sweet Chili Sauce (see p.296) or
   Spicy Tomato Jam (see p.298)

For the coating:
white flour (preferably unbleached) seasoned
   with salt and pepper
beaten egg
fine white bread crumbs

Put the cold milk into a saucepan, add the sprig of thyme, bring slowly to a boil, and simmer for 3–4 minutes. Strain, bring the milk back to a boil, and whisk in the roux bit by bit—it will get very thick but persevere. (The roux always seems like a lot too much, but you need it all, so don't decide to use less.)

Season with salt and freshly ground pepper. Cook for 1–2 minutes over gentle heat, then remove from the heat. Stir in the egg yolks, cheese, and thyme leaves. Taste and correct the seasoning. Spread out on a flat tray to cool.

When the mixture is cold or at least cool enough to handle, shape into balls about the size of a walnut. Roll first in seasoned flour, then in beaten egg, and then in fine bread crumbs. Chill until firm but bring back to room temperature before cooking, otherwise they may burst. Heat olive oil in a deep fryer to 300°F and cook the croquettes until crisp and golden. Drain on paper towels and serve hot with Sweet Chili Sauce or Spicy Tomato Jam.

Note: Cooked Cheddar Cheese and Thyme Leaf Croquettes can be kept warm in the oven for up to 30 minutes. They can also be frozen and reheated in the oven.

Alicia's Cheese Straws

MAKES ABOUT 12   (**P:** 20 mins./**C:** 15 mins.)

Alicia Wilkinson from Silwood Kitchens in Capetown gave me this delicious recipe.

9 ounces puff or rough puff pastry (or 1 sheet from a 17.3-ounce box of frozen)
1 cage-free, organic egg white, lightly whisked
4 ounces Parmesan cheese (about 1½-2 cups)
1 cup cheddar cheese
pinch of cayenne pepper

Preheat the oven to 375°F.

Roll the chilled puff pastry dough into a large rectangle on a floured marble slab. Brush the lower half of the dough with lightly beaten egg white.

Finely grate the two cheeses and mix with a good pinch of cayenne pepper. Sprinkle half the cheese and spice mixture liberally over the egg white, and press down gently.

Fold the upper half of the dough down over the lower half and press with a rolling pin to seal. Roll out the dough to the size of the first rectangle. Paint the entire sheet with egg white and cover with the remaining cheese and spice.

Chill for approximately 10 minutes. Cut the dough into thin strips ½-inch wide and twist into straws. Bake for 10–15 minutes or until golden brown and cooked through. Cool on a wire rack.

Serve in a tall glass or mug. We use a tall, scalloped zinc pot or children's tin sand buckets depending upon the occasion.

Top Tip: The raw prepared cheese straws can be laid on wax paper or parchment paper and frozen. If using parchment paper, you can place directly onto a baking sheet from the freezer and bake the straws as above, allowing a little extra cooking time. But don't try this with the wax paper.

Alicia's No-cook Chorizo con Marmalada de Sevilla

MAKES 36   (**P:** 5 mins.)

When Alicia Rios came to Ballymaloe to teach a tapas course with me, she created this unlikely but delicious tapa using our Seville orange marmalade—perfect for easy entertaining. Your guests will need paper napkins!

⅓ cup Seville orange marmalade
8 ounces chorizo sausage (about 2 cups sliced)
For serving: small rounds of bread (optional)

Chop the peel in the marmalade into short chunks. Cut the chorizo into slices and top each slice with a little Seville orange marmalade.

Serve as is or on little slices of French bread or baguettes.

Chorizo with Sherry

SERVES 4   (**P:** 5 mins./**C:** 5 mins.)

Don't forget this simple tapa—it's one of our favorites. Enjoy it with a chilled fino or manzanilla sherry.

7 ounces chorizo (the semi-cured type suitable for cooking is perfect)—about 1⅔ cups
⅓ cup fino or medium-dry sherry
a drizzle of extra virgin olive oil
For serving: crusty bread
toothpicks

Cut the chorizo into slices about ¼ inch thick.

Heat a frying pan over medium heat and add a drizzle of olive oil. When the oil begins to smoke, add the chorizo and fry until it starts to crisp. Turn over and fry the other side. When both sides are crisp, add the sherry. It will splutter but keep the pan over the heat for a few seconds to burn off the alcohol. Transfer the contents of the pan to a dish and tuck in immediately. Provide a few toothpicks, and some crusty bread to mop up the juices.

Melon and Spearmint Soup with Crispy Prosciutto Served in Shot Glasses

MAKES 2¹/₂ CUPS–12 SHOT GLASSES
(P: 10 mins./C: 10 mins.)

1 really ripe Ogen melon or canteloupe
juice of 1 large lemon
3-4 tablespoons sugar
2¹/₂ tablespoons chopped spearmint
4 ounces sliced prosciutto ham (about 1 cup)

For serving: 12 sprigs of mint

Peel and seed the melon. Puree the flesh in a blender with the lemon juice and spearmint, and add sugar to taste. Chill.

Meanwhile preheat the oven to 350°F.

Spread the prosciutto slices in a single layer on a baking tray. Lay another tray on top. Cook for 5–8 minutes or until the prosciutto is crisp and the fat has melted. Let cool, then break the prosciutto into long slivers.

To serve, pour the melon "soup" into shot glasses. Top with a splinter of prosciutto and a sprig of fresh mint.

Mussels with Dill Mayo and Cucumber, Red Onion, and Fennel Salsa

MAKES 60   (P: 20 mins./C: 5 mins.)

60 large fresh mussels
coarse sea salt or Kosher salt

*For the Cucumber, Red Onion, and Fennel
Salsa:*
1 crisp cucumber seeded and finely chopped
1¹/₂ small red onion finely chopped
¹/₂ cup finely chopped fresh fennel
  (¹/₄ cup dill may be used instead)
A few drops of white wine vinegar
Salt, freshly ground pepper, and sugar

For serving: Dill Mayonnaise (see p.297)

Check that all the mussels are closed. If any are open, tap each mussel on the counter, and discard all that do not close within a few seconds. (A good maxim with shellfish: "If in doubt, throw it out.") Wash the mussels well in several changes of cold water.

Spread them in a single layer in a pan, cover with a lid, and cook over gentle heat. As soon as the shells open the mussels are cooked—this usually takes 2–3 minutes. Remove from the pan immediately or they will shrink in size and become tough.

Remove the beard and discard the top shell from each mussel. Loosen the mussel from the bottom shell, but leave it in the shell. Open the rest in the same way. Set aside until quite cold. Coat a serving dish evenly with coarse salt. Arrange the mussels in their half shells on the salt.

Next make the salsa. Mix all the ingredients together. Taste and correct the seasoning. It should taste sweet and sour. Spoon the salsa over half of the mussels and put a blob of dill mayo on the others. Serve at room temperature or chilled.

Parmesan Toasts

MAKES 20   (P: 10 mins./C: 30 mins.)

What began as a way to use up leftover bread has become a delicious nibble to serve with drinks or as an accompaniment to tomato, onion, cauliflower, pumpkin, or kale soups.

day-old yeast or sourdough bread, or
  good-quality baguette, cut into ¹/₈-inch-
  thick slices (cut the baguette diagonally)
extra virgin olive oil
Parmesan cheese, grated

Preheat the oven to 300°F.

Brush one side of each slice of bread with olive oil. Sprinkle with Parmesan.

Arrange in a single layer on a baking tray and bake slowly until golden brown and crisp, about 30 minutes. Serve warm.

Cheat's Tarts with Various Fillings

MAKES 20   (P: 5 mins./C: 10 mins.+
                       TIME TO PREPARE FILLING)

I'm frightfully snooty about sliced bread but this is a brilliant trick shown to us by one of my favorite cookery writers and joint-owner of "Books for Cooks" in London, Eric Treuille, when he came to teach at the school a few years ago. I've listed a number of fillings you could use. Look in your fridge, experiment, and use fresh herbs and herb flowers. Unfilled Cheat's Tarts will keep in an airtight tin for several days.

ready-sliced white bread
filling of your choice (see suggestions, right)

rolling pin
mini muffin tray
1³/₄-inch cookie cutter

Preheat the oven to 400°F.

Cut the crusts off the bread. Roll the bread out very thinly with a rolling pin—it should be completely flat. Stamp out circles with the cookie cutter. Fit into the mini muffin pans and press down hard into the muffin cups.

Bake for 5–7 minutes until crisp and pale golden in color. Remove from the tray while hot. Cool on a wire rack and add your chosen filling.

Suggested fillings
Wild salmon pâté (Salmon Rillettes, see p.74) with Cucumber Pickle Relish (see p.73) and dill
Chicken liver pâté with sun-blush tomatoes
Goat cheese and Kumquat Compote (see p.267)
Goat cheese with pesto and cherry tomatoes
Shrimp with guacamole and cilantro
Crab mayonnaise (crabmeat mixed with a little mayo)
Smoked mussels with mayo
Goat cheese, piquillo pepper, and basil leaves
Smoked Mackerel and Dill Pâté (see p.73)
Crab, ginger, and lime (see p.60)

Ragged Phyllo Tartlets

MAKES 20   (**P:** 20 mins./**C:** 65 mins.)

4 ounces phyllo dough (about 5-6 sheets)
$^1/_2$ cup (1 stick) butter, melted

mini muffin pans, bun trays, or muffin trays

For the crab, ginger, and lime filling:
9 ounces crabmeat, drained (about 1 cup)
2-4 teaspoons peeled and grated fresh
  ginger root
juice and finely grated zest of 1 lime
$^1/_2$ unpeeled English cucumber, chopped
  into $^1/_4$-inch pieces
1 avocado, chopped
$^1/_3$ cup homemade mayonnaise
  (see pp.296–297)
Tabasco sauce
sea salt or Kosher salt
cilantro leaves, for garnishing

Preheat the oven to 350°F.

Using a wide pastry brush, brush 1 sheet of phyllo dough with the melted butter. Cut into roughly 4$^1/_2$-inch square pieces—adjust the size to fit your tartlet trays or mini muffin cups. Butter the muffin cups and line each one with 3 buttered phyllo dough squares placed at slightly different angles. (It is easier to assemble the stacks before pressing into the pan.) Repeat until all the dough has been used. Bake to a rich golden brown, about 6–8 minutes.

Carefully remove the tartlets from the pans and let cool completely on a wire rack. These tartlets can be baked a few days in advance. Store in an airtight container at room temperature.

To make the filling, mix the crabmeat with the ginger, lime zest, cucumber, avocado, and mayonnaise. Add a few dashes of Tabasco, a little lime juice, and salt. Taste and adjust the seasoning if needed. Close to the time of serving, divide the crab mixture among the ragged phyllo tartlet cases. Garnish with cilantro leaves.

Top Tip: Keep the phyllo dough covered with a damp cloth until ready to use otherwise it will become dry, brittle, and unusable.

Quesadillas with Tomato Salsa and Guacamole and Various Fillings

SERVES 8   (**P:** 5 mins./**C:** 5 mins.
+ TIME TO PREPARE FILLING)

Quesadillas are a favorite snack in Mexico. On Sundays in Oaxaca there are little stalls on the streets and squares with women making and selling these delicious stuffed tortillas. They flavor them with an aromatic leaf called hoja santa. Cut into 6 or 8 wedges, they make delicious finger food. There are masses of delicious filling combinations. Experiment and have fun! Serve with Guacamole, Tomato and Cilantro Salsa, and refried beans.

16 corn tortillas or 4 wheat flour tortillas
$2^{1}/_{4}$-$4^{1}/_{2}$ cups mild cheddar cheese, grated, or a mixture of cheddar and mozzarella
1 onion or 8 scallions, sliced
4 green chiles, sliced (optional)

For serving: Guacamole (see p.294), Tomato and Cilantro Salsa (see p.294), Refried Beans (see p.21)

Heat a wide iron pan, griddle, or heavy nonstick pan. Lay a tortilla on the hot pan. Sprinkle about $^{1}/_{4}$ cup grated cheese on top, depending upon size, keeping it a little from the edge, then add a few onion rings and some sliced chile (if using). Cover with another tortilla. Cook for a minute or two. As soon as the cheese begins to melt, carefully turn the assembly over. Cook for 1–2 minutes on the other side.

Serve just as it is or cut into wedges, accompanied by Guacamole, Tomato and Cilantro Salsa, and, if you like, Refried Beans.

Quesadillas with Cheese and Zucchini Blossoms
A favorite filling for quesadillas in Oaxaca is simply grated Oaxacan string cheese (mozzarella is our nearest equivalent) and fresh zucchini blossoms. Thinly sliced green chile is sometimes added for extra excitement!

Quesadillas with Spicy Pork or Chicken and Slices of Avocado
Add spicy pork or chicken and slices of avocado to the basic recipe.

Quesadillas with Shredded or Smoked Chicken, Mango, Brie, and Lime
Substitute slices of Brie for the cheddar cheese in the basic recipe and add some cooked shredded chicken, chopped mango, and lime.

Quesadillas with Pappadew Peppers, Mozzarella, and Basil Leaves
Sprinkle some sliced pappadew peppers over the grated mozzarella cheese in the basic recipe. Top with a layer of basil leaves.

Quesadillas with Chorizo
Add some chopped or thinly sliced chorizo to the basic recipe.

Seafood Quesadillas
Prawns or strips of smoked salmon (lox) can also be delicious.

Quesadillas with Spicy Chicken, Mozzarella, and Cilantro
Spread some cooked spicy chicken, mozzarella, chopped scallions and fresh cilantro leaves over the tortilla and continue as in the basic recipe.

Quesadillas with Mozzarella and Tapenade or Pesto
Spread tapenade (see p.75) or pesto (see p.297) on a tortilla and top with grated mozzarella. Top with another tortilla, cook, and serve as before.

Quesadillas with Anchoïade and Mozzarella
Substitute anchoiade for tapenade or pesto in the above recipe.

Quesadillas with Ballymaloe Country Relish and Cheddar Cheese
Spread a tortilla with Ballymaloe Country Relish, top with grated cheddar cheese, and sprinkle with chopped parsley and scallions. Cook and serve as before.

Marinated Black Olives

SERVES 10   (**P:** 10 mins.)

Marinated olives are so easy to make—we always have some ready to nibble with drinks. Prepare at least a few days ahead of serving.

1³/4 cups black olives, such as Kalamata
1 garlic clove, crushed
1/2 teaspoon smoked paprika
1 tablespoon sherry vinegar or red wine vinegar
pinch of freshly ground cumin
a little grated orange zest (optional)
1/4 cup extra virgin olive oil

Stir all the ingredients together and store in a Mason jar or canning jar. Cover the olives completely with oil and they will keep for several weeks.

Marinated Green Olives

SERVES 10   (**P:** 5 mins.)

1³/4 cups Spanish green olives
2–4 garlic cloves, lightly crushed
1/4 cup extra virgin olive oil
1 tablespoon finely chopped fresh oregano or annual marjoram
For serving: wild garlic or chive flowers

Stir everything together and store in a Mason jar or canning jar. Serve at room temperature, sprinkled with wild garlic or chive flowers.

Roasted Kalamata Olives

SERVES 20   (**P:** 5 mins./**C:** 15 mins.)

4 cups black olives, such as Kalamata
5 large garlic cloves, bashed
1 teaspoon chopped fresh rosemary or thyme
3–4 strips lemon or orange zest (scrub the fruit first if it's not organic)
extra virgin olive oil, for drizzling

Preheat the oven to 350°F.

Mix the olives, garlic, chopped herb, and citrus zest in a small roasting pan and drizzle with olive oil. Roast for 10–15 minutes. Serve warm.

Spicy Candied Nuts

SERVES 6–8   (**P:** 5 mins./**C:** 10 mins.)

1 cup walnut halves
1/3 cup sugar
1/2 teaspoon ground cinnamon
1/2 teaspoon ground coriander
1/4 teaspoon ground star anise

Preheat the oven to 350°F.
Spread the walnuts in a single layer on a baking tray and toast them for 4–5 minutes until they smell rich and nutty.

Meanwhile, mix the sugar with the spices and spread this mixture over the bottom of a frying pan in an even layer. Scatter the walnut halves on top. Cook over medium heat until the sugar melts and starts to color. Carefully rotate the pan until the walnuts are completely coated with the amber-colored spicy caramel. Turn out onto nonstick, parchment paper or an oiled baking tray. Let cool and harden. Store in an airtight container until needed.

Edamame with Sea Salt

SERVES 4–8   (**P:** 20 mins./**C:** 65 mins.)

These fresh soybeans in their pods are one of our favorite nibbles—they are not widely available fresh, but can be found frozen and then cooked in minutes.

5 cups water
1 pound edamame
1 tablespoons sea salt (or Kosher salt)

Bring the water to a boil and add the edamame beans. Return to a boil and cook for 3–4 minutes. Taste. If sufficiently cooked, they'll have a slight bite. Drain and sprinkle with the sea salt. Serve cold.

tips on finger food

The essence of good finger food is fantastic ingredients. Find a good deli or farmers' market and buy lots of top-quality bocconcini, heirloom tomatoes, salami, juicy olives, and a really good smoked fish and that will happily make up half of your menu.

Finger food does not need to be complicated—a fat shrimp on some brown bread with a spoonful of mayonnaise and a sprig of parsley or dill—what could be more delicious, but the quality of ingredient is key to this simplicity, and good-quality ingredients make it easier. If the tomatoes and mozzarella taste good to start with, you don't have to work so hard. Or serve miniature portions of your favorite recipes with a saucy herb garnish or spoonful of crème fraîche or sour cream and jazz up the presentation—sprigs of woody herbs, such as rosemary, make creative alternatives to the usual toothpicks and skewers, and Virginia creeper leaves, vine leaves, and even fig leaves are also very effective.

Food should be no larger than single mouthfuls and you should reckon on 5–7 pieces per person, less if this is an appetizer. Make sure that there are at least two vegetarian choices and if one of your guests cannot eat gluten, for example, do take care to explain the ingredients as you present them. Consider what will be popular dishes and make more of them than, for example, something containing tapenade, which not everybody likes.

Put the toppings on at the last-possible minute, otherwise they will melt through, especially when using porous bases such as shrimp chips. Nonetheless you can do a little preparation: arrange the bases on serving trays and have the garnish ready to go. Then it's just a simple matter of warming up the topping, loading up the tray, and off you go.

Cocktail party (see pp.46–49)
Bloody Mary Jellos (see p.66)
Melon and Spearmint Soup with Crispy Prosciutto (see p.57)
Mussels with Salsa Cruda, Dill Mayo, and Cucumber (see p.59)
Mixed Bruschetta (see p.52)

To drink
A classic margarita (p.290) will work here but if you want to provide a wine alternative, the most effective choice is probably a New World sparkling wine with plenty of ripe fruit character. Champagne or even Prosecco would be a little too austere. Go for something that combines elegant bubbles with a touch of tropical fruits. Names like Lindauer, Deutz, Jansz, and especially Pelorus (from Cloudy Bay in New Zealand) are worth seeking out.

Around the world menu
Sushi (see p.44)
Thai Chicken on Chinese Spoons (see p.51)
Mini Poppadoms with Spicy Chicken, and Banana and Cardamom Raita (see p.54)
Teeny Yorkshire Puddings (see p.54)
Quesadillas with Tomato Salsa (see p.61)
Marinated Black Olives (see p.62)

To drink
Sushi goes brilliantly with two starkly contrasting wines: Australian dry Riesling and fino or manzanilla sherry. The Riesling will also work with Thai chicken—and everything else on this menu with the possible exception of the quesadillas. These ideally need something with more fruit, perhaps a New World chardonnay. If you must have one wine, stick to a fresh Chilean sauvignon blanc, it will do a pretty good job.

Vegetarian party
Tomato and Coconut Milk Soup in Espresso Cups (see p.51)
Crostini with Spiced Eggplant (see p.53)
Bocconcini, Olive, Sun-Blush Tomato, and Pesto on Skewers (see p.55)
Cheddar Cheese and Thyme Leaf Croquettes (see p.55)
Alicia's Cheese Straws (see p.56)
Cruditées with Hummus and Eggplant Puree (see pp.213, 118, 119)

To drink
Both the crostini and the croquettes need a fruity red with a bit of bite: Montepulciano d'Abruzzo will fit the bill perfectly. Although a lot of people turn their noses up at it, retsina works magically well with both hummus and eggplant. But chill it very thoroughly and do bear in mind that some people think it's the wine equivalent of turpentine!

appetizers

A taste of things to come, an appetizer should tempt your tastebuds but leave your guests wanting more. Here are ideas for crostini, dips, and pâtés as well as ceviche and spring rolls. Many other recipes can double up as appetizers, so do also have a look in Soups and Salads as well as Finger Food—just remember to keep portions small. Appetizers don't have to be served at the dinner table—if you want to introduce people informally, choose dishes that can be passed around with an aperitif.

Campari and Blood Orange Granita

SERVES 10   (P: 10 mins. + FREEZING TIME)

An irresistible and deliciously non-fattening appetizer. Of course it can be made with juicy oranges at any time of the year, but keep an eye out for blood oranges from January to March. A non-alcoholic version with blood orange juice alone is also perfectly delicious.

4 cups freshly squeezed blood
   orange juice, or a mixture of blood orange
   juice and ordinary orange juice
1 3/4 cups sugar, plus extra if needed
1/2 cup Campari
1 cage-free, organic egg white (optional)
1–2 blood oranges, segmented, and mint
   leaves, for garnishing (optional)

Mix the orange juice with the sugar and Campari. Stir and taste, and add more sugar if needed. Make the granita in one of the following three ways:

1 Pour the mixture into a stainless steel or plastic container and put into the freezer. After about 4–5 hours, when the mixture is semi-frozen, remove from the freezer and whisk until smooth; then return to the freezer. After a few hours, whisk again. Return to the freezer until needed.

2 Let the mixture freeze completely in a stainless steel or plastic container, then break into large pieces and whizz in a food processor for a few seconds. Add the slightly beaten egg white, whizz again for another few seconds, then return to the bowl and freeze until needed.

3 Pour into the drum of an ice cream maker or sorbetière and freeze for 20–25 minutes. Scoop out and serve immediately, or store in a covered bowl in the freezer until needed. This method produces a less granular texture, which might be called a sherbet rather than a granita.

To serve, scoop out the granita and serve just as it is in chilled cocktail glasses, white bowls or plates, or, if you wish, garnished with segments of blood orange and some mint leaves.

Bloody Mary Jellos

SERVES 8   (P: 10 mins. +SETTING TIME)

1 tablespoon vodka
dash of Tabasco
two 1/4-oz envelopes gelatin
1/4 cup water
micro greens and a few tender celery stalks,
   chopped, for garnishing

8 shot glasses

For the fresh tomato juice:
1 pound (about 3 medium) very ripe
   tomatoes, skinned, halved, and seeded
1 scallion with a little green on it or
   1 slice onion, 2 inches in diameter,
   3/8-inch thick
3 fresh basil or spearmint leaves
2 teaspoons white wine vinegar
1/2 cup cold water
1 teaspoon salt
1 teaspoon sugar
freshly ground black pepper

First make the fresh tomato juice. Blend all the ingredients together in a blender, then strain. Taste and correct the seasoning if necessary.

Add the vodka and a dash of Tabasco to the fresh tomato juice. Taste.

Remove the top pan of a double boiler, and heat water in the bottom pan to simmering. Add the 1/4 cup water to the top pan and sprinkle the gelatin over it. Once it's spongy, place over the simmering water until the gelatin melts completely.

Stir some of the tomato juice into the gelatin, then mix with the remaining juice, stirring well. Pour into 8 shot glasses or oiled molds. Let them set in the fridge for several hours.

Serve with some micro greens and a little chopped tender stalks from the heart of celery.

Warm Mushroom and Arugula Salad with Shavings of Desmond Farmhouse Cheese

SERVES 8   (**P:** 10 mins./**C:** 10 mins.)

This is a poshed-up version of mushrooms on toast. Virtually all fungi are delicious on toast, so this can be a very humble or very exotic dish depending upon the mushroom variety chosen.

extra virgin olive oil, for frying
2 pounds wide-capped mushrooms or oyster
  mushrooms, or better still a mix of shiitake,
  enoki, oyster, and beech mushrooms, sliced
  into biggish chunks (leave the enoki whole)
salt and freshly ground pepper
1/2 cup coarsely chopped fresh marjoram
1 garlic clove, crushed (optional)
lots of arugula leaves
shavings of Desmond farmhouse cheese
  or Parmesan

For serving: crostini or charbroiled bruschetta
  (see p.52)

Heat a little olive oil in a hot frying pan. Cook the mushrooms in batches and keep warm while you cook the rest. Season each batch with salt and freshly ground pepper, and sprinkle with chopped marjoram and some crushed garlic, if you like. When all are cooked, taste and, adjust the seasoning if needed.

Arrange a fistful of arugula leaves on each plate and top with the mushrooms. Sprinkle a few shavings of Desmond farmhouse cheese or Parmesan on top and serve immediately with crostini or charbroiled bruschetta.

This salad is just as good if the mushrooms have cooled to room temperature.

Peach, Gorgonzola, and Watercress Salad

SERVES 8   (**P:** 20 mins.)

A gorgeous summer appetizer salad that can be made in minutes. For a light lunch, add a few strips of pangrilled chicken breast.

4 ripe peaches or nectarines
3–4 tablespoons lemon juice
sugar to taste
watercress sprigs or arugula leaves
8 ounces Gorgonzola cheese, or Crozier or
  Wicklow Blue (about 2 cups)
1 cup shelled walnuts, coarsely chopped
4 scallions, thinly sliced

For the dressing:
2 1/2 tablespoons white wine vinegar
1/2 cup walnut oil
1 teaspoon whole-grain mustard
1 teaspoon honey
sea salt, or Kosher salt and freshly
  ground pepper

First make the dressing. With a fork, whisk all the ingredients together in a little bowl. Taste, and adjust the seasoning as needed.

Cut the fruit in half and remove the pits, then slice into 6–8 pieces. If you are not serving immediately, sprinkle the fruit with some lemon juice and sugar and toss gently.

Scatter a few watercress sprigs or arugula leaves on each plate, tuck a few peach or nectarine slices in here and there, and crumble some gorgonzola or other blue cheese over the top. Drizzle some dressing over it, and sprinkle the walnuts and thinly sliced scallions on top. Serve soon.

Top Tip: Add a few strips of pangrilled chicken breast for a light lunch.

Salad of Goat Cheese with Arugula, Figs, and Pomegranate Seeds

SERVES 8   (P: 10 MINS)

1 fresh pomegranate
32 fresh walnut or pecan halves
enough arugula leaves for 8 helpings
a few radicchio leaves
4 small fresh goat cheeses
8–12 fresh figs or plump dried figs (try to find
  the Turkish ones on a raffia string)

For serving: crusty bread

For the dressing:
1/2 cup extra virgin olive oil
1/4 cup freshly squeezed lemon juice
1/2–1 teaspoon honey
salt and freshly ground pepper

Cut the pomegranate in half and break each side open. Flick out the glistening, jewel-like seeds into a bowl, avoiding the bitter, yellowy pith. Alternatively, if you are in a hurry, put the cut side down on the palm of your hand over a bowl and bash the skin side firmly with the back of a wooden spoon—this works really well but it tends to be a bit messy, so be sure to protect your clothes with an apron as pomegranate juice really stains.

Next make the dressing. Just whisk the oil, lemon juice, and honey together in a bowl. Season well with salt and freshly ground pepper.

Toast the walnut or pecan halves in a dry pan over medium heat until they smell sweet and nutty.

Just before serving, toss the arugula leaves and radicchio in a deep bowl with a little of the dressing. Divide between 8 large white plates. Cut each cheese into 6 pieces. Cut the figs into quarters from the top, keeping each one still attached at the bottom. Press gently to open out. Divide the cheese between the plates, 3 pieces per plate, and place a fig in the center.

Sprinkle with pomegranate seeds and freshly roasted nuts. Drizzle with a little extra dressing and serve immediately with crusty bread.

Ciabatta Stuffed with Good Things

MAKES 12 SMALL PIECES
                    (P: 10 mins./C: 15 mins.)

Serve as an appetizer, finger food, or for a yummy snack.

1 loaf ciabatta bread
extra virgin olive oil, for brushing
12 thin slices prosciutto or serrano ham
Roasted red and yellow peppers (see p.298)
1/2 cup Pesto (see p.297) or
  Tapenade (see p.75)
8 ounces soft white cheese, such as
  mozzarella, sliced (about 2 cups)
arugula leaves

Preheat the oven to 450°F.

Cut the bread in half lengthwise and remove some of the soft bread from both the top and bottom with your fingers (save it for making bread crumbs). Brush the bottom with olive oil. Lay the slices of prosciutto on the bottom, allowing them to drape over the sides of the bread.

Top with roasted red and yellow peppers and drizzle with pesto or tapenade. Cover with slices of cheese and drizzle with more pesto or tapenade. Top with some arugula leaves and fold the prosciutto over them to enclose the filling. Lay the other half of the bread on top and press gently.

Place the stuffed ciabatta on a baking tray and cook for 10–15 minutes. Transfer to a cutting board and cut into pieces about 1 1/2 inches wide. Serve warm.

Other yummy fillings
Tapenade, mozzarella cheese, and arugula leaves
Tomato, mozzarella cheese, balsamic vinegar, and basil leaves
Chorizo sausage, mozzarella cheese, roasted red and yellow pepper, and marjoram leaves

Salmon Spring Rolls with Cilantro Dipping Sauce

MAKES 12   (**P:** 20 mins./**C:** 10 mins.)

1 pound wild salmon, about 1 inch
  thick, skinned
12 rice paper wrappers (*bahn trang*),
  6¹/₂ inches square
48 cilantro leaves
¹/₃ cup finely chopped scallion greens
salt and freshly ground pepper
vegetable oil, for frying
cilantro sprigs, for garnishing

For the marinade:
¹/₃ cup extra virgin olive oil
¹/₃ cup fresh lime juice
3 tablespoons chopped cilantro leaves
1 teaspoon peeled and grated fresh ginger

For the cilantro dipping sauce:
Juice of 2 limes
2¹/₂ tablespoons rice vinegar
4 teaspoons soy sauce
2¹/₂ teaspoons sugar, or to taste
2 teaspoons peeled and grated fresh ginger
3 tablespoons chopped cilantro leaves

Whisk the marinade ingredients together in a large bowl and season with salt and pepper to taste.

Cut the salmon crosswise into 12 pieces, each about 4 x 1 inch and add them to the marinade. Let marinate, turning the pieces occasionally, for 30 minutes.

Meanwhile make the dipping sauce. Whisk all the ingredients together except the chopped cilantro, and add 1 tablespoon water.

Remove the salmon from the marinade and pat dry. Fill a wide, shallow bowl with hot water. Soak a rice paper wrapper for about 10 seconds, until very pliable. Drain. Lay it on a cutting board and arrange a salmon piece on the bottom half of the wrapper, leaving a 1-inch border on the bottom edge and on each side. Top the salmon with about 4 cilantro leaves, 1 teaspoon scallion greens, and salt and pepper to taste. Roll up the rice paper wrapper around the filling, folding in the sides after the first roll to enclose the filling completely. Make the remaining spring rolls in the same way.

In a deep 12-inch wide nonstick pan or a deep fryer, heat ¹/₄ inch oil over a medium-high heat until hot but not smoking. Fry 4 spring rolls at a time, turning once, until they are golden brown and the salmon is cooked through, about 3 minutes. Drain on paper towels. Repeat the procedure with the remaining spring rolls.

Stir the chopped cilantro into the dipping sauce. Garnish the spring rolls with sprigs of cilantro, and serve as a first course or as finger food, accompanied by the dipping sauce.

Mexican Seviche

SERVES 10–12
    (**P:** 10 mins. + 5¹/₂ HOURS TO MARINATE)

The fish is "cooked" by the action of the lime juice.

2 pounds fillets of very fresh white fish, such
  as monkfish (angler fish), cod, or flounder
2 lemons
4 limes
salt and freshly ground pepper
2 garlic cloves, finely chopped
¹/₄-¹/₃ cup chopped cilantro leaves
²/₃ cup onion, finely sliced
1–2 fresh red or green chiles
1 red pepper, finely chopped
1 green pepper, finely chopped
For serving: crusty white bread

For the garnish:
crisp lettuce, such as Bibb
2 ripe avocados, sliced
4 scallions, sliced at an angle

Skin the fish, slice or cube it into ¹/₂-inch pieces, and put them into a deep, stainless steel or china bowl. Squeeze the juice from the lemons and limes and pour it over the fish. Sprinkle with salt, freshly ground pepper, and chopped garlic. Cover, put in the fridge, and let marinate for 3–4 hours.

Add the chopped cilantro, sliced onion, chiles, and half of the chopped red and green peppers. Cover and return to the fridge for 1¹/₂ hours. Then serve or keep covered in the fridge until later

To serve, arrange a few crisp lettuce leaves on each plate and place a tablespoon of seviche in the center. Decorate with slices of avocado, the remaining chopped peppers, and the sliced scallions. Serve with crusty white bread.

Vine-ripened and Sun-blush Tomato Salad with Mozzarella, Prosciutto, and Basil

SERVES 8   (**P:** 10 mins./**C:** 15 mins.)

The mozzarella can be wrapped in the prosciutto ahead of time and refrigerated until needed.

8 small balls of buffalo mozzarella
8 slices of Parma ham (prosciutto)
8 large or 16 small vine-ripened tomatoes
salt and freshly ground pepper
24 sun-blush tomatoes
extra virgin olive oil, for drizzling
balsamic vinegar, for drizzling,
sugar or honey, to taste
pesto (see p.297)
lots of fresh basil leaves

For serving: crusty bread

Wrap the mozzarella balls in prosciutto, cover loosely with plastic wrap, and keep chilled in the fridge until needed. This can be done ahead of time.

Preheat the oven to 475°F.

Slice the fresh tomatoes into 1/4-inch thick slices and season with salt and freshly ground pepper. Drizzle a little olive oil and balsamic vinegar over them, taste, and add a little sugar or honey if needed.

Put the prosciutto-wrapped mozzarella onto a baking tray and place in the oven until the prosciutto is beginning to crisp and the mozzarella is starting to melt, about 10 minutes. Meanwhile arrange a circle of slightly overlapping tomato slices on individual serving plates (we like to use wide, deep soup bowls). Arrange 3 pieces of sun-blush tomatoes on top. Heat some balsamic vinegar and reduce it to make it a little syrupy and concentrate the flavor. Drizzle a little pesto and balsamic vinegar around the edges and over the top.

When the prosciutto and mozzarella balls are ready, pop them on top of the tomatoes. Scatter lots of fresh basil leaves over them, and drizzle some olive oil on top. Serve with crusty bread.

Baja-style Fish Tacos with Chipotle Mayonnaise

SERVES 10   (**P:** 20 mins./**C:** 10 mins.)

10 small fillets of fresh white fish, such as
  haddock, brill, flounder, or lemon sole
flour seasoned with salt and pepper
oil, for deep-frying

For the chili beer batter:
1 2/3 cups white flour
2 teaspoons mustard powder
2 teaspoons chili powder
1 teaspoon salt
2 teaspoons sugar
3 cage-free, organic eggs, beaten
1 cup beer

For the chipotle mayonnaise:
1 cup homemade mayonnaise
  (see p.296)
1 1/2 tablespoons pureed chipotle chiles in
  adobo sauce
juice of 1 lime
1 tablespoon chopped cilantro leaves

For the accompaniments:
10 flour tortillas
20 lettuce leaves
Guacamole (see p.294)
Tomato and Cilantro Salsa (see p.294)

First make the chili beer batter. Sift the flour into a bowl and add the mustard powder, chili powder, salt, and sugar. Make a well in the center, drop in the eggs, and gradually add the beer, whisking all the time from the center to the edge of the bowl in ever-increasing concentric circles until all the flour is incorporated. Cover and let stand.

Make the mayonnaise in the usual way, then add the chiles in adobo sauce, lime juice, and chopped cilantro.

Preheat the oven to 350°F. Wrap the tortillas in aluminum foil and heat through in the oven for 5–10 minutes. Meanwhile, prepare the rest of the accompaniments.

Heat the oil in a deep-fat fryer to 375°F. Dip each fish fillet in the batter, cook until crisp, and drain on paper towels.

Put a few lettuce leaves on half a warm tortilla, top with a piece of crispy fish, some chipotle mayonnaise, Guacamole, and Tomato and Cilantro Salsa, fold over and enjoy!

Carpaccio with Slivers of Parmesan, Arugula and Truffle Oil

SERVES 12   (P: 15 mins.)

Carpaccio is a brilliant recipe to make a little really good beef go a very long way. For this I use our own organically reared free-range Aberdeen Angus, or some Pol Angus beef from our local butcher Kevin Day.

1 pound tenderloin of beef, preferably
  Aberdeen Angus, Hereford, or Shorthorn
  (fresh not frozen)
about 5 arugula leaves per person, depending
  on the size
4–5 very thin slivers Parmesan cheese per
  person
Maldon or Halen Mon sea salt (or Kosher salt)
freshly cracked pepper
truffle oil or extra virgin olive oil
24–36 black Kalamata olives (optional)

For serving: focaccia or ciabatta bread

Chill the meat. Slice the beef with a very sharp knife to ¼-inch thick. Place each slice on a piece of wax paper and cover with another piece of wax paper. Roll gently with a rolling pin until the meat is almost transparent and has doubled in size. Peel the wax paper off the top, turn the meat onto a chilled plate, and gently peel away the other layer of paper.

Arrange the arugula leaves on top of the beef and scatter a few very thin slivers of Parmesan over the leaves. Sprinkle with sea salt and freshly cracked pepper. Drizzle with truffle oil or with your very best extra virgin olive oil.

Scatter a few black olives (if using) over each portion and serve immediately with crusty bread—focaccia or ciabatta is best.

A little drizzle of Tapenade (see p.75) is delicious instead of truffle oil and olives.

Smoked Mackerel and Dill Pâté with Cucumber Pickle Relish

SERVES 8   (P: 10 mins. + 1 HOUR IN FRIDGE)

8 ounces undyed smoked mackerel, skinned,
  boned, and flaked
¹/₃ cup (³/₄ stick) unsalted butter, softened
¹/₃ cup full-fat cream cheese
juice of ¹/₂ lemon
2¹/₂ tablespoons chopped fresh dill
1 generous tablespoon chopped fresh parsley
sea salt or Kosher salt and freshly ground
  pepper
sprigs of dill and dill flowers, for garnishing

For the accompaniments:
generous amount of watercress leaves
extra virgin olive oil
white wine vinegar
angular toast

For the cucumber pickle relish (serves 10–12):
2¹/₄ pounds unpeeled, English cucumber,
  thinly sliced
3 small onions, thinly sliced
1³/₄ cups sugar
2¹/₂ tablespoons salt (be very accurate
  with salt)
1 cup cider vinegar

Put the flaked mackerel in a blender and add the butter, cream cheese, and lemon juice. Whizz to a smooth puree. Transfer to a bowl and fold in the dill and parsley. Add salt and pepper to taste.

Divide between ramekins or small bowls. Top each with a sprig of dill and a dill flower. Cover and chill for at least an hour.

Fo serving, toss the watercress leaves in a little olive oil and a dash of white wine vinegar. Sprinkle with salt and pepper and toss. Put some of the leaves on each plate, along with a ramekin of pâté; serve with angular toast and the cucumber pickle relish.

To make the relish, put the cucumber and onion slices in a large pyrex or stainless steel bowl. In a separate bowl, mix together the sugar, salt, and vinegar, and pour them over the cucumber and onion; toss well. Cover tightly and chill in the fridge for at least 1 hour or, ideally, several hours to overnight before using. The relish keeps well for up to a week in the fridge.

A Dozen Oysters and a Pint of Murphy's or Guinness

SERVES 1–2   (P: 10 mins.)

What could be easier or more delicious than freshly shucked oysters with Irish wheaten bread and a pint of gorgeous creamy stout? If you come from County Cork, Murphy's is the sacred drop—Guinness is not quite the same, but we have to admit it makes a good substitute.

12 native Irish oysters

For the accompaniments:
seaweed or sea salt (or Kosher salt)
1 lemon wedge
Wheaten Bread (see p.37) or Ballymaloe
  Brown Yeast Bread (see p.35)
2¹/₂ cups Murphy's stout or Guinness

First wash the oysters if necessary, then open with a shucking knife or stubby, short-tipped knife. When opening oysters, it's wise to protect your hand with a folded towel. Wrap the towel around your hand, then set the deep shell on it with the wide end on the inside. Grip the oyster firmly in your protected hand, insert the tip of the knife into the hinge, and twist to lever the two shells apart; you'll need to exert quite a lot of pressure, so protect your hand well. Then slide the blade of the knife under the top shell to detach the oyster from the shell. Discard the top shell, then loosen the oyster from the deep shell and flip it over to reveal the plump side—don't lose the precious briny juice.

Make a bed of seaweed or sea salt on a plate and arrange the oyster shells over the top. Serve with a lemon wedge, some wheaten bread, and a pint of the black stuff!

Salmon Rillettes with Piquillo Pepper Crostini

SERVES 12–16   (P: 20 mins./C: 5 mins.)

As well as a fine appetizer this also makes great finger food.

3 tablespoons butter, plus 1¹/₂ cups
  (3 sticks) butter, softened
12 ounces smoked wild or organic Irish
  salmon
12 ounces fresh salmon, cooked
pinch of grated nutmeg
lemon juice, to taste
chopped fennel (optional)
salt and freshly ground pepper

For the crostini:
extra virgin olive oil, for frying
3–5 thick slices of really good-quality French
  baguette per person, cut diagonally

For the accompaniments:
1 x 14-ounce can piquillo peppers
brocco shoots (if you can't find these, use
  alfalfa or radish sprouts, or small arugula
  leaves or sprigs of purslane
sea salt or Kosher salt

Melt the 3 tablespoons butter in a pan over low heat; add the smoked salmon and 1 tablespoon water. Cover and cook for 3–4 minutes or until the salmon no longer looks opaque. Let it get quite cold.

Cream the cup and a half of softened butter in a bowl. With two forks, shred the smoked and cooked fresh salmon and mix well together. Still using a fork (not a food processor), mix them with the creamed butter. Sprinkle in some grated nutmeg and season with salt and pepper. Taste, and add lemon juice as necessary, and some chopped fennel if you have it. Salmon rillettes will keep perfectly in the fridge for 5–6 days, provided they are sealed with clarified butter (see p.108).

Not long before serving, make the crostini. Add olive oil to a frying pan to a depth of ¹/₄ inch and heat until very hot. Cook the crostini a few at a time, turning them as soon as they are golden. Drain on paper towels.

For serving, scoop a spoonful of salmon rillettes on a warm crostini and top with a strip or twirl of piquillo pepper. Top with brocco shoots or a tiny arugula leaf or sprig of purslane and a few flakes of sea salt.

Other good things to do with salmon rillettes:
1 Serve in individual containers or in a ceramic mold with cucumber pickle relish (see p.73).
2 Use to fill pappadew peppers, and serve with a salad of arugula leaves.
3 Serve as an appetizer or a light lunch.

Dips

Choose from these delicious dips and eat with grilled flat bread (see p.40).

Beetroot and Ginger Relish

SERVES 8–20   (P: 10 mins./C: 30 mins.)

This sweet-and-sour relish is particularly good with cold meats and coarse country pâtés, or used simply as a dip.

3 tablespoons butter
8 ounces onions, chopped (about 2 cups)
1/4 cup sugar
salt and freshly ground pepper
1 pound raw beets, peeled and grated (about 3 cups)
2 tablespoons sherry vinegar
1/2 cup red wine
2 teaspoons peeled and grated fresh ginger

Melt the butter in a pan and, over a very low heat, cook the onion until very soft. Add the sugar and salt and pepper to taste, and add all the remaining ingredients and cook over a low heat for 30 minutes. Leave to cool then pour into a sterilised screwtop jar and refrigerate until needed (the relish will keep for ages). Serve cold.

Tapenade

MAKES 1 CUP   (P: 5 mins.)

The strong, gutsy flavor of tapenade can be an acquired taste—however, the black olive paste becomes addictive and has become a "new basic" for me.

1²/₃ black olives (do not buy ready-pitted olives)
4 canned anchovy fillets
2 garlic cloves, chopped
1/3 cup extra virgin olive oil

In a food processor, whizz together the olives, anchovy fillets, and garlic, gradually adding the olive oil (alternatively, use a mortar and pestle.) Blend to a coarse or smooth puree, as you prefer. It will keep for months in the fridge.

Serve with crudités, bruschetta and crostini, lamb dishes, pasta, goat cheese…

Tapenade Oil
Add lots of extra virgin olive oil and store in a sterilized jar. Use it to drizzle over goat cheese, etc.

Tuna and Olive Tapenade
Flake a can of Ortiz tuna and add tapenade to taste. Serve with flat bread, tiny pita breads, hot crusty bread, or toast.

Dukkah

MAKES 1 CUP   (P: 10 mins./C: 15 mins.)

This Middle Eastern mix of spices and nuts can be served with crudités, warm pita bread and a bowl of best olive oil. Just dip a piece of crisp vegetable or a strip of bread into the olive oil and then into the dukkah. It is also delicious with all manner of things such as hard-boiled eggs or sprinkled over grilled meats as seasoning.

1/2 cup shelled hazelnuts
1/3 cup sesame seeds
2¹/₂ tablespoons whole coriander seeds
2 tablespoons whole cumin seeds
2 teaspoons black peppercorns
1 teaspoon ground cinnamon
pinch of salt

Preheat the oven to 400ºF. Put the hazelnuts on a baking tray and roast for 10 minutes or until the skins start to loosen. Let cool and rub off the loose skins. Chop finely or whizz them in a food processor for just a few seconds. Be careful not to overblend or the nuts will mush into a paste.

Heat a small, heavy frying pan over medium heat and add the sesame seeds. Shake gently until they turn a shade darker and release a nutty aroma. Tip into a bowl. Repeat with the coriander and cumin seeds.

Place the roasted seeds and peppercorns in a clean spice grinder or coffee grinder and whizz quickly to give a coarse, dry powder. Mix with the cinnamon and salt, then add the chopped nuts. Taste and adjust the seasoning if needed.

Store in a screw-top jar or airtight container. It will keep for months but loses its fragrance and oomphf over time.

soups and salads

Perfect as an appetizer or light meal, there are endless variations of soups and salads, so feel free to play around with ingredients and garnishes. Soups can be hot or cold, thin, thick, or solid, and a basic soup can be livened up with a few fresh herbs or spices. Salads rely on the best-quality ingredients and a great dressing. Think about the balance of color and texture. But don't just think of them as appetizers. Soup can be served as a canapé in miniature cups, bowls, or shot glasses or in a chunky mug for a cheering winter lunch or late-night snack. A salad can be beefed up into a summer lunch by adding some boiled potatoes, croûtons, or delicious cold meat.

Thai Chicken, Galangal, and Cilantro Soup

SERVES 8   (**P:** 10 mins./**C:** 10 mins.)

A particularly delicious example of how fast and easy making a Thai soup can be. Serve in Chinese porcelain bowls if available. The kaffir lime leaves and galangal (a type of ginger used in Thai cooking) are served but not eaten. The chile may of course be nibbled. Shrimp can be substituted for the chicken in this recipe with equally delicious results.

4 cups homemade chicken broth (see p.295)

4 kaffir lime leaves

2-inch piece of galangal, peeled and sliced, or smaller piece of fresh ginger

$1/3$ cup fish sauce (*nam pla*)

$1/2$ cup freshly squeezed lemon juice

8 ounces free-range organic chicken breast, very finely sliced (about 1 cup)

1 cup coconut milk

1–3 Thai red chiles

7 tablespoons cilantro leaves

Put the chicken broth into a pot and add the lime leaves, galangal or ginger, fish sauce, and lemon juice. Bring to a boil, stirring continuously, then add the finely sliced chicken and coconut milk. Continue to cook over high heat for 1–2 minutes until the chicken is just cooked.

Crush the chiles with a knife or Chinese chopper, add to the soup along with the cilantro leaves, and cook for just a few seconds. Ladle into hot Chinese rice bowls and serve immediately.

Noodle Soup

Blanched and refreshed rice noodles are a great addition to this soup—hey presto, you have a main course. Serve in wide pasta bowls, with lots of fresh cilantro scattered over the top.

Top Tip: Fresh lime leaves are not available in every store, so buy them any time you spot them and pop them into a bag and freeze.

Bacon and Cabbage Soup

SERVES 6   (**P:** 15 mins./**C:** 15 mins.)

Bacon and cabbage are a quintessential rustic meal, and a favorite flavor combination of mine. Cabbage soup is also delicious. Spinach or watercress, Swiss chard or kale can be substituted for cabbage.

$1/4$ cup ($1/2$ stick) butter

5 ounces potatoes, chopped into $3/8$-inch pieces (about 1 cup)

4 ounces onions, chopped into $3/8$-inch pieces (about 1 cup)

salt and freshly ground pepper

5 cups light chicken broth or vegetable broth (see p.295)

9 ounces Savoy cabbage leaves (stalks removed), chopped (about 4–$4^{1/2}$ cups)

$1/4$–$1/2$ cup ceam or creamy milk

8 ounce piece of bacon, in 1 piece, boiled

a little oil, for frying

$2^{1/2}$ tablespoons chopped parsley

Melt the butter in a heavy pot. When it foams, add the potatoes and onion and turn them in the butter until well coated. Sprinkle with salt and freshly ground pepper. Cover and sweat over low heat for 10 minutes.

Add the broth and boil, covered, until the potatoes are soft, then add the cabbage and cook with the lid off until the cabbage is cooked (keeping the lid off will preserve the green color of the cabbage). Do not overcook or the vegetables will lose both their fresh flavor and their color.

Remove from the heat and stir in the cream or creamy milk to thin to desired texture. Puree the soup in a blender. Taste, and adjust the seasoning if needed.

Just before serving, cut the bacon into strips. Heat a very little oil in a frying pan and toss in the bacon to heat through and get a little crispy. Add to the soup and sprinkle in some parsley.

Cabbage and Caraway Soup

Add 1–2 teaspoons freshly crushed caraway seeds to the potatoes and onions in the frying pan. Omit the bacon garnish.

Top Tip: If this soup is not served immediately, reheat until it just boils and serve. Prolonged boiling spoils the color and flavor of green soups.

Mediterranean Fish Soup with Rouille

SERVES 6–8   (**P:** 1 HOUR/**C:** 30 mins.)

I can't pretend that this gutsy fish soup is either quick or easy to make—it is a labor of love but worth every minute. Fish soups can be made with all sorts of combinations of fish. Don't be the least bit bothered if you don't have exactly the fish I suggest, but use a combination of whole fish and shellfish. In my opinion the crab adds almost essential richness.

5$^1/_2$ pounds mixed fish, such as 1 whole flounder, $^1/_2$ cod, and 2 small whiting
$^2/_3$ cup extra virgin olive oil
10 ounces onions, chopped (about 2 cups)
1 large garlic clove, crushed
5 large very ripe tomatoes, sliced, or one 14-ounce can tomatoes
5 sprigs of fennel
2 sprigs of thyme
1 bay leaf
3 swimming crabs or 1 common crab
6–8 mussels and 8–10 shrimp, including heads
5 cups fish stock or water, to cover
$^1/_4$ teaspoon saffron strands
pinch of cayenne pepper
salt and freshly ground pepper
chopped parsley, for garnishing

Prepare the fish. Remove the gills and cut the fish into chunks, bones, heads, and all.

In a large, deep pot, heat the olive oil until smoking, add the onions and garlic and stir for a minute or two. Add the tomatoes, fennel, thyme, and bay leaf, then the fish and shellfish, and cook, stirring occasionally, for 10 minutes. Pour in enough fish stock or water barely to cover, boil, and cook for another 10 minutes. Add more liquid if it reduces too much.

Soak the saffron strands in a little fish stock or water. Pick the mussel shells and crab shells out of the soup. Remove the crab meat from the shells and add to the soup. Add cayenne, salt, and pepper to taste, then add the saffron and its soaking liquid.

Push the soup through a food mill or strainer. This may seem like an impossible task but you'll be surprised how effective it is—there will be just a mass of dry bones left, which you discard.

Next make the rouille.

Rouille

SERVES 8   (**P:** 10 mins.)

This is a spicy mayonnaise from the Mediterranean.

1 piece of French baguette bread, about 2 inches long
4 garlic cloves
1 cage-free, organic egg yolk
pinch of saffron strands
$^1/_2$ cup extra virgin olive oil
salt and freshly ground pepper

Cut the bread into cubes and soak in about $^1/_2$ cup of the hot fish soup. Squeeze out the excess liquid and mix to a mush in a bowl.

Crush the garlic to a fine paste, preferably using a mortar and pestle, then add it to the soggy bread along with the egg yolk and saffron. Season with salt and freshly ground pepper. Mix well and whisk it into the oil drip by drip, as if making mayonnaise. If the mixture looks too thick or oily, add 2 tablespoons of hot fish soup and continue to stir.

Croûtons

(**P:** 10 mins./**C:** 10 mins.)

8 thin slices of French baguette bread
3–4 ounces Gruyère cheese, grated (about $^3/_4$-1 cup)

Food mill (Mouli legume)

Toast the bread until the slices are dry and crisp. Spread the croûtons with rouille and sprinkle with the Gruyère cheese.

Return the soup to a boil. Serve each guest a bowl of fish soup garnished with some parsley and 3–4 croûtons, a little bowl of rouille, and a little bowl of freshly grated Gruyère cheese.

To eat, spread the croûtons with rouille, sprinkle with Gruyère cheese, and float in your bowl of soup—exquisite.

Cauliflower Cheese Soup with Cheddar and Walnut Crisps

SERVES 6–8   (**P:** 20 mins./**C:** 25 mins.)

1 medium organic cauliflower, with green
  leaves retained
4 cups chicken or vegetable broth
  (see p.295), plus a bit extra if needed

For the mornay sauce:
2¹/₂ cups milk, with a dash of cream
1 slice of onion
3–4 slices of carrot
6 peppercorns
sprig of thyme or parsley
roux (see p.139)
5 ounces cheddar cheese, grated or
  a mixture of Gruyère, Parmesan, and cheddar
  (about 1¹/₄ cups)
¹/₂–1 teaspoon Dijon mustard, to taste
salt and freshly ground pepper

For serving: Cheddar and Walnut Crisps
  (see recipe below) or cubes of cheddar
  cheese, chopped parsley, and croûtons

Remove the cauliflower's outer leaves and wash both the vegetable and the leaves well. In a pot just large enough to take the cauliflower, put an inch water and add a little salt in. Chop the leaves into small pieces and break the cauliflower into florets. Put the leaves into the pan, then the cauliflower pieces on top of the leaves, cover, and simmer for about 10–15 minutes until the cauliflower is cooked. Test by piercing a stalk with a knife; it should be quite soft. Remove the cauliflower and the leaves to an ovenproof serving dish.

While the cauliflower is cooking, make the mornay sauce. Put the milk into a large saucepan with the slice of onion, carrot slices, peppercorns, and the thyme or parsley. Bring to a boil, simmer for 3–4 minutes, then remove from the heat and let it infuse for 10 minutes.

Strain out the vegetables from the milk, return the milk to a boil, and thicken with roux to a light coating consistency. Add the grated cheese and a little mustard, salt, and freshly ground pepper, then taste and adjust the seasoning if needed. Add the cauliflower, its cooking water, and the chicken or vegetable broth. Puree the soup in batches, adding more broth if necessary to create your desired consistency. Taste and adjust the seasoning if needed.

Serve with Cheddar and Walnut Crisps or cubes of cheddar cheese, chopped parsley, and croûtons.

Cheddar and Walnut Crisps

MAKES ABOUT 50   (**P:** 10 mins./**C:** 5 mins.)

**Yummy to serve with Cauliflower Cheese
Soup or as a nibble with drinks.**

3 ounces aged cheddar cheese, grated
  (about ²/₃ cup)
3 ounces Parmesan cheese, grated (about
  ²/₃ cup)
¹/₂ cup walnuts, chopped
1 tablespoon thyme leaves

2 baking sheets lined with parchment paper
  or foil

Preheat the oven to 350F.

Mix the cheeses in a bowl with the chopped walnuts and thyme leaves.

Drop spoonfuls of the mixture onto the lined baking sheets. Flatten with the back of a spoon. Bake for about 5 minutes or until bubbling and golden around the edge.

Remove the baking sheets from the oven and let cool for a few minutes. Lift off the crisps with a spatula and cool on a wire rack.

Potato Soup with Harissa Oil and Coriander Seed Grissini

SERVES 6   (P: 10 mins./C: 20 mins.)

Most people would have potatoes and onions in the house even if the cupboard were otherwise bare, so one could make this simply delicious soup at a moment's notice. It can be served completely unadorned, or it can be embellished with a variety of garnishes: wild garlic, parsley pesto, melted leeks, sizzling garlic butter, or chorizo and flat-leaf parsley. We sometimes pile homemade potato chips on top and pour some sizzling garlic butter over them at the last moment!

$1/4$ cup ($1/2$ stick) butter
1 pound potatoes, cut into $1/2$-inch cubes
   (about 3 cups)
4 ounces onions, cut into $1/2$-inch chunks
   (about 1 cup)
salt and freshly ground pepper
4 cups homemade chicken broth or
   vegetable broth (see p.295)
$1/2$ cup creamy milk, or to taste
harissa oil (see recipe below)
flat parsley leaves, for garnishing
coriander seed grissini (Breadsticks, see p.35,
   rolled in crushed coriander seeds before
   baking), for serving

Melt the butter in a heavy pot. When it foams, add the potatoes and onions and toss them in the butter until well coated. Sprinkle with salt and a few grinds of pepper. Lay a "paper lid" such as a butter wrapper directly on the sweating vegetables, and put the cover on the pot. Sweat over low heat for about 10 minutes.

Meanwhile return the stock to a boil. When the vegetables are almost soft but have not yet colored, add the hot stock and cook until the vegetables are soft.

Puree the soup in a blender. Taste and adjust the seasoning if needed. Thin with creamy milk to the required consistency. Serve in warm bowls, with a drizzle of harissa oil and a few flat parsley leaves on top, accompanied by coriander seed grissini.

Harissa Oil

MAKES 1 CUP   (P: 5 mins.)

My brother Rory O'Connell gave me this delicious recipe. Serve with grilled meat, fish, and vegetables, and drizzle into soups.

6 chiles, roasted, peeled, and seeded
$1/2$ cup tomato puree
8 garlic cloves, crushed
1 tablespoon cumin seeds, toasted and ground
1 tablespoon coriander seeds, toasted
   and ground
$1/2$ cup extra virgin olive oil, plus extra
   if needed
1 teaspoon red wine vinegar
$1/4$ cup chopped cilantro leaves
salt, freshly ground pepper, and sugar, to taste

Place the prepared chiles, tomato paste, garlic, and ground spices in a food processor. Puree until smooth and continue blending while you drizzle in the olive oil and vinegar.

Transfer to a lidded jar and add the cilantro leaves. Add salt, pepper, and a little sugar to taste, and add a little more olive oil if needed. It keeps for several weeks or longer in the fridge.

Chilled Cucumber, Melon, and Mint Soup

SERVES 8   (P: 20 mins. + TIME TO CHILL)

1 large or 2 small organic cucumbers
1 ripe melon (e.g., Honeydew)
2 cups plain whole-milk yogurt (not low-fat)
$1/3$ cup chopped mint, plus extra leaves
   for garnishing
$1/3$ cup lime juice
sugar, to taste (4–5 tablespoons depending
   on the sweetness of the melon)
salt

Peel the cucumber and the melon and cut into chunks. Working in batches, put some cucumber and melon in a blender, and add yogurt, chopped mint, and lime juice. Add some sugar and a pinch of salt. Puree, taste, and add more sugar if needed.

When all has been pureed, place in the fridge to chill until needed.

Serve in little bowls, with a few mint leaves scattered on top.

Gazpacho

SERVES 4–6   (P: 40 mins.)

We love to make this cold soup in the summer, when the vine-ripened tomatoes in the greenhouses are bursting with flavor. Serve it as an appetizer or as a refreshing drink for picnics.

1¹/₂ pounds very ripe tomatoes, skinned and
   finely chopped
3 thick slices of good-quality stale bread, crusts
   removed, and roughly chopped
4 teaspoons red wine vinegar
2–3 garlic cloves, crushed
2 cups fresh tomato juice (see p.66)
4 ounces onions, chopped (about 1 cup)
2 red peppers, roasted and peeled
1 medium cucumber, chopped
¹/₃ cup extra virgin olive oil
2¹/₂ tablespoons homemade Mayonnaise
   (see p.296; optional)
salt, freshly ground black pepper, and sugar,
   to taste

For the garnishes:
2 red peppers, seeded and finely chopped
1 small cucumber, finely chopped
4 very ripe tomatoes, finely chopped
4 slices of bread, cut into small pieces and
   fried in extra virgin olive oil
2¹/₂ tablespoons chopped black olives, or
   small whole olives
1 small onion, chopped
1–2 tablespoons chopped mint
extra virgin olive oil, for drizzling
ice cubes (optional)

Put the chopped tomatoes into a food processor or blender and add the chopped bread, red wine vinegar, crushed garlic, tomato juice, chopped onions, roasted red peppers, chopped cucumber, olive oil, and mayonnaise. Season with salt, freshly ground pepper, and sugar, and whizz until smooth. Dilute with water if necessary to loosen up the soup—how much you need depends upon how juicy the tomatoes are.

While the soup is chilling in the fridge, you can prepare the garnishes.

Before serving, taste the soup and adjust the seasoning if needed. Serve the garnishes on separate plates and everybody can help themselves—the soup should be thick with garnishes.

Drizzle with olive oil, and on a very hot day, add an ice cube or two if you wish.

Gazpacho Smoothie
Make as above, adding a little iced water if necessary. Serve chilled as a delicious drink.

Cannellini, Chorizo, and Cabbage Soup

SERVES 6   (P: 10 mins./C: 15 mins.)

Assorted cans of beans, canned tomatoes, and chorizo or kabanossi sausages are excellent secret ammunition to have on hand. Salads, omelets, and bean stews can all be whipped up literally in minutes. For this recipe, if you don't have fresh or frozen broth, use bouillon cubes.

2¹/₂ tablespoons extra virgin olive oil
6 ounces onions, chopped (about 1¹/₂ cups)
6 ounces chorizo or kabanossi sausage, sliced
   (about 1¹/₄-1¹/₂ cups)
1 x 14¹/₂-ounce can tomatoes
salt, freshly ground pepper, and sugar, to taste
5 cups homemade chicken broth,
   (see p.295)
1 x 15-ounce can cannellini, navy beans,
   or black-eyed peas, drained
¹/₄ Savoy cabbage
¹/₃ cup chopped parsley
1 teaspoon fresh thyme leaves

For serving: crusty bread

Heat the oil in a sauté pan or frying pan over medium heat, add the onions, cover, and sweat over low heat until soft but not colored. Add the chorizo or kabanossi slices and toss for 2–3 minutes until they begin to get slightly crisp—the fat should run. Transfer to a large pot.

Chop the tomatoes fairly finely in the can and add them with all the juice to the pot, then season with salt, freshly ground pepper, and a little sugar. Bring to a boil and cook over high heat for 5–6 minutes. Meanwhile, bring the broth to a boil in another pan.

Add the boiling broth and canned beans to the soup pot and return to a boil. Thinly slice the cabbage and add it to the pot. Cook for another 2–3 minutes, then add the chopped parsley and thyme leaves. Taste and adjust the seasoning if needed, and serve with lots of crusty bread.

Moroccan Harira Soup

SERVES 6–8
      (P: OVERNIGHT + 10 mins./**C:** 2 HOURS)

In Morocco this soup is served as an important part of the festivities of Ramadan. It's the traditional soup to break the fast. My brother Rory O'Connell shared this particularly delicious version with us.

$^3/_4$ cup dried chickpeas, soaked overnight
  and drained
$^1/_2$ cup dried Puy lentils
1 pound leg or shoulder of lamb, cut into
  $^1/_2$-inch cubes (about 2 cups)
6 ounces onions, chopped (about 1 $^1/_2$ cups)
1 teaspoon ground turmeric
$^1/_2$ teaspoon ground cinnamon
$^1/_4$ teaspoon each ground ginger, saffron
  strands, and paprika
salt, freshly ground pepper, and sugar, to taste
$^1/_4$ cup ($^1/_2$ stick) butter
$^1/_2$ cup long-grain rice
4 large ripe tomatoes, skinned, seeded,
  and chopped
2$^1/_2$ tablespoons chopped cilantro leaves
$^1/_3$ cup chopped flat-leaf parsley

For serving: lemon quarters

Tip the soaked chickpeas and dry lentils into a large pot. Add the lamb, onions, turmeric, cinnamon, ginger, saffron strands, and paprika, then pour in 6 cups water. Season with salt and freshly ground pepper.

Bring to a boil, skimming all the froth from the surface as the water begins to bubble, then stir in half the butter. Reduce the heat and let it simmer, covered, for 1$^1/_2$–2 hours until the chickpeas are tender, adding a little more water from time to time if necessary.

Towards the end of the cooking time, cook the rice. Bring 4 cups water to a boil in a saucepan, sprinkle in the rice, and add the rest of the butter and salt to taste. Cook until the rice is tender. Drain, reserving $^1/_4$ cup of the liquid.

To finish the soup, put the chopped tomatoes in a small pan, add the reserved rice-cooking water, and season with salt, pepper, and sugar. Cook over medium heat for 5 minutes or until the tomatoes have "melted." Add this and the drained rice to the soup and simmer for another 5 minutes to allow the flavors to mix.

Taste and adjust the seasoning if needed. Add the chopped herbs, stir once or twice, and serve accompanied by lemon quarters.

Roast Red Pepper Soup with Tapenade Strips

SERVES 4   **(P:** 10 mins./**C:** 10 mins.)

4 onions
6 red peppers
3 ripe tomatoes
salt and freshly ground pepper
1 chile (optional)
$^1/_3$ cup extra virgin olive oil, plus extra
  for serving
2$^1/_2$ tablespoons balsamic vinegar
5 cups homemade chicken or
  vegetable broth (see p.295)
a few basil leaves

For the tapenade strips:
4 slices of good white bread
Tapenade (see p.75)

Preheat the oven to 400°F.

Peel the onions and cut each into 4 pieces, cut each pepper into 4 pieces and seed them, and cut the tomatoes in half.

Put the vegetable pieces into a stainless steel roasting pan and season well with salt and pepper. Add the chile (if using) and drizzle with the olive oil and balsamic vinegar. Roast for 15–20 minutes, until the vegetables are roasted and soft. Meanwhile, heat the broth over low heat.

Remove the skins from the peppers and tomatoes, and remove the stalk and seeds from the chile (if using). Put the contents of the roasting pan and all the juices into a blender and add the basil leaves, then whizz until smooth. Transfer to a pot and mix in the hot broth. Taste and adjust the seasoning if needed.

To make the tapenade strips, cut the crust off the bread, spread the slices with tapenade, and cut into thick strips.

To serve, reheat the soup if necessary, drizzle a little olive oil over each bowl, and serve with a few tapenade strips.

You could use eggplant puree (see p.119) instead of tapenade. Pesto strips or breadsticks are also delicious with this soup.

A Retro Salad with Traditional Cream Dressing

SERVES 4   (P: 30 mins.)

This simple, old-fashioned salad is one of my absolute favorites. It is the sort of thing you would have had for tea during a visit to your granny on a Sunday evening, perhaps served with a slice of meat left over from the Sunday roast. It can be quite delicious when it's made with a crisp lettuce, good home-grown tomatoes and cucumbers, cage-free eggs, and home-preserved beets. If on the other hand you make it with pale eggs from intensively-reared chickens, watery tomatoes, tired lettuce, and aged cucumber—and, worst of all, vinegary beets from a jar—you'll wonder why you bothered. The salad cream dressing was popular before the days of mayonnaise. The recipe comes from Lydia Strangman, the previous occupant of our house.

2 cage-free, organic eggs
1 butterhead lettuce
4 tiny scallions
2–4 ripe tomatoes
16 cucumber slices
4 radishes, thinly sliced
8 slices home-pickled beets (see recipe below)

For the traditional cream dressing:
2 cage-free, organic eggs
4 teaspoons dark soft brown sugar
pinch of salt
1 teaspoon English mustard powder
4 teaspoons brown malt vinegar
1/4-1/2 cup cream

For the garnish:
chopped scallion
watercress
chopped parsley

Hard-boil the eggs for the salad and the dressing. Bring a small saucepan of water to a boil, gently slide in the eggs, and boil for 10 minutes (12 minutes if they are very fresh). Strain off the hot water and cover with cold water to cool them, then peel them.

Wash and dry the lettuce and scallions, and set aside.

Next make the dressing. Cut 2 of the eggs in half. Remove the yolks, place in a bowl, add the sugar, a pinch of salt and the mustard powder. Blend in the brown malt vinegar and enough cream to make a pouring consistency. Chop the egg whites and add some to the sauce, setting the rest aside to scatter over the salad. Cover the dressing until needed.

To assemble the salad, arrange a few lettuce leaves on each plate. Cut the tomatoes into quarters and arrange on the lettuce. Cut the remaining 2 hard-boiled eggs into quarters and add to the plates, then place a few slices of cucumber, some sliced radish, and 2 slices of beet on each plate. Garnish with some chopped scallion and watercress, scatter the reserved chopped egg white (from the dressing) and some chopped parsley on top.

Put a tiny bowl of traditional cream dressing in the center of each plate and serve immediately, while the salad is crisp and before the beet starts to run.

Pickled Beets

SERVES 5–6   (P: 10 mins./C: 2 HOURS)

This is an excellent standby to keep on hand and is great with goat cheese.

1 pound raw beets (about 2 3-inch beets)
salt
2 cups water
1 cup sugar
1 cup white wine vinegar

To prepare the beets, leave 2 inches of the leaf stalks on top and the whole root on the beet. Hold the beet under cold running water and gently wash off the mud with the palms of your hands; ensure you don't damage the skin, otherwise the beet will bleed during cooking.

Put the beets in a pan, cover with cold water, and add a little salt and sugar. Cover the pan, bring to a boil and simmer on top of the stove, or in the oven, for 1–2 hours depending upon size.

The beets are usually cooked when the skin rubs off easily and when they dent when pressed. If in doubt, test with a skewer or the tip of a knife. Drain, let the beets cool, then gently peel and slice them, and transfer to a bowl.

Pour the measured water into a saucepan and add the sugar. Stir to dissolve, then bring to a boil. Remove from the heat, stir in the vinegar, pour it over the sliced beets and let cool. Refrigerate until needed.

A Salad of Crozier Blue Cheese with Ripe Pears and Spicy Candied Nuts

SERVES 8   (P: 25 mins./C: 5 mins.)

Much of this salad can be made in advance: the prepared salad greens can be stored in the fridge, the spicy candied nuts in an airtight container, and the dressing in a sealed jar. Cashel Blue, Bellingham Blue, Stilton, or Gorgonzola cheese would be delicious alternatives to Crozier Blue.

selection of salad greens, including
   chicory and watercress
Spicy Candied Nuts (see p.62)
ripe Crozier Blue cheese
3–4 ripe pears (Bartlet or Anjou)
sprigs of chervil, for garnishing

For the dressing:
2$\frac{1}{2}$ tablespoons red wine vinegar
$\frac{1}{2}$ cup extra virgin olive oil
salt and freshly ground pepper

Preheat the oven to 350°F.

Gently wash the greens and dry them, then transfer to a bowl, cover, and refrigerate.

Prepare the candied nuts.

To make the dressing, whisk the vinegar and oil together and season to taste.

To serve the salad, cut the cheese into cubes or small wedges. Sprinkle the salad greens with the dressing and toss gently until the greens glisten. Taste and add more seasoning if needed. Divide the salad greens between the plates, making a little mound in the center. Slice the pears and tuck 3–4 slices in between the greens on each plate. Scatter with a few cubes of cheese and some Spicy Candied Nuts. Sprinkle with a few sprigs of chervil and serve.

Clair McSweeney's Wakame Seaweed Salad

SERVES 8   (P: 40 mins./C: 10 mins.)

I first tasted this delicious salad at a meeting of the Cork Free Choice Consumer's Group on using seaweed. Clair McSweeney gave me the recipe and it has become a favorite—it's great with fried fish or tempura. Seaweeds are full of goodness and trace elements not found in other foods.

1$\frac{1}{2}$ ounces dried wakame seaweed
1 large cucumber
1 tablespoon salt
1 handful of pickled ginger
$\frac{1}{2}$ pickled daikon, finely chopped

For the dressing:
$\frac{1}{2}$ cup rice wine vinegar
$\frac{1}{4}$ cup soy sauce
2$\frac{1}{2}$ tablespoons sugar

Put the wakame seaweed into a large bowl, pour lots of cold water over it, and let it rehydrate for about 15 minutes.

Peel the cucumber in strips along the length, cut it in half lengthwise, scoop out the seeds, and slice thinly. Put about a cup of water into a bowl and add the salt and the sliced cucumber. Let it soak for 20 minutes.

In a saucepan, mix the ingredients for the dressing and warm over a low heat until the sugar has dissolved.

Drain the seaweed, rinse in cold water, then drain again thoroughly. Drain the cucumber and press out any excess water. Mix the cucumber and seaweed together, and add the pickled ginger and diced daikon. Refrigerate for about 30 minutes before serving, so the salad becomes cool and crisp.

Mexican Chicken Salad with Chile and Cilantro Cream

SERVES 12   (P: 45 mins./C: 15 mins.)

4 chicken breasts
1 large romaine lettuce, torn into 1-inch strips
2 cups cooked black beans or one 15¹/₂-ounce
  can black beans
12 ounces fresh corn kernels (about 1¹/₃ cups)
12 cherry tomatoes, cut in half
2 medium red onions, chopped
4 small ripe but firm avocados, chopped
12 ounces cheddar cheese, grated (about
  3 cups)
8 ounces tortilla chips (about 8 cups)

For the spicy dressing:
³/₄ cup cider vinegar
4 teaspoons sea salt
4 teaspoons freshly ground black pepper
¹/₃ cup Worcestershire sauce
2 teaspoons English mustard powder
2¹/₂ tablespoons honey

juice of ¹/₂ lemon
4 garlic cloves, crushed
¹/₂ cup tomato paste
1 teaspoon red pepper flakes
³/₄ cup extra virgin olive oil
1 cup sunflower oil
1 tablespoon cumin seeds, toasted and
  ground

For the chile and cilantro cream:
1 cup sour cream or crème fraîche
4 teaspoons chopped jalapeño chile
3 tablespoons roughly chopped fresh
  cilantro
salt and freshly ground pepper

For the garnish:
1 bunch scallions, thinly sliced diagonally
  (use equal amounts of white and green parts)
fresh cilantro

First panbroil the chicken until cooked. Let it cool and cut into ¹/₂-inch cubes.

Make the spicy dressing (this recipe makes more than you need but it keeps very well in a covered jar in the fridge). Whisk all the ingredients together in a bowl, taste, and add a little water if the flavor is too intense.

Make the chile and cilantro cream by mixing all the ingredients together in a bowl. Keep chilled until needed.

Put the lettuce, chicken, beans, corn, tomatoes, onion, avocado, cheddar cheese, and tortilla chips in a large bowl. Add ¹/₂–²/₃ of the spicy dressing and toss gently. Serve on individual plates, with a spoonful of chile and cilantro cream, a sprinkle of scallions, and some fresh cilantro.

Pasta, Bocconcini, and Tomato Salad

SERVES 6–8   (P: 20 mins./C: 10 mins.)

1 pound penne pasta (mostaccioli, quills)
  or tiny shells (about 6 cups)
1 pound cherry tomatoes (about 3 cups),
  preferably vine-ripened and organic
1 pound bocconcini (baby mozzarella cheeses)
lots of fresh basil or mint or marjoram leaves
4 scallions, sliced diagonally
salt and freshly ground pepper
12–18 Picholine or Kalamata olives (green or
  black)

For the dressing:
³/₄ cup extra virgin olive oil
¹/₄ cup balsamic vinegar or white wine
  vinegar
2 garlic cloves, crushed
Pesto (optional; see p.297)

Cook the pasta in a large pot of boiling salted water until al dente (still slightly firm).

Meanwhile, cut the tomatoes in half. Whisk together all the dressing ingredients in a bowl, then add the tomatoes, bocconcini, herbs, and scallions. Season to taste with salt and freshly ground pepper. Drizzle some of the dressing over the salad and toss gently.

When the pasta is ready, drain it, toss immediately in the remaining dressing and let it cool. Then combine the pasta with the salad and add the olives. Taste and adjust the seasoning and add more herbs and pesto if you wish.

Tomato and Mint or Basil Salad

SERVES 8   (P: 10 mins.)

12 very ripe firm tomatoes
12 leaves, coarsely chopped mint or torn basil
salt, freshly ground black pepper, and sugar
Ballymaloe French Dressing (see p.94)

Remove the core from each tomato and cut into 3–4 slices (around the equator) or into quarters. Arrange in a single layer on a flat plate. Sprinkle with salt, sugar, and several grinds of black pepper. Toss immediately in just enough French dressing to coat the fruit and sprinkle with coarsely chopped mint or basil. Taste for seasoning. Tomatoes must be dressed as soon as they are cut to seal in their flavor.

Chicken Salad with Pomegranate, Pine Nuts, and Raisins

SERVES 8   (**P:** 25 mins./**C:** 5 mins.)

Use up leftover morsels of chicken in a delicious way.

1¹/₂–2 pounds roast chicken
1 pomegranate
²/₃-1 cup pine nuts, pecans, or
  walnuts
selection of salad greens, including watercress,
  frisée, and arugula leaves
lots of fresh mint leaves
¹/₄ cup raisins, Lexia if possible
salt and freshly ground pepper

For serving: crusty bread

For the dressing:
¹/₂ cup extra virgin olive oil or walnut
  oil
2¹/₂ tablespoons best-quality white wine
vinegar
1–2 teaspoons honey
¹/₂ teaspoon whole-grain mustard

If the chicken has been refrigerated, bring it to room temperature.

Whisk all the ingredients for the dressing together. Taste and adjust the seasoning if needed. Cut the pomegranate in half and flick the seeds into a bowl, ensuring you do not include any of the pith.

Toast the nuts briefly, then chop them coarsely.

Just before serving, put the salad greens and mint in a deep bowl. Sprinkle a little of the dressing over them and toss gently—there should be just enough dressing to make the leaves glisten. Add a little dressing to the pomegranate seeds and toss.

Slice the chicken into chunky pieces and place in a shallow dish. Sprinkle a little dressing over it and toss gently.

Combine the salad, pomegranate seeds, chicken pieces, raisins, and salt and pepper to taste. Divide pleasingly between the plates and sprinkle with the chopped nuts. Serve immediately, with some crusty bread.

Variation
Pheasant, guinea fowl, or free-range turkey instead of chicken would also be delicious in this salad; a few green grapes also make a good addition. A combination of walnut and sunflower oil may be used for the dressing if you wish.

Red Cabbage with Dried Cranberries, Walnuts, and Apple

SERVES 6   (**P:** 15 mins.)

3 eating apples
¹/₃ cup dried cranberries
1 pound red cabbage (about ¹/₂ a medium
  head)
small handful of flat-leaf parsley leaves
¹/₂ cup shelled walnut halves

For the dressing:
¹/₂ cup red wine vinegar
2¹/₂ tablespoons walnut oil
1 small teaspoon honey
salt and freshly ground pepper

First make the dressing. Whisk the vinegar, oil, and honey together and season with salt and pepper.

Cut the apples, unpeeled, into cubes. Transfer to a bowl, toss in a little of the dressing, and add the dried cranberries.

Cut the red cabbage into quarters and slice thinly crosswise. Transfer to a large serving bowl, add the cut-up apples and cranberries, the parsley, and some more dressing. Toss gently to coat evenly and add the walnut halves. Taste and adjust the seasoning if needed.

Serve on its own or as an accompaniment to cold duck, goose, pork, or ham.

Basmati Rice, Pea, Fava Bean, and Dill Salad

SERVES 6–8   (**P:** 5 mins./**C:** 20 mins.)

1¹/₃ cups basmati rice
salt and freshly ground pepper
extra virgin olive oil, for drizzling
freshly squeezed juice of 1–2 lemons
³/₄ cup peas (shelled)
³/₄ cup fava beans (shelled)
¹/₃ cup chopped fresh dill

Cook the rice in lots of boiling salted water. Drain, transfer to a wide bowl, and drizzle with olive oil and some freshly squeezed lemon juice. Let it cool.

Meanwhile, cook the peas and fava beans separately in boiling salted water, then drain them. Let cool.

Combine the rice, peas, fava beans, and dill. Toss, taste, and adjust the seasoning as necessary.

Spicy Green Salad

SERVES 4   (P: 10 mins./C: 10 mins.)

1 handful cilantro leaves
1 handful parsley leaves
1/2 handful mint leaves
4 scallions, white and green part,
    sliced diagonally
4 kaffir lime leaves, finely shredded (optional)
1–2 red chiles, seeded and thinly sliced

For the sweet-and-sour dressing:
2 1/2 tablespoons soft brown sugar
2 1/2 tablespoons white sugar
2 1/2 tablespoons fish sauce (*nam pla*)
2 1/2 tablespoons lime juice

First make the dressing. Put all the sugar into a small saucepan and add 2 1/2 tablespoons water. Place over medium heat and stir to dissolve, then bring to a boil and continue to boil for a minute or two, or until it becomes liquid. Remove from the heat and mix in the fish sauce and lime juice. Pour into a jar or small bowl.

Put the cilantro, parsley, and mint leaves into a bowl, then add the sliced scallions, shredded kaffir lime leaves (if using), and sliced chiles.

Just before serving, toss the leaves with enough dressing to make them glisten. Serve as soon as possible.

Shrimp and Rice Noodle Salad

SERVES 8   (P: 20 mins.)

1 pound rice vermicelli or fine rice noodles
1 small organic cucumber
48 miniature shrimp or 32 regular shrimp,
    cooked and peeled
8 scallions, sliced diagonally
1 cup cilantro leaves
1 cup mint leaves
3/4 cup peanuts or cashews,
    roasted and chopped

For serving: lime wedges

For the dressing:
1/2 cup soy sauce
1/4 cup rice vinegar or cider vinegar
1/4 cup extra virgin olive oil
1 red chile, seeded and thinly sliced
1 teaspoon peeled and grated fresh ginger
2 1/2 tablespoons brown sugar or palm sugar

Put the noodles into a large bowl. Cover with boiling water and let stand for 5–7 minutes or until just tender.

Meanwhile, make the dressing by combining all the dressing ingredients in a bowl. Stir until the sugar has dissolved.

Drain the noodles well and toss them in the dressing while still warm.

Cut the cucumber in half lengthwise. Scoop out the seeds with a melon baller or a sharp spoon and discard. Cut the cucumber into thin diagonal slices.

Add the cucumber slices to the noodles, along with the shrimp, the sliced scallions, and the cilantro and mint. Toss well. Taste and adjust the seasoning if needed. Scatter with the coarsely chopped nuts and serve with wedges of lime.

Top Tip: Noodles of all types are something you must keep in stock—there are a million delicious salads you can make. They are also great added to soup, or as an extra something in spring rolls.

Puy Lentil and Walnut Salad with Pomegranate Molasses

SERVES 6–8   (P: 15 mins./C: 15 mins.)

2 cups dried Puy lentils
1/2–1 pomegranate (optional)
1/4–1/2 cup shelled walnut halves
3–4 scallions, sliced diagonally
1/3 cup chopped flat-leaf parsley leaves
salt and freshly ground pepper

For the dressing:
4 teaspoons pomegranate molasses
2 1/2 tablespoons extra virgin olive oil
freshly squeezed juice of 1/2 lemon
1/2 teaspoon cumin seeds, toasted and ground

Cook the lentils in boiling salted water for 10–15 minutes or until just cooked.

Meanwhile, cut the pomegranate (if using) into pieces and flick the seeds into a bowl.

Drain the lentils and place in a large bowl. Whisk all the ingredients for the dressing together and pour it over the warm lentils. When cool, add the walnut halves, chopped scallions, and parsley; scatter with the pomegranate seeds (if using). Taste and add salt and freshly ground pepper as needed.

Sticky Asian Pork with Herb and Roasted Peanut Salad

SERVES 6   (**P:** 10 mins./**C:** 20 mins.)

You can cook the meat without marinating, but it is better marinated. This recipe would also work well with chicken or duck.

1/3 cup unsalted peanuts

18 ounces pork tenderloin, preferably free-range

1 tablespoon five-spice powder

sunflower oil, for frying

enough salad greens for 6 (include 1/2 large romaine lettuce, some arugula, and other crisp leaves)

handful each of basil, mint, and cilantro leaves

1 organic cucumber, cut lengthwise, seeded and sliced

1/4 cup Asian Dressing (see p.95)

4 scallions, diagonally sliced

For the marinade:

4 teaspoons fish sauce (*nam pla*)

1/4 cup soy sauce

1 lemongrass stalk, trimmed and shredded

3 large mild red chiles, seeded and chopped

2 large garlic cloves, crushed

3 shallots, finely chopped (if unavailable, use 3 tablespoons finely chopped mild onion)

2 1/2 tablespoons soft brown sugar

Preheat the oven to 400°F.

Spread the peanuts into a roasting tray and roast for about 15 minutes, shaking once or twice. Take the tray outdoors and blow off the loose skins (sounds very odd but it's exactly what everyone does in Asia). If the peanuts are not already golden brown all over, return them to the oven briefly. Chop coarsely.

Slice the tenderloin into 1/2-inch-thick pieces and put into a bowl, then toss with the five-spice powder.

To make the marinade, mix all the ingredients together in a bowl. Add the pork and toss well. Let it marinate for 30 minutes, better still 1 hour.

Heat a little sunflower oil in a heavy frying pan. Drain the marinated pork, retaining the marinade. Fry the meat for about 1 minute on each side, then add the remaining marinade and cook for another few minutes.

Meanwhile, tear any large salad greens in 3–4 pieces. Put them into a large, wide salad bowl with the other leaves and herbs, and add the cucumber. Sprinkle the Asian dressing over them and toss well. Add the pork with all the sticky caramelised bits. Scatter the scallions and roasted peanuts over them and serve as soon as possible.

Top Tip: Chicken breasts work excellently in this recipe instead of pork.

Panzanella

SERVES 8   (**P:** 20 mins.)

Every culture has a variety of recipes for using up leftover bread in a delicious way. This is a Tuscan bread salad, but don't attempt it unless you have really good yeast or sour dough bread.

1 1/2 pounds very ripe tomatoes

1 pound 2-day-old country bread (about 1/2 loaf)

1/2 cup extra virgin olive oil,

2 1/2 tablespoons lemon juice or red wine vinegar

3 garlic cloves, crushed

1 large red onion, sliced or coarsely chopped

sea salt (or Kosher salt) and freshly ground black pepper

sugar, if needed

24 basil leaves, roughly torn, or 1/4 cup fresh marjoram or tarragon leaves

arugula leaves (optional)

slivers of Parmesan cheese (optional)

Cut the tomatoes into 1/2-inch cubes or small chunks. Transfer to a colander, sprinkle with a little salt, and let drain while you prepare the remaining ingredients.

Cut the bread into slices about 1/2-inch thick, then tear or cut into uneven cubes. (I sometimes pop them into the oven for a few minutes just to crisp the edges.)

In a bowl, mix the olive oil, lemon juice or vinegar, and garlic. Add the drained tomatoes and sliced or chopped red onion. Season with salt, pepper, and a little sugar if the tomatoes are not sweet enough. Add lots of torn basil leaves or marjoram or tarragon. Toss gently, then add the stale bread and toss well. Taste and adjust the seasoning if needed.

A few peppery arugula leaves on the bottom of each plate, and slivers of Parmesan on top, make delicious additions to this rustic salad.

Top Tip: Although in Tuscany panzanella is a summer salad, there's no reason why one can't have fun during the other seasons. For instance, we make a delicious autumn version with sautéed wild mushrooms. Large flat mushrooms or portabellos are also great with lots of marjoram or thyme leaves, chopped arugula or watercress leaves, and shavings of Parmesan—it tastes as good as it sounds! In winter we add cubes of roast butternut squash or Jerusalem artichoke, with kale and pecorino cheese; in late spring, asparagus and fava beans.

A Green Salad for Every Season

The herb and vegetable gardens beside the Ballymaloe Cookery School are bursting with a myriad of lettuce and salad greens and edible flowers. We eat a green salad with lunch and dinner. The lettuces, salad greens, and wild things vary throughout the seasons.

Spring Green Salad

For this salad, use a selection of organic
  lettuces and salad greens:
Butterhead lettuce, iceberg lettuce, radicchio,
  chicory, endive…
Watercress
Buckler leaf sorrel
Arugula leaves
Claytonia
Mysticana
Wild garlic leaves and flowers

Summer Green Salad

A selection of fresh organic lettuces and
  salad greens:
Butterhead lettuce, oakleaf lettuce, iceberg
  lettuce, lollo rosso, frisée, Bibb…
Mesclun or Saladisi
Red Orach
Mizuma
Mibuna
Arugula
Edible chrysanthemum leaves
Green pea shoots or fava bean tips
Tiny chard and beet leaves
Wild sorrel leaves or buckler leaf sorrel
Salad burnet
Fresh herb leaves such as lemon balm, mint,
  flat-leaf parsley, golden marjoram, annual
  marjoram, tiny sprigs of dill, tarragon,
  or mint
Edible flowers such as chive flowers,
  marigold petals, young nasturtium leaves
  and flowers, borage or hyssop flowers,
  zucchini or squash blossoms

Autumn and Winter Green Salad

A selection of autumn and winter lettuces:
Butterhead lettuce, oakleaf lettuce, lollo
  rosso, radicchio, chicory, endive…
Watercress
Buckler leaf sorrel, lamb's tongue, and wood
  sorrel leaves
Arugula leaves
Mâche
Tender leaves of kale

Winter purslane
Mysticana
Tips of purple sprouting broccoli are also
delicious, and if you feel like something
more robust use some finely shredded
Savoy cabbage and maybe a few shreds of
red cabbage. Finely shredded stalks of fresh
Swiss chard are also good.

How to Make a Green Salad

A good green salad should have a contrast
of texture, color, and flavor. The mixture of
lettuce and salad greens should ideally
reflect the seasons. Seek out salad greens
that have been grown in rich, fertile soil
rather than hydroponically; they will not only
have more flavor but will also be more
nutritionally complex.

Wash and carefully dry the lettuce and salad
greens. Leave the leaves whole or, if too
large, tear into bite-sized pieces. Put them
into a deep salad bowl, then add the herb
sprigs and edible flowers. Toss, cover, and
store in the fridge until needed. Washed
organic salad greens seem to keep perfectly
in a plastic bag in the fridge for 4–5 days.

Immediately before serving, toss the salad in
just enough dressing to make the leaves
glisten, then taste and add a little more
seasoning if needed.

*Note: It is really worth investing in a good
salad spinner to dry the leaves, otherwise
the residual water will dilute the dressing
and spoil the salad.*

Salad Dressings

Green salad must not be dressed until just
before serving, otherwise it will look tired
and unappetizing. The flavor of the dressing
totally depends on the quality of the oil and
vinegar. We use best-quality, cold-pressed
oils and superb wine vinegars to dress the
precious organic lettuce and salad greens.
The quantity needed is so small it's really
worth spending as much as you can afford
on best quality—it makes all the difference.
All salad dressings need a good shake
before serving.

Simple French Dressing

MAKES ENOUGH TO DRESS A SALAD FOR
8 PEOPLE

1/2 cup extra virgin olive oil
2 1/2 tablespoons white or red wine vinegar
sea salt (or Kosher salt) and freshly
  ground pepper

Just before the salad is to be eaten, put all
the ingredients into a small bowl or jar.
Whisk with a fork until the dressing has
emulsified.

Ballymaloe Cookery School Dressing for Salad Greens

MAKES 2/3 CUP

1/2 cup extra virgin olive oil
2 teaspoons balsamic vinegar
1 teaspoon honey
1 garlic clove, crushed
1/2 teaspoon English mustard powder or
  1/2 teaspoon Dijon mustard
sea salt (or Kosher salt) and freshly
  ground pepper

Just before the salad is to be eaten, put all
the ingredients into a small bowl or jar.
Whisk with a fork until the dressing has
emulsified.

Honey and Whole-grain Mustard Dressing

MAKES JUST OVER 1 CUP

3/4 cup extra virgin olive oil or a
  mixture of olive and other oils, such as
  sunflower
1/4 cup white wine vinegar
2 teaspoons honey
2 heaped teaspoons whole-grain honey
  mustard
2 garlic cloves, crushed
sea salt (or Kosher salt) and freshly ground
  pepper

Mix all the ingredients together in a small
bowl or jar. Taste and adjust the seasoning if
needed. Whisk well before use.

Verjuice Dressing

MAKES JUST OVER 1 CUP

Verjuice is made from the juice of tart fruit e.g., apples or grapes, and was a popular medieval flavoring in the days before lemon juice was available. It is not technically a vinegar because it does not ferment. Verjuice is still used today in Middle Eastern cooking and in the making of commercial mustard.

1/4 cup verjuice
1 tablespoon lemon juice
3/4 cup extra virgin olive oil
1 teaspoon honey
sea salt (or Kosher salt) and freshly
   ground pepper

Mix all the ingredients together in a small bowl or jar. Taste and adjust the seasoning if needed. Whisk well before use.

Yogurt and Mint Dressing

MAKES 2/3 CUP

1/2 cup plain yogurt
1 tablespoon freshly squeezed lime or
   lemon juice
1 tablespoon extra virgin olive oil
1 teaspoon honey
1 tablespoon chopped mint
sea salt (or Kosher salt) and freshly
   ground pepper

Mix all the ingredients together in a small bowl or jar. Taste and adjust the seasoning if needed. Whisk well before use.

Herbed Vinaigrette Dressing

MAKES JUST OVER 1 CUP

3/4 cup extra virgin olive oil
1/3 cup cider vinegar
1 teaspoon Irish honey (or a locally-produced
   honey)
1 garlic clove, crushed
2 1/2 tablespoons chopped mixed herbs,
   such as parsley, chives, mint, watercress, and
   thyme
sea salt (or Kosher salt) and freshly
   ground pepper

Put all the dressing ingredients into a screw-topped jar, adding salt and freshly ground pepper to taste. Shake well. Alternatively whizz all the ingredients together in a food processor or blender for a few seconds.

You could also use 1/3 cup lemon juice or wine vinegar instead of cider vinegar.

Asian Dressing

MAKES 1 1/2 CUPS

2 Thai chiles, seeded and finely sliced
1 large garlic clove, crushed
1/4 cup white sugar
1/3 cup fish sauce (*nam pla*)
1/3 cup lime juice
1/3 cup rice wine vinegar
1/4 cup extra virgin olive oil

Mix all the ingredients together in a small bowl or jar. Taste and adjust the seasoning if needed. Whisk well before use.

Use it to dress salad greens, or omit the olive oil and use as a dip.

quick and easy meals

If you have a well-stocked cupboard and a folder of recipes that you can whip up in minutes, unexpected visitors need not faze you. The recipes in this chapter are perfect for when you have very little time to prepare—mussels, for example, make a wonderful meal in an instant and meat or fish can be pan-broiled in minutes.

Bowl of Warm Cockles or Mussels with Homemade Mayonnaise or Asian Mayonnaise

ALLOW 2¹/₂ CUPS PER PERSON)
(**P:** 20 mins./**C:** 5 mins.)

This is one of our favorite simple suppers. Just pop a few teeny weeny rolls into the oven, whizz up a bowl of mayonnaise, and cook the shellfish—the entire feast will be on the table in less than 30 minutes.

2¹/₂ cups per person cockles or mussels
  (if unavailable, use little neck or
  cherrystone clams)
homemade Mayonnaise (see p.296) or
  Asian Mayonnaise (see p.297)

For serving: Wheaten Bread or rolls (see p.37)
  and green salad

Check that all the cockles or mussels are tightly shut. Tap any that are slightly open on the counter: if they refuse to close, discard them. Wash them under lots of cold running water.

Preheat a wide pan for which you have a lid. Put a batch of cockles or mussels in a single layer in the pan, cover, and cook over medium heat for 1–2 minutes. As soon as they open, tip the whole lot into a serving bowl, discarding any that have not opened. Continue cooking in batches in the same manner. They are most delicious while still warm, but they're also good cold or at room temperature. Cockles are eaten just as they are but you will need to remove the "beard" from the mussels before eating.

Serve with freshly baked wheaten bread, a bowl of homemade mayonnaise, and a good green salad.

Spicy Omelet Sambo with Tomato and Red Onion Salsa

SERVES 1   (**P:** 15 mins./**C:** 5 mins.)

1 portion of focaccia bread or 1 crusty roll
butter
1 tablespoon extra virgin olive oil
2 cage-free, organic eggs
¹/₄–¹/₂ teaspoon cumin seeds, toasted and
  ground
1 teaspoon chopped flat-leaf parsley
salt and freshly ground pepper
a few arugula leaves
Tomato and Red Onion Salsa (see p.294)

Preheat the oven to 400°F.

Warm the piece of focaccia or roll in the oven. Split it in half and smear with butter.

Heat the olive oil in a nonstick pan over high heat and warm a plate. Whisk the eggs in a bowl, add the cumin and parsley, and season with salt and pepper.

Pour the egg mixture into the hot pan. It will start to cook instantly, so quickly pull the edges of the omelet towards the center with a plastic spoon or spatula, tilting the pan so that the uncooked egg runs to the sides; repeat this process 4–5 times, until most of the egg is set and will not run any more; the center will still be soft and uncooked but will continue to cook on the plate. To fold the omelet, flip the edge just below the handle of the pan into the center, then hold the pan almost perpendicular over the plate so that the omelet will flip over again; finally half roll, half slide the omelet onto the plate so that it lands folded in three. (It should not take more than 30 seconds in all to make the omelet.)

Scatter a few arugula leaves over the bottom of the bread, top with the omelet, and finally a generous spoonful of Tomato and Red Onion Salsa. Serve immediately.

Roast Chicken Pasta with Portobello Mushrooms and Pancetta

SERVES 8   (**P:** 15 mins./**C:** 15 mins.)

Bubbly superchef Merrilees Parker did this yummy recipe when she came to teach at the school in 2004. We have adapted it somewhat, but it was really her idea. It's a great recipe for using up delicious morsels of roast chicken—be sure to include the crispy skin. Alternatively use panbroiled chicken breasts.

salt
18 ounces spaghetti or linguine
sea salt (or Kosher salt) and freshly
  ground black pepper
2¹/₂ tablespoons extra virgin olive oil
8 ounces pancetta or bacon (about 8 strips),
  cut into ¹/₄-inch-wide strips
8 ounces portobello or field mushrooms,
  sliced (about 2¹/₃ cups)
2¹/₂ tablespoons fresh thyme leaves
  (preferably lemon thyme) or annual
  marjoram leaves
12 ounces leftover roast chicken or
  panbroiled chicken breast, coarsely
  shredded (about 2-2¹/₂ cups)
²/₃ cup heavy cream
2 large handfuls mixed salad greens, such as
  arugula or baby spinach, roughly chopped
4 ounces Parmesan cheese, grated
  (about 2 cups)

Bring 6 quarts water to a boil in a large pot and add 2 tablespoons salt. Curl in the pasta and stir gently. Return to a boil and cook for 2 minutes. Turn off the heat, cover with a tight-fighting lid, and let it continue cooking in the hot water for about 5 minutes until al dente (cooked but still slightly firm).

Meanwhile, heat a wok or a large, heavy frying pan. Add 1 tablespoon of the olive oil and then the bacon strips. Cook over a high heat for 4–5 minutes until really crispy. Remove to a plate. Add the remaining oil to the wok or frying pan and toss in the sliced mushrooms. Cook over a high heat for 3–4 minutes, stirring frequently.

Drain the pasta. Tip into the wok or frying pan on top of the mushrooms. Add the crispy bacon, thyme or marjoram leaves, and chicken, and toss really well. Season with salt and pepper. Pour the cream into the pan and bring to a boil. Taste and adjust the seasoning if needed, then toss thoroughly again.

Finally add the fresh leaves and half the Parmesan, mixing gently. Serve immediately, in warmed deep bowls, with the remaining Parmesan sprinkled over the top.

Pasta with Mushrooms and Ginger

SERVES 6   (P: 5 mins./C: 30 mins.)

1 pound penne pasta (mostaccioli)—about
  6 cups
4$^1/_2$ quarts water
2 tablespoons salt

Mushroom à la Créme with Ginger (see p.241)

Cheat's Method of Cooking Dried Pasta

We developed this method of cooking pasta when we taught a "survival course" for students in bedsits or small apartments with limited cooking facilities. Italians are usually shocked, but it works perfectly.

Choose a large, deep pot; two handles are an advantage for ease of lifting. To cook 1 pound pasta, bring 6 quarts of water to a boil and add 2 tablespoons salt. Tip the pasta in all at once, stir well to ensure the strands or shapes are separate, and cover the pot to bring the water back to a boil quickly.

Cook for 2 minutes for spaghetti and fettuccine, or 4 minutes for penne, small shells, and so on. Keep the pot covered. Then turn off the heat and let the pasta continue to cook in the hot water for the time indicated on the package. Test, drain, and proceed as usual.

Add the drained penne to the Mushroom à la Créme and toss well. Taste and adjust the seasoning if needed. Serve immediately.

Pasta with Garlic and Herbs

SERVES 4–6   (P: 10 mins./C: 20 mins.)

This is a terrific standby recipe and an excellent basic no-cream sauce for pasta. Really fresh herbs are a must. If you don't have an herb garden to pick and snip at, pop down to your local garden center and plant up a hanging basket or window box right away.

1 pound spaghetti or thin noodles
salt
2–4 ounces Parmesan cheese, grated
  (about 1-2 cups)
chive flowers and wild garlic in season (use
  both leaves and bulbs), for garnishing

For the herb butter:
$^1/_4$-$^1/_3$ cup ($^1/_2$-$^3/_4$ stick) butter, or half
  butter and half extra virgin olive oil
2$^1/_2$ tablespoons chopped parsley
1 tablespoon chopped mint
2$^1/_2$ tablespoons chopped watercress or
  arugula, scallions, or chives
$^1/_2$ tablespoon chopped basil or lemon balm
2 large or 4 small garlic cloves, crushed

Cook the spaghetti in lots of boiling salted water until al dente—this can range from 2–3 minutes for homemade pasta, to up to 20 minutes for dried pasta. Or use the "Cheat's Method", above.

Meanwhile, make the herb butter. Melt the butter in a small pan and add all the herbs and the crushed garlic. Cook over a very low heat for 2 minutes, no longer.

Drain the spaghetti and place in a dish. Pour the herb butter over it and toss well. Serve with the grated Parmesan. Sprinkle chive flowers and wild garlic over the top for extra excitement.

Variations

1 Add 8 ounces cooked, sliced, wild or cultivated mushrooms (about 1$^1/_3$ cups) to the herb butter—chanterelles are great.
2 Add some halved cherry tomatoes to the herb butter.
3 Add 1 teaspoon red pepper flakes to the herb butter.
4 Add 4–8 ounces chopped (about 1-2 cups) chorizo to the herb butter.

Linguini with Chile, Crab, and Cilantro

SERVES 8   (**P:** 10 mins./**C:** 15 mins.)

salt and freshly cracked pepper
1 pound linguini or spaghetti
1/2 cup extra virgin olive oil
2 garlic cloves, crushed
1–2 red chiles, chopped
1 green chile, chopped
2 1/2 tablespoons coarsely chopped
  flat-leaf parsley
2 1/2 tablespoons coarsely chopped cilantro,
  plus extra for garnishing
grated zest and juice of 1 lemon
9 ounces crabmeat, freshly cooked
  (about 1 1/4 cups)
8 lime wedges for serving

Put 6 quarts cold water into a large pot and bring to a fast, rolling boil. Add 2 tablespoons salt, then add the pasta and stir gently. Cover the pot and continue to boil for 2 minutes, then turn off the heat and let the pasta continue to cook in the covered pot for 8–10 minutes or until al dente (cooked but still just firm).

Meanwhile, heat the olive oil in a sauté pan or frying pan, add the garlic, chile, parsley, and cilantro. Cook for 1–2 minutes.

Drain the pasta and return it to the pot. Add the crab to the herb and chilli oil, heat through for 1–2 minutes, and pour it over the pasta. Add the lemon zest and a good squeeze of juice and lots of cracked pepper. Toss well, taste, and adjust the seasoning if needed.

Serve immediately, with cilantro leaves scattered over the top and some lime wedges.

Panbroiled Fish with Flavored Butter

SERVES 4   (**P:** 10 mins./**C:** 5 mins.)

8 fillets of very fresh fish, such as mackerel,
  sea bass or red snapper, skin attached,
  scales removed where necessary (allow
  6 ounces fish for main course, 3 ounces
  for an appetizer)
flour seasoned with salt and pepper
small pat of butter
flavored butter of your choice (see below,
  p.156 and p.231)
segments of lemon and parsley, for garnishing

Heat the grill pan. Dip the fish fillets in the flour. Shake off the excess flour and then, using a knife, spread a little butter on the flesh side, as though you were buttering a slice of bread rather sparingly.

When the grill pan is quite hot but not smoking, place the fish fillets, butter side down, on the grill—the fish should sizzle as soon as it touches the pan. Turn down the heat slightly and let the fillets cook for 4–5 minutes, then turn them over. Continue to cook on the other side until crisp and golden. Serve on hot plates with a few slices of flavored butter: it may be served directly on the fish or, if you have a pretty shell, serve the butter on the side in the shell. Garnish with segments of lemon and parsley.

Note: Fillets of any small fish are delicious panbroiled in this way. Fish under 2 pounds, such as mackerel, herring, and brown trout, can also be grilled whole on the pan. Fish over 2 pounds can be filleted first and then cut across into portions. Large fish of 4–5 1/2 pounds can also be grilled whole. Cook them for about 10–15 minutes on each side and then put in a hot oven 350ºF for another 15 minutes or so to finish cooking.

Flavored Butters

Mâitre d'Hotel Butter
1/2 cup (1 stick) butter
2 1/2 tablespoons finely chopped parsley
few drops of freshly squeezed lemon juice

Cream the butter, add in the parsley and a few drops of lemon juice at a time. Roll into butter pats or form into a roll and wrap in waxed paper or foil, twisting each end to seal. Refrigerate to harden.

Lemon Butter
Omit the parsley and add the rind of the lemon to the Mâitre d'Hotel Butter recipe.

Mustard and Parsley Butter
Add 4 teaspoons Dijon mustard to the Mâitre d'Hotel Butter recipe.

Cashel or Crozier Blue Cheese Butter
1/2 cup (1 stick) unsalted butter
2 ounces Cashel Blue cheese (about 1/2 cup)
1 teaspoon freshly ground pepper
4 teaspoons chopped parsley, optional

Mix all the ingredients together in a bowl or better still, whizz in a food processor. Form into a roll in tin foil or plastic wrap, tighten the ends. Chill or freeze until needed.

friends' supper party

A participation party, where the guests get involved in the cooking is one of the simplest and fun ways to entertain a group of people. Make up some crêpe batter (see p.106), lay out a range of fillings, and then get your guests to cook their own crêpe. Not only does this save on cooking time, it also means that the menu is really flexible and you can cater for all your friends' tastes and dietary choices. And if any of your guests have specific needs, they can bring their own fillings and still be involved in the preparation.
Note: Suggest making a batch of gluten-free crêpe batter, too, that way you're covered if you have any coeliacs coming and if you don't, others won't be able to tell they're gluten-free.

This is also a really good way to have a casual supper. If you are having good friends over you may not necessarily want the formality of sitting around a dining room table. The food may also not be the focal point of the evening—you may have gathered to plan a wedding or reunion, to have a film night or TV marathon or a sewing or games evening—and this kind of dining allows you to combine food with other activities.

Once you have made your crêpes, you can curl up on sofas and cushions around the TV or get on with the evening's entertainment. People can get up and make more crêpes as they like and you just need to keep an eye on the batter and put out more fillings as needed.

participation party

Omelets (see p.108) are perfect for participation parties, and are the quintessential "quick and easy meal." Tacos and fajitas (p.109) can also be served in this fashion, but they will need a little more preparation. If you have more time, sushi (see pp.44–45) is also great fun to make together.

Make sure you have a good salad and dessert (for the lemon meringue pie, see p.265) for guests to help themselves to, although with a crêpe party you can simply move onto sweet fillings.

Have some wine, beers, and soft drinks on a table, together with the appropriate glasses, and people can refill when their glasses are low.

You will need very little in the way of place settings or decoration as the food itself will provide plenty of color and entertainment. Find lots of generous bowls or chunky plates to set the fillings out on—or use square white plates for a more graphic look.

If you are worried about your guests' culinary skills, provide aprons and don't use your best crêpe pan. Don't forget to get everybody to help with clearing up!

A Crêpe Party

MAKES 12–15 CRÊPES   (**P:** 15 mins.
+ 1 HOUR TO REST/**C:** 2 mins. + FILLING)

A kitchen party is the best fun. Get everybody involved in cooking their crêpes as well as their filling. Make large quantities of basic crêpe batter, provide lots of fillings both sweet and savory, a few nonstick pans and maybe a few aprons for the more flamboyant cooks. This kind of participation party is great for catering for special diets— you can even ask guests to bring a filling or two themselves.

For the crêpe batter:
1¹⁄₃ cups white flour, preferably
   unbleached
good pinch of salt
2 large cage-free, organic eggs,
   plus 1–2 egg yolks,
2 cups milk or, for very crisp, light,
   delicate crêpes, milk and water mixed
2¹⁄₂ tablespoons melted butter

For the sweet crêpe batter:
As above, plus 1 tablespoon sugar (if
   the crêpes are to be served with sugar
   and lemon juice, use 2 tablespoons
   sugar and the finely grated zest of ¹⁄₂ lemon)

filling of your choice (see right), for serving

Note: If you make both batters, be careful not to mix them up.

To make the batter, sift the flour, salt, and sugar (if making sweet batter) into a bowl. Make a well in the center and drop in the eggs and yolks. With a whisk or wooden spoon, starting in the center, mix the eggs and gradually bring in the flour from the sides. Add the milk gradually, beating all the while, until the batter is covered with bubbles. Alternatively, just throw all the ingredients into a blender and whizz—it works beautifully.

Let the batter stand in a cold place for 1 hour or so—longer will do no harm. Just before you cook the crêpes, stir in the melted butter. This will make all the difference to the flavor and texture of the crêpes, and will make it possible to cook them without greasing the pan each time.

To cook the crêpes, heat a nonstick frying pan until very hot. Pour in just enough batter to cover the bottom when you tilt and swirl the pan. Put the pan back on the heat and loosen the crêpe around the edge with a non-metal spatula. Flip over and cook for a few seconds on the reverse side. Slide onto a plate. Repeat until all the batter has been used up. To fill the crêpes, lay some of your chosen filling on the crêpe and roll into a cigar or fold like an eggroll or a fan shape depending upon the filling.

Crêpes can be made ahead and finished later. They will keep overnight, covered, in the fridge. They will peel apart easily, so there's no need to interleaf them with waxed paper. To reheat, cover with aluminum foil and put in an oven at 350°F.

Suggested Fillings

Savory
Creamed spinach
Mushroom à la Crème (see p.241)
Tomato Fondue (see p.240)
Piperonata (see p.243)
Spicy chicken with almonds
Crispy chorizo
Grated cheese
Smoked mackerel flakes
Cream cheese mixed with lots of dill and freshly ground pepper
Lots of chopped herbs in little bowls, such as parsley
Thin slices of cooked ham and Gruyère cheese
Smoked salmon and dill
Marmite and sardines
Shrimp and scallions

Sweet
Freshly squeezed lemon juice, melted butter, and sugar
Toffee Sauce (see p.28) and bananas
Chocolate fudge sauce and bananas
Green Gooseberry and Elderflower Compote (see p.229)
Poached Apricots with Sweet Geranium Leaves (see p.29)
A shake of confectioners' sugar
A shake of cocoa powder
Chocolate spread
Chopped toasted hazelnuts, almonds, pecans, or walnuts

30-second Classic French Omelet

SERVES 1 (**P:** 10 mins./**C:** 30–45 SECONDS)

A classic French omelet has to be the quintessential easy entertaining recipe, so if a pal or several suddenly turn up and look as though they are not about to leave until they are fed, you can always whizz up an omelet! They are also great for participation parties—as with the crêpes (see p.106), prepare a huge batch of omelet batter and line up a ton of fillings. People can then create their own masterpieces.

As ever, the quality of the eggs really matters. The key to a successful omelet is to get the pan hot enough and to use clarified butter if at all possible. Ordinary butter will burn if your pan is as hot as it ought to be. The best tender golden omelets take no more than 30 seconds to cook—45 seconds if you are adding a filling. Time yourself: you'll be amazed.

2 cage-free, organic eggs
2 teaspoons water or milk
salt and freshly ground pepper
filling of your choice (see right)
2 teaspoons clarified butter or olive oil

Omelet pan, preferably nonstick,
  9-inch diameter

Warm a plate in the oven. Whisk the eggs with the water or milk in a bowl with a fork or whisk, until thoroughly mixed but not too fluffy. Season with salt and freshly ground pepper. Put the warm plate beside the stove. Have your chosen filling close at hand, hot, if necessary, with a spoon at the ready.

Heat the omelet pan over high heat and when it is almost smoking, add the clarified butter or the olive oil—it should sizzle immediately. Pour in the egg mixture. It will start to cook instantly, so quickly pull the edges of the omelet towards the center with a plastic spoon or spatula, tilting the pan so that the uncooked egg runs to the sides. Continue until most of the egg is set and does not run when the pan is tilted; the center will still be soft and uncooked at this point but will continue to cook on the plate. If you are using a filling, spoon the hot filling in a line across the center of the omelet.

To fold the omelet, flip the edge just below the handle of the pan into the center, then hold the pan almost perpendicular over the plate so that the omelet will flip over again, then half roll, half slide the omelet onto the plate so that it lands folded in three. Serve immediately.

Suggested Fillings
Tomato Fondue with or without pesto
Piperonata (see p.243)
Mushroom à la Crème (see p.241)
Crispy bacon, chopped cooked ham or chorizo sausage
Goat cheese, grated cheddar, Gruyère, or Parmesan cheese or a mixture and lots of fresh herbs
Fine herbs: add 1 teaspoon each of chopped parsley, chives, chervil, and tarragon to the eggs
  just before cooking or scatter them over the omelet just before folding
Smoked salmon (lox) or smoked mackerel: add about 3 tablespoonsful and perhaps a little
  finely chopped parsley or dill

How to Clarify Butter
Clarified butter is excellent for cooking because it can withstand a higher temperature as the salt and milk particles have been removed.

Melt 1 cup (2 sticks) butter gently in a saucepan or in the oven. Let it stand for a few minutes, then skim the crusty white layer of salt particles from the top of the melted butter. Underneath this crust is a clear liquid butter—the clarified butter. The milky liquid at the bottom can be discarded or used in a white sauce. Cover and store. It will keep covered in the fridge for several weeks.

Beef Fajitas with Tomato and Cilantro Salsa and Guacamole

SERVES 6–8   (**P:** 20 mins. + 1 HOUR
                    MARINATING/**C:** 5 mins.)

This is another great recipe for a participation party, although here you might want
to prepare the beef and fillings before your
guests arrive and then let them put their
fajitas together themselves.

1 pound round steak, 1-inch thick,
   cut into steaks
12–16 flour tortillas
salt and freshly ground black pepper
handful of shredded lettuce, such as iceberg
   or romaine
Tomato and Cilantro Salsa (see p.294)
Guacamole (see p.294)
1/2 cup sour cream

For the marinade:
2 garlic cloves, crushed
1 chile, seeded and chopped, or
   1/2 teaspoon red pepper flakes
1 teaspoon ground cumin
4 teaspoons chopped fresh marjoram
21/2 tablespoons Mexican beer
21/2 tablespoons extra virgin olive oil

To make the marinade, put all the marinade ingredients in a pie dish and mix well. Add the steak and turn to coat well. Cover and refrigerate for 1 hour.

When ready to cook, heat a grill pan. When it is very hot, drain the steaks and cook to your taste. Transfer to a plate and let it relax for 5 minutes.

Meanwhile, heat a frying pan and flip the tortillas over to heat through. When the meat has relaxed, carve it into 1/2-inch-thick slices.

To prepare the fajitas for serving, put the sliced steak on the warm tortillas. Sprinkle with salt and freshly ground pepper. Top with lettuce, Tomato and Cilantro Salsa, Guacamole, and sour cream. Roll up or fold over the tortillas and serve hot.

Alternatively, put a stack of warm tortillas on the table, set out the Tomato and Cilantro Salsa, Guacamole, sour cream, lettuce, and sliced steak, and let your guests have fun making up their own fajitas—a delicious interactive supper.

Taco Party

SERVES 20   (**P:** 10 mins./**C:** 2–3 HOURS)

Another fun way to have a carefree party.
Although the pork takes a couple of hours
to cook, this recipe can be made in advance
and it is easy to serve.

1 pork shoulder, boned
2 onions, peeled and quartered
4 celery stalks, chopped
3 garlic cloves
6 black peppercorns
1 bouquet garni
sea salt (or Kosher salt)
about 60 warm flour tortillas

For the accompaniments:
Refried Beans (see p.21)
Tomato and Cilantro Salsa (see p.294)
sour cream
tomatilla salsa (optional; available in delis)
grated cheddar cheese
lots of fresh cilantro
lime segments for squeezing (optional)

Put the pork into a heavy pot or pan just large enough to hold the meat and vegetables comfortably. Add the onions, celery, garlic, peppercorns and bouquet garni. Cover with cold water and bring to a boil. Reduce the heat to medium and simmer for 11/2–2 hours or until the meat is soft and tender.

Transfer the pork to a plate, strain the liquid, and discard the vegetables. Skim the fat off the liquid, return to the pan, and cook over medium heat until reduced to about 1 cup liquid.

Meanwhile, preheat the oven to 325ºF. Using two forks, pull the pork into shreds. Spread the shreds out on two baking trays and season with sea salt. Pour the reduced cooking liquid over the shredded pork and transfer to the oven. Cook until the edges of the meat start to brown and crisp, about 15 minutes. Taste, and adjust the seasoning if needed. The dish may be prepared ahead to this point.

Set out the hot pork, preferably in an earthenware casserole dish, on the table with the accompaniments. Warm the tortillas or, if it's a casual kitchen party, have an iron or nonstick frying pan over low heat so guests can warm their own.

To serve, take a warm tortilla, sprinkle a line of shredded pork down the center, top with some Refried Beans, sour cream, salsa, grated cheese, and cilantro, and squeeze a little lime juice over the top if you like.

Ballycotton Shrimp Whole in their Shells with Watercress and Dill Mayo

SERVES 8   (P: 10 mins./C: 5 mins.)

Not cheap, but always a wow. If you can, buy the shrimp already cooked from the person at your fish counter—great, but they are very simple to cook. Homemade mayo is a must to embellish beautiful fresh shrimp.

40–48 large very fresh raw shrimp
4 quarts water
1/4 cup salt

For the accompaniments:
1/3–2/3 cup homemade dill mayonnaise
  (see p.297)
lemon wedges
wild watercress leaves
crusty whole-wheat soda bread (see p.38)
butter

First cook the shrimp. In a large pot, bring the water to a boil, add the salt, and stir briefly to dissolve (the quantity given may sound a lot, but this is the secret of real flavor when cooking prawns or shrimp). Add a half or a third of the shrimp and, as soon as the water returns to a rolling boil, test to see if the shrimp are cooked—they should be firm and white, not opaque or mushy. Remove the cooked shrimp immediately; very large ones may take another 30 seconds–1 minute in the boiling water. Repeat in batches until all the shrimp are cooked. Spread them in a single layer on a tray, uncurl the tails and allow to cool.

Put 5–6 cooled whole shrimp on each plate. Spoon a tablespoon or two of dill mayonnaise into a little bowl or oyster shell on the side of the plate, and add a wedge of lemon. Garnish with some fresh wild watercress. Serve with crusty whole-wheat soda bread and Irish butter.

Note: Do not be tempted to cook too many shrimp together, otherwise they may overcook before the water even returns to a boil. Cook them in 2–3 batches. Smaller shrimp can be cooked in the same way, but take 2–3 minutes to cook.

Seared Fresh Salmon with Vine-ripened Tomatoes and Herbs

SERVES 8   (P: 5 mins./C: 5 mins.)

2-pound fillet of salmon, scales removed
salt, freshly ground pepper, and sugar, to taste
1/2 cup extra virgin olive oil or clarified
  butter (see p.108), plus extra for frying
8 very ripe vine tomatoes, coarsely chopped
1/3 cup each chopped basil, marjoram,
  and mint

Cut the salmon fillet into strips about 2½ inches wide. Season well with salt and pepper.

Heat a little olive oil or clarified butter in a frying pan or grill-pan, and fry the fish carefully so the fish doesn't fall apart—about 3–4 minutes on each side. Transfer to a serving dish, skin side up.

In a bowl, mix the chopped tomatoes and the herbs, then add the olive oil or clarified butter and season with salt, pepper, and sugar. Spoon this over the fish. Serve warm or cold.

Other good things to serve with roast or seared salmon
Dill butter and Tomato Fondue (see p.240)
Teriyaki sauce with new potatoes and bok choy
Rhubarb, cucumber, and mint salsa

Great Beans and Sausages

SERVES 6   (P: 5 mins./C: 10 mins.)

1 quantity well-seasoned Tomato Fondue
  (see p.240)
2½ tablespoons chopped fresh rosemary
15-ounce can cannellini or navy (Gt. Northern)
  beans, drained
1 pound best pork sausages
flat-leaf parsley leaves, for garnishing

Heat the Tomato Fondue in a sauté pan or frying pan. Add the chopped rosemary and beans, and bubble for 6–8 minutes.

Meanwhile, in a wide frying pan, cook the sausages until golden on all sides.

Taste the beans and adjust the seasoning if needed. Serve with the sausages and scatter with lots of parsley. Serve with crusty bread.

Pork with Rosemary and Tomatoes

SERVES 6   (**P:** 10 mins./**C:** 30 mins.)

2 pounds trimmed pork fillet
2¹/₂ tablespoons butter
2 shallots, finely chopped
1 pound very ripe but firm tomatoes,
   (about 3 medium) skinned and cut
   into ¹/₂-inch slices
salt, freshly ground pepper, and sugar
1 cup cream
4 teaspoons chopped fresh rosemary,
   plus whole sprigs for garnishing
1¹/₂ tablespoons extra virgin olive oil

Cut the trimmed pork fillet into slices about ³/₄-inch thick.

Melt 2 tablespoons of the butter in a pan. When it foams add the shallots, cover with a butter wrapper, and sweat gently for 5 minutes. Remove the butter wrapper, increase the heat slightly, add the tomatoes in a single layer, and season with salt, pepper, and sugar. After 2 minutes, flip the tomatoes and season on the other side, then add the cream and chopped rosemary. Simmer gently for 5 minutes. The sauce should not be too thick—just a light coating consistency. Check the seasoning.

Place the remaining butter and the olive oil in a sauté pan or frying pan over high heat. Season the pork, and when the butter and oil are quite hot, arrange the pork in the pan in a single layer. Allow the pork to turn a rich golden brown on the underside before turning the slices over. Reduce the temperature and finish cooking on the other side. The meat should feel slightly firm to the touch. Be careful not to overcook the pork or it will be dry and tasteless.

Add the pork to the sauce, taste, and correct the seasoning. The dish may be prepared ahead to this point. Garnish with rosemary sprigs and serve immediately or reheat later.

Orzo or rice make a delicious accompaniment and will mop up the herby sauce. This recipe is also great made instead with chicken breasts.

Lamb Chops with Cumin and Dill Tzatziki

SERVES 8   (**P:** 5 mins./**C:** 30 mins.)

16 lamb chops, preferably side loin (the chops
   with the rib loin)
extra virgin olive oil, for brushing
¹/₄ cup cumin seeds, toasted and
   ground
sea salt (or Kosher salt) and freshly
   ground pepper
Dill Tzatziki (see p.297)
roast cherry tomatoes (optional)

Trim the chops of excess fat and score the back fat. Lay the chops in a single layer on one or two flat dishes, brush with olive oil, and season with the ground cumin seeds and pepper. Let them sit for at least 15 minutes, better still an hour.

Heat a grill pan, season the chops with sea salt, and cook in batches for a few minutes each side until crisp on the outside, but slightly pink and juicy on the inside. Make sure the fat is crisp, so that those who love a little sweet fat can enjoy it.

Serve 2 chops per person, with a little bowl of Dill Tzatziki on each plate; a branch of roast cherry tomatoes is a delicious addition if you have time.

Top Tip: If you'd rather not stand over a grill pan in your good clothes, buy 2 racks of lamb. Score the skin in a diamond pattern, rub well with cumin seeds, and drizzle with olive oil as above. Roast in the oven preheated to 400°F for 20–30 minutes depending on the size of the racks of lamb. Serve as above.

Spiced Chicken and Red Peppers with Orzo

SERVES 6–8   (**P:** 5 mins./**C:** 30 mins.)

A simple recipe that works really well if cooking for a lot of people.

4 teaspoons coriander seeds
4 teaspoons cumin seeds
1/2 teaspoon ground turmeric
good pinch of cayenne pepper
2 teaspoons salt
1 teaspoon sugar
4 ounces onion, roughly chopped
  (about 1 cup)
1-inch piece of fresh ginger root, peeled and
  sliced
3 garlic cloves, crushed
1/4 cup shelled almonds, blanched
12 ounces red peppers, seeded and
  coarsely chopped (about 2 cups)
6 1/2 tablespoons sunflower oil

2 pounds boned chicken thighs, cut into
  finger-sized strips; alternatively use breast meat
2/3 cup water
2 1/2 tablespoons lemon juice, plus
  extra to taste

In separate dry pans, toast the coriander and cumin seeds, ensuring the seeds do not burn. Grind them using a mortar and pestle. Transfer the ground seeds to a food processor and add the turmeric, cayenne, salt, sugar, chopped onions, ginger, garlic, almonds, and peppers. Whizz to a smooth paste.

Heat the oil in a sauté pan or frying pan, add the spice paste, and cook for about 10 minutes until reduced. Add the chicken pieces, water, and lemon juice, and stir well. Taste and adjust the seasoning, adding a little more lemon juice if needed. Cover and cook over low heat for 15–30 minutes or until the chicken is tender.

Serve with orzo or pilaf rice (see recipe below).

Note: If you like a hot curry, increase the amount of cayenne pepper to 1/2 teaspoon.

Orzo with Fresh Herbs

SERVES 4   (**P:** 5 mins./**C:** 30 mins.)

Orzo looks like fat grains of rice but is in fact made from semolina (flour).

2 1/2 quarts water
1 cup orzo
salt and freshly ground pepper
4 teaspoons chopped fresh parsley
4 teaspoons chopped fresh chives
4 teaspoons fresh thyme
butter

Bring the water to a rolling boil and add 1 1/2 teaspoons salt. Sprinkle in the orzo and cook for 8–10 minutes or until just cooked. Drain, rinse under hot water, and toss with the herbs and a little butter. Season with freshly ground pepper.

Orzo with peas
Add 1 1/2 cups blanched peas to the orzo.

Pilaf Rice

SERVES 8   (**P:** 5 mins./**C:** 30 mins.)

Although a risotto can be made in 20 minutes, it entails 20 minutes of pretty constant stirring, which makes it feel laborious. A pilaf on the other hand looks after itself once the initial cooking is under way. It is also versatile—serve it as a staple or add whatever tasty bits you have at hand. Ensure all additions are seasoned and balanced.

2 tablespoons butter
2 1/2 tablespoons finely chopped onion
  or shallot
2 cups long-grain rice, preferably basmati
salt and freshly ground pepper
4 cups homemade chicken broth
  (see p.295)
2 1/2 tablespoons chopped fresh herbs such as
  parsley, thyme, or chives (optional)

Melt the butter in a heavy pan, add the onion, and let it sweat for 2–3 minutes. Add the rice and toss for a minute or two, just long enough for the grains to change color. Season with salt and freshly ground pepper, add the chicken broth, cover, and bring to a boil. Reduce the heat to a minimum and then simmer on top of the stove, or in the oven preheated to 325ºF, for about 10 minutes. By then the rice should be just cooked and all the water absorbed. Just before serving, stir in the fresh herbs (if using).

Spicy Thai Fish Cakes with Cucumber Relish or Arjard

SERVES 4   (P: 10 mins. + 30 mins.
STANDING TIME/C: 5 mins.)

10 ounces cod (rockfish or red
  snapper fillets are used in Thailand)
2¹/2 tablespoons red or green curry paste
1 cage-free, organic egg
¹/4 cup fish sauce (*nam pla*)
1 teaspoon sugar
5 kaffir lime leaves, stems removed and very
  finely shredded
2 ounces green beans, finely sliced across
  (about ¹/2 cup)
sunflower or peanut oil, for deep-frying
cilantro leaves and chili powder,
  for garnishing

For the Thai cucumber relish:
1 large cucumber
¹/3 cup rice vinegar
2–4 teaspoons sugar

1 teaspoon salt
1 small red chile, seeded and chopped
1 shallot, very thinly sliced

First make the cucumber relish. Peel the cucumber and cut in half lengthwise. With a melon baller or sharp spoon, scoop out the seeds from the center and discard them. Slice the cucumber diagonally into thin slices.

Mix the remaining relish ingredients in a glass bowl, add 2¹/2 tablespoons hot water, and stir well to dissolve the sugar and salt. Add the cucumber slices and toss well. Let the relish stand for at least 30 minutes before serving.

Put the fish into a food processor, add the curry paste, egg, fish sauce, and sugar, and blend well. Transfer to a medium bowl. Add the lime leaves and green beans and mix well. Shape the mixture into little 2-inch-wide patties, ¹/4-inch thick.

Heat the oil to deep-fry the fish cakes, then fry them for 4–5 minutes or until golden.

Serve the fish cakes with the cucumber relish, and garnish with fresh cilantro and chili powder.

Puff Pastry Tart with Tomato, Chorizo, Mozzarella, and Basil Leaves

SERVES 4   (P: 5 mins./C: 30 mins.)

**A piece of puff pastry dough is definitely an
invaluable standby to make a quick tart.**

8 ounces puff pastry dough
4–6 very ripe tomatoes or Tomato Fondue
  (see p.240)
salt, freshly ground pepper, and sugar, to taste
4 ounces chorizo, sliced (about 1 cup)
2 balls buffalo mozzarella cheese, thinly sliced
extra virgin olive oil, for drizzling
¹/3 cup pesto (see p.297)
basil leaves, for garnishing
green salad, for serving

Preheat the oven to 450°F.

Roll out the puff pastry dough to a sheet about ¹/4-inch thick. Cut into a square or rectangle that will fit a baking tray, or stamp into four 5-inch circles. Transfer to a cold baking tray. Prick the bottom with a fork. Chill for a few minutes in a fridge

Cut the tomatoes into ¹/4-inch-thick slices. Arrange overlapping slices on the pastry dough or else spread a thin layer of Tomato Fondue over it. Season with salt, freshly ground pepper, and some sugar. Tuck in slices of chorizo here and there, and top with slices of mozzarella. Sprinkle some pesto on top, and drizzle some olive oil over it. Bake for 10–20 minutes depending upon size.

Drizzle with a little pesto, scatter a few fresh basil leaves on top, and serve immediately, with a good green salad.

Son-in-law's Eggs Khai Loog Kheoy

SERVES 6   (**P:** 15 mins./**C:** 15 mins.)

Wasinee Beech, the lovely Thai cook, gave me this family recipe, which can be prepared ahead of time.

6 cage-free, organic eggs
6$^1/_2$ tablespoons extra virgin olive oil
3 garlic cloves, crushed and finely chopped
$^1/_2$ cup free-range organic ground pork
5 fresh shiitake mushrooms, sliced, or dried Chinese mushrooms, soaked for 20 minutes and sliced (reserve the water)
2$^1/_2$ tablespoons palm sugar or soft brown sugar
2$^1/_2$ tablepoons fish sauce (*nam pla*)
6$^1/_2$ tablespoons tamarind water (see p.126)
4 teaspoons lemon juice
3 scallions, sliced into $^1/_2$-inch lengths
8 shallots, thinly sliced, and 2 dried red chiles, thinly sliced, both fried in a little oil or roast until fragrant but not burnt
plain boiled rice, for serving

For Wasinee's Arjard cucumber salad:
$^1/_4$–$^1/_3$ cup sugar
$^1/_3$ cup white wine vinegar
$^1/_3$ cup water
$^1/_2$–1 teaspoon salt
1 cucumber, quartered lengthwise and thinly sliced
2 shallots, finely sliced (if unavailable, use $^1/_2$ a mild onion)
1 red chile, seeded and sliced
1 green chile, seeded and sliced

To make Wasinee's Arjard cucumber salad, mix together the sugar, vinegar, water, and salt in a small saucepan. Bring to a boil and simmer for 5 minutes. Let cool. Meanwhile, mix together in a bowl the cucumber, shallots, and red and green chiles. When the sauce has cooled, pour it over the vegetables.

Cook the eggs gently in boiling salted water for 7 minutes to hard-boil them. Drain and cover with cold water. When cool, shell and set aside.

Heat 4 tablespoons of the olive oil in a wok, add the cooked and shelled eggs and fry until golden brown all around. Transfer to a serving dish. Cut each egg in half and arrange nicely.

Clean the wok and heat the remaining olive oil. Stir-fry the garlic until golden. Add the ground pork and mushrooms. Stir and fry until the pork is cooked. Add the palm or brown sugar, fish sauce, tamarind water, and lemon juice. If more liquid is needed, add a little bit of water from soaking the mushrooms, or some plain water.

Taste and adjust the seasoning if needed. Add the scallions, give a quick stir, and spoon the sauce over the arranged eggs. Top with the crispy shallots and chiles. Serve with plain boiled rice and Wasinee's Arjard cucumber salad.

Shermin's Lamajun (Turkish Lamb Pizza)

MAKES ABOUT 8–10   (P: 10 mins./C: 5 mins.)

This little gem of a recipe was given to me by Shermin Mustafa, whose food I love. It's fantastic for an informal kitchen party or for a family supper.

2 cups all-purpose white flour, plus extra for
  dusting
1 cup plain yogurt
lemon wedges and lots of sprigs of flat-leaf
  parsley, for serving

For the topping:
1 tablespoon extra virgin olive oil or butter
1 large onion, finely chopped
1 cup ground lamb
4 ripe tomatoes, finely chopped
2 1/2 tablespoons chopped flat-leaf parsley
salt and freshly ground pepper

First make the topping. Heat the oil in a frying pan and cook the onion over low heat until soft but not colored. Let cool completely. Mix the onion with the remaining topping ingredients and season well with salt and pepper.

Preheat a heavy iron frying pan, preheat the broiler, and warm a baking sheet.

Mix the flour with the yogurt to form a soft dough. Divide into 8–10 pieces and roll each out until it's as thin as possible, using lots of flour to dust over the counter and the dough. Spread a few tablespoonfuls of the topping mixture on each circle of dough as thinly and evenly as possible.

Fold the dough in half, then in quarters, slide your hand underneath, then transfer to the pan and open out gently; there is no need to oil the pan. Cook over a high heat for about 2 minutes or until golden on the bottom. Remove from the pan and slide onto the warm baking sheet, then place under the hot broiler and cook for another 2–3 minutes or until the meat is cooked. Repeat with the remaining pizzas.

Serve with 3–4 lemon wedges and plenty of sprigs of flat-leaf parsley for each helping.

To eat the lamajun, squeeze lots of lemon juice over the surface. Pluck 4–5 parsley leaves and sprinkle over the top. Either eat flat like a pizza or rolled up like a tortilla.

Tortilla Pizza

SERVES 8   (P: 5 mins./C: 5 mins.)

A cheat's version of a very-thin-crust pizza, but so easy and delicious. Keep a package of corn or flour tortillas in your freezer or cupboard, check what's in the fridge for suitable toppings, and have fun.

8 soft corn or flour tortillas

Suggested toppings:
Tomato Fondue (see p.240) with mozzarella
  cheese and basil leaves
Piperonata (see p.243) with crispy pancetta
  or chorizo sausage
Mushroom à la Crème (see p.241) with lots of
  marjoram
Crumbled blue cheese with rosemary and
  caramelized onions
Pesto (see p.297), mozzarella cheese, and
  arugula leaves
Four-cheese pizza: Cheddar, mozzarella, Cashel
  Blue, and Durrus cheese, and arugula leaves
Smoked salmon, cream cheese, and crispy
  capers and chive blossoms

Preheat the broiler. Pop the tortillas under the broiler for 2–3 minutes per side. Top with your chosen topping, and pop back under the hot broiler, or into a preheated oven at 450°F, for 3–4 minutes. Scatter with fresh herbs or leaves as appropriate and serve immediately.

Frittata with Oven-roasted Tomatoes, Chorizo, and Goat Cheese

SERVES 6–8   (**P**: 10 mins./**C**: 30 mins.)

A frittata is an Italian omelet. Along with "kuku" and "Spanish tortilla," it sounds much more exciting than a flat omelet, although that's basically what they all are. Unlike their soft and creamy French cousin, these omelets are cooked slowly over a very low heat, during which time you can be whipping up a delicious salad to accompany them! A frittata is cooked on the stove and under the broiler, then cut into wedges like a piece of cake. Omit the tomato and chorizo given here and you have a basic recipe flavored with grated cheese and a generous sprinkling of herbs. As is the case of the omelet, though, you'll occasionally want to try other variations. For a yummy vegetarian alternative, omit the chorizo and use a cup of grated Gruyère cheese to add extra zing. Other tasty morsels include spinach, ruby chard, calabrese or broccoli, asparagus, smoked mackerel... the list is endless, but be careful: don't use a frittata as a trash can—think about the combination of flavors before you empty your fridge!

A frittata can also be cooked in a preheated oven at 320°F. You could also bake mini versions in muffin pans (about 15 minutes in the oven)—perfect for taking on a picnic (see p.220) as the pans will protect them on the journey.

1 pound ripe or sun-blush tomatoes
   (about 3 medium)
salt and freshly ground black pepper
8 large cage-free, organic eggs
2 1/2 tablespoons chopped parsley
4 teaspoons fresh thyme leaves
4 teaspoons chopped fresh basil, mint, or
   marjoram
4–6 ounces chorizo, thickly sliced and each
   slice quartered (about 1 cup)
1 1/2 ounces Parmesan cheese, grated
   (about 3/4 cup)
2 tablespoons butter
4 ounces soft goat cheese (about 1/2 cup)
green salad and olives, for serving

If using fresh tomatoes, preheat the oven to 350°F. (If using sun-blush tomatoes, there is no need to roast them.) Cut the fresh tomatoes in half around their equator, arrange them cut side up in a single layer in a nonstick roasting pan and season with salt and pepper. Roast for 10–15 minutes until almost soft and slightly crinkly. Remove from the oven and let cool.

Whisk the eggs in a bowl and add salt and pepper, the herbs, chorizo, and grated cheese. Add the tomatoes and stir gently.

Melt the butter in a nonstick frying pan. When the butter starts to foam, tip in the egg mixture. Reduce the heat to as low as it will go. Divide the goat cheese into walnut-sized pieces and drop gently into the frittata, spacing them regularly. Let the frittata cook on a heat-diffuser mat for 15 minutes, or until the underneath is set. The top should still be slightly runny. Meanwhile preheat the broiler.

Pop the frittata under the broiler for 1 minute to set and barely brown the surface. Slide the frittata onto a warm plate and serve cut into wedges, with a good green salad and a few olives.

Middle Eastern Mezze with Chile and Cilantro Flat Bread

SERVES 10   (**P**: 5 mins./**C**: 30 mins.)

salad greens and fresh herbs, tossed with a
  little vinaigrette
Eggplant Puree (see p.119)
Hummus Bi Tahini (see recipe below)
feta cheese with walnut and mint
Tunisian Spicy Carrot Salad (see p.119)
Roasted Red Peppers (see p.298)
generous amount of pine nuts, toasted
1 teaspoon paprika, or to taste
2¹/₂ tablespoons extra virgin olive oil
generous amount of chopped flat-leaf parsley
cooked chickpeas, for scattering
sprigs of mint
2¹/₂ tablespoons olives, or to taste
chopped cilantro, for garnishing

For the accompaniment:
10 flour tortillas or other flat bread (see
  p.40), and extra virgin olive oil, chopped
  chile, and sea salt (or Kosher salt)
or Pita Chips (see p.119)
or tortilla chips

Prepare and make all the mezze components.

Put some salad in the center of each plate. Around the salad drop a spoonful of Eggplant Puree, Hummus Bi Tahini, some feta with walnut and mint, and some Tunisian Spicy Carrot Salad.

Lay a strip or two of roasted red pepper on top of the eggplant and sprinkle with toasted pine nuts. Mix some paprika with the olive oil and drizzle over the top of the hummous. Sprinkle with chopped parsley and a few chickpeas. Drop a sprig of mint on the feta and scatter a few olives on the plate. Sprinkle cilantro on the mezze.

To make the chile and cilantro flat bread, brush the flour tortillas or flat bread with olive oil, sprinkle with chopped chile and sea salt, and warm through in the oven for about 5 minutes. Cut the bread into triangular portions.

Serve the mezze with the chile and cilantro flat bread, the Pita Chips, or tortilla chips.

Hummus Bi Tahini

SERVES 4–8   (**P**: 10 mins.)

Hummus with tahini's rich, earthy taste has got quite a cult following. Strange to the palate on first encounter, this flavored puree of chickpeas and sesame seed paste soon becomes addictive. It makes an excellent appetizer, served as a dip with pita bread, but is also delicious with kabobs or as a salad with a main dish.

1 cup dried chickpeas, cooked,
  (reserve the cooking water) or 1 x15-ounce
  can chickpeas, drained
juice of 2–3 lemons, or to taste
2–3 garlic cloves, crushed
²/₃ cup tahini (sesame seed paste,
  available from health food stores and
  delicatessens)
1 teaspoon ground cumin
salt
2¹/₂ tablespoons olive oil
¹/₄ teaspoon paprika
flat-leaf parsley, for garnishing
pita or any crusty white bread, for serving

Drain the chickpeas, retaining the cooking liquid. Put the chickpeas in a food processor, add the lemon juice, and whizz to a thick paste. Add the garlic, tahini, cumin, and salt, blending to a soft, creamy paste; add a little of the chickpea cooking liquid if needed. Taste and adjust the lemon juice and salt until you are happy with the flavor. Transfer to a serving bowl.

Mix the olive oil with the paprika and drizzle over the top of the hummus. Scatter with parsley and serve with pita or other crusty bread.

Eggplant Puree with Olive Oil and Lemon

SERVES 6   (**P:** 10 mins./**C:** 10 mins.)

This is one of my favorite ways to eat eggplant. It is served throughout the southern Mediterranean region, and there are many delicious variations.

4 large eggplants
5–6 tablespoons extra virgin olive oil
juice of 2 lemons, unwaxed
2 garlic cloves, crushed (optional)
salt and freshly ground pepper

Roast or broil the eggplants depending upon the flavor you prefer. Let cool. Peel the eggplants, retaining every little morsel of flesh. Discard the skin and drain the flesh in a strainer or colander.

Transfer to a bowl and mash the eggplant flesh with a fork or chop with a knife depending upon the texture you like. Add the olive oil and lemon juice, garlic (if using), and salt and freshly ground pepper to taste.

Other good things to add

1 In Turkey, some thick Greek-style yogurt is often added. Reduce the olive oil in the recipe by half and add 6–8 tablespoons yogurt. This also makes a delicious "sauce" for pasta if you use ricotta instead of the yogurt, and chopped fresh herbs, such as marjoram.

2 A spicier version from Morocco includes 1 teaspoon harissa, 1 teaspoon cumin seeds, toasted and ground, and $2\frac{1}{2}$ tablespoons coarsely chopped cilantro leaves.

3 In Syria they add some pomegranate molasses—our new "flavor of the month." Use $\frac{1}{4}$–$\frac{1}{3}$ cup instead of the lemon juice.

4 *Julia's eggplant puree:* Roast or broil the eggplants as above, peel, drain, and mash the flesh, and mix with 2 small garlic cloves, finely chopped, $\frac{1}{2}$–1 teaspoon ground roasted cumin seeds, 1–$2\frac{1}{2}$ tablespoons chiffonade of mint (roll into a cigar shape and chop), the freshly squeezed juice of $\frac{1}{2}$–1 lemon, and some freshly ground pepper or chili oil if you prefer. Mix well.

Tunisian Spicy Carrot Salad

SERVES 6   (**P:** 5 mins./**C:** 30 mins.)

A delish salad to serve alone or as part of a mezze plate.

$1\frac{1}{2}$ pounds carrots
$\frac{1}{4}$–$\frac{1}{3}$ cup extra virgin olive oil
$\frac{1}{4}$ cup white wine vinegar
2 garlic cloves, crushed
1 teaspoon harissa, or to taste, or 1 teaspoon
  paprika and a good pinch of chili powder
$1\frac{1}{2}$ teaspoons freshly ground cumin seeds
salt
black olives (optional)

Peel the carrots and cut into large pieces. Cook them in a little boiling salted water until tender. Drain and mash them with a potato masher or fork. Mix in the olive oil, white wine vinegar, crushed garlic, harissa or paprika and chili powder, cumin, and some salt. Taste and adjust the seasoning if needed. Sprinkle with a few black olives if you like. Refrigerate until needed and serve cold or at room temperature.

Pita Chips

mini pita breads, cut in half crosswise
extra virgin olive oil, for brushing
cumin seeds, freshly ground and toasted
salt

Preheat the oven to 400°F.

Cut the pita into triangular wedges. Brush evenly with olive oil, and sprinkle with cumin and salt. Spread in a single layer on a baking tray and bake in the middle of the oven for 3 minutes or until crisp and golden. Serve immediately.

Chicken with Chorizo, Tomato, and Chili

SERVES 8–10   (**P:** 15 mins./**C:** 20 mins.)

This works well for large numbers. Of course, it can be made ahead and reheated. When ready to eat, cook some pasta and serve.

2 tablespoons butter

1 tablespoon finely chopped fresh rosemary

1 1/2 pounds ripe tomatoes, skinned,
  seeded, and cut into 1/2-inch cubes
  (about 3 cups), or 1 1/2 x 14 1/2-ounce cans
  tomatoes, chopped

salt, freshly ground pepper, and sugar, to taste

8 free-range, organic chicken breasts,
  whole or sliced

6 ounces chorizo (about 1 1/2 cups, cut up)

pinch of red pepper flakes

3/4 cup cream

2 tablespoons finely chopped flat-leaf parsley,
  plus extra, chopped, for garnishing

1 pound fresh noodles or fettuccini

1/3 cup grated Parmesan cheese

Melt the butter in a large sauté pan or frying pan and add the chopped rosemary and tomatoes. Season with salt, freshly ground pepper, and some sugar to taste. Cook over medium heat until the tomatoes have just begun to soften into a sauce, about 5 minutes. Add the chicken breasts.

Cut the chorizo into 1/2-inch slices and add them to the pan along with the crushed red pepper flakes. Add the cream and chopped parsley and let it bubble for 5–10 minutes, depending upon the size of the chicken pieces, stirring frequently, until the chicken is cooked through. Remove the pan from the heat and set aside.

Cook the pasta in a large pot of boiling salted water (it should be al dente, or still just firm). Drain and toss with the sauce, then add the grated Parmesan. Toss again, and check and adjust the seasoning if needed. Sprinkle with lots of chopped flat-leaf parsley and serve at once.

Chicken Breasts with Honey and Mustard

SERVES 8   (**P:** 5 mins./**C:** 30 mins.)

1/3 cup honey

1/3 cup Dijon mustard

8 free-range organic chicken breasts

extra virgin olive oil, for drizzling

salt and freshly ground pepper

For serving: green vegetables and potatoes,
  rice, or orzo

Preheat the oven to 350°F.

In a large bowl, mix together the honey and mustard. Toss the chicken in this mixture until well coated. Arrange in a single layer in a roasting pan. Drizzle with oil and season with salt and pepper. Bake for 20–30 minutes until the chicken is cooked through.

Serve with fresh green vegetables and potatoes, rice, or orzo.

Phillippa's Magret de Canard with Port Sauce

SERVES 4   (**P:** 10 mins./**C:** 35 mins.)

This is one of Phillippa Canning's favorite recipes for easy entertaining.

1 tablespoon extra virgin olive oil

1/2 cup (1 stick) butter

2 medium onions, chopped

2 tablespoons brown sugar

1/2 cup port

1 cup crème fraîche (or, if unavailable,
  sour cream)

3–4 duck breasts

salt and freshly ground pepper

sprigs of flat-leaf parsley, for garnishing

First make the sauce. Pour the olive oil into a heavy pan and add the butter, then heat gently until the butter has melted. Add the chopped onions and brown sugar, and cook for 15 minutes over a low heat until the onions are soft and slightly sticky.

Add the port, followed by the crème fraîche, and simmer very gently for about 10 minutes until the sauce has reduced a little and has thickened slightly. This can be made in advance and reheats very well later in the day.

Score the skin of the duck breasts and put, skin-side down, on a cold grill pan. Cook over a low heat for 15–20 minutes or until the skin is crisp and the fat has rendered out. Season with salt and freshly ground pepper. Turn the duck breasts onto the flesh side and cook for another 5–10 minutes depending upon size. Let rest for 10–15 minutes before serving. Meanwhile, reheat the sauce. Thinly slice the duck breasts and serve with a generous pool of sauce. Garnish with flat-leaf parsley sprigs.

Mexican Spiced Pork Chops with Pineapple, Chile, and Lime Salsa

SERVES 8   (**P:** 5 mins. + 2 HOURS/**C:** 20 mins.)

8 pork loin chops, preferably free-range, organic
   with a nice layer of fat (1-inch thick)
salt

For the marinade:
4 garlic cloves, crushed
1 teaspoon chopped fresh marjoram
1 teaspoon ground cumin
$1/2$ teaspoon ground coriander
$1/4$ teaspoon ground cinnamon
$2^{1}/_2$ tablespoons red wine vinegar
$1/4$ cup orange juice
4 teaspoons honey
$1/3$ cup extra virgin olive oil
freshly ground black pepper

In a bowl or glass measuring cup, mix together all the marinade ingredients.

Put the chops in a large dish and pour the marinade mixture over them, turning them several times to coat thoroughly. Cover and refrigerate for a couple of hours if you have time.

Season the chops with salt. Panbroil or barbecue over medium-hot coals until fully cooked but still juicy, 8–10 minutes per side. Season the chops with salt. Serve hot, with the Pineapple, Chile, and Lime Salsa.

Pineapple, Chile, and Lime Salsa

SERVES 8   (**P:** 5 mins./**C:** 30 mins.)

$1/2$ pineapple, cored and finely chopped
1 fresh red chile, seeded and finely chopped
1 red onion, finely chopped
$2^{1}/_2$ tablespoons chopped cilantro or mint
grated zest of 1 lime
$1/4$ cup lime juice
salt and sugar

In a bowl, mix together the pineapple, chile, onion, cilantro or mint, lime zest, and lime juice. Add salt and sugar to taste. Cover and let stand at room temperature for 30 minutes for the flavors to blend. Serve this at room temperature or chilled if you prefer.

Bubbly Pork Chops with Gruyère Cheese and Thyme Leaves

SERVES 8   (**P:** 5 mins./**C:** 20 mins.)

extra virgin olive oil, for drizzling
8 pork chops, preferably free-range, organic
salt and freshly ground pepper
6 ounces Gruyère or Coolea cheese, grated
   (about $1^{1}/_2$ cups)
$2^{1}/_2$ tablespoons Dijon mustard
$1/3$ cup cream
1 teaspoon fresh thyme leaves

For serving: new potatoes, Colcannon (see
   p.236) or watercress mash

If you want to cook the meat in the oven, preheat the oven to 450°F.

Heat a grill pan over a high heat. Drizzle a tiny drop of olive oil on the chops and season the chops with salt and pepper. Working in batches if necessary, place the meat on the grill pan (don't overcrowd the pan or the meat will stew) and seal on both sides. Transfer to the oven and cook for about 10 minutes until just cooked through; alternatively, turn the burner down to medium and continue to cook.

Meanwhile, mix the grated cheese with the mustard, cream, and thyme leaves.

Transfer the pork chops to a wide, ovenproof serving dish. Spread a layer of the cheesy topping evenly over each pork chop. Return to the oven or pop under a preheated broiler for a few minutes until the top is hot, bubbly, and golden brown.

Serve with new potatoes or Colcannon or watercress mash.

Pork or Lamb Chops with Tapenade
Sauté the lamb chops in the usual way. Spread a little tapenade (see p.75) over one side, sprinkle with grated cheese, and pop under the broiler for a couple of minutes until the cheese melts. Yummy!

Martha Rosenthal's Red Lentil Dahl

SERVES 6   (**P**: 15 mins./**C**: 25 mins.)

This is the quickest dahl to cook—it takes only 20 minutes without using a pressure cooker. The orange/red color of the lentils becomes pale yellow once they are cooked. The dahl keeps very well, so I usually double or triple this recipe.

The *Baghar* is an indispensable process in South Asian cooking—a lot of dishes, mostly dahls, are finished with this process. It is used as a garnish to perfume a dish and is essentially seasoning in sizzling oil; i.e., the frying of spices in hot oil to release their fragrance and aromas, which is then added to the dish just before serving.

1 cup orange/red lentils
14-ounce can coconut milk
1 teaspoon ground turmeric
4 teaspoons lemon juice
1 teaspoon Garam Masala (see recipe below)
1 teaspoon salt

For the Baghar:
4 teaspoons sunflower oil
1 teaspoon cumin seeds
1 teaspoon cayenne pepper
1 teaspoon ground coriander

For the garnish:
6 slices of onion, sautéed until golden
a few chopped cilantro or mint leaves

For the accompaniments:
basmati rice
Tamarind Relish (see recipe below)

Put the lentils in a heavy pan and add the coconut milk and turmeric. Bring to a boil and simmer for about 20 minutes, by which time the lentils will be soft, almost mushy. Turn off the heat, add the lemon juice, Garam Masala, and salt.

To make the baghar, heat the oil in a heavy pan, add the cumin seeds, and fry for 2 minutes, then turn off the heat. Add the cayenne and coriander, stir, and pour them over the cooked lentils. Mix well and garnish with sautéed onion slices and chopped cilantro or mint leaves.

Serve with basmati rice and Tamarind Relish.

Top Tip: Martha sometimes adds 2 ripe tomatoes, quartered, just before serving.

Garam Masala

What adds flavor to the simple dahl recipe (above) is to make your own garam masala. I usually make triple the quantity as it stores well.

3 tablespoons cumin seeds
1/2 cup coriander seeds
1 1/2 teaspoons cardamom seeds
1 1/2 teaspoons black peppercorns
15 whole cloves
2-inch piece of cinnamon stick
1/4 cup fennel seeds
1 tablespoon brown mustard seeds
1/2 teaspoon red pepper flakes

Preheat a heavy frying pan over medium-low heat. Add all of the ingredients and dry-fry, stirring occasionally or, until they darken slightly, about 8–10 minutes. Transfer to a coffee grinder or blender and grind to a powder. Use while fresh or store in an airtight container for up to 1 month.

Tamarind Relish

2 teaspoons tamarind concentrate
1 cup boiling water
1 teaspoon peeled and grated fresh ginger root
1/4 cup chopped dates or raisins,
  or an equal combination of both
1/2 teaspoon dry-roasted cumin seeds,
  crushed
1/4–1/2 teaspoon cayenne pepper, or to taste
salt, to taste

Mix the tamarind paste with the boiling water until dissolved, then add the ginger. Stir and add the dates and/or raisins. Mix well, then add the cumin, cayenne, and salt to taste.

This sauce keeps, refrigerated, for 2–3 weeks.

Chili, Salt, and Pepper Squid with Frizzled Cilantro

SERVES 4–6   (P: 20 mins./C: 5 mins.)

Squid is divine, but can be a serious chew unless you have cooked it in a twinkle— otherwise it will toughen. You can substitute five-spice powder for the chili powder, if you like.

1¹/₂ pounds whole squid (tiny ones are best but not easy to come by)
peanut or sunflower oil, for frying
8–12 sprigs of cilantro
lemon segments, for garnishing
Sweet Chile Sauce (see p.296), for serving

For the coating:
³/₄ cup white flour
2¹/₂ tablespoons sea salt (or Kosher salt)
4 teaspoons freshly ground black pepper
1–2 teaspoons chili powder

Clean and prepare the squid (see below), then cut into strips. Alternatively, ask the person at your fish counter to do it for you.

Mix the coating ingredients together in a bowl. In a deep-fryer, heat the oil to 350°F. Toss the squid in the coating mixture. Shake off any excess flour and drop the squid pieces, one at a time, into the hot oil, ensuring you do not overcrowd the basket or pan; if necessary, cook the squid in batches. Fry for 1–2 minutes, then remove and drain on paper towels.

If you wish you can put the cilantro sprigs in the oil as well and cook for a few seconds until they frizzle up. This has a tendency to spit, so be careful. Drain on paper towels.

Divide the squid between 4 plates. Top with the crispy or uncooked cilantro.

Garnish with a lemon segment and serve immediately with a little bowl of Sweet Chile Sauce on each plate.

How to Prepare Squid
Cut off the tentacles just in front of the eyes. Pull the entrails out of the sac and discard. Remove the beak. Catch the tip of the quill and pull it out of the sac. Pull off the wings and scrape the purplish membrane off them and the sac. Cut the sac into ¹/₄-inch rings and cut the wings into ¹/₄-inch slices. Trim the two long tentacles; leave the remaining light tentacles intact. Wash all the pieces under cold water. Drain.

Seared Chicken Breasts

SERVES 4   (P: 5 mins./C: 15 mins.)

4 free-range, organic chicken breasts, skinless and boneless
extra virgin olive oil
salt and freshly ground pepper
accompaniment of your choice (see below right)

Heat a grill pan until quite hot. Brush each chicken breast with olive oil and season with salt and freshly ground pepper.

Put the chicken breasts on the pan for about 1 minute, then turn them around by 90° so that the grill pan sears criss-cross marks on the chicken. Turn the breasts over and repeat. If the chicken breasts are large, put in the oven, preheated to 350°F, for about 8–15 minutes, depending upon size, until they are cooked through.

Serve with one of the good things below.

Ten Good Things to Serve with Seared Chicken Breasts
1 Tomato Fondue (see p.240) with cilantro. Add 1–2¹/₂ tablespoons chopped cilantro.
2 Mushroom à la Crème with Ginger Root (see recipe given on p.241).
3 Sweet Chile Sauce (see p.296) mixed with lime juice. Drizzle this over the seared chicken and sprinkle with toasted sesame seeds and serve with an herb salad.
4 Honey, mustard, and rosemary. For 4 chicken breasts, use ¹/₄ cup honey, 2 teaspoons whole-grain mustard, and 1 teaspoon finely chopped fresh rosemary. Smear over both sides of the panbroiled chicken breasts and serve.
5 Spiced Eggplant Puree (see p.119) and arugula leaves.
6 Brush the chicken breasts with harissa before panbroiling. Serve with couscous, coarsely chopped sun-blush tomatoes, red onion, cubed feta cheese, and fresh mint leaves.
7 Satay sauce and Thai Cucumber Salad (see p.115).
8 Combine 1 tablespoon soy sauce, 1 tablespoon French mustard, and 2 tablespoons honey and marinate the chicken breasts for 30 minutes before panbroiling.
9 Banana and Cardamom Raita (p.294) with Ballymaloe Relish or a good tomato relish and poppadoms.
10 Salmoriglio and arugula salad.

Monkfish with Coconut Milk

SERVES 4–6 (**P:** 15 mins./**C:** 15 mins.)

This curry can be made in advance—it reheats beautifully as all the flavors have had time to rise to the occasion.

3 tablespoons coconut oil or sunflower oil

2¹/₂ tablespoons chopped shallot (or mild onion)

4 teaspoons peeled and grated fresh ginger root

2 green chiles, split lengthwise

³/₄ teaspoon ground turmeric

1 teaspoon sugar

³/₄ teaspoon chili powder

1 teaspoon ground coriander

1³/₄ cups coconut milk (preferably fresh) or 14-ounce can condensed coconut milk

salt

1¹/₂ pounds well-trimmed monkfish (angler fish) cut into 2-inch pieces

For the tamarind water:

2 tablespoons tamarind paste

¹/₄ cup hot water

For the tempering:

4 teaspoons coconut oil

4 teaspoons fresh curry leaves

1 teaspoon black mustard seeds

For the accompaniments:

lots of fresh cilantro leaves

rice

poppadoms

First make the tamarind water. Put the lump of tamarind paste into a small bowl and cover with the hot water. Let it soak for 15–30 minutes. Squeeze with your fingers to loosen the seeds and fiber from the pulp. Press through a strainer and discard the seeds and fiber. Reserve the strained tamarind water for use in the curry.

Heat the coconut or sunflower oil in a sauté pan or frying pan. Add the chopped shallot, grated ginger, and green chiles. Cook for about 5 minutes or until they start to turn golden.

Add the turmeric, sugar, chili powder and ground coriander. Cook for another 2 minutes. Add the coconut milk and tamarind water. Season with salt and add the fish. Cover and poach the fish until cooked, about 5–6 minutes.

Meanwhile, prepare the tempering. Heat the coconut oil in small pan and when it is smoking hot, add the curry leaves and mustard seeds (they will pop and crackle). When the mustard seeds finish crackling, pour the tempering over the curry.

Sprinkle with plenty of cilantro leaves and serve with rice and poppadoms.

Shermin's Thai Green Chicken Curry

SERVES 4–6 (**P:** 10 mins./**C:** 15 mins.)

12 ounces chicken thighs

14-ounce can coconut milk

4 teaspoons green curry paste

1 Thai green chile, seeded and pounded (optional—add if you like a hotter curry)

³/₄ cup chicken broth (see p.295)

2 eggplants, cut into ¹/₂-inch cubes, or 20–24 pea eggplants

2 kaffir lime leaves

2 teaspoons palm sugar, or a little less soft brown sugar

2¹/₂ tablespoons fish sauce (*nam pla*)

1 large red chile, seeded and pounded

20 basil leaves

1 tablespoon soy sauce

For serving: steamed rice

Remove the skin and bones from the chicken thighs, then cut the meat into thin strips.

Heat a wok over low heat. Pour ¹/₂ cup of the coconut milk into the wok. Add the green curry paste and the pounded green chile (if using), and mix well.

Add the chicken strips and increase the heat to medium. Cook until the chicken changes color, then add the broth, the remaining coconut milk, the eggplant cubes,* kaffir lime leaves, palm or brown sugar, fish sauce, pounded red chile, and half the basil leaves. Stir continuously until the curry boils and foams up. Reduce the heat and simmer, stirring continuously or the sauce may separate—it should be cooked in about 10 minutes.

Add the remaining basil leaves, taste, and add soy sauce if necessary to perk it up. Serve hot, with steamed rice.

* If using pea eggplants, add them 1–2 minutes before the end of cooking.

making meals quick and easy

Always be prepared—make sure you have all the basic ingredients for two or three quick-and-easy recipes on hand at all times. Frittatas and omelets are easy to prepare and can be bolstered by a good selection of cold meats, olives, and cheese from a deli. But your freezer should be your first port of call. Keep some buttermilk in the freezer so you can make up soda bread. The next time you make a lasagne, stew, or curry (see the recipes in Prepare-Ahead Suppers), double the quantities and freeze the extra in small quantities. Then in times of need, you can just pull one out, defrost, and hey presto, a ready meal you will really enjoy.

Don't forgot to have a couple of bottles of wine on hand, too—have a look at Tom Doorley's wise words on p.11.

Even if you don't have much notice, there are a few things you can do to spruce up a room. Quickly bundle papers, magazines, and everyday clutter into the nearest cupboard or the back of your closet. Then look around your house for decorative inspiration. Keep a selection of fabrics to use as tablecloths and a roll of colored paper or cardboard that can quickly be turned into place mats. Use a colorful, chiffon scarf as a table runner or throw it over a lampshade (but never on a naked bulb) to soften the light. Dig out your collection of pebbles or sea shells and scatter them on the table—the shells will also make great salt and pepper holders. Strings of tiny Christmas lights add glamour to any evening and a stock of candles or tea lights will always be useful. A bowl of ripe peaches, cherries, greengage plums, or apricots make an irresistible centerpiece which can double up as dessert.

Bright and breezy lunch

Bocconcini, Olive, Sun-blush Tomato, and Pesto on Skewers (see p.55)
Tortilla Pizza or Yufka (Turkish flat bread) (see p.116 or p.40)
Banana with Lime Syrup (p.259)

To drink

Red wines don't come any brighter or breezier than the light and gulpable Bardolino from Italy's Veneto region, but what you choose must be good. Choose a sound producer like the organically-minded Guerrieri-Rizzardi. Banana with lime syrup simply demands a Late Harvest Riesling from Australia.

Vegetarian option

Ciabatta Stuffed with Good Things (p.68)
Spicy Omelet Sambo with Tomato and Red Onion Salsa (p.98)
Poached Apricots with Sweet Geranium Leaves (p.29)

To drink

Bardolino will work here too but vegetarian food often needs something a little more robust. Good Beaujolais or Beaujolais cru (such as Fleurie or Morgon) may not be the height of fashion but it is worth seeking out. Serve it cool but not quite chilled in order to emphasize the fruit. Cabernet Franc wines from the Loire, such as Chinon, can be treated the same way. The apricots provide one of the few occasions where a Muscat de Beaumes de Venise, served fairly cold, will taste really good.

Deceptively easy

Basmati Rice, Pea, Fava Bean, and Dill Salad (p.90)
Seared Fresh Salmon with Vine-ripened Tomato and Herbs (p.110)
Chocolate Truffle Tree (p.251)

To drink

The choice here is very straightforward: an unoaked or very lightly oaked New World chardonnay will have the exuberant fruit that you need but without any danger of overpowering the food. Shaw & Smith of South Australia make several excellent examples. Try to find their M3 chardonnay. Cool Banyuls from Provence will merge deliciously with the chocolate.

prepare-ahead suppers

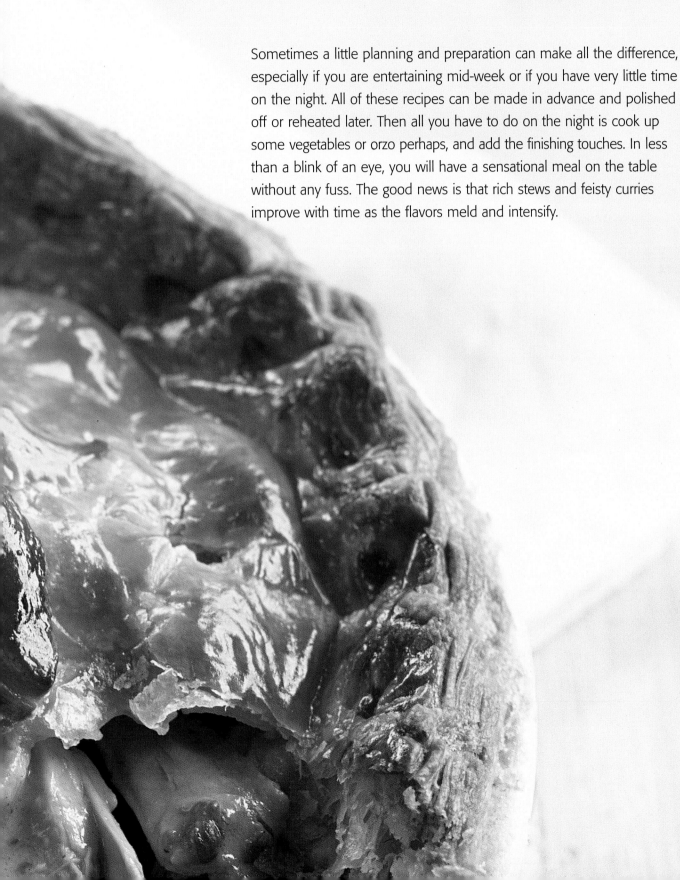

Sometimes a little planning and preparation can make all the difference, especially if you are entertaining mid-week or if you have very little time on the night. All of these recipes can be made in advance and polished off or reheated later. Then all you have to do on the night is cook up some vegetables or orzo perhaps, and add the finishing touches. In less than a blink of an eye, you will have a sensational meal on the table without any fuss. The good news is that rich stews and feisty curries improve with time as the flavors meld and intensify.

Beef Rendang

SERVES 8   (P: 30 mins./C: 2 HOURS)

Rendang is a wonderful slow-cooked dish from Malaysia, Indonesia and Sumatra usually served for feasts and celebrations. It should be chunky and dry, yet succulent.

3 pounds brisket, or good stewing steak
5 shallots, or 2 small mild onions, chopped
4 garlic cloves, chopped
1¹/₂ inches ginger root, peeled
  and roughly chopped
4 red chiles, seeded and roughly chopped,
  or 2 teaspoons chili powder
1 bay leaf
1 stalk fresh lemon grass, bruised
salt and freshly ground pepper
1 teaspoon turmeric
8 cups coconut milk
mint leaves (optional) and lime segments

Cut the meat into 1¹/₂-inch cubes. Puree the shallots, garlic, ginger, and chiles in a food processor. Put all these ingredients in a wide sauté pan or a wok, add the bay leaf, lemon grass, salt, turmeric, and meat, and cover with coconut milk. Stir and bring to a boil over medium heat, uncovered. Reduce the heat and let bubble gently for 1¹/₂ hours, stirring from time to time. By this time the coconut milk should be quite thick. Continue to cook, stirring frequently, until the coconut milk starts to get oily. Keep stirring until the oil is reabsorbed by the meat. Taste and add more salt if necessary.

Serve hot with a bowl of fluffy rice. I like to serve some fresh mint leaves and segments of lime with the rendang.

Note: Rendang keeps well in the fridge, and reheats perfectly.

Lamb Korma with Fresh Spices, Basmati Rice, Mangoes and Lime, Tamarind and Banana Chutney, Ballymaloe Relish, and Bread

SERVES 8   (**P:** 20 mins./**C:** 90 mins.)

2 pounds boneless lamb (leg or shoulder)
1 tablespoon peeled, grated, and pounded
  fresh ginger
salt
1/4 cup (1/2 stick) clarified butter (see p.108)
4 onions, sliced into rings
4 garlic cloves, crushed
1 teaspoon green cardamom pods
2 teaspoons coriander seeds
2 teaspoons black peppercorns
8 whole cloves
4 teaspoons ground turmeric
2 teaspoons sugar
freshly squeezed lime juice

For the nut milk:
1 cup whole almonds
1 pint (2 cups) light cream

For the accompaniments:
basmati rice
Mangoes and Lime (see recipe below)
Tamarind and Banana Chutney (see below)
Ballymaloe Country Relish or mango chutney
paratha, nan bread, or poppadoms

Trim the meat of the majority of the fat. Cut the meat into 1-inch cubes and mix it with the ginger and a generous sprinkling of salt.

To make the nut milk, blanch, peel, and coarsely chop the almonds. Put into a small saucepan with the cream and simmer for 4–5 minutes. Turn off the heat and let them infuse for 15 minutes.

Melt the butter in a heavy ovenproof pan and cook the onion rings and crushed garlic over gentle heat for 5 minutes.

Meanwhile, remove the seeds from the cardamom pods and measure 1/2 teaspoon. Discard the pods. Grind the seeds with the other whole spices in a clean spice grinder or coffee grinder.

Add these to the onions and cook over medium heat for 2–3 minutes. Remove the onions from the pan and set aside, then add the meat to the pan. Stir over high heat until the meat changes color.

Return the onions to the pan. Add the nut milk, turmeric, and sugar, and stir well. Cover and simmer gently on top of the stove, or better still in the oven, preheated to 325°F, until the meat is cooked, about 1 hour. Finish by adding a few drops of lime juice, to taste. This recipe can be prepared several days in advance up to this point and kept in the fridge.

Serve with basmati rice and other curry accompaniments which might include, apart from the suggestions listed, tomato chutney, mint chutney, raita, sliced bananas and chopped apples. A hot chili sauce is also good and, of course, a selection of Indian breads—paratha, nan, poppadoms…

Mangoes and Lime

2 ripe mangoes
juice of 1 lime

Peel and finely chop the ripe mangoes and add the lime juice. Toss, taste, and add more lime juice if needed.

Tamarind and Banana Chutney

SERVES 4–6

A piece of tamarind, the size of a
  mandarin orange
1–21/2 tablespoons sugar
1 teaspoon salt
1 teaspoon freshly roasted ground
  cumin seed
1/2 teaspoon cayenne pepper (optional)
1 banana

Soak the tamarind overnight or at least 2 hours in 3/4 cup hot water in a small non-metallic bowl or cup (make sure the water covers the tamarind).

Break up the lump to make a thick uneven pulp. It is more effective to use hands for this, but you could use the back of a wooden spoon. Then push the tamarind pulp through a strainer, with the back of a spoon. Keep pressing until just the fibers and seeds are left in the strainer. Scrape all the strained pulp from the outside of the strainer. Use extra water, if necessary, to separate all the pulp from the fibers. Discard the seeds and fiber.

Mix the pulp with the sugar, salt, cumin, and cayenne. Slice a peeled banana into 1/2-inch slices and mix with tamarind pulp.

Taste and balance the flavors if necessary.

Portuguese Pork, Bean, and Chorizo Stew

SERVES 10   (P: 30 mins./C: 2¹/₂ HOURS)

Oh, I so love this big, gutsy stew inspired by the version I enjoy at one of my favorite London pubs, The Eagle, on Farringdon Road.

1¹/₄ pounds dried cannellini beans, navy beans, lima beans, or black beans (3 cups)
2¹/₂ pounds belly pork
1¹/₂ pounds bacon or pancetta
1 pound ham hock
¹/₃ cup extra virgin olive oil
4 garlic cloves, sliced
1 pound onions, roughly chopped (about 3¹/₂ cups)
1 pound carrots, sliced a good ¹/₄-inch thick (about 3¹/₂ cups)
2 green peppers, seeded and chopped
1 sprig of thyme
1 bay leaf
1 pound very ripe tomatoes, skinned and chopped (about 2¹/₂ cups), or 14¹/₂-ounce can tomatoes
1 pound chorizo sausage, cut in ¹/₄-inch slices (about 3¹/₂ cups)
1 teaspoon hot or smoked paprika
freshly ground pepper
parsley stalks (optional)
generous amount of coarsely chopped cilantro or parsley, for garnishing
crusty bread, for serving

Soak the beans overnight in plenty of cold water.

When ready to cook, remove the pork and back rind and cut the meat into 1–1¹/₂-inch chunks. Cut the ham hock into chunks also. Working in batches, heat a little oil in a frying pan and brown the pork, ham hock, and bacon or pancetta on all sides. Transfer to a large heavy pan.

If you are going to cook the stew in the oven, preheat it to 325°F.

Pour off excess fat from the frying pan but leave enough to fry off the garlic, onions, carrots, and peppers with the sprig of thyme and bay leaf. Cook over low heat, stirring every now and then, for 5–6 minutes.

Transfer the vegetables to the heavy pan and add the chopped tomatoes, chorizo, paprika, and some pepper. Add just enough water almost to cover the meat. Bring to a boil, put the lid on (add a big bunch of parsley stalks if you have them), and transfer to the oven for 2–2¹/₂ hours; alternatively, reduce the heat to low and simmer gently on top of the stove for the same amount of time.

Meanwhile, drain the beans, place in a pot, and cover with fresh cold water. Bring to a boil and simmer until cooked—about 40–90 minutes depending upon the type of beans.

Add the cooked beans to the stew 15–20 minutes before the end of cooking. Taste and adjust the seasoning if needed—it's unlikely to need salt. This recipe can be prepared in advance up to this point.

Serve in deep, wide soup bowls, sprinkled with lots of coarsely chopped cilantro or parsley. You'll need crusty bread to mop up the juices.

Italian Beef Stew with Polenta

SERVES 6–8   (P: 30 mins./C: 3 HOURS)

A hearty stew that can be made in large quantities—it reheats and freezes excellently.

3 pounds aged stewing beef or lean flank
¹/₃ cup extra virgin olive oil
10 ounces onions, sliced (about 2¹/₄ cups)
2 large carrots, cut into ¹/₂-inch slices
²/₃ cup red wine
²/₃ cup beef or chicken broth (see p.295)
1 cup tomato puree (see p.294), or best-quality canned tomatoes, pureed and strained
2 tablespoons white flour
salt and freshly ground pepper
6 ounces mushrooms, sliced (about 1³/₄ cups)
1¹/₂ tablespoons chopped parsley

For the accompaniments:
Polenta (see p.298), mashed potatoes, or noodles, and green salad.

Preheat the oven to 325°F.

Trim the meat of any excess fat and cut into 1¹/₂-inch cubes. Heat 2 tablespoons of the olive oil in a heavy, ovenproof pan, then reduce the heat to very low, add the onions and carrots, cover, and cook for 10 minutes.

Mix the wine, broth, and tomato puree together in a bowl or glass measuring cup. Heat the remaining olive oil in a frying pan until almost smoking. Sear the pieces of meat on all sides, then stir in the flour and cook for just 1 minute.

Transfer the meat to the ovenproof pan. Add the prepared wine and broth, mix, season with salt and pepper, and cover. Place in the oven and cook for 2¹/₂–3 hours until the meat is tender. About 30 minutes before the end of cooking, sauté the mushrooms and add them to the pan along with the parsley.

Serve with polenta, mashed potatoes, or noodles and a good green salad.

This recipe can be prepared a couple of days in advance, kept in the fridge, and reheated when needed.

Pork and Ginger Stew

SERVES 10   (**P:** 20 mins./**C:** 1 1/2 HOURS)

The quality of the pork is as ever crucially important for this rustic pork stew. Because we have free-range pigs, the children, grandchildren, and all their friends love this dish. It is such a brilliantly easy way to feed lots of hungry people—one can, of course, cut the recipe in half. It can be prepared ahead and then heated up.

6 pounds free-range, organic shoulder
   of pork
2 pounds carrots, cut into large chunks
   (leave new carrots whole and unpeeled)
10 onions, roots trimmed and cut in half
6 shallots
12 garlic cloves, barely crushed
2 1/2 ounces fresh ginger root, peeled and
   sliced (about 5 tablespoons)
salt and freshly ground black pepper
2–3 thyme stalks
2–3 parsley stalks
4 cups chicken broth (see p.295)
roux (optional; see p.139)
chopped flat-leaf parsley, for garnishing
baked potatoes, for serving

Trim the fat off the pork and cut the meat into 1 1/2-inch cubes. In a hot frying pan, render down some of the fat (the fat runs out of the meat) while you prepare the other ingredients.

Preheat the oven to 350°F.

Working in batches, fry the pork and let it brown well on all sides. Transfer to a large heavy, flameproof and ovenproof pan. Build up the stew with a layer of pork, then a mixture of carrots, onions, shallots, garlic, sliced ginger, and then another layer of pork. It's crucially important to season each layer well with salt and black pepper. Tuck a little bunch of thyme and parsley stalks into the center (tie into a bouquet garni). Pour in the chicken broth. Bring to a boil over medium heat, then cover and transfer to the oven for about 1 1/2 hours. Check after 1 hour to see how it is progressing. (The stew can be simmered gently on top of the stove, but we usually transfer it into the oven for ease of cooking and to free up the stove top.)

When the meat is tender and succulent, strain the cooking liquid into a saucepan. Skim the fat off, then bring to a boil, and whisk in just enough roux to thicken slightly if you wish.

Remove the bouquet garni from the stew and discard. Pour the liquid back over the stew and return to a boil on top of the stove. Taste and adjust the seasoning if needed. This recipe can be prepared in advance up to this point.

Scatter lots of parsley over the top and serve. You could transfer the stew into serving bowls, but we just bring the pan to the table and tuck in. Serve with lots of floury potatoes baked in their skins.

Tagine of Lamb with Medjool Dates

SERVES 6   (**P:** 10 mins./**C:** 1 1/4 HOURS)

Tagines are excellent for easy entertaining and although this takes a while to cook, it is remarkably easy to make and, if you multiply up the quantities, it's great for large numbers. The word "tagine" refers both to the distinctive North African earthenware cooking pot, with its shallow base and conical top, and to a multitude of stew-like dishes cooked in it. This lamb tagine, which Emer Fitzgerald and I worked on together, has become our new favorite.

3 pounds boned shoulder of lamb
2 teaspoons ground cinnamon
1 teaspoon peeled and grated fresh ginger root
1/2 teaspoon paprika
1 teaspoon freshly ground black pepper
generous pinch of saffron strands
1/4 cup (1/2 stick) butter
2 onions, chopped

2 garlic cloves, finely chopped
1 1/4 cups tomato juice
salt
6 ounces Medjool dates (about 1-1 1/4 cups)
2 1/2 tablespoons chopped cilantro

For serving: couscous

For the garnish (optional):
1 tablespoon oil
1/2 cup sliced almonds
cilantro leaves

Trim the lamb, discarding excess fat, and cut into 1 1/2-inch cubes. In a large bowl, mix together the cinnamon, ginger, paprika, pepper, and saffron with 1/3 cup water. Toss the lamb in this mixture. If you have time, let it marinate in the fridge for up to 24 hours.

Melt the butter in a large, wide pan. Add the lamb, onions, garlic, tomato juice, and some salt, and pour in enough water to come halfway up the meat mixture. Bring to a boil, reduce the heat to bring it to a gentle simmer, and cover. Cook for about 45 minutes, stirring occasionally, until the meat is meltingly tender. Add the dates and cilantro. Continue to simmer, uncovered, for another 30 minutes or so until the sauce is thick and unctuous. Taste and adjust the seasoning if needed. The dish can be prepared ahead to this stage. Serve with couscous.

If you like, garnish the dish. Heat the oil and fry the sliced almonds until pale golden. Drain on paper towels, sprinkle them over the dish, and throw a few cilantro leaves on top before serving.

A Scrummy Chicken Pie

SERVES 6–8   (P: 30 mins./C: 2¹/₂ HOURS)

This can be prepared ahead of time—refrigerate until needed and increase the cooking time by a few minutes.

4 cups homemade chicken broth
  (see p.295) or water
2 large carrots, cut into chunks
2 large unpeeled onions, quartered
2 celery stalks, cut into small chunks
6 black peppercorns
1 bouquet garni
1 large free-range, organic chicken or
  boiling fowl
1 sprig of tarragon (optional)
16 small flat wide-capped mushrooms
2 tablespoons butter
salt and freshly ground black pepper
16 pearl onions, peeled
1 pound bacon in a piece, cooked
  (if unavailable, use sliced)
1 cup peas—frozen are fine (optional)
18 ounces puff pastry dough
egg wash (1 egg beaten with 1 tablespoon milk)
green salad, for serving

For the sauce:
²/₃ cup dry white wine
¹/₂ cup roux (see p.139)
1 cup light cream

Preheat the oven to 350°F.

In a heavy ovenproof and flameproof pan, pour chicken broth or water to a depth of 2 inches and add the vegetables, peppercorns, and bouquet garni. Lay the chicken on top. Add a sprig of tarragon if available, and cover with a tightly fitting lid. Bring to a boil and then transfer to the oven. Cook for 1–1¹/₂ hours, depending upon the size of the bird—when it is cooked, the leg joints should feel loose and there should be no trace of pink. Ensure that it does not boil dry—check from time to time and add more liquid as necessary. The cooking liquid should be deliciously rich and may be a little fatty.

Meanwhile, fry the mushrooms in a little of the butter in a hot pan and season with salt and pepper. Sweat the onions in butter in a small covered pan until soft. Cut the cooked bacon into cubes. Transfer the chicken from the ovenproof pan onto a large platter, reserving the cooking liquid. Do not turn the oven off, but increase the temperature to 450°F.

Carve the chicken flesh. Arrange the sliced chicken in layers in a deep pie dish or casserole dish (or in 6–8 small individual pie dishes), covering each layer with bacon, onions, and mushrooms. Add the peas if using (no need to pre-cook).

Next make the sauce. Strain the cooking liquid and remove any fat from it. Put 2¹/₂ cups of the cooking liquid and the dry white wine into a saucepan and bring to a boil. Whisk in the roux. Cook until thick and smooth. Add the cream and bring to a boil again, then remove from the heat. Taste and adjust the seasoning if needed. Let it cool.

Pour the cooled sauce over the chicken and vegetables in the pie dish and cover with puff pastry dough. Have fun decorating the top with the leftover puff pastry—we sometimes make funny faces, write messages such as "yummy," "scrummy" or "yippee," or put a fine pastry cockerel on top!

Just before cooking, brush the top of the crust with egg wash. Bake for 10 minutes, then reduce the temperature to 400°F and bake for another 15–20 minutes or until golden brown. Serve with a good green salad.

Lamb Chili con Carne

SERVES 6–8   (P: 10 mins./C: 35 mins.)

¹/₃ cup extra virgin olive oil
1 large onion, chopped
2 garlic cloves
1–2 chiles, seeded and chopped
1 red pepper, seeded and cut into
  ¹/₄-inch pieces
1 teaspoon smoked or sweet paprika
1 teaspoon ground cumin
1¹/₂ pounds leg or shoulder of lamb,
  chopped into ¹/₄-inch pieces
2 x 14¹/₂-ounce cans tomatoes, chopped
1 tablespoon tomato paste
grated zest of ¹/₂ unwaxed lemon
4 teaspoons chopped fresh marjoram
1 teaspoon thyme leaves

1 teaspoon soft brown sugar
salt and freshly ground pepper
2 x 15-ounce cans red kidney beans or
  black beans, rinsed and drained

For the accompaniments:
basmati rice
sour cream
Tomato and Red Onion Salsa (see p.294)
tortillas
fresh cilantro leaves

Heat the oil in a heavy pan, add the chopped onion, garlic, and chiles, and sweat over medium heat for about 5 minutes. Add the red pepper, toss, and continue to cook for 1–2 minutes. Add the paprika and cumin and continue to cook for a few

minutes. Add the lamb and toss until it changes color.

Add the chopped tomatoes and their juice, the tomato paste, lemon zest, and herbs. Add the sugar and season with salt and pepper. Bring to a boil and cook for 30 minutes.

Add the beans and cook for another 15 minutes. Taste and adjust the seasoning if needed. This dish can be prepared in advance up to this point.

Serve with basmati rice, sour cream, Tomato and Red Onion Salsa, and lots of warm tortillas and fresh cilantro.
Beef or pork is also great in this recipe.

Vegetarian Lasagne

SERVES 12   (**P:** 1 1/2 HOURS/**C:** 30 mins.)

Lasagne is basically a formula—once I realized that simple fact, I started to play around and now we make many versions with meat, fish, and vegetables. The end result needs to be bubbly and juicy with lots of filling.

1 pound fresh spinach lasagne
   or 13 ounces dried plain lasagne or spinach
   lasagne
6 quantities Béchamel Sauce (not too
   thick; see recipe below)
1 quantity Piperonata (see p.243)
8 ounces grated Parmesan (about 4 cups)
   or shredded aged cheddar cheese
   (about 2 1/2 cups) or a mixture of both
1 quantity Buttered Spinach (see recipe below)
2 quantities Mushroom à la Crème (see p.241)
salt and freshly ground pepper
green salad, for serving

1 large or 2 medium-sized lasagne dishes

First taste each component to make sure it is delicious and well seasoned.

Preheat the oven to 350°F.

Cook the lasagne pasta as directed on the package. Spread a little Béchamel Sauce on the bottom of a large lasagne dish, then cover with strips of lasagne and a layer of Piperonata. Top with another layer of lasagne. Spread this with Béchamel Sauce, sprinkle with grated cheese, and add a layer of Buttered Spinach. Cover with another layer of lasagne, then the Mushroom à la Crème. Top with another layer of lasagne. Carefully spread more Béchamel Sauce over it and finally sprinkle liberally with cheese. Make sure all the pasta is under the sauce.

Bake in the oven for 10–15 minutes for fresh pasta, or 30 minutes for dried pasta, or until bubbly and golden on top. If possible, let it stand for 5–10 minutes before cutting to allow the layers to compact. Serve with a good green salad.

Other ideas for layers

Buttered Zucchini with marjoram or basil, panbroiled eggplant, Roasted Red Pepper (see p.298) and Pesto (see p.297), Spiced Eggplant (see p.243) with raisins.

Béchamel Sauce (White Sauce)

This is a marvelous quick way of making Béchamel Sauce if you already have roux. Put the cold milk into a saucepan with the carrot, onion, peppercorns, thyme, and parsley. Bring to a boil, simmer for 4–5 minutes, remove from the heat, and let it infuse for 10 minutes.

1 1/4 cups milk
few slices of carrot
few slices of onion
3 peppercorns
1 small sprig of thyme
1 small sprig of parsley
3 tablespoons roux (see p.139)
salt and freshly ground pepper

Strain and discard the vegetables. Put the milk back in the pan and bring to a boil. Thicken with roux to a light coating consistency. Season with salt and freshly ground pepper, taste, and correct the seasoning if necessary.

Buttered Spinach

SERVES 4–6

Here are three different basic methods of cooking spinach—a huge improvement on the watery mush that frozen spinach often unfortunately ends up as!

1/4–1/2 cup (1/2–1 stick) butter
2 pounds fresh spinach, with stalks removed
   (about 24 cups)
salt, freshly ground pepper
a little freshly grated nutmeg

Method 1: Melt a scrap of butter in a wide frying pan or pot, toss in as much spinach as will fit easily, season with salt and freshly ground pepper. As soon as the spinach wilts and becomes tender, strain off all the liquid, increase the heat, and add some butter and freshly grated nutmeg. Serve immediately.

Method 2: Wash the prepared spinach and drain. Put into a heavy pot over very low heat, season with salt and pepper, and cover tightly. After a few minutes, stir and replace the lid. As soon as the spinach is cooked, about 5–8 minutes, strain off the copious amount of liquid that spinach releases and press between two plates until almost dry. Chop or puree in a food processor if you like a smooth texture. Increase the heat, add butter, correct the seasoning, and add a little freshly grated nutmeg to taste.

Method 3: Cook the spinach uncovered in a large pot of boiling salted water until soft, about 4–5 minutes. Drain and press out all the water. Continue as in method 2. Method 3 produces a brighter-colored spinach.

Chicken and Zucchini Lasagne

SERVES 8   (**P:** 2 HOURS/**C:** 20 mins.)

1 quantity Chicken and Zucchini Gratin
  (see below)
8–9 sheets best-quality lasagne
salt
3 ounces Parmesan cheese, grated
  (about 1^1/$_2$ cups)
green salad, for serving

Preheat the oven to 400°F.

Cook the chicken and zucchini, following the instructions for Gratin of Chicken with Zucchini and Marjoram (see recipe below) up to the seasoning with salt and freshly ground pepper.

Bring a large pot of salted water (2 tablespoons salt to 6 quarts water) to a boil. Working in 2–3 batches, drop the lasagne sheets into the pot, return to a boil, and blanch them. Refresh them under cold running water.

Spread a little sauce on the bottom of a lasagne dish. Cover first with a layer of lasagne, then a layer of chicken, then sauce, and then a layer of zucchini. Repeat with another similar sequence of layers. Then cover with a layer of lasagne, then a layer of chicken pieces only, then a final layer of lasagne, and finally a layer of chicken sauce. The dish may be prepared ahead to this point.

Sprinkle grated Parmesan over the top and pop into the oven for 15–20 minutes or until bubbling and golden. Let it rest for 5 minutes. Serve with a good green salad.

Variations
Chicken and Piperonata Lasagne—replace the zucchini with Piperonata (see p.243).
Chicken and Tomato Fondue Lasagne—replace the zucchini with Tomato Fondue (see p.240).

Gratin of Chicken with Zucchini and Marjoram

SERVES 4–6

3^1/$_2$-pound free-range, organic chicken
2 onions, sliced
2 carrots, sliced
sprig each of thyme and tarragon
a few peppercorns
2^1/$_2$ cups homemade Chicken Broth
  (see p.295)
8 ounces mushrooms, sliced (about 2^1/$_3$ cups)
1^1/$_2$ cups milk
3–4 tablespoons annual marjoram
roux (see p.139)
pat of butter
2 pounds zucchini, green and
  golden, cooked
2 ounces Buttered Crumbs (see p.142),
  about ^{1}/$_2$-1 cup
2–4 ounces grated aged cheddar
  cheese (about ^{1}/$_2$-1 cup)

2 x lasagne dish 10 x 8 in.

Put the chicken into a large heavy pan along with the onions and carrots, and add a sprig of thyme, tarragon, and a few peppercorns. Pour in the broth, bring to a boil, cover, and simmer for 1–1^1/$_4$ hours or until the chicken is tender.

Sauté the mushrooms in the butter in a hot pan, season with salt and freshly ground pepper, and set aside.

When the chicken is cooked, remove the meat and carve into bite-sized pieces.

Strain the cooking liquid and remove the fat, add the milk to the pan, bring to a boil, and add the annual marjoram. Simmer for a few minutes, thicken to a light coating consistency with roux, then add the chicken to the sauce. Season with salt and freshly ground pepper.

Butter an ovenproof lasagne dish, put a layer of cooked zucchini on the bottom, scatter the mushrooms on top, and cover with the creamy chicken mixture.

Mix the Buttered Crumbs with the grated cheese and sprinkle over the surface. Reheat in a moderate oven (350°F) for 15–20 minutes and flash under the broiler until the top is crunchy and golden. Serve immediately.

Gratin of Chicken with Broccoli
Substitute 2 pounds broccoli florets cooked al dente for the courgettes.

Gratin of Chicken with Cauliflower
Substitute cauliflower florets for broccoli in the above recipe and substitute tarragon for marjoram.

Classic Daube of Beef Provençale with Melted Leek Champ

SERVES 8   (P: 30 mins./C: 2 HOURS)

This stew has a rich, robust flavor. It's classic French country winter food at its most comforting. It reheats perfectly and can also be made ahead and frozen. The meat should be cut and served in large chunks.

3 pounds lean well-aged stewing beef
   (rump or chuck)
extra virgin olive oil
1 pound bacon, cut into 1/2-inch lardons
14 ounces tomatoes, chopped
   (about 2 1/2 cups)
2/3 cup beef stock
6 ounces mushrooms, sliced (about 1 3/4 cups)
2 1/2 tablespoons olive oil
10 canned anchovy fillets
2 1/2 tablespoons capers
2 1/2 tablespoons chopped parsley
2 garlic cloves, crushed
1/4 cup wine vinegar
roux (optional, see p.139)
chopped parsley, for garnishing

For the marinade:
2 1/2 tablespoons extra virgin olive oil
1 1/4 cups dry white or red wine
1 teaspoon chopped fresh thyme, sage, or
   annual marjoram
1 bay leaf
2 garlic cloves, crushed
1 large carrot, thinly sliced
1 large onion, thinly sliced
1 teaspoon salt
plenty of freshly ground pepper

For the accompaniment:
Melted Leek Champ (see p.139) or fluffy
   mashed potatoes

Cut the beef into large chunks, around 3 inches wide. In a large bowl, mix together the marinade ingredients. Add the meat, cover, and marinate in the fridge or a cool pantry overnight.

The next day, drain on a wire rack over a roasting pan to collect the marinade. Strain the marinade, and reserve the vegetables and marinade separately.

Heat the oil in a heavy frying pan, cook the bacon lardons until crisp, then transfer to a flameproof casserole dish. Dry the beef with paper towels. Add to the hot frying pan and cook briefly, stirring, to seal on all sides. Add the beef, along with the marinated vegetables and the tomatoes, to the pan containing the bacon.

Skim and discard the fat from the juices in the frying pan. Place the juices over a high heat, pour in the marinade and the beef stock, and stir to deglaze, then add to the stew. Bring the stew to a boil and simmer very gently on top of the stove (or transfer to a preheated oven at 325°F) for 1 1/2–2 hours.

Meanwhile, sauté the mushrooms in the olive oil in a hot pan and set aside.

When the meat is soft and tender, blend the anchovies with the capers, parsley, garlic, and wine vinegar. Add to the stew along with the mushrooms. Simmer the stew gently for 8–10 minutes to combine the flavors. Taste and adjust the seasoning if needed. Skim off the fat and, if necessary, thicken the boiling liquid by whisking in a little roux. Sprinkle with chopped parsley and serve with Melted Leek Champ or fluffy mashed potatoes.

Melted Leek Champ

SERVES 6   (**P:** 15 mins./**C:** 15 mins.)

We cook the potatoes in their skins—this means much more flavor and much less waste.

4 organic medium leeks, total weight around
  3 pounds
$1/2$–$3/4$ cup (1–$1^1/2$ sticks) butter
salt and freshly ground pepper
6–8 unpeeled floury potatoes
$1^1/4$–$1^1/2$ cups milk
4 teaspoons chopped fresh chives

Trim off the dark green leaves from the top of the leeks—they're not needed for this recipe but you could use them, washed, in making broth or green leek soup. Slit the white part of the leeks about half way down the center and wash well under cold running water. Slice into $1/4$-inch rings.

Melt $1/4$ cup ($1/2$ stick) of the butter in a heavy pan. Once it foams, add the sliced leeks and toss gently to coat. Season with salt and pepper. Cover closely with a paper lid such as a butter wrapper and then with a close-fitting pan lid. Reduce the heat and cook very gently for 8–10 minutes, or until almost soft and moist. Turn off the heat and let it continue cooking in the residual heat of the pan.

Scrub the potatoes and boil them in their skins. Meanwhile, bring the milk and chives to a boil, simmer for about 3–4 minutes, turn off the heat, and let them infuse.

Drain the potatoes well. Peel the potatoes while hot, mash immediately, and mix with most of the infused milk. Add the drained leeks and beat in another $1/4$ cup of the butter. Add the remaining milk for a softer consistency if you like. Season to taste with salt and pepper. Serve in 1 large or 6 individual bowls, with a pat of butter melting in the center.

Melted Leek Champ may be set aside and reheated later in the oven, preheated to 350°F. Cover with aluminum foil while it reheats so that it doesn't get a skin.

Roux

Really useful stuff to have in your fridge. Use it to thicken sauces or gravies.

$1/2$ cup (1 stick) salted butter
4 ounces all-purpose flour (about $3/4$-1 cup)

Melt the butter in a small saucepan over low heat, add the flour, and cook for 2 minutes, stirring occasionally.

Roux can be stored in a cool place and used as needed, or made up on the spot if you prefer. It will keep at least two weeks in the fridge.

Gravadlax with Sweet Mustard and Dill Mayonnaise

SERVES 12–16 AS AN APPETIZER
(**P:** 20 mins. + 25 HOURS TO MARINATE)

This is a simply wonderful standby, miles more impressive than smoked salmon. We use it for canapés, appetizer salads, and as a main course for a light summer lunch, accompanied by pickled cucumber, deliciously runny semi-hard-boiled eggs, and salad greens. It keeps for up to 1 week. Fresh dill is essential but we also have fun with black peppercorns, coriander seeds, whole grain mustard, vodka…

1^1/$_2$–2 pound tail piece of fresh wild salmon
2 tablespoons sea salt (or Kosher salt)
2 tablespoons sugar
1 teaspoon freshly ground black pepper
2^1/$_2$ tablespoons finely chopped dill, plus whole sprigs for garnishing
Sweet Mustard and Dill Mayonnaise (see below)
bread and butter, for serving

Fillet the salmon and remove all the bones with a tweezer. In a bowl, mix together the salt, sugar, pepper, and dill. Place the fish on a piece of plastic wrap and scatter the mixture over the surface of the fish. Wrap tightly in plastic wrap and refrigerate for a minimum of 24 hours. If you have 2 pieces of fish, place one on top of the other, flesh side together.

To serve, wipe the dill mixture off the salmon and slice thinly, cutting straight down to the skin. Arrange a few slices on a white plate (square for preference) with a zig-zag of Mustard and Dill Mayonnaise over the top.

Alternatively, arrange in a rosette shape and fill the center of the rosette with Sweet Mustard and Dill Mayonnaise. Garnish with fresh dill.

Serve with brown bread and butter—Brown Yeast Bread (see p.35) or pumpernickel works particularly well.

Sweet Mustard and Dill Mayonnaise

1 large cage-free, organic egg yolk
2^1/$_2$ tablespoons French mustard
4 teaspoons sugar
^{2}/$_3$ cup peanut or sunflower oil
4 teaspoons white wine vinegar
4 teaspoons finely chopped dill
salt and freshly ground white pepper

In a bowl, whisk the egg yolk with the mustard and sugar.

Add the oil, drop by drop, whisking all the time, then add the vinegar and dill and season to taste.

Gravadlax with Cucumber Ribbon Salad and Mustard and Dill Mayonnaise

SERVES 8   (**P:** 15 mins.)

8–12 ounces gravadlax (see recipe above)
Mustard and Dill Mayonnaise (see recipe above)
brown bread, for serving

For the pickled cucumber strips:
1 cucumber
2 teaspoons salt
^{1}/$_2$ cup sugar
^{1}/$_3$ cup cider vinegar

For the garnish:
sprigs of dill
chive or wild garlic flowers
freshly cracked black pepper

Prepare the gravadlax 2–3 days before serving.

The cucumber ribbon salad should be prepared on the day. Cut the cucumber in half, then cut into strips using a potato peeler. Put the cucumber strips into a deep bowl and add the salt, sugar, and cider vinegar. Toss gently and let it macerate for at least 30 minutes.

To assemble, unwrap the gravadlax and, using a thin, sharp knife, carefully cut down to the skin in thin slices.

Drain the cucumber strips. Arrange the cucumber strips and gravadlax in a haphazard way on each serving plate. Drizzle with Mustard and Dill Mayonnaise. Garnish with tiny sprigs of dill and chive or wild garlic flowers.

Finally, sprinkle a little freshly cracked black pepper over each serving. Serve with Brown Yeast Bread (see p.35).

Haddock with Dijon Mustard Sauce

SERVES 6   (P: 15 mins./C: 15 mins.)

This is an excellent recipe for easy entertaining. Virtually any round fish may be used in this recipe—for instance cod, hake, and pollock.

1/4 cup (1/2 stick) butter
8 ounces onions, chopped (about 2 cups)
2 pounds haddock fillets
salt and freshly ground pepper
2 1/2 cups milk
1/4 cup cream
3 tablespoons white flour
2 1/2 tablespoons Dijon mustard
2 1/2 tablespoons whole-grain mustard
1 1/2 tablespoons chopped parsley
1 3/4 pounds mashed potato, (about
   3 1/2 cups (optional)

Melt the butter in a saucepan and sweat the onions, covered, until golden brown.

Meanwhile, skin the haddock and cut into 6 portions. Season with salt and pepper. Put the fish into a wide sauté pan or frying pan, cover with the milk and cream, bring to a boil, and simmer gently for 4–6 minutes, depending upon the thickness of the fish. Using a slotted spoon, remove the fish carefully to a serving dish, reserving the cooking liquid.

Add the flour to the onions, stir, and cook for 2 minutes. Add the reserved hot cooking liquid and bring back to a boil, then simmer for 3–4 minutes. Add the mustard and chopped parsley, taste, and adjust the seasoning if needed, then pour it over the fish and serve.

For a retro version, mashed potato may be piped around the dish. It can also be prepared in advance: let it cool, refrigerate, and reheat later in the oven, preheated to 350°F, for about 20 minutes.

Variations

1 Sprinkle 1–1 3/4 cups sliced sautéed mushrooms over or under the fish before adding the sauce.
2 Sweat 1 pound finely sliced leeks (about 6 cups) in 2 tablespoons butter in a covered heavy pan over gentle heat and use instead of the mushrooms in Variation 1.
3 Peel pieces of cucumber and sweat in 1–2 tablespoons butter with 2 teaspoons chopped dill in a covered heavy pan over gentle heat. Use instead of the mushrooms in Variation 1, and omit mustard from the sauce.

Hake with Gruyère Cheese and Buttered Crumbs

SERVES 6–8   (P: 10 mins./C: 35 mins.)

This is a sort of "basic" recipe, which like the recipe above, can be used for almost any round fish such as pollock, haddock, or red snapper. It is a perfect recipe for entertaining because it can be prepared ahead, refrigerated, and reheated later. Cheddar or Parmesan cheese, or a combination of the two, may also be used.

2 1/4 pounds hake fillets (or cod, haddock
   or similar fish)
salt and freshly ground pepper
1 tablespoon butter
2 1/2 cups milk
1/4 cup roux (see p.139)
1/4 teaspoon mustard, preferably Dijon
6 ounces Gruyère cheese, grated (about
   1 1/2 cups)
2 pounds fluffy mashed potato or
   Scallion Champ, about 4 cups (optional;
   see p.237), for serving

For the buttered crumbs:
2 tablespoons butter
2 ounces soft white bread crumbs (about 1 cup)

Skin the fish and cut into 6–8 portions. Season with salt and pepper.

Lay the pieces of fish in a lightly buttered sauté pan or frying pan and cover with the cold milk. Bring to a boil and simmer for 4–5 minutes, or until the fish has changed color. With a slotted spoon, remove the fish to a serving dish or dishes, reserving the milk.

Return the milk to a boil and thicken with roux to a light coating consistency. Add the mustard and two thirds of the grated cheese; set aside the remaining cheese. Season with salt and pepper, taste, and correct the seasoning if necessary.

Preheat the oven to 350°F.

Next make the buttered crumbs. Melt the butter in a pan and stir in the bread crumbs. Remove from the heat immediately and let cool.

Coat the fish with the sauce. Mix the remaining grated cheese with the buttered crumbs and sprinkle them over the fish. For a more substantial dish, pipe a ruff of fluffy mashed potato or champ around the edge. The recipe can be prepared in advance up to this point.

Bake for 15–20 minutes or until the fish and sauce are heated through and the top is golden brown and crisp. If necessary, place under the broiler for a minute or two before serving, to brown the edge of the potato.

Note: This dish may be served in individual dishes; scallop shells are fun, completely ovenproof, and can be used over and over again.

preparing ahead

If you have very little time on the day of the event, preparation is everything. You will need to shop and cook in advance, leaving only the finishing touches just before the guests arrive. Choose the recipes several days in advance and make two shopping lists—one for the food to be prepared in advance, and the second for what must be bought at the last minute—herbs and salad ingredients, for example. Take the time to read each recipe and work out when you need to make each stage. Most important of all, check if you need to marinate meat or allow batter or pastry dough time to rest and plan this extra time into your schedule.

On the day, take the prepared meal out to defrost if you need to, and organize what you have to do for the accompanying dishes. Bear in mind that salad dressings are best made at the last minute. While the food is heating, you will have time to get yourself and the room ready and be ready to welcome your guests without any fuss or flapping!

To avoid last-minute rushing around, set out the number of plates, cutlery, glasses, and napkins you need in the morning. Pick up some flowers with your last-minute shopping. Or, the weekend before, hunt out dried flowers or tiny cacti potted in colorful containers (look for cacti with eye-catching shapes, smoldering colors, or striped succulents) for the table. A pile of glass beads can be used to great effect, and stuffing tiny Christmas lights into a glass vase is one of the simplest ways to illuminate and decorate a side table or mantelpiece.

A taste of India
Mini Poppadoms with Spicy Chicken, Banana, and Cardamom Raita (p.54)
Rogan Josh (p.130)
Indian Paratha Bread (p.39)
Yogurt and Cardamom Cream with Apricot and Saffron Syrup (p.266)

To drink
Don't serve just any old beer with this Indian menu. It deserves the best and many of the world's best beers come from the Czech Republic. Pilsener Urquell, Staropramen, or Budvar all have real character and style. The yogurt and cardamom cream cries out for a vendage tardive Gewürztraminer from Alsace which will be expensive. Cheaper dessert wines from the same grape come from South Africa.

Veggie delight
Fougasse (p.38)
Salad of Goat Cheese with Arugula, Figs, and Pomegranate Seeds (p.68)
Vegetarian Lasagne (p.136)
A Seasonal Green Salad (p.94)
Molten Chocolate Puddings (p.246)

To drink
To be geographically correct with the fougasse you need to look to Provence. A red Bandol will deliver plenty of fruit with an herby edge, while a white Bandol will be good with the salad. Domaine Tempier is a brilliant producer. Goat cheese, on the other hand, is always best with a sauvignon blanc, even a basic one from Chile or Touraine. Chocolate pudding would defeat most wines, even sweet ones, but a good LBV Port from Taylor's, Fonseca, or Noval is well up to the job.

The healthy choice
Gravadlax (p.140)
Hake with Gruyére Cheese in Buttered Crumbs (p.142)
Carrigeen Moss Pudding with Gooseberry and Elderflower Compote (p.232)

To drink
Hake always suggests a Spanish white, especially the trendy wines made from Albarinho. The most fashionable and most expensive ones come from Rias-Baixas, but they are still quite affordable. These crisp, slightly sea-scented whites will deal equally well with the gravadlax where the dill flavor would overpower many other wines. The pudding, because of the heady elderflower scent, will work best with a sweet muscat. Brown Brother's Late Picked Muscat is fresh, aromatic, ripe, and still delicate.

slow food

The Slow Food Movement, which started in Italy in 1986, has taken the world by storm—it now has in excess of 80,000 international members who respond to its concerns about the standardizing effects of fast food and the frenetic pace of life in the fast lane. Slow Food is not just about long, slow cooking, although it can be. It celebrates differences in flavors, artisanal food production, and small-scale agriculture. It is about using products that are produced in a time-honored, sustainable, usually non-intensive way. Slow Food links ethics and pleasure. In a word, eco-gastronomy. Food with a feel-good factor.

Slow-cooked Lamb Shanks with Navy Beans and Tomatoes with Lots of Fresh Herbs

SERVES 8   (**P:** 20 mins./**C:** 3 HOURS)

Lamb shanks can be from the back leg or the shoulder. Choose one or the other so they cook evenly—the shoulder takes much longer to cook. Gutsy herbs like rosemary or thyme are an excellent accompaniment, as are beans, lentils, or robust mashed potato with added root vegetables or kale.

8 lamb shanks
8 small sprigs of rosemary or thyme
8 slivers of garlic
salt and freshly ground black pepper
1/4–1/3 cup extra virgin olive oil or
  2 tablespoons goose or duck fat
2 carrots, roughly chopped
2 celery stalks, roughly chopped
1 leek, roughly chopped
1 onion, roughly chopped
4 garlic cloves, bruised
2/3 cup good red wine
2/3 cup chicken broth (see p.295)
  or lamb stock
1 sprig of thyme
2 sprigs of rosemary
2 bay leaves
2 strips of dried orange peel

For the navy beans and tomatoes:
2 tablespoons olive oil
8 ounces bacon, cut into lardons (about
  1 1/3 cups) and blanched
2 quantities Tomato Fondue (see p.240)
2 x 15-ounce cans navy or Gt Northern
  beans, drained

For garnishing:
Lots of flat-leaf parsley, cilantro, mint,
  and chives

Preheat the oven to 300°F.

Make an incision in each lamb shank and insert a small sprig of rosemary or thyme and a sliver of garlic. Season the meat with salt and freshly ground black pepper. Heat the olive oil or fat in a heavy sauté pan or ovenproof frying pan and sauté the meat in it until well browned on all sides.

Remove the meat from the pan. Add the carrots, celery, leek, onion, and bruised garlic, and cook over high heat until it starts to brown. Pour the red wine into the pan, bring to a boil, and bubble for a minute or two. Add the broth, herbs, and orange peel to the pan, then arrange the lamb shanks on top, bones pointing upwards. Bring to a boil. Cover and cook in the oven for 1 1/2–2 1/2 hours depending upon size—the meat should be almost falling off the bones.

Meanwhile, for the navy beans and tomatoes, heat the olive oil in a saucepan and brown the bacon in it until golden and fully cooked. Add the Tomato Fondue and navy beans. Cover and simmer for 5–10 minutes.

When the lamb has finished cooking, remove the lamb shanks to a deep, wide serving dish. Strain the liquid and press to extract all the delicious juices. Discard the vegetables, which have by now contributed all their flavor. Return the juices to the pan and cook to reduce and concentrate the flavor if necessary. Meanwhile, reheat the beans and tomatoes. Add the concentrated juices. Taste and correct the seasoning. Spoon the beans over the lamb shanks and scatter with a fistful of roughly chopped herbs.

Other Good Things to Serve with Lamb Shanks
Root Vegetable Mash (see p.236), Colcannon (see p.236), or Parsnip Mash (see p.151)
Chickpeas with Tomato Fondue (see p.240) and cumin
Lentils or couscous

Paella

SERVES 10–12   (**P:** 20 mins./**C:** 40 mins.)

Paella is a fantastic dish to make for large numbers of people. In Spain you can buy a portable stove with a large gas burner especially for cooking paella on a picnic— how wonderful is that?

1/2 cup extra virgin olive oil
8 ounces belly pork, preferably organic,
  cut into 1-inch cubes
2 large onions, chopped
8 garlic cloves, sliced
1 each large green and red pepper, seeded
  and cut into 1/2-inch cubes
1 free-range organic chicken,
  cut into smallish pieces
salt and freshly ground pepper
1 chorizo sausage, thickly sliced
1 teaspoon saffron strands
2–2 1/2 quarts homemade chicken
  broth (see p.295)
2 1/4 pounds paella rice (about 5 1/4 cups)
1 pound frozen peas (about 3 1/2-4 cups)
1 pound mussels, in their shells
12 shrimp, in their shells

For garnishing:
4 very ripe tomatoes, chopped
sprigs of flat-leaf parsley and coarsely chopped
  chives

Paella pan, about 18 inches

Warm the olive oil in the paella pan. Add the pork and cook for a few minutes until the fat begins to run.

Add the onions, garlic, and peppers and cook for 4–5 minutes. Add the chicken and season with salt and freshly ground pepper, then add the sliced chorizo. Cook, stirring regularly, for 15 minutes. Meanwhile, soak the saffron strands in a cup of warm chicken broth.

Add the saffron and its soaking liquid to the pan, then stir in the uncooked rice. Add broth almost to cover and stir to blend. Add the peas and then don't stir again unless absolutely necessary. Bring to a boil, reduce the heat, and simmer very gently uncovered for about 20 minutes until the meat is fully cooked through. About 5 minutes from the end of cooking, add the mussels and shrimp in their shells. Continue to cook, stirring occasionally, until the mussels open and the shrimp are cooked; discard any mussels that do not open.

Bring the paella pan to the table. Scatter with chopped tomatoes, lots of flat-leaf parsley sprigs, and some chives. Serve immediately, directly from the pan.

Slow-roasted Shoulder of Lamb with Cumin Seeds

SERVES 8–10 (P: 20 mins./C: UP TO 7 HOURS)

A shoulder of lamb is much trickier to carve than a leg, but it's so sweet and juicy that it is certainly worth the struggle. I sometimes put this dish into the low oven of our 4-door Aga in the morning. By 7.30pm, it is cooked—how easy is that! The cumin seeds give a delicious flavor to the meat.

2 tablespoons cumin seeds
1 whole shoulder of lamb on the bone,
  7–8 pounds
salt and freshly ground pepper
extra virgin olive oil, for drizzling

For the cumin gravy:
2$\frac{1}{2}$ cups homemade lamb stock or chicken
  broth (see p.295)
1–2 teaspoons cumin seeds, toasted and ground
roux (optional; see p.139)

For serving: roast potatoes

Preheat the oven to 275°F.

Warm the cumin seeds slightly in a pan, then crush them using a mortar and pestle. Score the skin of the meat in a diamond pattern with a sharp knife. Transfer to a flameproof roasting pan. Sprinkle the meat with salt, pepper, and the ground cumin seeds, and drizzle with olive oil.

Roast for 6–7 hours—this gives a delicious, juicy, succulent texture. (Alternatively preheat the oven to 325°F and roast for 2–2$\frac{1}{2}$ hours.) Transfer to a serving dish and leave in a warm place while you make the gravy.

To make the cumin gravy, spoon the fat off the roasting pan and discard. Add the stock to the remaining cooking juice. Boil for a few minutes on top of the stove, stirring and scraping the pan well to dissolve the caramelized meat juices (I find a small whisk is ideal for this). Add the ground toasted cumin. Thicken with a very little roux if you like. Taste, and add salt and pepper if needed. Strain and transfer to a gravy boat.

Carve the meat into thick slices so that everybody gets some crushed cumin seeds. Serve with the cumin gravy, and crusty roast potatoes.

Lamb Roast with Coriander
Substitute coriander seeds for the cumin seeds, both for roasting the lamb and flavoring the gravy. Alternatively use a mix of cumin and coriander seeds.

Cocido

Spain's national lunchtime stew epitomizes easy entertaining. You can reduce the temperature and let it cook for 6–7 hours or speed it up by semi-cooking the chickpeas first. This robust dish has the added advantage of producing two courses in one—soup and a main dish.

SERVES 8   (P: 30 mins./C: 4 HOURS)

1 pound dried chickpeas
generous pinch of saffron strands
4$\frac{1}{2}$ quarts light chicken broth (see p.295),
  or water
4 free-range organic chicken thighs and
  4 drumsticks
11 ounces chorizo
1 pound belly of pork, cut into large chunks
8 shallots
8 garlic cloves
6 sprigs of rosemary
3 sprigs of thyme
salt and freshly ground pepper
9 ounces little pasta shapes, such as stellini
  (stars), orzo, or medolinne (melon seed)
$\frac{1}{3}$–$\frac{1}{2}$ cup chopped flat-leaf parsley
4 ounces Parmesan or Manchego cheese
  (about 2 cups, grated)

Put the chickpeas in a bowl, cover with plenty of water, and let soak overnight. Next day, preheat the oven to 300°F.

Put the saffron into a little bowl and cover with $\frac{1}{4}$–$\frac{1}{3}$ cup boiling broth or water. Soak the saffron while preparing the other ingredients.

Drain the chickpeas and put them into a large heavy ovenproof pan or, better still, a flameproof earthenware pot. Add the chicken, chorizo, pork, shallots, garlic, rosemary, and thyme. Add the saffron, its soaking liquid, and the remaining broth or water. Season well with salt and pepper. Bring to a boil over medium heat on top of the stove, then cover and pop into the oven. Cook for 3–4 hours or until the chickpeas and meat are completely tender.

When the cocido has cooked, cook the pasta in boiling salted water for 8–10 minutes depending upon size. Drain and divide between 8 soup bowls. Add some chopped parsley and a ladleful of cocido broth to each bowl. Eat the pasta soup with some grated Parmesan or Manchego and lots of crusty country bread.

Put the cocido in the center of the table and serve it as the main course. Follow with a good green salad and some seasonal fresh fruit.

Beef and Oxtail Stew with Parsnip Mash

SERVES 8   (**P:** 1 HOUR/**C:** 3 HOURS)

Oxtail makes an extraordinarily rich and flavorsome winter stew, considering how cheap it is. The stew is best cooked ahead and reheated, and is so comforting and yummy eaten with champ, colcannon, or parsnip mash.

2 tablespoons beef drippings or
   extra virgin olive oil
4 ounces bacon, cut into 1-inch cubes
   (about 2/3 cup)
8 ounces onions, finely chopped
   (about 2 cups)
8 ounces carrots, cut into 3/4-inch cubes
   (about 1 1/2-2 cups)
2 ounces celery, chopped (about 1/3-1/2 cup)
1 pound stewing beef, cut into
   1 1/2-inch cubes
2 oxtails, cut into pieces
2/3 cup red wine
2 cups beef stock
1 bay leaf
1 sprig of thyme
parsley stalks, plus 2 tablespoons chopped
   parsley for garnishing
1 1/2 tablespoons tomato paste
salt and freshly ground pepper
butter, for frying
6 ounces mushrooms, sliced (about 1 3/4 cups)
1 tablespoon roux (see p.139)

For serving:
Parsnip Mash (see p.151)

If you want to cook the stew in the oven, preheat the oven to 325°F.

Heat the drippings or olive oil in a frying pan, add the bacon, and sauté for 1–2 minutes until the fat runs. Add the onions, carrots, and celery, and continue to cook for 2–3 minutes, stirring occasionally. Transfer to an ovenproof pot or casserole dish.

Put the beef and oxtail pieces in the frying pan, a few at a time, and cook until the meat is beginning to brown. Add to the casserole dish. Pour the wine and 2/3 cup of the stock into the pan. Bring to a boil and use a whisk to dissolve the caramelized meat juices, then return to a boil. Add to the casserole dish and mix in the bay leaf, thyme, and parsley stalks, the remaining stock, and the tomato paste. Season with salt and pepper. Cover and cook in the oven, or if using a flameproof pot, over a low heat on top of the stove, for 2–3 hours or until the beef, oxtail, and vegetables are very tender. The meat should be falling off the bones.

Meanwhile, melt a little butter in a frying pan and cook the sliced mushrooms for 2–3 minutes. Season with salt and pepper. About 5 minutes before the stew is fully cooked, stir in the mushrooms.

Transfer the meat and vegetables to a hot serving dish and keep warm. Remove and discard the bay leaf, thyme, and parsley stalks. If necessary, transfer the stew liquid to a flameproof pan. Bring the liquid back to a boil. Whisk in a little roux and cook until slightly thickened. Return the meat and vegetables to the pan and add the chopped parsley. Bring to a boil, taste, and adust the seasoning. Serve with Parsnip Mash.

Parsnip Mash

SERVES 8   (P: 15 mins./C: 20 mins.)

1¹/2 pounds parsnips
1¹/2 pounds fluffy mashed potatoes
  (about 3 cups)
¹/4–¹/3 cup (¹/2–³/4 stick) butter
salt and freshly ground pepper
chopped parsley

Peel the parsnips thinly. Cut off the tops and tails and cut the parsnips into wedges. If the inner core seems to be at all woody, remove it. Divide the wedges into ³/4-inch cubes. Cook them in boiling salted water for 15–20 minutes until quite soft.

Drain and mash the parsnips. Mix in the mashed potato and a nice bit of butter, and season well with salt and pepper. The texture should not be too smooth. Scatter with chopped parsley.

Steamed Raisin Pudding

SERVES 4   P: 30 mins./C: 2 HOURS)

Oh, my goodness, does this bring back memories or what? Serve a steamed pudding for an autumn or winter dinner party and everyone of a certain age will dissolve into a sepia tinted haze of nostalgia!

1 tablespoon butter, melted, plus ¹/2 cup
  (1 stick) butter, at room temperature
¹/3–¹/2 cup golden raisins pitted or ¹/2 cup
  stoned Lexia or Muscatel raisins
¹/2 cup sugar
grated zest of ¹/2 unwaxed organic lemon
2 cage-free, organic eggs
6 ounces all-purpose white flour (about
  1¹/3 cups)
¹/2 teaspoon baking powder
1–2¹/2 tablespoons milk

For the homemade custard:
¹/2 vanilla bean or a few drops of
  vanilla extract
1¹/4 cups rich milk
2 cage-free, organic egg yolks
1 tablespoon sugar

5-inch pudding bowl or ovenproof bowl

Brush the pudding bowl with the melted butter. Press some of the golden raisins or pitted and split raisins around the sides. In another bowl, cream the remaining butter, add the sugar and lemon zest, and beat until light and fluffy. Gradually add the eggs, beating well after each addition. Stir in the flour and baking powder and enough milk to make the mixture just loose enough to drop from a spoon, then add the remaining raisins. Spoon into the pudding bowl.

Cover with a tight-fitting lid or a pleated piece of double aluminum foil and tie it down. (The foil is pleated to allow for expansion.) Bring a saucepan of water to a boil and put in the pudding bowl—the water should come halfway up the sides. Cover and steam for 2 hours.

Meanwhile, make the custard. Put the vanilla bean (if using) into the cold milk and bring slowly to a boil. Whisk the egg yolks with the sugar in a bowl. Remove the vanilla bean from the milk and pour the milk onto the egg mixture, whisking all the time. At this point add the pure vanilla extract (if using). Return the mixture to the saucepan and stir over a gentle heat until it thickens just enough to coat the back of a spoon—be careful not to boil it. Pour into a cold bowl and stir occasionally as it cools.

Turn out the pudding and serve with the custard.

Raspberry Jam Pudding
Another children's favorite. Substitute ¹/3–¹/2 cup raspberry jam for the raisins, spreading it over the sides and bottom of the pudding bowl. Serve with a warm raspberry jam sauce (thin the jam with a little water) and lots of lightly whipped cream.

Jellied Ham Hock and Parsley Terrine

SERVES 12–16   (**P:** 1 HOUR/**C:** 2½ HOURS)

Jambon persillé **is a classic in French charcuteries. When I first looked up recipes for it they would always go into a long ramble about making a clear jelly with calves' feet. I tried it once and was exhausted by the effort, and forgot about it until recently when I ate a delicious version at a friend's house. I was wildly impressed— my goodness, he must have spent days, I said. Nonsense, he replied, just use gelatin! So now it's child's play and makes a super dish for a summer lunch. It can be prepared several days ahead; it's also a terrific way to use up leftover ham or bacon.**

9 pounds ham hocks, or a 6-pound piece of
    dry-cured ham (bacon or oyster cut is good)
dash of dry white wine
2 onions, each stuck with 1 clove
2 carrots
1 celery stalk
1 small bay leaf
few sprigs of thyme
10 black peppercorns
4 rounded teaspoons powdered gelatin
2 ounces parsley, finely chopped,
    about 1 cup (stalks reserved)

For serving:
Tomato and Mint or Basil Salad (see p.89)
scallions
gherkins
green salad

If the ham is salty, soak it in cold water for a few hours, preferably overnight. Discard the soaking water. Put the ham in a large pot, cover with fresh water, and bring to a boil; as soon as it boils, discard the water, cover with fresh water, and bring to a boil again. Repeat two or three times depending upon how salty the ham is.

Finally, cover with fresh water and a dash of white wine. Add all the remaining ingredients except the gelatin and chopped parsley, but do include the parsley stalks. Bring to a boil, cover, and reduce the heat, then simmer for 2–2½ hours—a skewer should go through easily. Remove the ham and strain the cooking liquid through a fine strainer or one lined with cheesecloth into a shallow dish. Skim the fat off the liquid and let it cool.

Remove the rind from the ham and cut the meat into 1-inch cubes.

Measure the cooking liquid—you won't need much more than 2½ cups. Put ⅓ cup of the cooking liquid into a small bowl, sprinkle 4 rounded teaspoons of gelatin on it—this amount will gel 2½ cups liquid, and let it soak for a few minutes. Meanwhile, bring a small saucepan of water to a boil. Put the bowl into the simmering water to dissolve the gelatin. When the gelatin is clear, add a little of the measured cooking liquid, stir well, and then mix with the remaining liquid, finally stirring in the chopped parsley. Mix well. Put the cubed ham into an oiled bowl or terrine (it should be about 4 inches deep) and pour the liquid over it. Try to flatten the top so it does not wiggle around too much when you take it out. (In France it is traditionally made in a round-bottomed bowl.) Cover and refrigerate overnight.

Serve in slices with summer salads.

Slow-roasted Belly of Pork with Crackling and Spiced Eggplant

SERVES 6–8   (**P:** 30 mins./**C:** 2 HOURS)

5 pounds belly of free-range organic pork
    with the rind intact. (You will most certainly
    need to order this ahead to ensure that
    the rind is still on—no rind, no crackling!)
sea salt (or Kosher salt) and cracked
    black pepper

For serving:
Spiced Eggplant (see p.243)
arugula leaves

Score the pork rind at ¼-inch intervals running with the grain—let your butcher do this if possible because the skin, particularly of free-range pork, can be quite tough. This is to give you really good crackling and make it easier to carve later.

Preheat the oven to 325°F. Put the pork, skin side up, on a cutting board and season with salt and pepper. Pour ½ inch water into a roasting pan and roast the pork on a wire rack in the roasting pan. Allow 30–35 minutes per pound. Baste with the rendered pork fat every now and then.
Just before the end of the cooking time remove the pork to another roasting pan. Return to the oven and increase the temperature to 450°F, to crisp the crackling a bit more, for 10–15 minutes. When the pork is cooked, the juices should run clear. Let it rest for 10–15 minutes in a low oven before carving.

Degrease the cooking juices and reduce to a few tablespoons (if your roasting pan is not flameproof, scrape juices into another pan to degrease). Serve the pork sprinkled with some flakes of sea salt along with the degreased juices, the Spiced Eggplant and arugula. Rustic roast potatoes and a good green salad would also be great.

why slow cook?

Slow food requires time and patience, but the results are well worth it and it is something that I am passionate about. How does this fit into a book on easy entertaining? Well, most of these recipes require no more preparation than any other, but can be left to cook happily by themselves for several hours.

Moreover, if you love to cook, then you will find these recipes all the more rewarding because the resultant taste makes it all worth while. The meat will be so juicy and succulent, full of flavor and coaxed into such tenderness that your guests will talk about it for weeks. These recipes are perfect for when you have a whole day or weekend to prepare, or if you have house guests for a lazy weekend—you can start in the morning and check on it every so often. As with all recipes, read them carefully and work out when you will need to get started on each stage

Another joy is that you can spend the cooking time getting ready for the party. Why not make your own cordials or lemonade, fruit ice cubes for drinks, and whip up a divine dessert to finish off. With 2–3 hours to spare, you also have plenty of time to get the house in order and you can really go to town on the decoration. If you are the least bit artistic, take the time to create some simple table settings and placemats using wrapping paper, cardboard, or tissue paper and pinking shears for a funky finish. Or edge the cardboard with matching ribbon. Then devote some time to yourself—a long bath or a home manicure, all the while sipping some bubbly—what better way to prepare for a party.

Traditional
A Plate of Cured Meats
Beef and Oxtail Stew with Parsnip Mash (p.150)
Steamed Raisin Pudding (p.151)

To drink
Cured meats go best with red wines that are big on fruit but low on tannin. Beaujolais or Sancerre Rouge are ideal and they are best served quite cool, especially if the weather is warm. By contrast, fino or manzanilla sherry, the classic partner of tapas, will do the same job but in a very different way. The stew requires something much more gutsy and full-bodied. A southern Rhône red, such as Gigondas or Vacqueyras, has the concentration for the job. Really intense New World reds, especially Californian zinfandel or Hunter Valley Shiraz, which are often a bit overpowering with food, will meet their match here. There are two ideal wines for steamed raisin pudding: the treacly Liqueur Muscats of Victoria and the sweetest of them all, Pedro Ximenez from Jerez.

Take it slow
Salmon Rillette with Piquillo Peppers (p.74)
White Yeast Bread (p.34)
Cocido (p.149)
A Great Lemon Meringue Pie (p.265)

To drink
The white wines of Spain's cool climate Rueda region, often using sauvignon blanc grapes, can tackle the combination of richness and smokiness that the rillettes present. Alternatively, a straight sauvignon blanc from Chile will do the job, or even a Muscadet, provided it's from a really good source. Cocido is quite a contrast, requiring a Spanish red with oodles of fruit, brawny structure, and some vanilla-scented oak. Think in terms of Rioja, Ribera del Duero, or Bierzo. An Australian GSM (i.e., Grenache, Shiraz, Mourvedre) blend is a good substitute.

formal suppers

A formal dinner party is the ultimate challenge. The first place to start is with pen and paper—think of it as you would a military operation. Make lots of lists—the guests, shopping list for ingredients, wine list. Consider drawing up a schedule of works—it may sound a bit like hard work, but it does avoid a mad dash before your guests arrive (remember to leave yourself at least half an hour to get yourself ready for dinner). There are lots of elegant suppers in this chapter that will wow your guests, and they can easily be complemented by recipes from earlier chapters. And take a look at Sweet Things and A Cheese Course for the finishing touches. My final tip—if you have time, have a practice run with the recipes, so you will be full of confidence on the night.

Striped Mullet or Sea Bass in a Salt Crust with Fresh Herb Butter

SERVES 2–4   (P: 15 mins./C: 30 mins.)

So easy and so elegant.

1 striped mullet or sea bass, 1¹/₂–2 pounds
1 cage-free, organic egg white, lightly beaten
  (optional)
2¹/₄ pounds sea salt or Kosher salt

For serving:
Herb Butter (see below)
tiny new potatoes
oven-roasted cherry tomatoes

1 large oval dish, preferably cast iron, large
  enough to hold the fish, cook the fish, and
  bring to the table

Preheat the oven to 425°F.

Gut the fish and wash out the inside well to remove any trace of blood (I often use a clean dish-washing brush). Do not remove the head. Use strong kitchen scissors to cut away the dorsal fin. Remove the scales, if needed, by holding the fish by the tail and pushing against the scales with the back of a knife from the tail to the head on both sides. (Gray sea mullet has scales as large as a thumbnail; other fish, such as sea bass or bream (porgy), need not necessarily be scaled.)

If you want a harder crust, mix the egg white with the salt. Spread one third of the sea salt evenly over the bottom of a large cast-iron dish. Lay the fish on top. Cover completely with the remaining sea salt. Bake for 18–20 minutes.

Meanwhile, make the herb butter (see below). Don't do this too far in advance or it will lose its fresh flavor and green color.

When the fish is cooked, bring the dish to the table, crack the hard crust on top. Remove the top crust to a plate and peel the skin off the fish. Lift the fillets off onto individual serving plates and spoon a little herb butter over them.

A few tiny new potatoes and maybe a branch of sweet oven-roasted cherry tomatoes on the side would be delicious with this.

Herb Butter

¹/₂ cup (1 stick) butter
4 teaspoons finely chopped mixed herbs,
  such parsley, chives, fennel, and thyme

Melt the butter in a small saucepan and stir in the herbs. Remove from the heat.

Fish in Fresh Fig Leaves with Nasturtium and Parsley Butter

SERVES 8   (P: 15 mins./C: 15mins.)

8 large fresh fig leaves
8 portions of fresh fish, such as sea bass,
  grouper, wild salmon, about 2¹/₂ pounds
extra virgin olive oil
salt and freshly ground pepper

For garnishing:
flat-leaf parsley and nasturtium flowers

For the nasturtium and parsley butter:
¹/₂ cup (1 stick) butter
freshly squeezed lemon juice
zest from 1 unwaxed lemon
1¹/₂ tablespoons chopped parsley
1 teaspoon chopped fresh chives
30 fresh nasturtium flowers, coarsely chopped

Preheat the oven to 400°F.

First make the nasturtium and parsley butter. Cream the butter and beat in the lemon juice bit by bit. Add the lemon zest and chopped parsley, chives, and nasturtium flowers. Form into a roll and wrap in waxed paper, twist the ends to seal, and chill in the fridge.

Wash the fig leaves in cold water. Dry gently. Skin the fish and dip each portion in extra virgin olive oil. Season well on both sides with salt and freshly ground pepper. Wrap each piece of fish individually in a fig leaf—it may not be perfectly enclosed but that's fine. Roast on a baking tray in the oven for 8–10 minutes depending upon the thickness of the fish.

Serve on hot plates. Open the fig-leaf packages and put a slice of nasturtium and parsley butter on top of the fish. Garnish with a sprig of flat-leaf parsley and a nasturtium flower. Serve immediately as the butter melts over the fish.

Pacific Oysters with Asian Vinaigrette

SERVES 8 AS AN APPETIZER   (P: 40 mins.)

Even though Pacific oysters are available all year round, they are best in winter (see the photograph on p.172).

32–40 Pacific oysters

For the Asian vinaigrette:
1/2–1 teaspoon peeled and finely grated fresh ginger
1/3 cup rice wine vinegar
1 teaspoon sugar
1 teaspoon soy sauce
1/2 cup sunflower oil
2 1/2 tablespoons extra virgin olive oil
1/2 tablespoon lemon juice

For garnishing:
fresh seaweed, if available
chives or cilantro sprigs

To make the Asian vinaigrette, mix all the ingredients in a glass jar, seal, and shake well.

If you can get some, place a little fresh seaweed on each plate. Arrange 4–5 oysters per person on top and spoon a little vinaigrette over each one.

Sprinkle the oysters with the finely chopped chives, or a crisscross of 2 longer chives, or a sprig of cilantro.

Top Tip: If you can find some fresh seaweed, such as bladder wrack, dip the fronds into boiling water for a second or two and it will turn bright green. Drop it right into a bowl of iced water to prevent it continuing to cook, and to set the color. It will make an attractive garnish, which you could eat if you were very hungry but it doesn't taste delicious! Use it soon otherwise it will go slimy.

Salad of Smoked Mackerel with Beets, Watercress, and Horseradish Sauce

SERVES 8   (P: 10 mins.)

4–6 fillets of smoked mackerel, skin on
Pickled Beets (see p.86)
generous amount of watercress and baby salad greens
sprigs of dill, for garnishing

For serving:
Ballymaloe Brown Yeast Bread (see p.35)
Horseradish Sauce (see below)

Cut the smoked mackerel into 1-inch pieces and the pickled beets into 1/2-inch cubes.

Strew the bottom of each plate with a mixture of watercress and baby salad greens. Put 5–6 pieces of mackerel on top. Scatter with some beet cubes, and top with a few little spoonfuls of horseradish sauce. A few sprigs of dill add to the deliciousness. Serve with Ballymaloe Brown Yeast Bread.

Horseradish sauce

SERVES 8–10   (P: 20 mins./C: 3 HOURS)

Horseradish is widely available in Irish greengrocers nowadays, but it also grows wild in many parts of Ireland. It looks like giant dock leaves. If you can't find it near you, plant some in your garden. It is very prolific and the root, which is the part you grate, can be dug up at any time of the year. Serve horseradish sauce with roast beef, smoked venison, or smoked mackerel.

This is a fairly mild horseradish sauce. If you want to really "clear the sinuses," increase the amount of horseradish.

enough horseradish root to make
    2–4 tablespoons grated horseradish
2 teaspoons white wine vinegar
1 teaspoon lemon juice
1/4 teaspoon Dijon mustard
1/4 teaspoon salt
pinch of freshly ground pepper
1 teaspoon sugar
1 cup lightly whipped cream

Scrub and rinse the horseradish root well, peel and grate. Put the grated horseradish into a bowl and mix in the vinegar, lemon juice, mustard, salt, freshly ground pepper, and sugar. Fold in the lightly whipped cream—do not overmix or the sauce will curdle.

Covered, the sauce will keep in the fridge for 2–3 days.

Chickpeas with Fresh Spices

SERVES 8–10

(**P:** 10 mins. IF USING CANNED CHICKPEAS,
70 mins. IF DRIED/**C:** 15 mins.)

A few little jars of fresh spices are a crucial part of any kitchen, they will add terrific zest and an exotic flavor to your food.

1²/₃ cups dried chickpeas, soaked overnight in cold water, or 2 x 15-ounce cans chickpeas
2 fresh green chiles
2-inch piece of fresh ginger root, peeled and roughly chopped
4 garlic cloves
¹/₄ cup extra virgin olive oil
8 ounces onions, finely chopped (about 2 cups)
1 teaspoon cumin seeds, crushed
2 teaspoons coriander seeds, crushed
8 very ripe tomatoes, skinned and chopped, or 1¹/₂ x 14¹/₂-ounce cans tomatoes
8 ounces spinach leaves (about 6 cups)
salt and freshly ground pepper
2 tablespoons chopped cilantro
1 tablespoon chopped mint

For serving:
yogurt, crème fraîche (or sour cream), fresh cilantro, and mint leaves
or
boiled rice and Tomato and Red Onion Salsa (see p.294)

Drain the soaked chickpeas (if using) into a pot, cover with fresh water, and cook until tender; this can take 30–60 minutes depending upon the quality. Drain and reserve the cooking liquid.

Meanwhile, remove the seeds from the chiles. Using a mortar and pestle or food processor, grind together the chiles, ginger, and garlic to a paste.

Heat the oil in a heavy sauté pan or frying pan and sweat the onions over low heat until soft but not colored. Add the chile paste, the crushed cumin and coriander seeds, and cook for a minute or two. Add the tomatoes, the drained chickpeas, and a little of their cooking liquid (save the rest for soup). If using canned chickpeas, add them at this point. Simmer gently for about 10 minutes until the flavors have mingled.

Add the spinach leaves, tossing gently until they wilt. Add salt and pepper to taste and sprinkle with chopped cilantro and mint. Serve immediately with plain boiled rice and Tomato and Red Onion Salsa (see p.294), or let cool and serve cold with yogurt, crème fraîche (or sour cream), and lots of fresh cilantro and mint leaves.

Goat Cheese, Scallion, "Pink Fir Apple" Potato, Chorizo, and Thyme Leaf Tart

SERVES 6   (P: 30 mins./C: 1 HOUR)

If you don't have access to these intensely flavored Pink Fir Apple potatoes, use some small new potatoes.

1/2 tablespoon butter
1 1/2 tablespoons extra virgin olive oil
4 ounces scallions (white and green
    parts), finely chopped (about 1 cup)
salt and freshly ground pepper
2 ounces (1/2 cup) chorizo, cut up, (optional)
3 cage-free, organic eggs, plus extra beaten
    egg for brushing
1/4 cup fresh thyme leaves
3/4 cup cream
4–6 Pink Fir Apple potatoes (or small new
    potatoes), cooked and sliced or cut
    into chunks
4 ounces soft goat cheese (about 1/2 cup)
thyme flowers, for garnishing (optional)

For serving:
green salad

For the pastry dough:
5 ounces white flour (a generous cup)
1/4 cup (1/2 stick) butter
1 cage-free, organic egg

1 x 8-inch quiche pan or flan ring
dried beans or baking beans

First make the pastry dough. Sift the flour into a bowl and rub in the butter until the mixture resembles coarse bread crumbs. Mix the egg with 2 tablespoons water, and mix in just enough to bind the dough, being careful not to make it too sticky. Chill for 15 minutes.

Roll out the dough to a thickness of about 1/8-inch and use to line the quiche pan. Line the dough with tin foil and fill to the top with dried beans or baking beans. Let it rest for 15 minutes.

Preheat the oven to 350°F.

Bake the pie crust for 20 minutes, then remove from the oven but do not turn off the oven.

Remove the beans and foil, brush the pie crust with beaten egg, and return to the oven for a minute or two. This seals the crust and helps to avoid a "soggy bottom."

To make the filling, melt the butter in a frying pan. Add the olive oil and scallions, sprinkle some salt over them, and cook over low heat for a few minutes until the scallions are soft but not colored. Add the chorizo (if using). Let cool.

Whisk the eggs and the thyme leaves in a bowl, add the cream, the softened scallions, and chorizo and cooked potatoes. Season well with salt and freshly ground pepper and pour into the pie shell. Scatter pieces of goat cheese into the pan. Bake for 40–45 minutes, or until just set in the center.

Sprinkle thyme flowers over the top, if available. Serve with a good green salad.

Glazed Baby Onion or Shallot Tarte Tatin

SERVES 6   (P: 30 mins./C: 1 HOUR)

1/4 cup (1/2 stick) butter
1 1/4 pounds baby onions or shallots
    (about 5 cups)
12 garlic cloves
1 1/4 cups homemade chicken or
    vegetable broth (see p.295)
7 ounces puff pastry
2 1/2 tablespoons sugar
1 1/2 tablespoons balsamic vinegar
2 teaspoons fresh thyme leaves
salt and freshly ground black pepper

For serving:
fresh arugula leaves

9-inch nonstick frying pan with a metal handle

Heat a large heavy frying or sauté pan. Melt half the butter in the pan, add the onions, and fry gently for about 10 minutes, tossing occasionally until golden. After about 5 minutes, add the garlic cloves. Pour in the broth, cover, and simmer for 5–10 minutes, depending upon the size of the onions—they should be tender when pierced with a sharp knife but still hold their shape. Using a slotted spoon, remove the onions and garlic to a plate, drain well, and pat dry with paper towels (save the remaining broth for sauces or soup). Let cool completely.

Roll out the pastry dough to a 10-inch circle. Chill for at least 30 minutes to let the dough rest. Preheat the oven to 400°F.

Melt the remaining butter in a 9-inch ovenproof, preferably nonstick, frying pan. Sprinkle the sugar over the bottom of the pan and cook until caramelized. Sprinkle the balsamic vinegar over the top, add the onions, toss until well coated—about 3 minutes—and remove from the heat. Tuck the garlic cloves in between the onions. Sprinkle with the thyme leaves.

Season with salt and pepper. Lay the dough on top, tucking the edges down around the inside of the pan, and prick all over with a fork. Bake for about 30 minutes or until the pie crust has risen and is golden brown. Let it rest for a few minutes, then loosen the sides with a knife and invert onto a flat serving plate. Serve warm or cold, with an arugula salad.

Tofu and Vegetable Stir-fry

SERVES 6 (**P:** 15 mins. PLUS 2 HOURS TO MARINATE (OPTIONAL)/**C:** 15 mins.)

Tofu is made from soy milk which is heated and stirred with coagulants. It solidifies into curds which are pressed to make blocks of tofu. It can be soft and silky or very firm. Chinese-style tofu is firm in texture and looks coarse but becomes smoother when cooked. It can be marinated for a longer period and is also good fried or grilled, or used for brochettes. It comes packed in water in a sealed plastic container, either in slabs or slices, and can be frozen. Always check the use-by date and keep refrigerated. Tofu should smell mild, sweet, and vaguely nutty. Once it begins to smell sour, it is not good to eat.

$2^1/2$ tablespoons soy sauce
$2^1/2$ tablespoons rice wine vinegar
1 tablespoon brown sugar
1 teaspoon peeled and grated fresh ginger root
1 chile, chopped, or 1 teaspoon red pepper flakes
2 teaspoons Chinese five-spice powder
12 ounces firm tofu, drained
$2^1/2$ tablespoons extra virgin olive oil
7 ounces mushrooms, sliced (about 2 cups)
salt and freshly ground pepper
1 large red pepper, quartered, seeded, and sliced at an angle
1 large yellow pepper, quartered, seeded, and sliced at an angle
7 ounces small broccoli or cauliflower florets, blanched and refreshed (about $3^1/2$ cups)
$1^1/2$ tablespoons sesame oil
2–4 scallions, chopped
$1^1/2$ tablespoons toasted sesame seeds

For serving:
Steamed Thai fragrant rice

Mix the soy sauce, vinegar, sugar, ginger, chile, and five-spice powder together. Cut the tofu into 1-inch cubes, place it in a small pie dish, cover with the spicy mixture, and let it marinate for 1–2 hours if possible.

Drain the tofu, reserving the marinade. Heat a wok or frying pan and add the olive oil. Cook the tofu in batches for 3–4 minutes until golden and transfer to a plate. Increase the heat. Add a little more oil if needed, toss in the mushrooms, and season with salt and freshly ground pepper. Toss until fully cooked through. Add the peppers, stir, and fry for a minute or two, then add the broccoli or cauliflower florets.

Drizzle with the sesame oil and stir-fry for 2–3 minutes. Add the tofu, chopped scallions, and the reserved marinade. Let it bubble up, taste, and correct the seasoning. Scatter with sesame seeds and serve immediately with Thai fragrant rice.

Warm Salad of Pigeon Breast with Spiced Pears and Mushrooms

SERVES 12 (**P:** 20 mins./**C:** 15 mins.)

6 ripe pears, such as Bose or Doyenné de Comice
1-inch piece of cinnamon stick
$1/2$ teaspoon allspice berries
1 teaspoon coriander seeds
$1/4$ teaspoon black peppercorns
1 star anise
1 tablespoon sugar
grated zest of 1 orange
8 ounces wide-capped mushrooms, sliced (about $2^1/3$ cups)
2 tablespoons butter
extra virgin olive oil, for frying
salt and freshly ground black pepper
12 pigeon breasts, skinned
flat-leaf parsley leaves, for garnishing
enough salad greens for 12 helpings

For the dressing:
$1^1/2$ tablespoons verjuice (see p.95)
$1^1/2$ tablespoons lemon juice
$1/2$ cup extra virgin olive oil
$1/2$ teaspoon Dijon mustard
1 teaspoon honey

Peel the pears and cut them into quarters.

Put the cinnamon stick in a spice grinder, add the allspice berries, coriander seeds, peppercorns, star anise, and sugar, and whizz to a powder. Transfer to a bowl. Add the grated orange zest. Toss the pears in the spice mixture.

Make the dressing by whisking all the dressing ingredients together in a bowl.

Heat the butter in a sauté pan or frying pan, add the pears, toss, and cook over low heat until the pears are tender. Keep warm.

Heat a little olive oil in a frying pan and sauté the mushrooms over a high heat. Season with a little salt and pepper, set aside, and keep warm.

Clean the frying pan and heat a little more olive oil over a very high heat. Season the pigeon breasts and fry very quickly—they should be sealed on the outside but still pink, otherwise they will be tough. Remove them to a plate to rest while you dress the salad greens.

Toss the greens in the dressing and divide between 12 plates. Divide the warm pears and mushrooms between the plates. Quickly slice the pigeon breasts and add to the plates. Scatter with the parsley and serve immediately.

Fettucine with Asparagus

SERVES 4   (P: 15 mins./C: 15 mins.)

You can use this as a basic creamy pasta sauce and add all sorts of good things.

Don't make this recipe with out-of-season asparagus that has been flown halfway around the globe. In Ireland and Britain, the asparagus season comes in May and June.

8 ounces fettucine or noodles
sea salt (or Kosher salt) and freshly
  ground pepper
16 spears of fresh asparagus, trimmed
1 cup cream
3 tablespoons butter, cubed
3 ounces Parmesan cheese, grated (about
  1 1/2 cups), plus extra for serving

First cook the pasta. Bring 6 quarts of water to a boil, add 2 tablespoons salt, and tip the pasta in all at once. Stir well to ensure the strands are separate, cover the pot just long enough to bring the water back to a boil. Cook, uncovered, until al dente, cooked but still firm to the bite—about 1–2 minutes for fresh pasta; for dried pasta follow the instructions on the box, but test 2–3 minutes before the suggested time. Drain the pasta as soon as it is cooked, but don't overdrain: fresh pasta and all long pasta should still be wet and slippery.

Meanwhile, cook the asparagus in very little water for 4–5 minutes or until almost soft or when the tip of a knife pierces the root end easily. Drain and set aside.

Next make the sauce. Heat the cream in a wide saucepan or sauté pan, add the butter, and simmer over medium heat for a minute or two until the cream and butter are incorporated and slightly thickened. Add the Parmesan and lots of pepper. Taste, and add salt if needed. Toss the drained pasta into the sauce.

Slice the still-warm asparagus at an angle, keeping the tip intact. Scatter it over the top of the pasta, toss gently, and serve immediately in hot pasta bowls.

Have an extra bowl of grated Parmesan for guests to sprinkle over the pasta at the table.

Other Good Additions
1 Instead of the asparagus, add 3/4 cup freshly cooked fava beans and lots of coarsely chopped flat-leaf parsley to the sauce.
2 To the basic sauce, add thin strips of freshly roasted and peeled sweet red pepper or piquillo (2 large ones should be enough) instead of the asparagus. Top with fresh arugula leaves.
3 Add some finely cut up roasted pumpkin, toasted pine nuts, and arugula leaves to the sauce instead of the asparagus.

Involtini di Melanzane alla Mozzarella

SERVES 6   (P: 40 mins./C: 10 mins.)

1 very large eggplant, about a pound,
  or 2 small ones
salt and freshly ground black pepper
extra virgin olive oil, for frying
9 ounces buffalo mozzarella cheese
12 basil leaves
freshly ground pepper

For serving:
Tomato Fondue (see p.240)
green salad (see p.94)

Slice the eggplant thinly, sprinkle with salt, and let it drain for 30 minutes. Rinse and pat dry. Brush with olive oil and panbroil until tender and slightly browned. Drain on paper towels.

Heat the broiler until it is really hot.

Cut the mozzarella into thin slices, place 2 basil leaves on each slice, and sprinkle with freshly ground pepper. Roll an eggplant slice around each piece of cheese and arrange in a single layer on an ovenproof plate.

Broil until the cheese melts. Serve at once with Tomato Fondue and a mixed green salad.

Spiced Vegetable Pie

SERVES 6   (P: 1 HOUR/C: 1 HOUR)

9 ounces onions, chopped (about 2 cups)

8 ounces potatoes, chopped
  (about 1¹/₂–1³/₄ cups)

9 ounces carrots, chopped (about 2¹/₄ cups)

8 ounces celeriac, chopped (about 2 cups)

4 ounces parsnips, chopped (about 1 cup),
  and/or 4 ounces mushrooms, sliced
  (about 1 cup) and sautéed

2¹/₂ tablespoons extra virgin olive oil

salt and freshly ground pepper

2 teaspoons cumin seeds

1 tablespoon coriander seeds

¹/₂ teaspoon cardamom seeds

2¹/₂ tablespoons flour

1 teaspoon ground turmeric

pinch of sugar

1¹/₄ cups vegetable broth (see p.295)

egg wash

green salad, for serving

For the hot water pastry dough crust:

1 pound flour (about 3¹/₂ cups)

pinch of salt

1 cup plus 2 tablespoons (2¹/₄ sticks) butter

³/₄ cup water

1 pan, 8 inches in diameter, 1¹/₂ inches deep

Cut the vegetables into uniform-sized cubes of about ¹/₂ inch. Heat the olive oil in a wide sauté pan or frying pan, add the onions, potatoes, carrots, celeriac, and parsnips. Season with salt and pepper, toss in the oil, cover the pot, and sweat over gentle heat for 4–5 minutes.

Meanwhile, heat the cumin, coriander, and cardamom seeds in a pan until they smell aromatic—just a few seconds. Crush lightly, add to the vegetables, and cook for 1–2 minutes. Remove from the heat, sprinkle the flour, turmeric, and sugar over them, and stir well.

Return to the heat and add the vegetable broth, stirring all the time. Cover the pot and simmer for 20–30 minutes or until the vegetables are almost tender but not mushy.

Meanwhile make the pastry dough. Sift the flour and salt into a mixing bowl and make a well in the center. Cut up the butter, put it into a saucepan with the water, and bring to a boil. Pour the liquid all at once into the flour and mix together quickly; beat until smooth. At first the dough will be too soft to handle, but as it cools, roll out until it is ¹/₈–¹/₂-inch thick and use two thirds of it to line a deep pan. The dough may be made into individual pies if you prefer. Keep back one-third of the dough to make the lid.

Preheat the oven to 450°F.

Fill the pastry dough-lined pan with the vegetable mixture, including the sautéed mushrooms (if using); the vegetables should be almost, but not quite, cooked and cooled a little. Brush the edges of the dough with the egg wash and put on the pie dough lid, pinching the edges tightly together. Roll out the trimmings to make pastry dough leaves or twirls to decorate the top of the pie. We sometimes make a smiley face. Make a hole in the center, then egg-wash the lid and the decorations, also.

Bake the pie for about 30 minutes. Serve with a good green salad.

Jeannie's Roast Lamb with Chocolate

SERVES 7–8   (P: 30 mins./C: 1¹/₂ HOURS)

This bizarre-sounding but utterly delicious recipe was given to me by the lovely bubbly Scottish cook Jeannie Chesterton, who with her husband Sam owns one of my favorite getaways in the whole world—Finca Buenvino at Los Marines in Andalucia.

1 leg of free-range organic lamb

salt and freshly ground pepper

1 head of garlic

extra virgin olive oil, for drizzling

2–2¹/₂ cups cold coffee or tea, strained

1–2 ounces good-quality dark chocolate,
  chopped (about 3-5 tablespoons), plus
  extra if needed

For serving:

new potatoes

Preheat the oven to 350°F.

Score the skin of the lamb and sprinkle with salt and pepper. Peel the garlic cloves and put into a roasting pan. Lay the leg of lamb on top of the garlic and drizzle with a little olive oil.

Pour the coffee or tea into the roasting pan—it should come about ¹/₂ inch up the side of the pan. Roast for 15 minutes per pound, about 1¹/₄–1¹/₂ hours depending upon the size of the leg.

When the meat is cooked, transfer it to a serving dish to rest.

Meanwhile, skim the fat off the juices in the roasting pan. If the pan is flameproof, put it over a low heat, add the chocolate, and whisk to emulsify (if it's not flameproof, scrape the juices into one that is). The sauce will thicken slightly and become darker brown in color. Taste, and adjust the seasoning and chocolate if needed.

Carve succulent slices of lamb and serve with the sauce and perhaps a few new potatoes. Surprisingly delicious!

Debbie's Thai Green Vegetable Curry

SERVES 6–8   (**P:** 30 mins./**C:** 45 mins.)

This is the yummiest vegetable curry. The recipe was given to me by Debbie Shaw, who originally came to the school as a student and is now a teacher. Her curry is great for everyone, including vegetarians who don't mind a drop of fish sauce!

4 tablespoons sunflower oil
4 medium zucchinis, cut into 1-inch
 cubes
salt and ground white pepper
12–14 ounces mushrooms, quartered
 (about 4-4$^{1}/_{2}$ cups)
4 tablespoons extra virgin olive oil
2 medium eggplants, cut into 1-inch
 cubes
$^{1}/_{2}$ head large cauliflower (about 1 pound),
 broken into large florets
1 large shallot or small onion (about
 2 ounces), finely chopped
2 large garlic cloves, finely chopped
1-inch piece of fresh galangal or
 ginger root, peeled and finely chopped
2 green chiles, finely chopped
1 tablespoon Thai green curry paste (add a
 bit more if you like it hot!)
2 x 14-ounce cans coconut milk
2$^{1}/_{2}$ tablespoons fish sauce (*nam pla*)
1$^{1}/_{2}$ tablespoons sugar
juice of 1 lime
$^{1}/_{4}$ cup roughly torn Thai basil leaves,
 or other basil
8 kaffir lime leaves
1$^{1}/_{2}$–1$^{3}/_{4}$ cups homemade
 vegetable broth (see p.295)
6 ounces frozen peas (about 1$^{1}/_{3}$-1$^{1}/_{2}$ cups)

For serving:
basmati rice or Thai noodles
herby green salad

Heat 1 tablespoon of the sunflower oil in a frying pan over medium heat and add the zucchini. Season lightly with salt and sauté until cooked and slightly browned. Set aside in a bowl. In the same pan, sauté the mushrooms in the same way; add them to the zucchini when cooked.

Heat 2 tablespoons of the olive oil over medium heat and fry the eggplants until cooked through and slightly brown. Season with a pinch of salt and white pepper. Remove from the heat and add to the bowl.

Cook the cauliflower florets in boiling salted water for 4–5 minutes or until cooked but still slightly crunchy. Add to the other vegetables.

Heat the remaining sunflower oil in a frying pan over medium heat. Fry the shallot or onion, garlic, chiles, and galangal or ginger for 2–3 minutes or until the shallot is cooked, but do not let it burn. Add the curry paste and continue to cook for another 3 minutes.

Add the coconut milk and simmer for 5–6 minutes, stirring, until the sauce thickens.

Add the fish sauce, sugar, half the lime juice, half the basil, and all the kaffir lime leaves. Stir in 1$^{1}/_{2}$ cups vegetable broth; if the sauce is too thick, add a little more broth. Bring to a boil and add the frozen peas. Reduce the heat and continue to cook for another 4 minutes, stirring occasionally.

Add all the cooked vegetables and the remaining basil and lime juice. Taste, and adjust the seasoning if needed.

Serve on warm dishes, with boiled basmati rice or Thai noodles and a green salad with lots of fresh herbs.

Note: Debbie stressed that when curry paste is newly opened, it is very hot, but will gradually become milder, so adjust the quantity accordingly.

Roast Pheasant with a Salad of Arugula, Pomegranate, and Game Chips

SERVES 2–3   (P: 30 mins./C: 1 1/4 HOURS)

A roast pheasant makes the perfect romantic dinner for two, and you'll probably have a little left over that may be eaten cold for a picnic the next day. This slightly unorthodox way of cooking the pheasant produces a moist, juicy bird. Guinea fowl is also wonderful cooked and served in this way.

1 young plump pheasant
2 tablespoons butter
1 1/4 cups game or chicken broth
   (see p.295)

For the stuffing:
3 tablespoons butter
3 ounces onions, chopped (about 2/3 cup)
2 1/2 ounces bread crumbs (about 1 1/2 cups)
1 1/2 tablespoons chopped mixed herbs,
   such as parsley, thyme, chives, and marjoram
salt and freshly ground pepper

For serving:
Salad of Arugula, Pomegranate, and
   Game Chips (see below)

Gut the pheasant if necessary and remove the crop, which is at the neck end; wash all over and dry well.

Preheat the oven to 375°F.

To make the stuffing, melt the butter in a small pan and sweat the onions over a low heat until soft but not colored. Remove from the heat and stir in the bread crumbs and herbs, then season with salt and pepper to taste. If you are cooking the bird right away, the stuffing can be used warm; otherwise let the stuffing get quite cold before you use it.

Season the pheasant cavity with salt and pepper and fill loosely with the stuffing. Sprinkle some more salt and pepper over the top of the bird. In a small saucepan, melt the butter and soak a piece of clean cheesecloth or a handiwipe in it. Wrap the pheasant completely in the cloth. Alternatively, smear the breast and legs generously with butter.

Roast for about 45–60 minutes, depending upon size. Test by pricking the thigh at the thickest point: the juices should run clear when the bird is cooked. Remove the cloth and keep the pheasant warm on a serving dish while you make the gravy.

Spoon off any surplus fat from the roasting pan (keep it for roasting or sautéing potatoes later). If the roasting pan is flameproof, put it over a high heat and pour in the game or chicken broth to deglaze. Otherwise, scrape the juices into a flameproof pan and proceed. Bring to a boil, and use a whisk to dislodge the crusty caramelized juices so they can dissolve into the gravy. Boil for a minute or two and adjust the seasoning to taste. Pour into a hot gravy boat.

Carve the pheasant and serve with some stuffing, gravy, and the Salad of Arugula, Pomegranate, and Game Chips.

Top Tip: This stuffing is also delicious for a chicken or a traditional roast turkey—multiply quantity by four.

Salad of Arugula, Pomegranate, and Game Chips

Game Chips (see p.167)
Generous amount of arugula leaves, or a
   mixture of arugula and other little leaves,
   such as mizuna, mibuna, bok choy, daytonia,
   mâche (corn salad) and buckler leaf sorrel
1/2 pomegranate
Pomegranate Molasses Salad Dressing
   (see p.167)

Make the Game Chips and drain on paper towels.

To prepare the salad, wash and dry the leaves and keep refrigerated.

Extract the pomegranate seeds by holding the pomegranate, cut-side down, over a bowl. Tap firmly with the bowl of a wooden spoon to loosen the seeds. Keep refrigerated.

Just before serving, assemble the salad. Remove the salad greens from the fridge and place in a deep bowl. Sprinkle some Pomegranate Molasses Salad Dressing over the green salad and toss gently to coat the greens. Add the pomegranate seeds and the Game Chips and toss gently again. Turn out onto a flat serving dish and serve with the roast pheasant.

Game Chips

SERVES 4   (P: 15 mins./C: 15 mins.)

Game chips are traditionally served with roast pheasant, but they are also very good with guinea fowl or just as a snack with a drink.

1 pound large even-sized potatoes
  (about 3 medium)
olive oil, for deep-frying
salt

Wash and peel the potatoes. For even-sized chips, trim each potato with a swivel-top peeler until smooth. Slice them very finely, preferably on a mandoline. Soak in cold water to remove the excess starch (this will also prevent them from discoloring or sticking together). Drain off the water and dry well.

Heat the olive oil to 350°F. Working in batches of a few dry slices of potato at a time, drop them in the oil and fry until golden and completely crisp. Drain on paper towels and sprinkle lightly with salt. Repeat until they are all cooked.

If they are not to be served immediately, they may be stored in a tin and reheated in a low oven just before serving.

Other Good Things to Do with Game Chips:
Use to scoop up a warm, melting Camembert or Brie cheese.
Pour sizzling garlic butter over a bowl of homemade chips and nibble immediately.

Pomegranate Molasses Salad Dressing

This versatile dressing is delicious with salad greens, but also with grilled fish, grilled chicken, and grilled vegetables.

Pomegranate molasses is made by reducing the juice of sour pomegranates to a thick, dark brown syrup that has a distinctive sweet-and-sour flavor. It's available from Indian grocery stores and good delicatessens.

2 garlic cloves, crushed
1/4 teaspoon ground cumin
1/2 teaspoon sugar, plus extra if needed
1/3 cup pomegranate molasses
2 1/2 tablespoons lemon juice
2/3 cup extra virgin olive oil
salt and freshly ground black pepper

In a bowl, mix the garlic, ground cumin, sugar, pomegranate molasses, and lemon juice. Whisk in the olive oil. Season to taste with salt and pepper, and add a little extra sugar if you think it's a bit too sharp.

It will keep for several weeks and there is no need to store it in the fridge.

Roast Rack of Lamb with Rosemary and Membrillo Aioli and Rustic Roast Potatoes

SERVES 8   (P: 20 mins./C: 3 HOURS)

I love this recipe. My good friend the Australian cook Maggie Beer, from the Barossa Valley, made this membrillo aioli when she taught a class at the Cookery School a few years ago. Membrillo, or quince paste, is available from delicatessens and many good cheese stores, and brings a delicious, fruity flavor to the dish.

4 racks of lamb, or 1 leg of spring lamb
3 tiny sprigs of rosemary and 1–2 garlic cloves
  (optional)
salt and freshly ground pepper
sprigs of rosemary, for garnishing

For serving:
Rustic Roast Potatoes (see p.237)

For the rosemary and membrillo aioli:
2 teaspoons finely chopped fresh rosemary
1 cup oil (sunflower, peanut, or olive
  oil, or a mixture; we use 6 parts sunflower oil
  and 2 parts extra virgin olive oil)
2 cage-free, organic egg yolks
1/4 teaspoon salt
dab of English mustard or 1/4 teaspoon
  French mustard
2 teaspoons white wine vinegar
1 garlic clove, crushed
1 1/2–2 ounces membrillo (quince paste),
  about 2–3 tablespoons

Preheat the oven to 425ºF. Score the skin of the lamb; you may like to insert a few tiny sprigs of rosemary and slivers of garlic here and there on the skin side. Season with salt and pepper.

Roast for 25–30 minutes for a rack or 1 1/4–1 1/2 hours for a leg, depending upon the age of the lamb and how well done you like it.

Meanwhile, make the aioli. Put the chopped rosemary into a little saucepan with 3 tablespoons of the oil and warm gently for 2–3 minutes, ensuring you do not burn the herb. Set aside.

Put the egg yolks into a bowl with the salt, mustard, white wine vinegar, and crushed garlic. Put the oil into a measuring cup. Take a whisk in one hand and the oil in the other, and drip the oil onto the egg yolks drop by drop, whisking at the same time. Within a minute you will notice that the mixture is beginning to thicken. When this happens you can add the oil a little faster, but not too fast or it will suddenly curdle—the egg yolks can absorb the oil only at a certain pace. Taste and add a little more seasoning and vinegar if needed.

(If the aioli curdles it will suddenly become quite thin, and if it is left sitting, the oil will start to float to the top of the sauce. If this happens you can quite easily rectify the situation: put another egg yolk or 1–2 tablespoons boiling water into a clean bowl, then whisk in the curdled aioli 1/2 teaspoon at a time until it emulsifies again.)

Chop the membrillo and warm gently in a little saucepan until it melts, then let it cool. When it is cold, add it to the aioli with the infused rosemary oil and chopped rosemary. Taste, and adust the seasoning if necessary, then store in the fridge until needed.

When the lamb is cooked, remove from the oven and let it rest for 5–10 minutes. Carve, allowing 2–3 cutlets per person if using rack of lamb. Garnish with a sprig of rosemary and serve with the rosemary and membrillo aioli and Rustic Roast Potatoes.

Guard of Honour

A guard of honour looks mightily impressive for a dinner party. It is made up simply of two interlinked racks of lamb, tied in one or two places to secure while cooking, similar to a crown roast but instead of a circular crown of bones, you have crisscrossed interlinked bones. Add 5–10 minutes extra cooking time on top of the above recipe.

Other Good Things to Serve with a Rack of Lamb, Guard of Honour, or Panbroiled Lamb Chops
1 Sauce Paloise (see Béarnaise Sauce, p.295).
2 Spiced Eggplant (see p.243).
3 Roast cumin and tzatziki.
4 Three sauces: Sauce Soubise (see p.296), Mint Sauce (see p.176), and red currant jelly.

Panbroiled Steak with Chipotle Chili Butter

SERVES 8   (**P:** 20 mins./**C:** 3 HOURS)

Chipotle in adobo is one of my favorite flavors. You can buy it in small cans from specialty food stores.

8 sirloin or tenderloin steaks, about 8 ounces
   each
1 garlic clove
salt and freshly ground pepper
extra virgin olive oil, for drizzling
watercress or arugula leaves

For garnishing:
chopped parsley

For the chipotle chili butter:
1/3 cup (3/4 stick) butter
2 1/2 tablespoons chipotle chili in adobo sauce
2 1/2 tablespoons chopped parsley

First make the chipotle butter. Cream the butter in a bowl and mix in the chipotle and chopped parsley. Shape into a roll, wrap in waxed paper, twist the ends to seal, and refrigerate until needed.

About 1 hour before cooking, prepare the steaks. If using sirloin steaks, score the fat at 1–inch intervals. Cut the garlic clove in half and rub both sides of each steak with the cut sides. Grind some pepper over the steaks and sprinkle a few drops of olive oil on them. Turn the steaks in the oil and set aside for about an hour.

Heat the grill pan, season the steaks with a little salt, and lay them on the pan. For the weight given (see left), the approximate cooking time for each side of the steaks is:

	Sirloin	Tenderloin
Rare	2 minutes	5 minutes
Medium rare	3 minutes	6 minutes
Medium	4 minutes	7 minutes
Well done	5 minutes	8–9 minutes

If using sirloin steaks, once they are cooked, turn them over onto the fat and cook for 3–4 minutes or until the fat becomes crisp.

Put the steaks on a plate and let them rest for a few minutes in a warm place. Transfer to individual serving plates, with a slice of chipotle butter melting on top and some watercress or arugula leaves on the side. Sprinkle some chopped parsley over them.

Other Good Things to Serve with a Steak
1 Mushroom à la Créme (see p.241).
2 Béarnaise Sauce (see p.295) and frites.

Roast Tenderloin of Beef with Béarnaise Sauce, and Twice-cooked Roasted Potatoes with Shallots and Thyme Leaves

SERVES 8–10   (**P:** 20 mins./**C:** 3 HOURS)

Caul fat is light, lacy fat which melts and bastes the meat during cooking.

1 whole tenderloin of well-aged dried beef,
   about 6 pounds, trimmed
1–2 garlic cloves
sea salt (or Kosher salt) and freshly
   cracked pepper
pork caul fat (if available), or extra virgin olive
   oil, for drizzling
2–3 sprigs of thyme

For serving:
Twice-cooked Roast Potatoes with Shallots
   and Thyme Leaves (see p.237)
wide-capped mushrooms
Béarnaise Sauce (see p.295)

Double over the tenderloin at the tapered end and tie it securely with fine butcher's cotton twine. Alternatively, ask your butcher to do the "butchering" for you.

Preheat the oven to 450°F.

Cut the garlic cloves in half and rub the tenderloin all over with the cut sides. Season well with lots of pepper and wrap loosely in caul fat (if using), then season well with sea salt; if you have no caul fat, season the meat well with salt and pepper and drizzle with olive oil.

Heat a cast iron grill-pan to very hot. Sear the beef until nicely browned on all sides.

Transfer it to a roasting pan and tuck a couple of sprigs of thyme underneath. Roast for 25–30 minutes. If you have a meat thermometer, the internal temperature should read 245°F. Alternatively, the meat should feel springy to the touch and when it is pierced with a skewer, the juices should be pale pink.

Transfer to a carving dish. Cover loosely with aluminum foil and let it rest for 15–20 minutes, by which time the juices will have redistributed themselves and the beef will be uniformly medium rare. Serve cut in 1/4-inch–thick slices, with Twice-cooked Roast Potatoes with Shallots and Thyme Leaves, wide-capped mushrooms (sautéed whole for 5–8 minutes depending upon size), and Béarnaise Sauce.

dinner for two

Dinner for two, what could be more romantic? In fact many of the principles for a successful dinner à deux can be applied to any formal dinner party.

This is an occasion when you want to make an impression so give yourself plenty of time to prepare. Firstly, check whether your guest has any dietary restrictions. Also, be clear about what time you want them to arrive—between 7:30 and 8P.M., for example. This will not only ensure that you are not caught in mid-preparation, but that you can time everything perfectly. For formal invitations, the guest's name is always hand-written in ink as is the envelope. For more informal and fun invitations you might fill the envelope with glitter or confetti or paper cut-outs.

Choose at least one recipe that can be prepared ahead or easily, "cheat's recipes" I call them. Think about the presentation—if a goat cheese salad calls for balsamic vinegar, serve it on a white plate with little drizzles. Likewise, a dusting of confectioners' sugar is stunning on dark china. Herb butter balls look gorgeous in oyster shells.

If you are having a large party, see if you can get some help—teenage children or students may be up for some extra cash in return for clearing the table and doing the dishes, between courses and at the end of the meal. If you are planning a romantic evening, warn any roommates or family and get them out of the way— bribe them with movie tickets if necessary, but make sure they know to be discreet.

arranging a formal supper

Creating an atmosphere is vital. Lighting should be your first consideration. Candles do a beautiful job—dot the room with stately church candles, pretty tea lights, or stylish candlelabras. Paper lampshades are cheap but incredibly effective, for example, red Chinese lanterns can bring a soft-colored hue to your table. Find some glass beads and thread colorful strings of them around the table to catch the candlelight. Velvet or satin ribbon can be used to tie bundles of breadsticks, napkins, and cutlery. Line the breadbasket with a square of satin fabric.

Flowers are essential. For a romantic evening, go for luscious peonies, antique papery roses, frilly parrot tulips, or gerberas with dark centers. For a formal dinner, aurum lilies or orchids are stunning, or ask your florist to create a centerpiece for your table.

Seating plans are helpful for large numbers. Not only do they avoid awkward dances around the table, but they are are a great way of introducing people. Even if you don't write it down, do give it thought.

Epicurean (see pp.170–172)
Pacific Oysters (see p.158)
Roast Pheasant with a Pomegranate Salad and Game Chips (see pp.166–167)
Molten Chocolate Puddings (see p.246)
A Plate of locally-made Cheddar

To drink
You can't go wrong with oysters and champagne but there are other possibilities such as Guinness or Guinness combined with champagne to make Black Velvet. Good Chablis, too, is, as they say, no hardship to drink with oysters. Roast pheasant with gamey red Burgundy is a classic combination but the sweetness of the pomegranate seeds complicates matters. A New Zealand pinot noir will have some Burgundy character but often with a touch more

ripeness to counteract the sweetness. Châteauneuf-du-Pape is another possibility. Banyuls, the Provençal red dessert wine, has a great affinity with chocolate, as does port.

Cheat's dinner
Salad of Goat Cheese with Arugula, Figs, Pomegranate Seeds (p.67)
Bowl of Warm Mussels with Homemade Mayonnaise (see p.98)
Brioche with Sugared Strawberries and Mascarpone (see p.254)
Piece of Local Cheese with Turkish Figs or Medjool Dates

To drink
In keeping with the ease and simplicity of the menu, you can serve a Sancerre or Pouilly-Fumé (or any other dry, fresh sauvignon blanc, perhaps from New Zealand or the Cape of South Africa) with both appetizer and main course. A light dessert Muscat will go with the brioche without overpowering it and provide an unusual accompaniment to the cheese, especially if it happens to be blue.

Vegetarian
Peach, Gorgonzola, and Watercress salad (see p.67)
Goat Cheese, Scallion, and Thyme Leaf Tart (see p.160)
A Good Green Salad (see p.94)
Frosted Black Currant Parfait with Black Currant Coulis (see p.252)
Homemade Cottage Cheese with Fresh Herbs and Crackers (p.274)

To drink
Once again, a Sancerre or Pouilly-Fumé will be perfect with both appetizer or main course, or you may prefer to try a sauvignon blanc from elsewhere. Such wines will enhance the fresh, clean flavors of the cottage cheese. If you want a red, keep it light: basic Bordeaux would be good.

Exotic
Moroccan Harira Soup (see p.54)
Seared Fresh Salmon with Tomatoes and Herbs (see p.110)
A Good Green Salad (see p.94)
Summerberry Tart with Rose Water Cream (see p.173)

To drink
In keeping with the exotic theme, why not choose an off-beat white? Perhaps a Viognier or a white Crozes-Hermitage, a Verdelho from Western Australia, a Roero Arneis from Piedmont, or even an Assyrtiko from Greece. The rosewater cream needs a dessert Muscat or Gewürztraminer.

festive meals

Easter, Halloween, Thanksgiving, Christmas—these are times to celebrate and party with friends and family. This chapter contains some of my favorite festive recipes, many of them with a clever twist. If you have served up the traditional turkey one too many times, you will love my spicy version. There is also spring lamb for Easter, Bacon and Cabbage for St. Patrick's Day, and pumpkin for Thanksgiving, not forgetting some boozy plum puddings for Christmas.

Roast Leg of Spring Lamb with Sea Salt, Mint Sauce, and Glazed Baby Carrots

SERVES 6–8   (P: 15 mins./C: UP TO
                            1³/₄ HOURS)

**Young spring lamb is sweet and succulent
and needs absolutely no embellishment,
apart from a dusting of salt and pepper and
a little fresh mint sauce—made from the first
tender sprigs of mint from the cold frame in
the kitchen garden. Follow it with rhubarb
tart made with the first pink spears of the
season. For me this is the
quintessential taste of Easter.**

1 leg of milk-and-grass-fed spring lamb
sea salt (preferably Halen Mon or Maldon)
  and freshly ground pepper

For the gravy:
2¹/₂ cups lamb or chicken broth
  (see p.295)
a little roux (see p.139)

For serving:
Glazed Baby Carrots (see p.238)
Roast Onions (see p.236)
Rustic Roast Potatoes (see p.237)
Mint Sauce (see recipe below)

If possible, ask your butcher to remove the aitchbone (or rump bone) from the top of the leg of lamb so that it will be easier to carve later, then trim the knuckle end of the leg.

Preheat the oven to 350°F.

Season the skin of the meat with sea salt and freshly ground pepper. Put the lamb into a roasting pan and roast—the time will depend upon size and cooking preference. For rare, roast for 1–1¹/₄ hours; for medium, 1¹/₄–1¹/₂ hours; or for well done, 1¹/₂–1³/₄ hours. When the lamb is cooked to your taste, remove the leg to a carving dish. Rest the meat for 10 minutes before carving.

Meanwhile, make the gravy. Skim the fat off the juices in the roasting pan and add the broth. Bring to a boil and whisk in a little roux to thicken slightly. Taste and let it bubble up and reduce until the flavor is concentrated enough. Adjust the seasoning if needed and serve hot with the lamb, Glazed Baby Carrots, Roast Onions, lots of Rustic Roast Potatoes, and Mint Sauce.

Mint Sauce

MAKES ABOUT 3/4 CUP   (P: 15 mins.)

**Traditional mint sauce, made with tender
young shoots of mint, takes only minutes to
make. It's the perfect accompaniment to
spring lamb, but for those who are expecting
a bright green jelly, the slightly dull color
and watery texture comes as a surprise.
That's how it ought to be—try it.**

2¹/₂ tablespoons finely chopped fresh mint
2¹/₂ tablespoons sugar
¹/₂–²/₃ cup boiling water
2¹/₂ tablespoons white wine vinegar or
  lemon juice

Put the chopped mint and the sugar into a bowl or sauce boat. Add the boiling water and vinegar or lemon juice.

Let it infuse for 5–10 minutes before serving.

Easter Egg Nests

MAKES ABOUT 24   (**P:** 15 mins./**C:** 15 mins.)

These nests are irresistible to kids of all ages, and grown-ups too!

6 ounces good-quality dark chocolate
  roughly chopped (about 1 cup)
4 ounces Rice Krispies (about 4¹/₂ cups)
72 mini chocolate eggs

paper baking cups or ring molds

Melt the chocolate in a large heatproof bowl over a pan of hot water. Bring the water just to a boil, turn off the heat, and let the chocolate melt in the bowl. Stir in the Rice Krispies.

Spoon the mixture into paper baking cups. Flatten a little and make a well in the center. Fill each one with three speckled mini chocolate eggs. Let them set and hide them from the grown-ups.

Spicy Roast Turkey with Banana and Cardamom Raita

SERVES 10–15   (**P:** 15 mins. + 3³/4 HOURS
MARINATING/**C:** 3 HOURS)

1 free-range, organic turkey, 10–12 pounds
extra virgin olive oil, for brushing
2 cups turkey or chicken broth (see p.295)
³/4 cup cream
roux (optional; see p.139)

For the spice paste:
2¹/2 tablespoons cumin seeds, toasted
   and ground
2¹/2 tablespoons paprika
2 teaspoons cayenne pepper
2¹/2 tablespoons ground turmeric
2 teaspoons sugar
2 teaspoons freshly ground pepper
1 tablespoon salt
4 garlic cloves, crushed
juice of 2 lemons
¹/3 cup extra virgin olive oil or vegetable oil

For serving:
relish or mango chutney
Banana and Cardamom Raita (see p.294)
jewelled rice
sprigs of cilantro

To make the spice paste, mix all the ingredients together in a bowl. Set aside 1–2¹/2 tablespoons for the sauce.

If you are cooking the turkey whole, put it into a roasting pan. Spread the spice paste all over the skin—breast, legs, wings—and tuck a little under the breast skin if possible. Alternatively, remove the breasts and legs. Bone the legs (retain the carcass and giblets to make a turkey broth). Spread the spice paste all over the surface of the turkey pieces and put them into a roasting pan. Cover and leave in the fridge for 3 hours, or better still overnight, to absorb the spicy flavors.

Preheat the oven to 350°F. Brush the turkey with a little oil and roast for 3–3¹/2 hours.* Check from time to time that the skin is not burning—you may need to cover loosely with aluminum foil about halfway through cooking.

Remove the turkey to a hot serving dish. Add the retained 1–2¹/2 tablespoons spice paste to the juices in the roasting pan. Stir and cook over low heat for 3–4 minutes. Spoon off any excess fat. Add the broth and cream to the pan and bring to a boil. Whisk in a little roux if necessary. Taste and adjust the seasoning if needed.

Carve the turkey, or serve the turkey pieces. Spoon a little spicy sauce over each helping. Serve with a good relish or mango chutney, Banana and Cardamom Raita, and jewelled rice with a green salad, and some sprigs of cilantro for garnishing.

* Note: When roasting turkey, allow about 15 minutes per pound plus an extra 15 minutes.

Zanne Stewart's Pumpkin Pie

SERVES 8   (**P:** 15 mins./**C:** 1 HOUR)

My quest for a pumpkin pie started and ended with my friend Zanne Stewart, food editor of *Gourmet* magazine. Zanne suggested I use the terrific Eagle brand recipe. We've baked the pie shell first. I serve the pumpkin pie topped with whipped cream and drizzle honey over the top as Zanne's grandmother did.

1 x 15-ounce can pumpkin puree
1 x 14-ounce can sweetened
   condensed milk
2 cage-free, organic eggs
1 teaspoon ground cinnamon
¹/2 teaspoon ground ginger
¹/2 teaspoon freshly grated nutmeg
¹/2 teaspoon salt

9-inch pie shell, baked blind,
   (see recipe on p.247)
whipped cream and honey, for serving

Preheat the oven to 425°F.

Whisk the pumpkin, condensed milk, eggs, spices, and salt in a bowl until smooth. Pour into the pie shell and bake for 15 minutes. Protect the edges of the crust if necessary. Reduce the temperature to 350°F and continue to bake for 35–40 minutes or until a knife inserted an inch from the crust comes out clean. Let it cool.

Serve topped with whipped cream and a drizzle of honey. Store any leftover pie in the fridge.

Other Yummy Toppings
1 Sour cream topping:
Mix ³/4 cup sour cream, 2¹/2 tablespoons sugar, and 1 teaspoon vanilla extract in a medium bowl. After the pie has been baked for 30 minutes at 350°F, spread this evenly over the top and bake for another 10 minutes.
2 Streusel topping:
Mix ¹/2 cup brown sugar and ¹/2 cup white flour in a bowl and rub in ¹/4 cup (¹/2 stick) cold butter until crumbly. Add a ¹/4 cup chopped almonds, pecans, or walnuts. After the pie has baked for 30 minutes at 350°F, sprinkle the streusel evenly over the top and continue to bake for 10 minutes.
3 Chocolate glaze:
In a small saucepan over low heat, melt 4 ounces chocolate chips (about ²/3 cup) and 1 teaspoon butter. Drizzle or spread over the top of the baked pumpkin pie.

Teeny Weeny Plum Puddings with Boozy Ice Cream

SERVES 8–10, IN TINY PUDDING BOWLS OR
ESPRESSO CUPS   (**P:** 2 DAYS/**C:** 1¹/₄ HOURS)

**It has always been the tradition in our
house to eat the year's first plum pudding
on the evening it is made. As children we
could hardly contain ourselves with
excitement—somehow that plum pudding
seemed all the more delicious because it
was our first taste of Christmas. It was
usually made in mid-November and
everyone in the family had to stir so we
could make a wish—I now know that it
helped to mix it properly. It's fun to put
silver plum pudding charms in the pudding
destined to be eaten on Christmas Day.**

1 cup muscat raisins
1 cup golden raisins
1 cup currants
³/₄ cup brown sugar
6 ounces white bread crumbs (3–3¹/₂ cups)
6 ounces organic beef suet, finely chopped
  (about ³/₄ cup)
2 ounces good-quality candied peel (¹/₂ cup)
1 cooking apple, finely chopped or grated
grated zest of 1 lemon
2 cloves, pounded
3 cage-free, organic eggs
¹/₄ cup Jamaica rum
¹/₄ cup shelled almonds, chopped
¹/₄ cup shelled hazelnuts, chopped
pinch of salt

For serving:
Irish whiskey or brandy, for flaming brandy
  butter, rum or whiskey cream or Boozy Ice
  Cream (see recipe below)

In a large bowl, mix all the ingredients together very thoroughly and leave overnight; don't forget—everyone in the family must stir and make a wish!

Next day, stir again for good measure. Fill into tiny bowls or espresso cups, then cover with aluminum foil or a double thickness of waxed paper. Tie tightly under the rims with cotton twine, making a twine handle also for ease of lifting.

Pour a little boiling water in a wide pan or baking tray, and place the bowls or cups in it—the water should come halfway up the side of the bowls or cups. Cover with a lid or aluminum foil and steam over medium heat for 1¹/₄ hours. Check regularly and top up with boiling water if needed.

Let cool completely and re-cover each pudding with fresh foil or waxed paper. Store in a cool, dry place until needed. It will keep for months.

On Christmas Day or whenever you wish to serve the plum puddings, steam as above for another 30 minutes.

Turn the plum puddings out onto very hot serving plates, pour some Irish whiskey or brandy over them, and ignite. Serve immediately on the very hot plates, with brandy butter, rum or whiskey cream, or Boozy Ice Cream.

This recipe will also make 1 large or 2 medium puddings. The large size will serve 5–6 people, the medium 3–4. Cook for 6 hours on the first day, re-cover, and store in a cool place. Steam for 2 hours in a covered saucepan on the day of serving.

Boozy Ice Cream with Nuts and Raisins

SERVES 20   (**P:** 20 mins. + 3 HOURS FREEZING)

**A gorgeous, rich ice cream with a scoopable
texture. Serve it in small helpings.**

¹/₂ cup (1 stick) butter
1 cup soft dark brown sugar
1 cage-free, organic egg
¹/₄ cup medium sherry
¹/₄ cup port
2¹/₂–3 pints cream, lightly whipped

For the nuts and raisins:
²/₃ cup muscat raisins
¹/₄ cup rum
¹/₄ cup sherry
¹/₂ cup fresh walnuts, chopped

two 9 x 5-inch loaf pans or one ¹/₂-gallon
  plastic container

Melt the butter, stir in the sugar, and let it cool slightly. Whisk the egg and add to the butter and sugar along with the sherry and port. Cool. Add the lightly whipped cream.

Pour into a plastic container, cover, and freeze. Alternatively line two loaf pans with plastic wrap, cover, and freeze.

Meanwhile, put the raisins into a bowl, cover with a mixture of rum and sherry and let them plump up. Chop the walnuts coarsely and add to the raisins just before serving.

Cut the ice cream in slices or serve in little glasses scattered with a few of the boozy raisins and some chopped walnuts. Sliced banana is also delicious with this combination.

Roast Bramley Apples with Amaretto Cream

SERVES 8   (**P:** 15 mins./**C:** 45 mins.)

8 large Bramley apples (if unavailable, use
  other large, tart cooking apples)
1/4 cup (1/2 stick) butter, softened
1/4 cup sugar
finely grated zest of 1 lemon
2 1/2 tablespoons golden raisins
2/3 cup whipping cream
1 1/2 tablespoons amaretto almond liqueur

Preheat the oven to 350°F.

First core the apples with an apple corer so the apples remain whole, and score the skin around the equator. Mix the butter with the sugar, lemon zest, and raisins. Stuff the butter mixture into the coring holes. Stand the apples in an ovenproof dish and pour about 2/3 cup water into the bottom of the dish.

Roast for 30–45 minutes. The apples should be beginning to burst—this is vital, so hold your nerve; they should look fat and squishy.

Meanwhile, whip the cream and add amaretto to taste. Serve the apples right from the oven, with the amaretto cream.

Top Tip: Stuff the apples with mincemeat or cinnamon sugar (see p.207).

Thanksgiving Turkey with Fresh Herb Stuffing, Spiced Cranberry Sauce, and Bread Sauce

SERVES 10–12   (**P:** 30 mins./**C:** 3 1/4 HOURS)

This is my favorite roast stuffed turkey recipe. You can cook a chicken in exactly the same way but use one-quarter of the stuffing quantity given.

For the fresh herb stuffing:
12 ounces onions, chopped (about 3 cups)
3/4 cup (1 1/2 sticks) butter
14–16 ounces (from a 1-pound loaf)
  soft bread crumbs
2 ounces (about 1 cup) chopped herbs
  such as parsley, thyme, chives, marjoram,
  savory, lemon balm
salt and freshly ground pepper

10–12-pound free-range, organic turkey,
  with neck and giblets
1 cup (2 sticks) butter
roux (optional; see recipe on p.139)
4 1/2 cups turkey or chicken stock
sprigs of parsley, watercress, or a sprig of holly,
  for garnishing

Large square of cheesecloth (optional)

For the spiced cranberry sauce:
2 1/3 cups sugar
1/2 cup wine vinegar
1/2 stick cinnamon, 1 star anise, 6 cloves, and a
  2-inch piece of fresh ginger root, peeled and
  sliced, 1 chile, split and seeded, all tied in a
  cheesecloth bag
1 pound cranberries (about 5 cups)
freshly squeezed lemon juice

To make the fresh herb stuffing, in a large pot, sweat the onions gently in the butter until soft, for about 10 minutes, then stir in the crumbs, herbs, and a little salt and pepper to taste. Let it get quite cold. If necessary, wash and dry the cavity of the bird, then season and half-fill with cold stuffing. Put the remaining stuffing into the crop at the neck end.

Preheat the oven to 350°F. Weigh the stuffed turkey and calculate the cooking time. Allow 15 minutes per pound, plus an additional 15 minutes.

Melt 1 1/2 tablespoons of the butter and, if you have a large piece of good-quality cheesecloth, soak it in the melted butter; cover the turkey completely with the cheesecloth, place in a roasting pan, and roast for 3–3 1/2 hours. The turkey browns beautifully, but if you like it even browner, remove the cheesecloth 10 minutes before the end of the cooking time. Alternatively, smear the breast, legs, and crop well with soft butter, and season with salt and freshly ground pepper. If the turkey is not covered with butter-soaked cheesecloth, it is a good idea to cover the whole roasting pan with aluminum foil. However, your turkey will then be semi-steamed, not roasted in the traditional sense of the word.

The turkey is cooked when the juices run clear. To test, prick the thickest part at the bottom of the thigh and examine the juices—they should be clear. Remove the turkey to a carving dish, keep it warm, and let it rest while you make the gravy.

To make the gravy, spoon off the surplus fat from the roasting pan. If the roasting pan is flameproof, deglaze the pan juices with the stock. If the roasting pan is not flameproof, scrape the pan drippings into one that is. Using a whisk, stir and scrape well to dissolve the caramelized meat juices from the roasting pan. Boil it up well, season, and thicken with a little roux if you like. Taste and correct the seasoning. Serve in a hot gravy boat.

To make the spiced cranberry sauce, place the sugar, a cup of water, the vinegar, and spice bag in a non-reactive saucepan and bring to a boil. Add the cranberries and simmer very gently until they become tender. Some will burst, but that's OK. Add a little lemon juice to taste.

Serve with the turkey garnished with parsley, watercress, or holly, roast potatoes (see recipe on p.237), along with the spiced cranberry sauce, the bread sauce, and the gravy.

Witches' Bread with Chocolate and Raisins

MAKES 1 LOAF or 8–10 MINI LOAVES
(P: 15 mins./C: 45 mins.)

1 pound all-purpose flour, preferably
  unbleached (about 3 1/3 cups)
1 teaspoon baking soda, sifted
1 teaspoon salt
2 teaspoons sugar
2 ounces good-quality dark chocolate,
  roughly chopped (about 1/3 cup)
1/3 cup raisins
1 3/4 cups buttermilk, or 1 1/2 cups
  buttermilk beaten with 1 cage-free, organic
  egg
butter, for serving

Preheat the oven to 425°F.

In a large bowl, sift the flour and baking soda, then add the salt, sugar, chocolate, and raisins. Make a well in the center and pour all the buttermilk in at once. Using one hand, mix in the flour from the side of the bowl to make a softish, but not too wet and sticky dough. When it all comes together, turn out the dough onto a floured counter. Wash and dry your hands.

With floured fingers, tidy up the dough gently, flip it over, and tuck it in underneath. Pat the dough into a round loaf about 1 1/2 inches deep. Cut a deep cross in the top with a sharp knife and then prick in the center of the four segments (to "let the fairies out").

Bake for 10 minutes, then turn the oven down to 400°F and continue baking for another 35 minutes or until cooked. If you are in doubt, tap the bottom of the loaf: it should sound hollow. Cool on a wire rack. Serve freshly baked, cut into thick slices and smeared with butter

Halloween Weeny Witches: make 8–10 mini loaves—don't forget to cut a cross in these too.

Lana Pringle's Barm Brack

MAKES 2 LOAVES   (P: 25 mins. + OVERNIGHT
SOAKING/C: 1 HOUR)

Halloween is a terrific time to have a party. In Ireland a barm brack is a must for this. The word "barm" comes from the old English "beorma," meaning yeasted fermented liquor. "Brack" comes from the Irish "brac," meaning speckled—which the cake is, with dried fruit and candied peel. Halloween has always been associated with fortune telling and divination, so various objects are wrapped up and hidden in the cake batter—a wedding ring, a coin, or a thimble (signifying spinsterhood). I treasure this recipe, which was given to me by Lana Pringle. Her breads and cakes are legendary among her friends. Lana dislikes the din of food processors, so all her cakes are creamed, beaten, and whisked by hand and baked in the Aga.

14 ounces mixed raisins and golden raisins
  (about 2 3/4-3 cups)
2 cups brewed strong tea
1/3 cup candied cherries, cut in half
1/3 cup good-quality candied peel, chopped
1/2 cup soft brown sugar
1/2 cup granulated sugar
1 cage-free, organic egg
14 ounces all-purpose white flour (about 3 cups)
scant 1/2 teaspoon baking powder
melted butter, for greasing

two 8 x 4 1/2-inch loaf pans, 2 1/2 inches deep

Put the raisins into a bowl, cover with the tea (Lana occasionally uses a mixture of Indian and Lapsang Souchong, but any good strong tea will do), and leave overnight for the fruit to plump up.

Next day add the cherries, candied peel, sugars, and egg, and mix well. Sift the flour and baking powder and stir in thoroughly. The mixture should be softish, so add a little more tea if necessary.

Preheat the oven to 350°F. Grease the pans with melted butter (Lana uses old pans, heavier-gauge than are available nowadays; light, modern pans may need to be lined with baking paper for extra protection.)

Divide the batter between the pans and bake for 1 hour or until the bread is cooked. Lana bakes her barm bracks in the Aga, and after 1 hour she turns the pans around and gives them another 10 minutes. Leave in the pans for about 10 minutes and then remove and cool on a wire rack.

Traditional Irish Bacon, Buttered Cabbage, Parsley Sauce, and Scallion Champ

SERVES 12–15   (P: 10 mins./C: 2 HOURS)

The Irish national dish of bacon and cabbage is real comfort food. When I serve this delicious peasant food for a dinner party everyone really tucks in and loves it to bits.

4 to 5-pound loin of bacon, smoked or
   unsmoked, with the rind on and a nice
   covering of fat
Buttered Cabbage (see recipe below)
Parsley Sauce (see recipe below)
Scallion Champ (see p.237)

Put the slab of bacon in a large pot, cover in cold water, and bring to a boil over medium heat. If the bacon is very salty there will be a white froth on top of the water, in which case it is preferable to discard the water and start again. Depending upon how salty the bacon is, it may be necessary to change the water several times. Finally, cover with hot water and simmer until fully cooked; allow 20 minutes for each pound. It is cooked when a skewer will come out easily and the rind will peel off easily.

Remove the rind and serve with Buttered Cabbage, Parsley Sauce, and Scallion Champ.

Parsley Sauce

SERVES 8–10   (P: 5 mins./C: 15 mins.)

2$\frac{1}{2}$ cups milk
salt and freshly ground pepper
2 ounces (about $\frac{1}{4}$ cup) roux (see p.139)
1–2 ounces chopped parsley (about $\frac{1}{2}$–1 cup)
a few slices of carrot (optional)
a few slices of onion (optional)
1 bouquet garni (optional)

If you are not using the vegetables or bouquet garni, bring the milk to simmering point. Season with salt and pepper and simmer for 4–5 minutes. Whisk in the roux until the sauce reaches a light coating consistency. Add the chopped parsley and simmer over a very low heat for 4–5 minutes. Serve hot.

If using vegetables and a bouquet garni, put them in a saucepan, add the cold milk, and bring to simmering point. Season with salt and pepper and simmer for 4–5 minutes. Strain out the vegetables and bouquet garni and bring the milk back to a boil. Whisk in the roux until the sauce reaches a light coating consistency and season. Add the chopped parsley and simmer over a very low heat for 4–5 minutes. Serve hot.

Buttered Cabbage

SERVES 4–6   (P: 10 mins./C: 5 mins.)

This method takes only a few minutes to cook, but first the cabbage must be sliced into fine shreds. It should be served the moment it is cooked.

1 pound Savoy cabbage
2–4 tablespoons butter, plus extra
   for serving
salt and freshly ground pepper

Remove the tough outer leaves from the cabbage and discard. Divide the cabbage into four. Cut out the core and then cut the cabbage crosswise into fine shreds. Put 2–3 tablespoons water into a wide pot and add the butter and a pinch of salt. Bring to a boil, add the cabbage, and toss continuously over a high heat for 3–4 minutes then set aside, covered, for a few minutes. Toss again and adjust the seasoning to taste. Add a pat of butter and serve.

Buttered Cabbage with Caraway Seeds
Add 1–2$\frac{1}{2}$ tablespoons caraway seeds to the cabbage at the start of cooking, and continue as per the above recipe.

Buttered Cabbage with Ginger
Add 2–3 teaspoons peeled and grated fresh ginger root to the butter in the pan, and continue as per the above recipe.

Buttered Cabbage with Smoky Bacon
Heat 1 tablespoon extra virgin olive oil in a frying pan. Add 4 ounces bacon slices (about $\frac{2}{3}$ cup), and cook until crisp. Add to the cooked cabbage, along with $\frac{1}{4}$ cup cream, and let it bubble for 2–3 minutes. Scatter with chopped parsley and serve.

Buttered Cabbage with Chorizo
Substitute chorizo for the bacon in the above recipe, and omit the cream.

fabulous festivities

Let the occasion be your inspiration. Easter is a time for eggs, so why not hard-boil some eggs and paint them in bright colors. Halloween is an excuse to play all sorts of old-fashioned games and to indulge in divination. Make some Witches' Bread or a Barm Brack and hide a ring, pea, stick, and rag inside so your guests can predict their fortune. Colcannon is another traditional Halloween dish—don't forget to put a little bowl on the windowsill for the fairies and to ward off evil spirits. To get everyone in the spirit of things, drape twists of black and orange crepe paper all over doors and windowframes. Weave cobwebby tangles of gray wool and make broomsticks from autumnal twigs and leaves. At Christmas, make old-fashioned orange pomanders (stud oranges with cloves) or mini puddings for your guests and leave brightly wrapped and beribboned gifts as place settings. Wrap the table in tinsel and long strands of ivy and the bottoms of thick church candles in colored foil. Less is not more at this time of year.

Christmas dinner
Campari and Blood Orange Granita (see p.66)
Spicy Roast Turkey (p.178)
Rustic Roast Potatoes (see p.237)
Spiced Eggplant (see p.243)
Arugula or Watercress Salad
Teeny Weeny Plum Puddings with Boozy Ice Cream (see p.179)

To drink
The ideal match with the turkey is a wine that many people feel poses difficulties for food: a ripe, buttery, oaky Chardonnay from the New World. Turkey cries out for it. There are lots of candidates but one of the best, because it's elegant and stylish as well as big and buttery, is the organic Bonterra Chardonnay from California. If you must have red try the Zinfandel from the same stable, or even the Sangiovese. Otherwise, any luscious red wine, such as Chilean pinot noir or an Argentinian Bonarda. The dark-brown, sugary Pedro Ximenez from Jerez is simply too sweet to drink on its own but with boozy ice cream and plum pudding, it's magic. You can even pour some over this dessert and drink the rest!

St. Patrick's Day
A Dozen Oysters and a Pint of Murphys or Guiness (see p.74)
Colcannon (see p.236)
Traditional Irish Bacon, Cabbage, Parsley Sauce, and Scallion Champ (see p.184)
Irish Rhubarb Tart (see p.271)

To drink
Murphys stout is what goes with oysters in Cork. If you want a bit more bite and bitterness, Guinness is the right partner. Alternatively, good Chablis, but this may seem curiously out of place for this day. Bacon and cabbage, strange as it may seem, are stunning with a Riesling Kabinett, which has the gentle sweetness and crisp backbone of a Granny Smith apple. Any good one will do, but ideally it should come from the Mosel. Ernst Loosen and von Kesselstatt are names to bear in mind. Rhubarb tart is very good, odd as it may seem, with a sweet Oloroso sherry from a top producer like Lustau or Valdespino.

Thanksgiving dinner
Thanksgiving Turkey with Fresh Herb Stuffing, Spiced Cranberry Sauce, and Bread Sauce (see p.181)
Twice-cooked Roast Potatoes with Shallots and Thyme Leaves (see p.237)
Zanne Stewart's Pumpkin Pie (see p.178)

To drink
Cranberries and turkey are a terrific combination. Unfortunately wine and cranberries are a bit of a nightmare, so we must tread cautiously. This is not the time to open cherished old bottles of fine claret; you need something cheap, cheerful, and pretty robust. Australian merlot, Chilean Carmanere, Argentinian Bonarda or Bonarda/Shiraz all stand a good chance of fighting their way through the cranberries. In keeping with the American theme, it might be an idea to try Bonny Doon's Big House Red or Cardinal Zin. Fetzer merlot is another candidate. Pumpkin pie will need a dessert wine with a citrus character and one of the tastiest comes from California: Quady's Essencia Orange Muscat.

children's food

Children's parties should be bright and colorful, with food to match. This is a time for treats and indulgence, but sneak in healthy vegetables in wraps and sandwiches and use nutritious fruit and milk to make lurid-colored smoothies. Give the recipes exciting names—crispy potato skins can become "dragon's skin" and sour cream "dinosaur milk."

Icky Sticky Sausage Wraps

MAKES 10   (**P:** 15 mins./**C:** 15 mins.)

1 tablespoon extra virgin olive oil, for frying
10 good-quality juicy pork sausages
1/3 cup Sweet Chile Sauce (see p.296)
1/3 cup soy sauce
2 1/2 tablespoons sesame seeds, for sprinkling
1–2 avocados, peeled and cut into wedges
10 small flour tortillas
some curly lettuce, we love Little Gem
  (Bibb or limestone lettuce)

If you want to cook the sausages in the oven, preheat it to 425°F.

For the oven, heat the oil in a roasting pan or, for the stovetop, heat it in a frying pan. Cook the sausages in the oven or the frying pan until golden on all sides.

In a bowl, mix the Sweet Chile Sauce with the soy sauce. Slip in the sausages and toss until all are well coated with the sweet sticky glaze. Sprinkle with sesame seeds and toss again.

To assemble, peel the avocados and cut into thick slices. Heat a frying pan and heat a tortilla on both sides. Put a sausage, a wedge or two of avocado, and some curly lettuce on the tortilla. Turn up the end and roll it to make an open-ended wrap. Prepare 9 more wraps in the same way. Serve immediately.

Lunch Wraps

Wraps were inspired by the Mexican burrito—originally invented as a convenient way for cowboys and farmers to carry a packed lunch! For years Americans have been eating burritos filled with Mexican ingredients such as refried beans, salsa, and cilantro, but more recently they have acquired a new name and are now stuffed with a multitude of fillings inspired by cuisines from all over the world. They are the perfect easy casual food for breakfast, lunch, or dinner. Have fun with the fillings!

flour tortillas
your choice of fillings

Heat a wide frying pan over medium heat, lay a tortilla on the pan, warm on one side for about 15–30 seconds, then turn over to warm the other side. This makes it soft and pliable.

Lay the warm tortilla on a cutting board and arrange the filling, in a rectangle roughly 2 x 5 inches in size, on the bottom half of the tortilla. Fold in the right and left edges, then fold the bottom edges over the filling and gently but firmly roll the tortilla over until the filling is completely enclosed.

Wraps can be made ahead, covered in plastic wrap or aluminum foil, and refrigerated. Depending upon the filling, they can also be reheated.

Open Wraps
Proceed as above but fold only in one side initially, and continue to roll until the filling is wrapped.

Fun Fillings
1 Lots of crunchy lettuce, goat cheese, Roasted Red Peppers (see p.298), Pesto (see p.297), and crispy bacon or prosciutto.
2 Lots of crunchy lettuce, smoked salmon, cream cheese and dill, cucumber strips, freshly cracked pepper, and a few crispy capers.
3 Lots of crunchy lettuce and arugula leaves, rare roast beef, Garlic Mayonnaise (see p.296), and crispy French-fried onions.
4 Lots of crunchy lettuce, roast chicken, fresh herb stuffing, Tarragon Mayonnaise (see p.218), and sun-dried tomatoes.
5 Lots of crunchy lettuce, spicy chicken, crème fraîche or sour cream, Cucumber Pickle (see p.73) and cilantro leaves.
6 Lots of crunchy lettuce, strips of Cheddar cheese, Cucumber Pickle Relish (see p.73), Ballymaloe Country Relish or mango chutney, and scallion.

children's birthday party

Birthday parties are a great opportunity to have as much fun as the children. Remove all the vases, ornaments, and fragile objects from the rooms and prepare for an invasion.

The food should be as simple as possible. Consider making lots of cupcakes instead of one big confection—they are much easier for young kids to eat. Use different-colored frostings, rainbow sprinkles, and candies. For decorating: Frost each cake with letters from the alphabet to spell out the birthday name, or make meringue initials so that children can spell out their own.

Make kiddie-friendly sandwiches using cookie cutters to cut out stars and circles, with alfalfa sprouts and slices of mini radishes for decorating—how grown up! Ice creams are a great treat and you can make them a bit special by decorating the cones with gingham ribbon. If you are a home-improvment whizz, you could make an ice cream holder box of MDF or Plexiglass with holes cut out to fit the cones.

Make lots of fruit juice or smoothies instead of soda so that they don't get too hyperactive, but serve them in fun plastic glasses with curly straws. Cut fresh fruit up into small chunks—if you make funny faces with banana and raisin eyes, berry noses, and a big strawberry mouth, children might think they are candies and be persuaded to eat them.

Party favor bags are a must—make them up from leftover pieces of fabric or sheets of tissue paper. Fill them with small toys, crayons, and candy. Tie them closed with ribbon and decorate them with big butterflies, cut from craft-store stencils.

balloons and sparklers

This is a time for a riot of color, pattern, and exuberance. Put away your best china and buy lots of rainbow-colored paper plates—plain, patterned, or with popular cartoon characters. Use lots of lacy doilies to decorate plates and protect the table, and blow up as many balloons as you can—the children will have a lot of fun catching and popping them. A sweet idea is to write each child's name on a balloon and tie it to a chair as place settings. Hang cut-out birds and butterflies and deck the room with bunting—craft and gift stores will have lots of paper creations.

Adorn the cupcakes with striped candles and little sparklers, but keep a close eye on the children when they are lit. Party poppers and streamers will fill the table with color. If you can find squares of origami paper, you can make little boxes for chocolate eggs.

Provide glamorous headgear—sailor and clown hats, tiaras, and play jewelry—and get the children to act out their costumes. And don't forget the old favorite games such as "pin the tail on the donkey" and "musical chairs."

Remember to organize lots of crowd control— make sure a couple of other parents stay to help you. Children tire quickly, so don't let the party go on for too long or you run the risk of tears and tantrums from all the excitement.

Party time

Something for lunch

Penny's Cupcakes

MAKES 36   (**P:** 15 mins./**C:** 20 mins.)

My daughter-in-law is famous for her yummy cakes. Depending upon how the cupcakes are decorated, they can fit any occasion—a wedding, christening, anniversary, children's party (see pp.190–195).

2 cups (4 sticks) butter, at room temperature
2 cups sugar
1 pound self-rising flour (about 3 1/3 cups)
6 large cage-free, organic eggs
1 1/2 teaspoons vanilla extract
1/2 cup milk

Frosting: see recipes below
Decorations: mixture of gum drops,
  jelly beans, crystallized flowers, chocolate
  buttons, fondant hearts or stars, M & Ms,
  streamers, tiny crackers, sparklers…

three muffin pans, each lined with 12 paper
muffin cups

Preheat the oven to 375°F.

Put all the cupcake ingredients except the milk into a food processor and whizz until smooth. Scrape down the sides, then add the milk and whizz again.

Divide the mixture between the muffin cups in the 3 muffin pans (you may need to make the cupcakes in 3 separate batches), and bake for 15–20 minutes until the cakes have risen and are golden. Remove from the trays and cool on a wire rack.

Make one or several frostings and smear them over the tops of the cupcakes, then decorate with a selection of little items.

Arrange in a pyramid on 2–3 cupcake stands or on a Plexiglass cake stand.

Lemon Frosting

MAKES ENOUGH FOR 12 CUPCAKES (**P:** 5 mins.)

4 ounces confectioners' sugar (about 1 cup)
finely grated zest of 1/2 unwaxed, organic
  lemon
1–2 1/2 tablespoons lemon juice

Sift the confectioners' sugar into a bowl. Mix in the lemon rind and enough lemon juice to make a softish frosting.

Dark Chocolate Frosting

MAKES ENOUGH FOR 12 CUPCAKES
                    (**P:** 15 mins./**C:** 5 mins.)

6 ounces confectioners' sugar (about 1 1/2 cups)
1/2 cup unsweetened cocoa powder
1/3 cup (3/4 stick) butter
1/3 cup water
1/2 cup granulated sugar

Sift the confectioners' sugar and cocoa powder into a mixing bowl. Put the butter, water, and granulated sugar into a saucepan. Set over a low heat and stir until the sugar has dissolved and the butter is melted. Bring just to a boil, then remove from the heat and pour at once into the sifted ingredients. Beat with a wooden spoon until the mixture is smooth and glossy. It will thicken as it cools.

Coffee Frosting

MAKES ENOUGH FOR 12 CUPCAKES
                    (**P:** 5 mins.)

8 ounces confectioners' sugar (about 2 cups)
scant 1 tablespoon Irel coffee essence
  (if unavailable, use any coffee-flavored syrup)
about 2 1/2 tablespoons boiling water

Sift the confectioners' sugar into a bowl. Add the coffee essence and enough boiling water to make the frosting the consistency of sour cream.

Chicken Goujons with Sweet Chile Dip

SERVES 6–8   (**P:** 10 mins./**C:** 10 mins.)

This is a clever, quick, and delicious way to make a little chicken go a long way and tempting enough to wean kids off processed chicken nuggets.

good-quality oil, for deep frying
3 free-range, organic chicken breasts, skinned and boned
salt and freshly ground pepper
flour seasoned with salt and pepper
beaten egg
fine white bread crumbs

For the Sweet Chile Dip:
1/2 cup Sweet Chile Sauce (see p.296)
freshly squeezed juice of 1/2–1 lime

Heat some oil in a deep-fryer. Cut the chicken breasts diagonally into 1/2-inch strips. Season with salt and pepper. Turn the pieces in the seasoned flour, the egg, and the bread crumbs, or simply in some milk and seasoned flour.

Drop pieces individually into the hot oil and fry for 2–3 minutes or until crisp and golden. Drain on paper towels.

Serve immediately, with a bowl of Sweet Chile Sauce mixed with lime juice, to taste.

Other Good Things to Serve with Goujons:

Garlic Mayonnaise
To 1 quantity of Homemade Mayonnaise (see p.296), add 2 1/2 tablespoons of crushed garlic and 2 1/2 tablespoons of chopped parsley.

Chile and Parsley Mayonnaise
To 1 quantity of Homemade Mayonnaise, add 1 roasted, peeled, seeded, and chopped fresh chile, and 2 1/2 tablespoons of chopped parsley.

Pesto Mayonnaise
Into 1 quantity of Homemade Mayonnaise, stir 3 generous teaspoons of Pesto (see p.297).

Garlic and Sun-dried Tomato Mayo
Add 4–5 chopped sun-dried tomatoes to the Garlic Mayonnaise.

Spicy Tomato Mayo
Add 2 1/2 tablespoons of Ballymaloe Country Relish or a good tomato chutney into 1 quantity of Homemade Mayo (see p.297).

Crispy Potato Skins with Dips

SERVES 4 (**P:** 15 mins./**C:** 1¹/₄ HOURS)

8 large floury potatoes
melted butter or extra virgin olive oil, for brushing
salt and freshly ground pepper

Preheat the oven to 400ºF.

Prick the potatoes once or twice. Bake for 45–60 minutes depending upon size. When they are cooked, remove from the oven and turn the oven up to 450ºF.

Slice the potatoes in half lengthwise. Scoop out the flesh, set aside in a bowl, and use later for mashed potato or potato fish cakes.

Cut the skins into 3–4 pieces and arrange in a single layer in a roasting pan. Brush well with melted butter or olive oil and season with salt and pepper. Bake for 10–15 minutes or until crisp and delicious. Serve with a selection of dips.

Dips
Sweet Chile Sauce (see p.296)
sour cream
tuna salad and cucumber
melted cheese and chorizo

Hot Chocolate with Churros for Dunking

SERVES 4   (**P:** 5 mins./**C:** 5 mins.)

3¹/2–4 ounces good-quality dark chocolate
  (about ²/3 cup broken up)
¹/4 cup water
2¹/2 cups whole milk
1–2 teaspoons sugar
4 large teaspoons whipped cream
churros (long Spanish spiral doughnuts) or
  ladyfingers, for dunking

Put the chocolate and water into a heavy saucepan and melt over very low heat. Meanwhile, in a separate saucepan, heat the milk until it just shivers before boiling. When the chocolate has melted, pour the milk into it, whisking all the time; the drink should be smooth and frothy. Taste and add some sugar if needed, and pour into warmed cups. Dunk the churros in the hot chocolate and enjoy!

Hot Chocolate with Marshmallows
Pop a fat marshmallow onto the top of the hot chocolate—luscious!

Chocolate Butterfly Buns

MAKES 24   (**P:** 25 mins./**C:** 20 mins.)

1 cup (2 sticks) butter, cut into cubes and at
  room temperature, plus extra for greasing
10 ounces all-purpose white flour,
  (about 2 cups) plus extra for dusting
1 cup sugar
¹/2 cup unsweetened cocoa powder
4 cage-free, organic eggs
2 teaspoons baking powder
¹/2 teaspoon vanilla extract

1¹/4 cups whipped cream
confectioners' sugar, sprinkles, and/or
  praline for dusting

Dark Chocolate Frosting (see p.196)
2 muffin pans

Preheat the oven to 425ºF. Grease the muffin pans and sprinkle with flour.

Put the butter cubes into a food processor, add the sugar, cocoa powder, flour, eggs, baking powder, and vanilla extract, and whizz for about 30 seconds. Clear the sides down with a spatula and whizz again until the consistency is nice and creamy, about 30 seconds more.

Spoon the mixture into the muffin cups and transfer to the oven. As soon as the buns begin to rise (about 10 minutes), reduce the temperature to 375ºF. Bake for 20 minutes in total. Cool on a wire rack.

Meanwhile make the Frosting.

To assemble, cut the top off each bun, cut the top in half vertically and set aside. Spread a layer of chocolate frosting on the bottom part of the bun. Pipe a ruff of whipped cream across the center and replace the two little top pieces, arranging them like wings. Dredge with confectioners' sugar, and scatter with sprinkles and/or praline.

Top Tip: Bake in a conventional rather than fan-assisted oven if you can—this applies to all cakes and cookies, but meringues benefit from fan-assisted ovens.

Strawberry Gelato in Sugar Cones

SERVES 6–8 (**P:** 20 mins./**C:** 3 HOURS FREEZING)

**This gelato is also yummy served alone on
chilled plates with fresh strawberry sauce.**

1 cup sugar
1¹/4 cups water
2 pounds very ripe strawberries
juice of ¹/2 orange
juice of ¹/2 lemon
3 cups whipped cream

6–8 sugar cones or regular ice cream cones
fresh mint leaves, for garnishing

For the strawberry sauce:
14 ounces strawberries (about 3¹/2–4 cups)
2 ounces confectioners' sugar (about ¹/3–¹/2 cup)
freshly squeezed lemon juice (optional)

In a small saucepan, dissolve the sugar in the water over medium heat and boil for 7–10 minutes. Set aside to cool.

Puree the strawberries in a food processor or blender, then strain the puree into a bowl. When the sugar syrup is cold, mix in the orange and lemon juice. Stir the flavored syrup into the strawberry puree and fold in the whipped cream.

Freeze immediately, preferably in a sorbetière, but if you don't have one, just stir once or twice during the freezing process. Store in the freezer, and transfer to the fridge 15–20 minutes before serving. Scoop the ice cream into balls and fill into the cones.

To make the strawberry sauce, clean and hull the strawberries and transfer to a blender. Add the confectioners' sugar and blend until smooth. Strain into a bowl, taste, and add lemon juice if you like.

Pour the sauce over scoops of strawberry gelato and garnish with some fresh mint leaves.

Mini Sponge Cakes with Raspberry Jam and Cream

MAKES 12   (**P:** 30 mins./**C:** 15 mins.)

A really terrific sponge cake recipe. If you'd rather make a regular-sized cake, divide the batter between two 8-inch round cake pans.

¹/₂ cup (1 stick) butter, softened, plus extra
    for greasing
6 ounces all-purpose white flour
    (about 1¹/₃ cups), plus extra for dusting
³/₄ cup sugar
3 cage-free, organic eggs
1 teaspoon baking powder
4 teaspoons milk

confectioners' sugar, for dusting

For the filling:
¹/₂ cup homemade raspberry jam
1¹/₄ cups whipped cream

2 x 12-cup sloping muffin pans

Preheat the oven to 350°F. Grease and flour the pans well.

In a large bowl, cream the butter and gradually add the sugar, beating until soft, light, and quite pale in color. Add the eggs one at a time, beating well between each addition. (If the butter and sugar are not creamed properly and if you add the eggs too fast, the mixture will curdle, resulting in a cake with a heavier texture.)

Sift the flour and baking powder and stir in gradually. Mix all together lightly and add the milk to moisten.

Divide the mixture evenly between the pans. Bake for 10–15 minutes or until golden and firm to the touch. Turn out onto a wire rack and let cool.

Slice each cupcake in half horizontally and sandwich the halves together, with raspberry jam and cream for the filling. Dust with confectioners' sugar.

Other Good Fillings for Mini Sponge Cakes
Kumquat Compote (see p.267) and cream
Blackberry jam and cream
Green Gooseberry and Elderflower Compote (see p.229)
Mango and passion fruit
Chocolate spread and cream
Lemon curd and cream

Meringue Initials

MAKES 20–30   (**P:** 45 mins./**C:** 2 HOURS)

2 cage-free, organic egg whites
¹/₂ cup sugar
edible food coloring (optional)

For decorating: candy shots, silver dragées,
    cocoa powder, or crystallized violets or rose
    petals
whipped cream, for sandwiching or Chocolate
    Ganache, see p.247 (optional)
sparklers (optional)

pastry bag and small star-shaped decorating
    nozzle ¹/₄-inch

Preheat the oven to 225°F (a fan-assisted oven is good for meringues).

Beat the egg whites until stiff but not yet dry. Fold in half the sugar and beat again until the mixture will stand in a firm, dry peak. Carefully fold in the remaining sugar. Add a few drops of food coloring to create your desired effect. Transfer to a pastry bag.

Line several baking trays with baking paper or foil. Pipe the initials you want onto the paper—do two of each if you would like to sandwich them together with cream. The letters can be sprinkled with candy shots, silver dragées, or cocoa powder, but don't get too carried away. Bake in the oven for 2 hours or until the meringue shapes will lift easily off the paper. Turn off the oven and let cool in the oven.

When the meringues are cold, sandwich them together with cream or Chocolate Ganache (see p.247).

It's fun to spell out children's names or write "happy birthday" or a funny message. A few sparklers here and there on the final assembly add to the impact and excitement. (We sometimes scatter crystallized violets or rose petals over the meringues for a more grown-up version.)

portable food

Food for picnics and barbecues needs to be robust enough to travel well and be easy to serve. Many of these recipes can be cooked on a barbecue or camp fire or else eaten cold. Some of my favorite meals have been eaten outside, so I hope you will pack up a hamper, crank up the barbie, and enjoy these recipes al fresco.

Paillarde of Chicken with Cucumber, Mango, and Spearmint Salsa

SERVES 8   (P: 20 mins./C: 10 mins.)

Butterflying chicken is an excellent way to ensure that it cooks faster and more evenly on a barbecue. This recipe is easy-peasy and so delicious!

8 free-range, organic chicken breasts
1/3 cup extra virgin olive oil
2 1/2 tablespoons chopped rosemary
   or marjoram
salt and freshly ground pepper

For serving:
arugula leaves
Cucumber, Mango, and Spearmint Salsa
   (see below)

First prepare the chicken paillarde. Remove the skin, and inner fillet from each chicken breast if it is still attached, and retain for use in another recipe. Slice the chicken breast horizontally from top to bottom, keeping it attached along one side—you should be able to open it like a book.

Flatten each breast with the palm of your hand to ensure that it is of an even thickness. In a shallow dish, mix the olive oil and chopped rosemary or majoram. Season the chicken with salt and pepper and coat evenly with the rosemary oil. Let it marinate until ready to cook.

Prepare the Cucumber, Mango, and Spearmint Salsa.

Cook the chicken on a barbecue or preheated grill pan for 3–4 minutes each side, turning it to give a crisscross effect. Serve on a bed of arugula leaves with the Salsa.

Other Good Things to Serve with Chicken Paillarde:
1 Sweet Chile Sauce (see p.296)
2 Banana and Cardamom Raita (see p.294)
3 Roast summer vegetables with Tapenade Oil (see p.75)

Cucumber, Mango, and Spearmint Salsa

SERVES 8   (P: 15 mins.)

1 small cucumber, cut into 1/4-inch pieces
salt
1 mango, peeled and cut into 1/4-inch pieces
1/4 cup coarsely chopped spearmint
1/4 cup coarsely chopped cilantro
1/4 cup shelled peanuts, roasted and
   coarsely chopped

For the dressing:
2 tablespoons soft brown sugar
1 tablespoon fish sauce (*nam pla*)
juice of 2 limes
1/2–1 chile, seeded and chopped

Put the chopped cucumber in a strainer over a bowl. Sprinkle with salt and let it release its juice.

To prepare the dressing, mix all the ingredients together.

Put the mango into a bowl, add the herbs, roasted nuts, and the cucumber, and spoon some dressing over it. Toss well and taste. Add more dressing if needed.

Wire-rack Salmon with Dill Butter and Roast Tomatoes

SERVES 10–20   (P: 15 mins./C: 15 mins.)

Fish cooks excellently on the barbecue, provided you put it in a "fish cage" for ease of turning. However, you can do a perfectly good job using two wire cake racks (see p.210).

1–2 sides of fresh wild salmon, unskinned
extra virgin olive oil or melted butter
sea salt (or Kosher salt) and freshly
   ground pepper

For the dill butter:
1/2–1 cup (1–2 sticks) butter
1/3–2/3 cup chopped dill

For the roast tomatoes:
10–20 branches of cherry tomatoes on the vine
extra virgin olive oil, for drizzling

Up to 1 hour before cooking, sprinkle the salmon generously with sea salt. Chill until needed.

Light the grill or barbecue. When ready, lay the salmon fillets, skin-side down, on one of the wire racks. Brush the flesh with oil or melted butter and sprinkle with pepper. Put the other wire rack on top. Lay it on the barbecue, 6–8 inches from the heat, and cook for 10–15 minutes. Turn the entire cage over and cook for another 5–6 minutes or until just cooked through—the time will depend upon the thickness of the fish. Transfer to a serving plate.

Roast Cherry Tomatoes
Drizzle a little olive oil over the tomatoes and season with salt and freshly ground pepper. Cook on the barbecue for 5–6 minutes until they are warm through and just beginning to burst.

Meanwhile, make the dill butter. Melt the butter and stir in the dill. Spoon a little dill butter over the salmon and serve with the Roast Cherry Tomatoes.

Camilla Plum's Spatchcock Chicken with Roasted Fennel and Pickled Lemon

SERVES 6–8   (**P:** 20 mins./**C:** 40 mins.)

1 free-range, organic chicken
salt and freshly ground pepper
chopped rosemary or thyme leaves
extra virgin olive oil, for drizzling
a few garlic cloves
4 fennel bulbs
4 pickled lemons (see p298)
8–24 potatoes, depending upon size
seeds from 4 cardamom pods, crushed
1 teaspoon saffron strands
2½ cups plain yogurt

Preheat the oven to 350ºF or heat the barbecue. Insert a heavy chopping knife into the top of the chicken, from the back end to the neck. Press down sharply to cut through the backbone. Or use poultry shears to cut along the outer length of the backbone as close to the center as possible. Open the bird out as much as possible. Season with salt and freshly ground pepper, sprinkle with rosemary or thyme, and drizzle a bit of olive oil over it.

Transfer to a roasting pan, skin-side upwards, and tuck the whole garlic cloves underneath. Roast in the oven for 40 minutes or until cooked through and golden. Alternatively barbecue about 6 inches away from the coals for about 40 minutes. Let it rest for 5–10 minutes.

Meanwhile cut the fennel bulbs into quarters through the root. Cut the lemons in half. If the potatoes are large, cut into chunks. Arrange all the vegetables on a roasting tray, drizzle with olive oil, and season. Add the cardamom and a good pinch of saffron to the yogurt. Mix well and pour it over the vegetables. Roast under the spatchcock chicken for 30–45 minutes. Serve.

Sticky Chicken Thighs with Soy and Ginger Sauce

SERVES 10   (P: 10 mins. + MARINATING/
                    C: 40 mins.)

10 free-range, organic chicken thighs
salt and freshly ground pepper

For the marinade:
1 cup soy sauce
1/4 cup sunflower oil
1/4 cup honey
1/4 cup rice wine or dry sherry
1 1/2 tablespoons peeled and grated fresh ginger
2 garlic cloves, crushed
1–2 chiles, seeded and finely chopped

For serving:
cucumber and lime wedges
Spicy Green Salad (see p.91)
Sweet Chile Sauce (see p.296)

Mix all the ingredients for the marinade in a bowl. Score the skin of the chicken thighs. Put them into a large dish, cover with the marinade, and turn well to coat. Cover and keep refrigerated for at least 1 hour, or even overnight.

Preheat the oven to 350ºF or heat the barbecue.

Drain the chicken pieces, retaining the marinade for basting. Arrange the chicken, skin-side up, in a roasting pan or on the barbecue. Season with salt and pepper. Roast or barbecue for about 30 minutes, then baste every 10 minutes or so with some of the reserved marinade. Continue to cook until the chicken is cooked through and there is no pink.

Serve with cucumber wedges, lime wedges, some Spicy Green Salad, and a bowl of Sweet Chile Sauce for dipping.

Oriental Marinated Chicken Wings

SERVES 4   (P: 20 mins. + MARINATING/
                   C: 75 mins.)

20 chicken wings (see photograph on p.209)
lime wedges

For the marinade:
2 garlic cloves, crushed
2 teaspoons peeled and grated fresh ginger
4 ounces onions, finely chopped (about 1 cup)
1 red chile, seeded
2 1/2 tablespoons dark soy sauce
2 1/2 tablespoons oyster sauce

For the dipping sauce:
1/2 cup plum sauce
2 1/2 tablespoons Sweet Chile Sauce
  (see p.296)
1 1/2 tablespoons dark soy sauce
1 1/2 tablespoons rice vinegar, or to taste

Divide the chicken wings into 3 joints and retain the 2 joints closest to the body—save the wing tips for a stockpot.

To make the marinade, mix all the ingredients together in a medium bowl. Add the retained chicken wing pieces and toss well. Cover and let marinate in the fridge for at least 1 hour, better still for several hours or overnight.

Preheat the oven to 350°F. To cook in the oven, transfer the chicken pieces to a deep roasting pan, cover with a lid or aluminum foil and cook for 15 minutes, then remove the cover and turn over the chicken pieces. Continue to cook, uncovered, for another 35–45 minutes until fully cooked through, adding a splash of water during cooking if the chicken becomes too dry.

Meanwhile, make the dipping sauce by mixing all the ingredients together.

Serve the sticky chicken wings with the dipping sauce and some wedges of lime, and eat with your fingers—you will need lots of napkins and a finger bowl.

Roast Bananas with Chocolate and Roasted Hazelnuts

SERVES 6   (P: 5 mins./C: 15 mins.)

6 ripe bananas
3–4 ounces good-quality dark chocolate, chopped (about 1/2–2/3 cup)
2 ounces roasted hazelnuts (or walnuts), chopped (about 1/2 cup)

For serving: crème fraîche or whipped cream

Cook the bananas, unpeeled, on the barbecue until black on all sides. Transfer to serving plates. Split the skin on one side and sprinkle some chopped chocolate and roasted nuts over the hot banana flesh. Serve immediately, with a spoonful of crème fraîche or lightly whipped cream. Alternatively cook in the oven preheated to 350°F.

Other Good Things to Serve with Roast Bananas
1 Cinnamon sugar—combine 1/2 cup sugar and 1–2 teaspoons ground cinnamon.
2 A mixture of rum-soaked raisins and chopped walnuts.
3 Toffee sauce and chopped pecans.

a summer barbecue

Barbecues are relaxed occasions where the food is a bit hit or miss, but the sunshine makes up for that. The key to a successful barbie is, like every other kind of entertaining, preparation. The best place to start is with top-quality meat and fish. If you have a gorgeous steak, all you need to go with it is some extra virgin olive oil, sea salt, black pepper, and fresh herbs. A good marinade works wonders on chicken wings and juicy shrimp. You will also need lots of dips and sauces, as well as plenty of fresh bread—the Tear and Share bread (see p.211 and p.34) is perfect for grabbing hunks to wrap around sausages and mop up plates.

Roast corn on the cob and baked potatoes can be cooked in aluminum foil, but put tomatoes on the vine straight onto the grill. A big green salad is also essential as well as a good flow of fresh fruit juice or lemonade. Pimms with lots of fruit and cucumber or a big bowl of punch is a good thing and stash bottles of white wine or champagne in a cool place—under the shade of a tree or in a bucket full of ice.

For dessert, wrap a banana in aluminum foil, bake in its skin, and serve with chunks of chocolate or chopped nuts. It's an old classic but a real crowd pleaser.

The best thing about a barbecue is that normally reluctant cooks will often suddenly take charge of all the cooking, but do give them a break every so often. Or, as they do in Australia, everybody brings something to put on the barbie and cooks it themselves.

alfresco dining

Before your guests arrive, make sure you have room for everybody to sit comfortably—bring out chairs, stools, and deckchairs and beg and borrow outdoor seating from neighbors and guests. Put lots of cushions on brick or stone walls, so people can perch on them and spread out rugs on grass.

Get hold of thick tumblers for both soft drinks and wine—wine glasses are too difficult in the open air. You can buy drink holders on spikes that you push into the ground as well as silly foam beer holders.

For an evening meal, put candles in terracotta flowerpots filled with sand or find some of those big outdoor candles on sticks. Hang jam jars with tea lights from branches or place them on paths to light the way back to the house. Outdoor Christmas lights are enchanting strung on trees, over bushes, or draped around the structure of the house.

A note of warning—be careful where you position the barbecue—don't put it under hanging branches or close to shrubs and avoid smoking out your neighbors—or just invite them to the party, too!

Periwinkles with Homemade Mayonnaise

We love to forage along the seashore. We've got lots of secret places where we gather cockles and mussels and razor claws—just enough for supper, and I always throw one of them back for good karma. Periwinkles are widely available: they nestle under stones and cling to the harbor walls. Not everyone finds the idea of eating wiggly little sea snails appetizing; I love them now, but as a child the thought completely repulsed me. I used to watch in fascination as my Dad devoured them with relish out of a newspaper cornet on holidays in County Clare. Now our grandchildren giggle with delight as they help us to collect periwinkles and miniature shrimp. When we picnic by the beach we light a fire in a small circle of stones so we can cook our little feast. (See photographs on p.221.)

fresh live periwinkles *or* miniature shrimp

For serving:
Homemade Mayonnaise or Garlic Mayonnaise
  (see p.296)
vinegar (optional)
freshly baked brown bread
lemon wedges
wild watercress

To cook the periwinkles, bring plenty of salted water to a boil—you need 2½–5 tablespoons salt to every 2½ quarts water. Add the periwinkles, then cook for 3–4 minutes, strain off the water, and let cool.

When cold, serve with Homemade Mayonnaise or Garlic Mayonnaise. Some people love to dip them in vinegar. Either way you will need to supply a large pin for each person to extract the winkles from the shells.

Miniature shrimp with Homemade Mayo
Miniature shrimp are cooked in much the same way, but need slightly less cooking time. Bring the salted water to a boil. Toss in the shrimp—they will change color from gray to pink almost instantly. Bring the water back to a boil and cook for 2–3 minutes; the shrimp are cooked when there is no trace of black at the back of the head. Drain immediately and spread out on a large serving plate to cool.

Serve with Homemade Mayonnaise and freshly baked brown bread, and perhaps a wedge of lemon and some watercress. Let the picnickers peel their own shrimp! (To peel, first remove the head, pinch the end of the tail and tug it, it will pull off half the shell. Remove the remaining shell with your fingers. Shrimp are much easier on the fingers than Dublin Bay prawns (scampi)!)

Cruditées with Garlic Mayonnaise in Polka-dot Plastic Cups

Cruditées (cut-up vegetables for dipping) with garlic mayonnaise or aioli are among my favorite appetizers. They fulfill all my criteria for a first course: small helpings of very crisp vegetables with a good garlicky homemade mayonnaise. The cruditées can be either very funky or frumpy, depending upon the presentation. Serve them in polka-dotted plastic cups or shot glasses or on simple white plates—it's your call!

Another great plus for this recipe, I've discovered, is that children love cruditées. They even love aioli, provided they don't hear some grown-up saying how much they dislike garlic, and you can feel happy to see your children polishing off plates of raw vegetables for their supper. It's really quick to prepare and full of wonderful vitamins and minerals.

Cruditées are a perfect first course for winter or summer, but for them to be really delicious one must choose very crisp and fresh vegetables. Cut the vegetables into bite-sized bits so they can be picked up easily. You don't need knives and forks because they are usually eaten with fingers. Use as many of the following vegetables as are in season.

ripe tomatoes, quartered, or whole with the calyx on if they are freshly picked
broccoli, broken (not cut) into florets
calabrese (green sprouting broccoli), broken into florets
cauliflower, broken into florets
green beans or snow peas
baby carrots, or larger carrots cut into sticks about 2 inches long
cucumber, cut into sticks about 2 inches long
tiny scallions, trimmed
red cabbage, cut into strips
tender celery, cut into sticks about 2 inches long
Belgian endive leaves
red, green, or yellow peppers, seeded and cut into sticks about 2 inches long
very fresh Brussels sprouts, cut in half or quartered
whole radishes, with green tops left on
fennel bulbs, cut into wedges
young asparagus
sugar peas, sugar snaps, or fresh peas in the pod
parsley, finely chopped
thyme, finely chopped
chives, finely chopped
sprigs of watercress

For serving:
Garlic Mayonnaise (see p.297)

Other Good Things to Serve with Cruditées
1 Tapenade (see p.75)
2 Dukkah (see p.75)
3 Hummus bi tahini (see p.118)

A typical plate of cruditées might include the following: 4 sticks of carrot, 2–3 sticks of red and green pepper, 2–3 sticks of celery, 2–3 sticks of cucumber, 1 whole radish with a little green leaf left on, 1 tiny tomato or 2 quarters, 1 Brussels sprout, cut in quarters, and a little pile of chopped fresh herbs.

Wash and prepare the vegetables. Arrange them on individual white side plates with contrasting colors next to each other, with a little bowl of Garlic Mayonnaise in the center. Alternatively, do a large dish or basket for the center of the table. Arrange little heaps of each vegetable in contrasting colors. Put a bowl of Garlic Mayonnaise in the center and then guests can help themselves.

Instead of serving the Garlic Mayonnaise in a bowl, you could make an edible container by cutting a slice off the top of a tomato and hollowing out the seeds. Alternatively, cut a 1 1/2-inch-long piece of cucumber and hollow out the center with a melon baller or a teaspoon. Then fill or pipe the mayonnaise into the tomato or cucumber and place in the center of the plate of cruditées.

Ballymaloe Irish Stew in a Haybox

SERVES 4–6   (**P:** 45 mins./**C:** UP TO 2 HOURS)

Irish stew is an excellent one-pot meal, a wonderfully comforting traditional dish, and great for entertaining. It's best made in early summer when the lamb is still young and sweet and the new-season onions and carrots are small and tender.

3 pounds lamb chops or leg chops,
  not less than an inch thick
6 medium onions or 12 baby onions
6 medium carrots or 12 baby carrots
salt and freshly ground pepper
4 cups lamb stock, chicken broth,
  (see p.295) or water
8–12 potatoes, or more if you like
sprig of thyme
1 tablespoon roux (optional; see p.139)
2¹/₂ tablespoons chopped parsley
1¹/₂ tablespoons chopped chives

If you intend to cook the stew in the oven, preheat the oven to 350°F.

Cut the chops into 2-ounce pieces and trim off some of the excess fat. Set aside. Render down the fat over low heat in a heavy pan (discard the rendered-down pieces).

Meanwhile, peel the onions and, if they are large, cut them into chunks; if they are small, they are best left whole; and if young, leave some of the green stalks on. Scrape or thinly peel the carrots and, if they are large, cut them into large chunks; if young, leave them whole and leave some of the green stalks on.

Toss the meat in the hot fat until it is slightly brown and then transfer the meat to an ovenproof and flameproof stewpot and season with salt and pepper. Briefly toss the onions and carrots in the fat in the first pan. Add them to the stewpot and season again. Deglaze the first pan with a little lamb or chicken broth, pour into the stewpot, along with the rest of the broth.

Peel the potatoes and lay them whole on top of the meat and vegetables, so they will steam while the stew cooks. Season the potatoes. Add a sprig of thyme and bring the stew to a boil on top of the stove. Cover and transfer to the oven, and cook for 1–2 hours depending upon whether the stew is being made with tender lamb or tougher mutton; alternatively, simmer for the same amount of time on top of the stove.

When the stew is cooked, pour off the cooking liquid, degrease it, and reheat it in another saucepan. If you like, thicken it slightly with a little roux. Taste and adjust the seasoning if needed, then add chopped parsley and chives and pour the liquid back over the stew. Bring it back up to boiling point and serve directly from the pot or in a large pottery dish.

Irish Stew with Pearl Barley
Add 2¹/₂ tablespoons barley to the stew along with the vegetables. Increase the liquid to 5 cups, as the barley absorbs a considerable amount of liquid.

The Essential Picnic Haybox
No home should be without a haybox. It's a brilliant invention that certainly dates back to wartime and possibly long before. The idea is to make an insulated box that can be transported in the back of the car to your picnic spot. Stew is the poshest nosh for an autumn or winter race meeting, football match, or chilly boat ride. I always get a wonderful response when I whip off the lid and produce a piping-hot stew hours after it was made!

Start with a wooden box with a separate lid. If you're handy, a couple of posh wine boxes can be adapted to make a haybox. Don't forget to add rope handles. Layer the bottom and sides with soft hay to a thickness of at least 2¹/₂–3 inches. When the casserole dish or earthenware pot of bubbling stew is ready, tuck it into the haybox, tightly pack more hay in around the sides, and cover with another thick layer of hay and then the wooden lid.

The haybox was initially invented to save fuel in wartime, as the food continues to cook by retained heat. My husband's family have very warm memories of a haybox, because his mother Myrtle used it to transport a delicious stew when they were at boarding school. How cool an idea is that?

Chest of Sandwiches with a Selection of Fillings Surrounded by Watercress

SERVES 8 (MAKES 24 SANDWICHES)

I was totally enchanted when my mother-in-law Myrtle Allen taught me how to make this chest of sandwiches soon after I arrived in Ballymaloe. It has been a delightful tradition in the family for several generations.

2-pound loaf of bread or round country loaf
1/4 cup (1/2 stick) butter, at room temperature
salt and freshly ground pepper

Sandwich fillings might include:
scrambled egg and chives
Gravadlax with Sweet Mustard and Dill Mayo
   (see p.140)
Roasted Peppers (see p.298), mozzarella,
   and Pesto (see p.297)
mature cheddar cheese with Ballymaloe
   Country Relish or mango chutney and
   Cucumber Pickle Relish (see p.73)
roast chicken with Roasted Red Pepper
   Mayonnaise (see p.297) and sunflower
   sprouts
tomato, buffalo mozzarella, Tapenade
   (see p.75), and basil leaves

For garnishing:
salad greens
watercress
flat-leaf parsley
cherry tomatoes
scallions

The "chest" that the sandwiches will go in is actually the loaf of bread itself, after you've carefully removed its insides, leaving an empty crust "chest" to fill with sandwiches, which you'll make from the block of bread you've removed from the "chest." You will need a long, sharp knife with a pointed tip. Insert the knife horizontally on the side of the loaf just over the bottom crust, and as close as you can get to one end of the loaf without cutting through that end. Push it through until it reaches, but does not go through, the crust on the opposite side. Without enlarging the cut through which the knife was inserted, work the knife in a fan shape as far forward as possible, then pull it out. Do the same from the opposite corner on the other side of the loaf. You should now be able to cut the bread away from the bottom crust inside without a noticeable mark on the exterior of the loaf.

Next cut through the top of the loaf to make a lid, carefully leaving one long side uncut, as a hinge.

Finally, with the lid open, cut the bread away from the sides. Ease it out carefully: it should turn out in a solid brick or a round piece, leaving an empty shell behind.

Cut the crustless bread into slices—long horizontal ones, square vertical ones, or round ones, depending upon the shape of the loaf. Carefully stack them, butter them, and fill them with your chosen filling or fillings in the order in which they were cut. Don't forget to season each sandwich with salt and pepper.

Press the sandwiches together firmly and cut into strips (I usually cut each into 6). Fill them back into the empty crust, still in order.

For a picnic, close the top of the "chest"—it will gape slightly because of the extra bulk of delicious filling. Cover with plastic wrap—the sandwiches will stay very fresh.

For a party, leave the lid slightly open. Decorate inside and out with lettuce and watercress leaves, small ripe cherry tomatoes, scallions, and so on, so that the loaf looks like a little hamper overflowing with fruit and vegetables.

Cherry Tomatoes on the Branch, and Tiny Scallions and Radishes

very ripe cherry tomatoes on the branch
tiny scallions, roots trimmed
lots of radishes, roots trimmed
unsalted butter
sea salt (or Kosher salt)

Fill 1–3 separate little baskets with cherry tomatoes, scallions, and radishes. Picnickers can pick and nibble as they choose. We love to eat radishes as the French do, with unsalted butter and sea salt.

Rum and Raisin Cake

(P: 35 mins./C: 60 mins.)

A favorite picnic cake (see opposite).

6 ounces raisins (about 1¼ cups)
½ cup Jamaica rum
1¼ cups (2½ sticks) butter, softened
¾ cup light brown sugar
4 cage-free, organic eggs
¼ cup milk
1½ teaspoons vanilla extract
10 ounces all-purpose white flour
   (about 2 cups)
4 teaspoons baking powder
2 ounces shelled walnuts, hazelnuts, or
   pecans, chopped (about ½ cup)
2 tablespoons dark brown sugar

9-inch round springform cake pan,
   buttered and floured

Soak the raisins in the rum for 30 minutes. Drain and reserve the rum, and set aside the raisins.

Preheat the oven to 350°F.

Cream the butter, add the sugar, and beat until light and fluffy. Separate the eggs and set the whites aside. Add the egg yolks, one at a time, to the creamed butter, beating well between each addition. Mix in the retained rum, the milk, and the vanilla extract.

Mix together the flour and baking powder and fold in, a little at a time, to the butter mixture.

In a clean bowl, beat the egg whites until stiff and fluffy. Working in batches of a third of the beaten egg whites at a time, fold into the cake batter; with the final third, add the raisins and chopped nuts.

Pour into the prepared pan, sprinkle with the dark brown sugar, and bake for 45–60 minutes, until the top is golden and the center set and firm. Let the cake cool a little in the pan. Then unhinge the sides and let the cake cool, still on its removable bottom, on a wire rack.

Gâteau Pithivier with Gruyère and Ham

SERVES 8   (P: 30 mins./C: 50 mins.)

So yummy for a picnic (see photograph on p.222), but also delicious for a summer lunch at home with a salad of organic greens.

1 pound puff pastry sheets

For the filling:
12 ounces cooked ham, thinly sliced
   (about 3 cups)
12 ounces Gruyère or Emmental cheese,
   very thinly sliced (about 3 cups)
¼ cup Dijon mustard
egg wash, for glazing

Preheat the oven to 450°F.

Divide the pastry dough in half and roll out each half to just under ¼-inch thick. Cut each into a circle about 10 inches in diameter. Sprinkle some water over a baking tray and put one of the pastry circles on it; put the other on a plate and chill both.

To assemble, alternate layers of the ham and cheese until you have 5 layers each. Lay some ham on the pastry in the baking sheet, top with a layer of cheese, and repeat until all are used. Dab the layers with a little Dijon mustard every now and then. Slightly dome the stack in the center, leaving a rim of about an inch free around the pastry edge.

Brush the rim with egg wash or water. Place the other circle of puff pastry dough over the top and press it down well around the edges. Flute the edges with a knife. Make a small hole in the center, brush the top with egg wash, and leave it for 5 minutes in the fridge.

With the back of a knife, nick the edge of the pastry 12 times at regular intervals to form a scalloped edge with a rose-petal effect. Mark long, curving lines from the central hole outwards to designate formal petals. Ensure you do not cut through the pastry—just score it.

Bake for 20 minutes, then reduce the oven temperature to 400°F and bake for another 30 minutes. This is best eaten warm, but it also reheats remarkably well.

Hard-boiled Eggs and Dips

Hard-boiled eggs (or semi hard-boiled eggs) with dips are a must-have for a picnic. Easy, munchable food—no fuss and very addictive!

10–12 cage-free, organic eggs
dips of your choice

Bring a pan of water to a boil. Gently slide in the eggs, bring the water back to a boil and simmer for 10–12 minutes.

Choose 3–5 dips: Tomato and Red Onion Salsa (see p.294), Spicy Mayonnaise (see below), Tarragon Mayonnaise (see below), Tapenade (see p.75), Anchovy and Flat-leaf Parsley Mayonnaise (see below), Dukkah (see p.75).

Sausages with Dips

1 pound best-quality pork sausages

Cook the sausages in the usual way and serve with 1 or more of the following dips.

Barbecue Sauce

MAKES ABOUT 1 CUP

This is yummy as a dip or sauce and can also be used to marinate the sausages, or pork, lamb, or chicken.

$1/3$ cup extra virgin olive oil
2 garlic cloves, crushed
4 ounces onions, finely chopped (about 1 cup)
1 x $14^1/2$-ounce can tomatoes, chopped
salt and freshly ground pepper
$2/3$ cup tomato puree (see p.294)
$1/2$ cup red or white wine vinegar
$1/3$ cup honey
$1/3$ cup Worcestershire sauce
$2^1/2$ tablespoons Dijon mustard

Heat the oil in a frying pan, add the garlic and onions, and cook over low heat for 4–5 minutes. Add the tomatoes and their juice and cook for another 4–5 minutes. Season with salt and freshly ground pepper. Puree in a blender or food processor. Return to the heat, mix in the remaining ingredients, and bring to a boil, then simmer for 4–5 minutes.

Anchovy and Flat-leaf Parsley Mayonnaise

To $1^1/4$ cups Homemade Mayonnaise, (see p.296), add 6 mashed canned anchovies and $2^1/2$ tablespoons chopped flat-leaf parsley.

Honey Grainy Mustard and Rosemary Dip

$1/3$ cup honey
$1/3$ cup grainy mustard
1–2 teaspoons finely chopped rosemary

Mix all the ingredients together and put into a deep bowl ready for dipping.

Sweet Chile Sauce Mixed with Lime Juice

$1/3$ cup Sweet Chile Sauce (see p.296)
$1/4$–$1/3$ cup freshly squeezed lime juice

Mix together, to taste (see photograph on p.223).

Tuna Salad

1 can of tuna
2 canned anchovies, crushed
$2^1/2$ tablespoons chopped parsley
$1^1/4$ cups Homemade Mayonnaise,
  (see p.296)

Mix all the ingredients together, to taste.

Tarragon Mayonnaise

To $1^1/4$ cups Homemade Mayonnaise (see p.296), add $2^1/2$ tablespoons chopped fresh tarragon.

Thai Green or Red Curry Mayonnaise

4 teaspoons Thai green or red curry paste
$1/3$ cup coconut milk
$1^1/4$ cups Homemade Mayonnaise,
  (see p.296)
$2^1/2$ tablespoons chopped cilantro leaves
1–2 tablespoons apricot jam (optional)

Cook the curry paste in a wok or heavy frying pan for 3–4 minutes. Add the coconut milk and let it bubble for a minute or two, then remove from the heat and let cool. Mix together with some mayonnaise and the chopped cilantro A bit of apricot jam is a delicious addition.

tips on portable food

Portable food is all about the packaging. Collect lots of plastic containers with lids—old take-out boxes, for example, and big yogurt cartons. A picnic hamper will help—many now come with straps and small compartments to hold cutlery and glasses, but you can improvise using an old small suitcase. If your destination is some hours away, don't take anything that will melt or lose its shape easily.

For barbecues, do try to marinate meat and make lots of dips and sauces. Set the barbecue up as near to the kitchen as possible, or keep a clear path. Be realistic: if you have a small kettle barbecue, don't try to cook a whole chicken or rack of ribs—stick to breasts and fillets. Fish will cook easily and quickly. Half-cook baked potatoes in the oven first, then transfer them to the barbecue, otherwise you will be waiting for hours. Remember not to leave uncooked meat in the open for too long and keep a bucket of water nearby, just in case.

Best barbecued (see pp.208–211)
Pasta, Bocconcini, and Tomato Salad (see p.89)
Dukkah (see p.75) with Fougasse (see p.38)
Tear and Share Bread (see p.34)
Edamame with Sea Salt (see p.62)
Dill Mayo (see p.297)
Cherry Tomatoes on the Branch (see p.217)
Wire-rack Salmon with Dill Butter (see p.204)
Oriental Marinated Chicken Wings (see p.207)
Marinated Olives (see p.62)
Roast Bananas (see p.207)

To drink
The ideal wine here is one that will work with all the elements in the meal. While there are plenty of white wines, such as Viognier or New World Marsanne or Rousanne, which will work well, most people seem to prefer a red. The salmon will need a pinot noir or, perhaps, a Chinon, Bourgeuil, or Saumur from the Loire, all of which will work well with the chicken, too. An unusual but effective choice might be a straight red Bordeaux or Bordeaux Supérieur. If you want a wine for the bananas, consider a late harvest sauvignon blanc from Chile or Torcolato from Italy.

An old-fashioned picnic (see pp.220–223)
Frittata with Oven-Roasted Tomatoes, Chorizo, and Goat Cheese (see p.117)
Periwinkles with Homemade Mayonnaise (see p.212)
Sausages with Dips (see p.218)
Gâteau Pithivier with Gruyère and Ham (see p.217)
Marinated Olives (see p.62)
White Soda Bread (see p.36)
Rum and Raisin Cake (see p.217)
Homemade Lemonade (see p.288).

To drink
Pink wines really come into their own in the open air and for picnics they have the added bonus of going with virtually every savory dish you care to mention. A good rosé—emphatically not Rosé d'Anjou or blush zinfandel, which are too flabby and sweet—has a lovely color, a crisp backbone of acidity, and a bone-dry finish. It may come from virtually anywhere in the wine world, but most often from the south of France or from Spain. You may want a red to accompany the sausages and the Pithivier, in which case a fruity Côtes du Rhone will do nicely. And for the rum and raisin cake you might like to chill a bottle of tawny port in a nearby stream.

Party picnic
Buttermilk Bread (see p.36)
Bloody Mary Jellos (see p.66)
Temari Sushi (see p.45)
Alicia's No-Cook Chorizo (see p.56)
Middle Eastern Mezze (see pp.118–119)
Sticky Chicken Thighs (see p.207)
Belgian Chocolate Biscuit Cake (see p.248)

To drink
As this is a party, kick off with some sparkling wine or even champagne if it's a very special occasion. This will serve as an aperitif and take you through to the sushi. The mezze and sticky chicken thighs won't object to decent fizz, but a chunky red wine will be better. Think in terms of ripe fruit: Malbec from Argentina, Grenache from Australia, or Tempranillo from Spain. Or be really adventurous with an Agiorghitiko from Greece.

picnic on the beach

Before you set out, make sure you have packed the food carefully. Everything needs to be well secured for the journey, so the simplest thing is to transport food in the dishes they were cooked, for example, make individual frittata in muffin cups, keep the cake in its cake pan and wrap it in a collar of waxed paper to protect it. The next priority is to keep food cool. Carry salad greens in a bucket of water to keep them fresh. If you freeze a couple of bottles of water or juice (don't fill the bottles completely or else they will explode when they freeze), not only will you have cold drinks on the picnic, but they will also keep neighboring food cool on the journey.

Don't forget plates, cutlery, napkins, and a corkscrew as well as condiments—salt, pepper, oil and vinegar—plus plenty of paper napkins and a big garbage bag to take the remnants home with you.

out in the open

Pies, especially the gâteau pithivier (see center photograph and p.217) are robust enough to survive a journey. Fat, juicy sandwiches and hard-boiled eggs are a picnic staple and cold sticky chicken wings are also a winner.

Part of the pleasure of eating outside is campfire cooking, so rather than bring everything fully prepared, see if you can build a small fire in a circle of stones to cook sausages or toast bread or marshmallows.

Choose a wine that does not need to be chilled. Rosé is great for the outdoors, but I have to say that there is nothing quite like champagne, drunk under the skies in plastic cups.

Freezable wine sleeves are handy to have as are padded coolbags. You will also need a good rug or two—plastic-backed to protect against damp ground—plus cushions to sit on, if you have room in the car. Director's chairs are cheap and fold up easily.

Simple food, a view to die for, and a friendly dog to eat up the leftovers, what could be better?

foraging

I love foraging and I particularly love to combine foraging with entertaining. How wild and free it feels to organize a blackberry or cockle-picking expedition or a mushroom hunt and then head back to the kitchen to cook the spoils. And how much will you enjoy the meal knowing that you have searched for and picked the ingredients!

Wild Mushroom Soup

SERVES 8–9   (**P:** 15 mins./**C:** 20 mins.)

Some years not a single mushroom pops up in the fields; other years they are so abundant that we are frantically making sauces, soups, and so on to use them up. In fact, the soup base of this recipe, without the broth, is a perfect way to preserve field mushrooms for another time. If wild mushrooms are unavailable, wide-capped mushrooms also make a delicious soup.

4 ounces onions (about 1 cup chopped)
2 tablespoons butter
2$^1/_2$ cups Homemade Chicken Broth
  (see p.295)
1 pound wild mushrooms, such as *Agaricus campestris*
3 tablespoons white flour
salt and freshly ground pepper
2$^1/_2$ cups milk
cream (optional)
sprig of flat-leaf parsley, for garnishing

Chop the onions finely. Melt the butter in a pot over low heat. Toss the onions in it, cover, and let them sweat until soft and completely cooked, about 7–10 minutes.

Meanwhile, heat the chicken broth to boiling point. Chop the mushrooms very finely, add to the onions, and cook over a high heat for 3–4 minutes. Stir in the flour, reduce the heat to low, and cook for 2–3 minutes. Season with salt and pepper, then gradually add the hot broth and the milk, stirring all the time. Increase the heat and bring to a boil. Taste, adjust the seasoning if needed, and add a dash of cream if you like. Serve right away or reheat later.

Top Tip: If you don't feel like chopping the mushrooms finely, just slice them. When the soup is cooked, whizz in a blender for a few seconds.

Spring Nettle Soup

SERVES 6   (**P:** 15 mins./**C:** 20 mins.)

This is now a "cool" soup for spring dinner parties. Nettles grow in profusion throughout the Irish countryside—go foraging in spring when they are young and tender. You'll need gloves when you are gathering them so as not to sting yourself! Nettles are high in iron and other minerals and trace elements. Traditionally, Irish people ate a feed of nettles during the month of May to clear the blood after winter, and to keep away "the rheumatics" for the coming year.

3 tablespoons butter
10 ounces potatoes, chopped
  (about 1$^3/_4$ cups)
4 ounces onions, chopped (about 1 cup)
4 ounces leeks, chopped (about 1–1$^1/_4$ cups)
salt and freshly ground pepper
4 cups Homemade Chicken Broth
  (see p.295)
5 ounces young nettle leaves
  (about 3$^1/_2$–4 cups), chopped
$^2/_3$ cup cream or creamy milk,
  plus extra, for serving

Melt the butter in a heavy pot. When it foams add the potatoes, onions, and leeks, and toss them until well coated. Sprinkle with salt and freshly ground pepper. Cover with a paper lid (to keep in the steam) and the saucepan lid, and sweat over low heat for 10 minutes or until the vegetables are soft but not colored.

Discard the paper lid, add the broth, bring to a boil, and boil until the vegetables are just cooked, about 10 minutes. Add the chopped nettles. Simmer, uncovered, for just a few minutes. Do not overcook or the vegetables will lose their flavor.

Add the cream or creamy milk and blend. Taste and adjust the seasoning if needed. Serve hot, with a swirl of cream on top.

Roast Rabbit with Potatoes, Onions, and Thyme Leaves

SERVES 8   (**P:** 30 mins./**C:** 1 HOUR)

Preheat the oven to 400°F.

Bring the roasting pan to the table and serve this dish family-style. Chicken is also delicious cooked in this rustic way.

2 rabbits
8–16 potatoes, depending upon size
8–16 shallots or baby onions
salt and freshly ground pepper
dry white wine, for drizzling
extra virgin olive oil, for drizzling
4 teaspoons thyme leaves
green salad, for serving

Cut up the rabbits into 6 or 8 pieces each. Peel the potatoes if necessary (new potatoes may not need it) and cut into halves or quarters depending upon size—they should be large chunks. Peel the onions, carefully trimming the root end so they keep intact during cooking; if the onions are large, cut in quarters through the root.

Transfer the rabbit, potatoes, and onions to 1–2 roasting pans. Season well with salt and pepper. Drizzle generously with white wine and olive oil. Sprinkle with the thyme leaves and toss well.

Roast for 45–60 minutes or until the rabbit is cooked and everything looks golden and slightly crispy at the edges. Serve with a good green salad.

A Salad of Rabbit (or Chicken) Livers with Apples, Hazelnuts, and Wild Garlic Flowers

SERVES 4   (**P:** 15 mins./**C:** 5 mins.)

First make the hazelnut oil dressing by whisking all the ingredients together.

1 sweet crisp dessert apple, such as russet
2¹/₂ tablespoons chopped hazelnuts
1 teaspoon butter
1¹/₂ tablespoons extra virgin olive oil
4 rabbit or chicken livers
a selection of salad greens, such as
  butterhead and oak leaf lettuce, curly chicory,
  wild sorrel, radicchio, arugula, salad burnet,
  and golden marjoram
wild garlic flowers or chive flowers,
  for garnishing

For the hazelnut oil dressing:
¹/₂ cup hazelnut oil
2¹/₂ tablespoons white wine vinegar
¹/₂ teaspoon Dijon mustard
salt, freshly ground pepper, and sugar, to taste

Cut the apple into thin julienne strips. Transfer to a bowl and mix with the hazelnuts and 1 tablespoon of the hazelnut oil dressing.

Heat the butter with the oil in a frying pan and cook the livers gently until just cooked (about 2–3 minutes, a little more if you prefer no trace of pink).

Meanwhile, toss the salad greens in enough dressing to make them just glisten, and divide between the serving plates.

Place a quarter of the apple and nuts on each salad, and then set the warm livers on top. Sprinkle with wild garlic flowers or chive flowers and serve immediately.

Pasta with Chanterelles, Tapenade, and Flat-leaf Parsley

SERVES 4–6   (**P:** 10 mins./**C:** 20 mins.)

4 quarts water
2 tablespoons salt
8 ounces penne, shells, or bow-tie pasta
8–16 ounces chanterelle mushrooms,
  or a mix of different types of wild mushrooms
2 tablespoons butter
salt and freshly ground pepper
¹/₂ cup heavy cream
3–4 tablespoons Tapenade (see p.75)
¹/₃ cup chopped flat-leaf parsley

Bring the water to a fast rolling boil in a large pot, then add the salt and the pasta. Stir and cook until *al dente*, or just cooked but still slightly firm, about 10 minutes.

Meanwhile, gently wash the mushrooms under cold running water. Trim the stalks and discard. Slice the mushrooms thickly.

Melt the butter in a large frying pan over a high heat. When it foams add the mushrooms and season with salt and pepper. Cook over a high heat—the juice will exude at first, but continue to cook until the mushrooms reabsorb it. Add the cream and let it bubble for a few minutes. Stir in the Tapenade and remove from the heat.

Drain the pasta well, then put it back into the pot and add the sauce. Sprinkle the parsley over it and toss gently. Turn into a hot bowl and serve immediately.

Elderflower Fritters with Gooseberry and Elderflower Compote

SERVES 8   (P: 20 mins./C: 5 mins.)

Elderflowers are in full bloom in hedgerows all over the Irish countryside in late May and June. Make cordials, elderflower champagne, syrups, compote, and fritters, and partner with gooseberries to impart a divine muscat flavor. Elderflower vinegar is also delicious.

4 ounces white flour (about 3/4–1 cup)
pinch of salt
1 cage-free, organic egg
2/3 cup lukewarm water
extra virgin olive oil or sunflower oil
8–16 elderflower heads
superfine sugar, for coating
Green Gooseberry and Elderflower Compote
  (see recipe below), for serving

Sift the flour and salt into a bowl. Make a well in the center and drop in the egg. Using a whisk, gradually bring in the flour from the edges, adding the water at the same time.

Heat the oil in a deep-fryer to 350°F. Hold the flowers by the stalks and dip into the batter. Fry until golden brown, about 1 minute. Drain the fritters on paper towels, toss in superfine sugar, and serve immediately, with Green Gooseberry and Elderflower Compote.

Green Gooseberry and Elderflower Compote

SERVES 6–8   (P: 10 mins./C: 15 mins.)

2 pounds green gooseberries
2–3 elderflower heads, plus extra
  for decorating
2 1/3 cups sugar
2 1/2 cups cold water

Top and tail the gooseberries.

Tie the elderflower heads in a little square of cheesecloth, put them in a stainless steel or enameled saucepan, add the sugar, and cover with the water. Bring to a boil over medium heat and continue to boil for 2 minutes. Add the gooseberries and simmer until the fruit begins to burst, about 5–6 minutes.

Let it cool. Serve in a pretty bowl and decorate with fresh elderflowers. This compote is also delicious with Yogurt and Cardamom Cream (see p.266), Carrigeen Moss Pudding (see p.232), or vanilla ice cream.

Compote of Blackberries and Apples with Sweet Geranium Leaves

SERVES 6   (P: 20 mins./C: 10 mins.)

A delicious autumn dessert.

1 cup sugar
2 cups water
8 large sweet geranium leaves
  (*Pelargonium graveolens*)
4 large dessert apples
10 ounces blackberries (about 2 cups)
shortbread cookies, for serving

Put the sugar in a saucepan and add the water and sweet geranium leaves. Bring to a boil, stirring occasionally to dissolve the sugar, and boil for 1–2 minutes.

Peel the apples thinly, keeping a good round shape. Cut them into quarters, remove the core, and trim the ends. Cut into segments 1/4-inch thick. Add to the syrup, bring to a boil, reduce the heat to low, and cover with a paper lid and then the saucepan lid. Poach until translucent but not broken, about 8–10 minutes. About 3–5 minutes before they have finished cooking, add the blackberries and simmer together so that they are both cooked at the same time. Let cool, then chill in the fridge. Serve chilled, with little shortbread cookies.

Compote of Cranberries and Apples
Substitute 6 ounces (about 1 1/2–2 cups) fresh cranberries for the blackberries in the above recipe.

Yogurt with Honey and Toasted Wild Hazelnuts

Delicious for either dessert or breakfast

best-quality thick, whole-milk yogurt
strongly flavored local honey
toasted wild hazelnuts, sliced

Serve a portion of chilled plain yogurt per person. Just before serving, drizzle generously with really good honey and sprinkle with toasted hazelnuts.

Yogurt with dates, bananas, and honey
Add some chopped dates and sliced banana to the yogurt and drizzle with honey.

Brown Trout with Marsh Samphire

SERVES 4   (**P:** 20 mins./**C:** 15 mins.)

A fat brown trout is a rare treat nowadays; if you cannot get hold of any, rainbow trout is available at virtually every fish market. Marsh samphire or sea asparagus grows in the salt marshes along the coast of the British Isles. It is in season from July to August and is so easy to cook and delicious as a vegetable and garnish. This combination is surprisingly delicious and very quick to make.

4 fresh trout, preferably brown
seasoned flour, for coating
butter
salt and freshly ground pepper
8–10 ounces marsh samphire
chopped parsley, for garnishing
lemon wedges, for serving

For the parsley butter:
¼ cup (½ stick) butter
2–4 teaspoons finely chopped parsley
few drops of lemon juice

First make the parsley butter. Cream the butter, and stir in the parsley and a few drops of lemon juice. Roll into butter pats or form into a roll and wrap in waxed paper or aluminum foil, twisting each end to seal. Refrigerate to harden.

Gut the trout and fillet it carefully, then wash and dry well. Put some seasoned flour in a shallow dish and coat the fillets. Shake off the excess flour and then spread a little butter on the flesh side, as if you were buttering a slice of bread rather stingily. Season with salt and freshly ground pepper.

Wash the marsh samphire well. Bring a large pot of unsalted water to a boil, add the marsh samphire, and return to a boil for 3–4 minutes. Drain and toss it in a little butter. Keep warm.

Heat a grill pan over a medium-high heat. When it is quite hot but not smoking, lay the fish fillets, buttered side down; the fish should sizzle as soon as they touch the pan. Reduce the heat slightly and cook for 3–4 minutes on the buttered side, then turn them over and continue to cook until crisp and golden, about 2–3 minutes. Serve immediately on hot plates with the marsh samphire, wedges of lemon, and some parsley butter melting over the top, and sprinkle with chopped parsley.

Insalata di Campo

A salad of wild leaves and flowers from the woods and hedgerows is always a delight. It might include any of the leaves and flowers suggested below.

For the leaves:
watercress
dandelion leaves
wood and field sorrel
salad burnet
red and green orach
chickweed
wild garlic leaves
lamb's tongue sorrel
wild thyme
bishop weed
samphire
daisy zucchini

For the flowers:
primroses
violets
wild garlic flowers
borage, blue and white

dressing of your choice (see pp.94–95)

Wash and carefully dry the leaves. Choose a dressing, such as Honey and Whole-grain Mustard, and toss the leaves in just enough of it to make them glisten. Scatter the flowers over the top and enjoy!

Carrigeen Moss Pudding

SERVES 6   (P: 20 mins./C: 2 HOURS)

We find that visitors to Ireland are fascinated by the idea of a dessert made with seaweed, and carrigeen moss just bursts with goodness. But if too much carrigeen is used in this dish it will be stiff and really unpalatable. This recipe is from my mum-in-law, Myrtle Allen. It's the best and most delicious recipe I know for carrigeen.

Fred Dawes taught me how to forage for and harvest carrigeen moss. The word "carrigeen" means "little rock" in Gaelic, and Fred picks it off the rocks in the small cove of Ballyandreen in East Cork, after the spring tides. He then spreads it out on the grass on the cliffs, where it is washed by the rain and bleached by the sun. He turns it over every few days, and when it's ready he stores it in a paper or plastic bag in a dry cupboard. Carrigeen keeps almost indefinitely and is one of the most valuable of all our wild foods; it's loaded with vitamins, minerals, and trace elements, particularly iodine. Another "cool food" with a story—it helps our metabolism to work to its optimum and so breaks down fats while giving us lots of strength and energy.

semi-closed fistful of cleaned, well-dried
  carrigeen moss (about 1/4 ounce)
4 cups whole milk
1 vanilla bean or 1/2 teaspoon vanilla extract
1 cage-free, organic egg
1 tablespoon sugar

For the accompaniments:
compote of fruit in season (see p.29 or p.229),
  or soft brown sugar and lightly
  whipped cream

Soak the carrigeen in a little bowl of tepid water for 10 minutes. It will swell and increase in size.

Strain off the water and put the carrigeen into a saucepan. Add the milk and vanilla bean (if using; if using vanilla extract, do not add it now). Bring to a boil, then reduce the heat and simmer very gently, covered, for 20 minutes.

At this point and not before, separate the egg and put the yolk into a bowl. Add the sugar and vanilla extract (if using) and whisk together for a few seconds.

Pour the hot milk and carrigeen moss through a fine mesh strainer onto the egg-yolk mixture, whisking all the time. The carrigeen will now be swollen and exuding jelly. Rub all this jelly through the strainer and beat it into the milky egg mixture. Test for a set on a chilled plate as you would with jam—a drop should set to a wobbly consistency within minutes. If it is too stiff, add a little more milk; if too runny, dip the strainer into the infused milk and push the carrigeen through again.

Beat the egg white stiffly. Fold it gently into the carrigeen mixture. It will rise to make a fluffy top. Let it cool completely, then chill.

Serve chilled with a fruit compote, such as poached rhubarb or Green Gooseberry and Elderflower (see p.229), or with soft brown sugar and whipped cream.

Wild Damson Jam

MAKES ABOUT 9–10 POUNDS
                    (P: 10 mins./C: 30 mins.)

Damsons, bullaces, or wild plums grow wild in many parts of Ireland, ripening towards the end of September. We love collecting them, and eat lots freshly picked; the surplus we make into damson pies, compotes, and jam. The fruit also makes a delicious sauce to accompany roast pork with crackling, and freezes perfectly. The new cultivated varieties of damson are much sweeter than the wild; if using cultivated fruit you would need to reduce the sugar to 4 pounds for 6 pounds fruit.

6 pounds damsons
butter
4 cups water
6 pounds sugar

Stainless steel canner
Hot sterilized jars

Preheat the oven to 325°F.

Pick over the fruit carefully, discard any damaged damsons, and wash and drain well. Grease a stainless-steel boiling-water canner with butter to prevent the damsons from sticking to the bottom, and add the fruit and water. Stew them over a low heat until the skins break, about 8–10 minutes, stirring regularly.

Meanwhile, put the sugar in an ovenproof dish and pop it into the oven to warm. Add it to the fruit and stir over a low heat until the sugar is dissolved. Increase the heat and boil steadily, stirring frequently. Skim off the pits and scum as they rise to the top. After 15 minutes boiling, test for a set—it should register 100°F on a sugar thermometer. Alternatively, put a little jam on a cold plate, and let it cool for 1–2 minutes. If it trembles when pressed with the tip of your finger, the jam is set.

Pour into hot sterilized jars and cover. Store in a cool dry place.

food from the wild

If you know what to look for, you can make a wonderful feast after a day in the wild. Wild food adds a whole new dimension to your menu and is a much welcome seasonal change from the familiar supermarket offerings. Cooked fresh herbs, plants, mushrooms, fruit, and fish will taste better than anything bought in a supermarket. And foraging is not limited to autumn, when there is such an abundance of wild food. Once you get in tune with your local area, you will find delicious treasures from the fields, woods, and seashore to incorporate into menus all year round: carrigeen moss, periwinkles, field sorrel, marsh samphire, watercress, elderflowers, crab apples, blackberries, sloes, damsons, hazelnuts, rosehips, and a myriad of shellfish along the shores if you live close to the sea. Go with an experienced forager the first few times—someone who knows one end of a mushroom from the other if you do not, or get a good book on the subject—and take a walk on the wild side.

A good day's work
Wild mushroom soup (see p.226)
Roast rabbit with potato, onion, and thyme leaves (see p.228)
Insalata di Campo green salad (see p.231)
Compote of blackberry and apples with sweet geranium leaves (see p.229)

To drink
Soup and wine generally don't strike up much of a relationship, but a small glass of dry—and it has to be dry—amontillado sherry makes each taste more intensely of itself. Roast rabbit with the scent of thyme is an easy match for any number of medium-bodied red wines, but Barbera d'Asti from Piedmont in northwest Italy is quite simply perfect. And if the budget allows, you could trade up to a Barolo to similar effect. The compote is more difficult but a 20-year-old tawny port will be no hardship to drink with it.

veg and spuds

The all-important side dishes. Here are some fantastic vegetable and potato dishes to accompany your meals. Many of the recipes in the previous chapters will have led you here, but feel free to pick and choose to suit your menu. Tomato Fondue, Mushroom à la Crème, Piperonata and Cucumber Neopolitana are all excellent examples of versatile vegetable dishes that can be cooked ahead, reheated, and frozen.

Root Vegetable Mash 1

SERVES 6   (**P:** 15 mins./**C:** 45 mins.)

8 ounces parsnips, cooked and mashed
  (about 1 cup)
8 ounces Jerusalem artichokes, braised and
  mashed (about 1 cup)
4 ounces celeriac, mashed (about 1/2 cup)
4 ounces potatoes, cooked and mashed
  (about 1/2 cup)
1–2 tablespoons chopped parsley (optional)
2–4 tablespoons butter
salt and freshly ground pepper

Mix all the mashed root vegetables and the
optional parsley together, beat in the butter,
and season well with salt and pepper.

Root Vegetable Mash 2

SERVES 6   (**P:** 15 mins./**C:** 45 mins.)

4 ounces rutabaga, cooked and mashed
  (about 1/2 cup)
8 ounces carrots, cooked and mashed
  (about 1 cup)
12 ounces parsnips, cooked and mashed
  (about 1 1/2 cups)
1–2 tablespoons chopped parsley (optional)
2–4 tablespoons butter
salt and freshly ground pepper

Mix all the mashed root vegetables and the
optional parsley together, beat in the butter,
and season well with salt and pepper.

Colcannon

SERVES 8   (**P:** 15 mins./**C:** 30 mins.)

**Songs have been sung and poems have been
written about colcannon. It's one of Ireland's
most famous potato dishes: comfort food at
its very best and terrific for a party.**

Did you ever eat colcannon
When 'twas made with yellow cream
And the kale and praties blended
Like a picture in a dream?
Did you ever scoop a hole on top
To hold the melting lake
Of the clover-flavoured butter
Which your mother used to make?

3 pounds floury potatoes, unpeeled
salt and freshly ground pepper
1 pound Savoy cabbage or spring cabbage
  or kale
1 cup milk
1/4 cup finely chopped scallions (optional)
1/4 cup (1/2 stick) butter

Scrub the potatoes, put them in a large pot of cold water, add a good pinch of salt, cover, and bring to a boil. When the potatoes are half cooked—about 15 minutes for floury potatoes—strain off two thirds of the water. Replace the lid on the pot, place over a low heat, and let the potatoes steam until they are cooked.

Meanwhile, remove the dark outer leaves from the cabbage and discard; wash the cabbage and cut into quarters, then remove and discard the core and slice the leaves crosswise (if using kale, remove the central rib). Put a little water in a large pot and bring to a boil. Add the cabbage or kale and cook until soft. Drain, season with salt and pepper, and add a little butter.

When the potatoes are just cooked, put the milk in a saucepan, add the scallion (if using) and bring to a boil. Pull the skin off the potatoes and discard. Mash quickly while they are still warm and beat in enough boiling milk to make a fluffy puree (if you like, beat the potatoes with an electric beater). Stir in the cooked cabbage and adjust the seasoning to taste.

For perfection, serve immediately in a hot dish, with a lump of butter melting in the center.

Colcannon can also be made ahead and reheated later: cover the dish so it doesn't get too crusty on top, pop it in an oven preheated to 350°F, and warm through for 20–25 minutes.

Roast Onions

SERVES 6–8   (**P:** 5 mins./**C:** 30 mins.)

**Just pop the onions into the hot oven—they
don't even need to be peeled. The flesh
becomes soft and melting. I'm always
surprised that so few people cook onions in
this ultra-simple way.**

1 pound small or medium onions, unpeeled
butter or extra virgin olive oil
sea salt (or Kosher salt)

Preheat the oven to 400°F.

Cook the onions on a baking tray until soft—this can take anything from 10 to 30 minutes depending upon size. Serve in their skins. To eat, cut off the root, squeeze out the onion, and enjoy with butter or olive oil, and salt.

Scallion Champ

SERVES 4–6   (P: 10 mins./C: 30 mins.)

A bowl of mashed potatoes, flecked with green scallions and with a blob of butter melting in the center, is "comfort food" at its best.

3 pounds floury potatoes, unpeeled
salt and freshly ground pepper
4 ounces scallions, chopped, about 1 cup
   (use both the bulb and the green stem), or
   2 ounces fresh chives, chopped (about 1 cup)
1¼–1½ cups milk
¼–½ cup (½–1 stick) butter

Scrub the potatoes and cook them in their skins in boiling salted water.

Put the chopped scallions or chives in a saucepan and cover with the milk. Bring slowly to a boil and simmer for 3–4 minutes, turn off the heat, and let them infuse.

Peel and mash the freshly boiled potatoes and, while they are hot, mix in the hot milk and scallions or chives, then beat in the butter. Season to taste. Serve in a large serving dish, or in individual bowls, with a pat of butter melting in the center.

Scallion champ may be put aside and reheated later, covered, in an oven preheated to 350°F for 20–25 minutes.

Scallion and Potato Cakes
Shape leftover Scallion Champ into potato cakes. Heat some butter, clarified butter (see p.108), or oil in a frying pan and cook the patties on both sides. Serve piping hot.

Wild Garlic Mash
Add 2–3 ounces (1–2 large handfuls) roughly chopped wild garlic leaves to the milk just as it comes to a boil. Continue as above.

Rustic Roast Potatoes

SERVES 4–6   (P: 10 mins./C: 45 mins.)

So quick and easy. Just scrub the spuds well, and don't bother to peel them.

6 large floury potatoes
extra virgin olive oil, beef drippings, or duck or
   goose fat, for drizzling
sea salt (or Kosher salt)

Preheat the oven to 450°F.

Scrub the potatoes well. Cut into quarters lengthwise, or into slices about ¾-inch thick. Put into a roasting pan, drizzle with olive oil, and toss so they are just coated (or heat the fat or drippings in the pan in the oven until sizzling and toss the potatoes in the fat). Roast for 30–45 minutes depending upon size. Sprinkle with sea salt and serve in a hot terracotta dish.

Rustic Roast Potatoes with Rosemary
Mix 6–8 sprigs of rosemary or some coarsely chopped fresh rosemary with the olive oil and cook as above. Serve garnished with fresh sprigs of rosemary.

Rustic Roast Potatoes with Cumin
Mix 1–2 teaspoons roasted and ground cumin seeds with the olive oil and cook as above.

Twice-cooked Roast Potatoes with Shallots and Thyme Leaves

SERVES 8–10   (P: 15 mins./C: 40 mins.)

I love to cook potatoes and shallots (or baby onions) in the roasting pan after I've roasted a duck. The duck fat and juices soak into the vegetables and give them a sublime flavor.

8–10 large potatoes, boiled in their skins
24–30 shallots
¼–⅓ cup duck or goose fat,
   or extra virgin olive oil
sea salt (or Kosher salt) and freshly
   ground pepper
3–4 tablespoons fresh thyme leaves

Preheat the oven to 450°F.

Peel the potatoes (no need if they are new potatoes) and cut into ¾-inch slices. Peel the shallots and cut in half if large.

In 1 or 2 roasting pans, heat the fat or oil. Put in the potato slices and shallots, season with salt and pepper, and add the thyme leaves. Toss gently to coat in the fat or oil. Roast for 30–40 minutes, turning regularly, until the outsides are all crisp and golden.

Mary Jo McMillin's Gratin Dauphinoise

SERVES 6–8   (**P**: 10 mins./**C**: 30–45 mins.)

Everyone loves this rich potato dish, and it is so easy; put it in the oven alongside a roasting chicken or leg of lamb.

2 garlic cloves, crushed
salt and freshly ground white pepper
1 cup milk, warmed
1/2 cup cream
3 tablespoons butter, sliced
21/4 pounds even-sized potatoes
11/2–2 ounces Gruyère cheese or cheddar
  cheese, grated (about 1/2 cup)

Preheat the oven to 400°F.

In a 21/2-quart baking dish, sprinkle the garlic, salt, and pepper. Add the milk, cream, and slices of butter and place the dish in the oven to heat.

Meanwhile, peel and thinly slice the potatoes. When the milk is bubbling at the edges, remove the dish from the oven but do not turn off the oven. Strew sliced potatoes into the dish and sprinkle with the cheese. Return to the oven and bake for 30–45 minutes or until the potatoes are tender and the top is golden brown.

Glazed Carrots

SERVES 4–6   (**P**: 10 mins./**C**: 10 mins.)

You might like to try this method of cooking carrots; admittedly it takes a little vigilance, but the resulting flavor is a revelation to many people.

1 pound organic carrots (Early Nantes and
  Autumn King have particularly good flavor)
1 tablespoon butter
1/2 cup water
salt and sugar, to taste
chopped parsley or mint, for garnishing

Cut off the tops and tips of the carrots, scrub, and peel thinly if necessary. Leave very young carrots whole, cut others into even slices a 1/2-inch thick, either straight across or diagonally.

Put them in a saucepan with the butter, water, and some salt and sugar. Bring to a boil, cover, and cook over a low heat until tender, by which time the liquid should have all been absorbed; if not, remove the lid and increase the heat until all the water has evaporated.

Taste and adjust the seasoning if needed. Shake the saucepan so the carrots become coated with the buttery glaze. Serve in a hot vegetable dish, sprinkled with chopped parsley or mint. Freshly roasted and ground cumin or coriander are also delicious.

Note: It is really important to cut the carrots to the same thickness, otherwise they will cook unevenly.

Baby Carrots
Scrub the carrots with a brush, but don't peel. Trim the tails, but if the tops are really fresh, leave a little of the stalks attached. Cook and glaze as above.

Melted Leeks

SERVES 6–8   (**P**: 10 mins./**C**: 20 mins.)

8 medium leeks
1/4 cup (1/2 stick) butter
salt and freshly ground pepper
chopped parsley or chervil, for garnishing

Cut off the dark green leaves from the top of the leeks. Slit the leeks from the top until about halfway down the center and wash well under cold running water. Slice into 1/4-inch rings.

Melt the butter in a heavy pan; when it foams, add the leeks and toss gently to coat with butter. Season with salt and pepper. Cover with a paper lid and then a close-fitting lid. Reduce the heat to very low and cook for 8–10 minutes, stirring every now and then, until semi soft and moist. Turn off the heat and let them continue to cook in the heat for 4–5 minutes. Serve on a warm dish, sprinkled with chopped parsley or chervil.

Melted leeks with rosemary: before tossing, add 1–2 tablespoons of freshly chopped rosemary to the leeks.

Melted leeks with ginger: Add 2 teaspoons freshly grated ginger to the foaming butter before adding the leeks.

Tomato Fondue

SERVES 6   (P: 10 mins./C: 25 mins.)

Tomato Fondue has a myriad of uses—we serve it as a vegetable dish, as a sauce for pasta, a filling for omelets, and topping for pizza or a base for bean stew.

1¹/₂ tablespoons extra virgin olive oil
4 ounces onions, sliced (about 1 cup)
1 garlic clove, crushed
2 pounds very ripe tomatoes, skinned, or
  2¹/₂ x 14¹/₂-ounce cans tomatoes
salt, freshly ground pepper, and sugar, to taste
1 tablespoon of one or a mix of any of these
  chopped herbs, such as mint, thyme, parsley,
  lemon balm, marjoram, or basil
few drops of balsamic vinegar

Heat the olive oil in a large non-reactive saucepan. Add the sliced onions and garlic, toss to coat them well in oil, cover, and sweat over low heat until soft but not colored. It is vital for the success of this dish that the onions are completely soft before the tomatoes are added.

Slice the tomatoes and add with all their juice to the onions. Season with salt, pepper, and some sugar (canned tomatoes need lots of sugar because of their high acidity). Add a generous sprinkling of herbs. Cook, covered, for 10 minutes, then remove the lid and continue to cook until the tomatoes soften (cook fresh tomatoes for a shorter time than canned, in order to preserve the lively fresh flavor). Just before the end of cooking, sprinkle in a few drops of balsamic vinegar to enhance the flavor.

Tomato Fondue with Chile

While the onions are sweating, add 1–2 chopped fresh chiles or 4 sliced Hungarian wax chiles.

Tomato Fondue with Chile and Cilantro

While the onions are sweating, add 1–2 chopped fresh chiles and ¹/₃ cup cilantro leaves.

Tomato Fondue with Kabanossi

Five minutes before the end of cooking, add 1–2 sliced kabanossi sausages—great with pasta.

Tomato Fondue with Chorizo

Ten minutes before the end of cooking, add 1 sliced chorizo.

Tomato Fondue with Chorizo and Black-eyed Peas or Cannellini Beans

Add 14 ounces (about 2¹/₂ cups) of cooked or canned black-eyed peas or cannellini beans to the recipe above, just before the end of the cooking time, and heat through.

Tomato Fondue with Green Olives and Marjoram

Add 4 ounces (about ³/₄ cup) green olives and 2 tablespoons of fresh marjoram to the above recipe 5 minutes before the end of cooking. Serve with meatballs or hamburgers.

Cucumber Neapolitana

SERVES 6   (P: 10 mins./C: 25 mins.)

A terrifically versatile vegetable dish that may be made ahead and reheats well. It is also delicious served with rice or pasta and makes a great stuffing for tomatoes. It is particularly good with roast lamb.

1 tablespoon butter
1 medium onion, sliced
1 large, organic English cucumber
4 very ripe tomatoes
salt, freshly ground pepper, and sugar
¹/₄ cup cream
2 teaspoons freshly chopped mint
Roux (optional; see p.139)

Melt the butter in a heavy saucepan. When it foams, add the onion, then cover and sweat for about 5 minutes until the onion is soft but not colored.

Meanwhile, peel the cucumber and cut into ¹/₂-inch cubes. Add to the onion, toss well, and continue to cook.

Scald the tomatoes with boiling water for 10 seconds. Skin the tomatoes and slice into the pan, then season with salt, freshly ground pepper, and a pinch of sugar. Cover the pan and cook for a few minutes until the cucumber is tender and the tomatoes have softened, then add the cream and bring back to a boil. Add the chopped mint. If the liquid is very thin, thicken it by carefully whisking in a little roux.

Cucumber Neapolitana keeps for several days and may be reheated.

Variation

Use 1 pound zucchini or patty pan squash instead of the cucumber.

Mushroom à la Crème

SERVES 8   (**P**: 10 mins./**C**: 20 mins.)

Like Tomato Fondue and Piperonata (see p.243), Mushroom à la Crème is another of our great convertibles. If you keep some in your fridge or freezer you can use it in a myriad of ways. It can be served as a vegetable, or as a filling for vol au vents, bouchées, or crêpes, or as a sauce for pasta, steak, or hamburgers. It may be used to enrich casseroles and stews or, by adding a little more cream or stock, it may be served as a sauce with beef, lamb, chicken, veal, or fish. A crushed clove of garlic or a teaspoon of freshly grated ginger can be added while the onions are sweating.

2 tablespoons butter
6 ounces onions, finely chopped
  (about 1^1/$_2$ cups)
1 pound mushrooms, sliced (about 5 cups)
squeeze of fresh lemon juice
1 cup cream
1^1/$_2$ tablespoons freshly chopped parsley
1^1/$_2$ tablespoons freshly chopped chives
  or marjoram (optional)
salt and freshly ground pepper

Melt half the butter in a large heavy saucepan until it foams. Add the chopped onions, cover, and sweat over a low heat for 5–10 minutes or until quite soft but not colored. Set aside.

Meanwhile, melt the rest of the butter in a frying pan and cook the sliced mushrooms, in batches if necessary. Season each batch with salt, pepper, and a tiny squeeze of lemon juice. Add the mushrooms to the onions in the saucepan over medium heat, then add the cream and herbs and let it bubble for a few minutes. Taste and adjust the seasoning.

Mushroom à la Crème keeps well in the fridge for 4–5 days and also freezes perfectly.

Wild Mushroom à la Crème

For the mushrooms in the recipe above, substitute wild field mushrooms or a mixture of mushrooms, such as oyster, enoki, shiitake, nameko, girolle, or chanterelle.

Mushroom à la Crème with Ginger

To the sweated onions add 1–2 teaspoons of grated fresh ginger—delicious with chicken breast, pasta, or a hamburger.

Buttered Zucchini with Marjoram

SERVES 4   (**P**: 5 mins./**C**: 10 mins.)

1 pound zucchinis, no longer than 5 inches
2 tablespoons butter
dash of extra virgin olive oil
3–4 tablespoons chopped marjoram
salt and freshly ground pepper

Top and tail the zucchinis and cut them into 1/4-inch slices. In a large frying pan, melt the butter over medium heat and add a dash of olive oil. Toss in the zucchini, coating them evenly in the butter and oil. Cook, tossing occasionally, for 4–5 minutes or until tender. Sprinkle in the chopped marjoram and season to taste. Turn into a hot serving dish and serve immediately.

Note: it is important to undercook the zucchini slightly as they continue to cook after they have been removed from the heat.

Broccoli with Anchovy Butter

SERVES 4   (**P**: 15 mins./**C**: 15 mins.)

1 pound broccoli
freshly ground pepper
1/4 cup (1/2 stick) butter
4 canned anchovy fillets, chopped

First cook the broccoli in boiling, salted water (use 1 tablespoon salt to 5 cups of water). Drain well.

Melt the butter in a small frying pan, add the anchovy fillets, and let them sizzle for just a minute. Add the broccoli, sprinkle on some pepper, toss, and taste. Adust the seasoning if needed.

Piperonata

SERVES 8–10   (P: 10 mins./C: 40 mins.)

Another excellent easy entertaining basic. We use this not only as a vegetable dish but also as a topping for pizzas, as a sauce for pasta, grilled fish, or meat, and as a filling for omelets and crêpes.

2^1/$_2$ tablespoons extra virgin olive oil
1 garlic clove, crushed
1 onion, sliced
2 red peppers
2 green peppers
6 large very ripe tomatoes
salt, freshly ground pepper, and sugar, to taste
a few basil leaves

Heat the olive oil in a heavy pan, add the garlic, and cook for a few seconds, then mix in the sliced onion and let it soften over a low heat, covered, for 5–10 minutes.

Meanwhile, prepare the peppers: cut them in half, remove the seeds, cut into quarters, and then into crosswise strips. Add to the onion and toss in the oil; replace the lid and continue to cook.

Skin the tomatoes (cover in boiling water for 10 seconds, then pour off the water and peel immediately). Slice the tomatoes and add them to the pan. Season to taste with salt, pepper, some sugar, and a few leaves of basil. Cook until the vegetables are just soft, about 30 minutes.

Piperonata, Bean, and Chorizo Stew
Add a can of rinsed navy beans, black-eyed peas, or chickpeas to the Piperonata, with 4 ounces sliced chorizo sausage (about 1 cup). Continue to cook for about 10 minutes or until the chorizo is fully cooked.

Spiced Eggplant

SERVES 6   (P: 15 mins./C: 20 mins.)

This is another of our favorite recipes and is completely delicious served with a rack of lamb or a few lamb chops. It is also great with pork, and divine partnered with soft goat cheese and a few arugula leaves as an appetizer. It keeps well in the fridge for 4–5 days.

1^3/$_4$ pounds eggplants
1 cup vegetable oil
1-inch cube of fresh ginger root, peeled and
    coarsely chopped
6 large garlic cloves, coarsely crushed
^{1}/$_4$ cup water
1 teaspoon whole fennel seeds
2 teaspoons whole cumin seeds
12 ounces very ripe tomatoes, skinned and
    finely chopped (about 1^3/$_4$–2 cups), or
    14^1/$_2$-ounce can tomatoes and 1 teaspoon
    sugar
4 teaspoons freshly ground coriander seeds
^{1}/$_4$ teaspoon ground turmeric
^{1}/$_4$ teaspoon cayenne pepper (more if you like)
sea salt (or Kosher salt)
^{1}/$_3$ cup raisins

Cut the eggplants into ^{3}/$_4$-inch-thick slices. Heat ^{3}/$_4$ cup of the oil in a deep 10–12-inch frying pan. When it is almost smoking, add a few eggplant slices and cook until golden and tender on both sides. Remove and drain on a wire rack over a baking sheet. Repeat with the remaining eggplant slices, adding more oil if necessary.

Put the ginger, garlic, and water into a blender. Blend until fairly smooth.

Heat the remaining oil in the frying pan. When it is hot, add the fennel and cumin seeds and stir for just a few seconds (careful not to let them burn). Add the tomatoes (and sugar if using canned tomatoes), the ginger/garlic mixture, coriander, turmeric, cayenne, and salt. Taste and correct the seasoning. Simmer, stirring occasionally until the spice mixture thickens slightly, about 5–6 minutes.

Add the fried eggplant slices and raisins, and coat gently with the spicy sauce. Cover the pan, turn the heat to very low, and cook for another 3–4 minutes. Serve warm.

The spiced eggplant mixture is also good served cold or at room temperature as an accompaniment to hot or cold lamb or pork.

sweet things

The best part of the meal. A good dessert will simply seduce you,
making your mouth water even before you dip a spoon in it. And once
you have—well, one spoonful is never enough. Light or heavy,
chocolatey or fruit-based, creamy or spicy, these will have your guests
humming with happiness. And don't forget, desserts can also be a meal
in themselves—time for tea, anyone?

Molten Chocolate Puddings

MAKES 6–8   (**P:** 45 mins./**C:** 10 mins.)

These are the most delectable little puddings (see photograph on p.171) and a cinch to make provided you find the right mold and time it correctly. The mixture can be made ahead, refrigerated overnight, or frozen.

1/2 cup (1 stick) butter, plus extra for greasing

2 teaspoons flour, plus extra for sprinkling

4 ounces good-quality semisweet dark chocolate, chopped (about 2/3 cup)

2 cage-free, organic eggs, plus 2 egg yolks

1/4 cup sugar

For serving: lightly whipped cream or crème fraîche
confectioners' sugar

6–8 molds—we use aluminum foil molds measuring 31/4 inches across at the top, 21/4 inches deep, and with a 2/3 cup capacity

If the puddings are to be baked immediately, preheat the oven to 450°F, and place a baking tray in the oven to heat.

Generously butter and flour the molds, then tap the molds upside-down on the counter to shake out the excess flour. Line the bottoms of the molds with baking parchment.

Put the chocolate and the butter in the top of a double boiler over hot water. Bring to a boil, turn off the heat, and let it sit until the chocolate is melted. Meanwhile beat the eggs and egg yolks with the sugar until thick and pale and doubled in volume. Add the melted chocolate and butter while still warm and mix gently but thoroughly. Sift the flour over the chocolate mixture and work in with a spatula until it is just combined. Spoon the mousse into the well-buttered molds until each is about two-thirds full.

If baking immediately, set the molds on the heated baking tray and bake for 6–7 minutes. Alternatively, the puddings may be covered lightly with plastic wrap, kept at room temperature, and baked later. They can also be refrigerated, but they must be brought to room temperature before baking.

When they come out of the oven, invert each pudding onto a warmed dessert plate, wait for 10 seconds, then lift off the molds. Dust with confectioners' sugar and serve with a spoonful of whipped cream or crème fraîche. They are also delicious with homemade vanilla ice cream.

Chocolate Tart with Fresh Raspberries

SERVES 8   (**P:** 20 mins./**C:** 10 mins.)

1 x 91/2-inch Sweet Pastry Dough (see recipe opposite)

For the filling:

7 ounces good-quality dark chocolate, chopped (about 1–11/4 cups)

2/3 cup (11/4 sticks) butter, preferably unsalted

2 cage-free, organic eggs, plus 3 egg yolks

21/2 tablespoons sugar

For serving: 11/2 pounds raspberries

For garnishing: mint leaves
confectioners' sugar

Preheat the oven to 375°F.

Begin by making the filling. Melt the chocolate and butter together in the top of a double boiler over hot but not simmering water. Beat together the eggs, egg yolks, and sugar with an electric beater until pale and thick (about 5 minutes). Fold in the melted chocolate and mix carefully to amalgamate.

Pour the filling into the blind-baked pie shell and bake for 8 minutes; the mixture should still be slightly molten—it cooks a little more as it cools. Let it cool slightly, then cut into slices and serve with the fresh raspberries. Garnish each slice with a sprig of mint and a little confectioners' sugar.

Chocolate Meringue Layer Cake

SERVES 10–12   (P: 45 mins./C: 45 mins.)

A luscious cake, very naughty and very nice (see photographs on pp.262–263).

For the meringue:
4 cage-free, organic egg whites
9^1/2 ounces confectioners' sugar
    (about 2–2^1/4 cups)
4 rounded teaspoons unsweetened
    cocoa powder

For the chocolate wafers:
3^1/2 ounces good-quality dark chocolate,
    chopped (about ^{2}/3 cup)

For the chocolate and rum cream:
3 ounces good-quality dark chocolate,
    chopped (about ^{1}/2 cup)
2^1/2 tablespoons Jamaica rum
2^1/2 tablespoons cream
2^1/2 cups lightly whipped cream

Sparklers (optional)

Preheat the oven to 300°F and set out 3 baking trays. Mark three 9-inch-diameter circles on baking paper and place a circle on each of three baking trays.

Put the egg whites into a bowl that is free from grease and is dry and spotlessly clean, add 1^3/4 cups of the confectioners' sugar all at once, and beat until the mixture forms stiff, dry peaks—this will take about 10 minutes.

Sift the cocoa powder and the remaining confectioners' sugar together and fold very gently into the beaten egg whites. Spread the mixture on the three paper circles with a palette knife or butter knife.

Bake immediately for 45 minutes or until just crisp. Turn off the oven and let cool completely in the oven. When cold, peel off the paper.

Meanwhile, make the chocolate wafers. Put the chocolate in the top of a double boiler over simmering water. Bring the water to a boil, turn off the heat immediately, and let the chocolate melt, sitting over the hot water. Stir until quite smooth.

Spread the chocolate on a flat piece of heavy, white notepaper, baking paper, or light card stock. Leave in the fridge until stiff enough to peel off and cut into square or diamond shapes.

Meanwhile, make the chocolate and rum cream. Very gently melt the chocolate with the rum in the top of a double boiler over hot water as before, and add the cream. Cool, and then fold in the lightly whipped cream (do not stir too much, as this may make it curdle).

Sandwich the three meringue discs together with the chocolate and rum cream, and decorate with chocolate wafers and sparklers—perfect for a celebration.

Alison Henderson's Sweet Pastry Dough

MAKES ENOUGH TO LINE 2 X 9^1/2-INCH OR
3 X 7-INCH TART PANS
                    (P: 45 mins./C: 20 mins.)

^{3}/4 cup (1^1/2 sticks) cold butter, cut into cubes
^{1}/4 cup granulated sugar
3 tablespoons confectioners' sugar
10^1/2 ounces white all-purpose flour
    (about 2^1/4 cups), plus extra for dusting
1 cage-free, organic egg, beaten, plus one
    beaten egg for egg wash

Put the butter into a food processor, add the granulated sugar, confectioners' sugar, and flour and pulse to give a coarse, "flat" bread crumb texture. Add the egg and pulse again until the dough comes together. Tip onto a sheet of plastic wrap, form into a roll, and refrigerate for at least 30 minutes. Meanwhile preheat the oven to 350°F.

Divide the dough between the number of tart pans. Roll each out on a floured counter, under a sheet of plastic wrap. Slip the bottom of the tart pan under the dough, lift the tart pan and press the pastry dough around the sides of the pan. Cover with plastic wrap and leave in the fridge to rest for 30 minutes, or freeze until needed. Remove the plastic wrap from the pie shell, line the pie crust with baking parchment or foil, and fill with dried beans or baking beans, and bake blind for about 15 minutes. Remove from the oven and brush with egg wash. Return to the oven for 2–3 minutes to dry off and seal. Let the pie crust cool, then patch any cracks with egg wash.

Mary Risley's Chocolate and Raspberry Truffles

MAKES ABOUT 24   (P: 45 mins.)

This recipe comes from my friend Mary Risley's terrific cookery book, *The Tante Marie's Cooking School Cookbook*, and Mary, in turn, got this recipe from Alice Medrich. The truffles are rather fiddly and a seriously messy job to make—but so worth it, because they taste divine.

8 ounces good-quality dark chocolate, chopped (about 1 1/3 cups)
1/3 cup (3/4 stick) unsalted butter
4 ounces raspberry jam (scant 1/2 cup), melted and strained
2 1/2 tablespoons raspberry liqueur (framboise) or kirsch

1/4 cup unsweetened cocoa powder
24 raspberries
24 tiny paper baking cups

Put the chocolate and the butter in the top of a double boiler over hot water, without letting the water touch the bottom of the top pan. Bring slowly to a boil, then turn off the heat and let the chocolate melt, stirring gently until smooth. Let the chocolate cool for a few minutes, then stir in the strained raspberry jam and the framboise or kirsch. Cover the bowl and let it chill in the fridge until firm.

To shape the truffles, sift the cocoa powder onto a plate. Scoop out a teaspoonful of the truffle mixture, press it gently around a fresh raspberry, then lift it with your fingertips and drop it into the cocoa. Roll the truffle around in the cocoa, then lift it with a fork to transfer it to a little paper cup. Repeat with the remaining raspberries. Place each truffle in its cup on a tray and leave the tray in the fridge for an hour or two or until the mixture sets and firms up.

Chocolate and Rosemary Mousse with Pouring Cream

SERVES 8   (P: 10 mins./C: 30 mins.)

The legendary British cookery writer, Jane Grigson, gave me this recipe when she came to teach at the cookery school in 1989.

1 cup sugar
1 cup dry white wine
juice of 1/2 lemon
2 1/2 cups heavy cream
1 long rosemary branch
6 ounces good-quality dark chocolate, chopped (about 1 cup)

For serving: light cream and rosemary sprigs

In a stainless steel saucepan over low heat, mix together the sugar, white wine, and lemon juice, stirring until the sugar is dissolved. Add the cream and bring to a boil; the mixture will thicken somewhat. Add the rosemary branch and chocolate. Stir, bring to a boil, then reduce the heat and let the mixture simmer very gently for 20 minutes, stirring occasionally. It should be the consistency of thick cream.

Let cool, tasting occasionally to see if the rosemary flavor is intense enough. Pour through a strainer into 8 ramekins or little shot glasses. Cover with plastic wrap and refrigerate until needed.

Serve with light cream and a sprig of rosemary.

Belgian Chocolate Cookie Cake

SERVES 8–10   (P: 30 mins.)

8 ounces good-quality dark chocolate, chopped (about 1 1/3 cups)
2 cage-free, organic eggs
2 teaspoons sugar
1 cup (2 sticks) unsalted butter
2 tablespoons raisins, soaked in boiling water
1/2 teaspoon vanilla extract
8 ounces plain cookies, broken
1/4 cup walnuts or toasted almonds, chopped

For serving: lightly whipped cream (optional)
raspberry coulis (optional)

Line a 5 x 8-inch loaf pan with non-PVC plastic wrap.

Melt the chocolate in the top of a double boiler over hot, but not simmering water, or in a very cool oven.

Beat the eggs and sugar together until light and fluffy. Melt the butter and while it is still hot, beat it into the egg and sugar mixture. The batter should thicken slightly. Next stir in the melted chocolate, drained raisins, and vanilla extract, and finally the broken cookies.

Press into the prepared loaf pan. Sprinkle with the chopped nuts and let it set in a cold place for a couple of hours or until firm enough to cut.

Cut into slices and serve with lightly whipped cream and/or a raspberry coulis.

Kara's Chocolate Boxes

MAKES 1 BOX   (**P:** 1 HOUR + 1 HOUR TO SET)

2–3 ounces good-quality dark chocolate,
  chopped (about 1/3–1/2 cup)

For the box frame:
1 empty 1-quart milk or buttermilk carton
small palette knife or rubber spatula

For serving: chocolate mousse
Homemade Ice Cream (see p.270)
fresh raspberries

Wash and dry the carton carefully. Cut the sides to the desired height – 5cm (2in) works well. Carefully cut down along all four corners. Align the edges and tape the sides together again with sellotape or masking tape.

Melt three quarters of the chocolate in your preferred manner (using a double boiler or microwave). Pour the melted chocolate into the box and quickly spread the chocolate with the aid of a palette knife so that it evenly coats the sides and bottom and all the corners. Turn upside-down on a wire rack set over a baking tray and let it set for 1–2 hours.

When solid, carefully peel off the tape. Gently pull back the sides of the carton, then pop out the bottom of the box. If necessary, smooth the top edges of the chocolate box by dipping a palette knife in warm water and using it to smooth each edge.

To make the top, melt the remaining chocolate and pour 2–3 tablespoons of melted chocolate into the empty carton, enough to cover the bottom. Make sure the entire surface is covered and let it cool. Pop it out when solid.

There is a lovely X pattern on the lid from the folding pattern at the bottom of the carton itself. Fill the box with mousse, ice cream, or a filling of your choice.

White Chocolate Mousse with Fresh Strawberry Sauce

SERVES 8–12   (**P:** 30 mins. + 3 HOURS TO SET)

2 teaspoons powdered gelatin
9 ounces good-quality white chocolate
  (about 1 1/2 cups broken up)
5 cage-free, organic egg yolks
1 3/4 cups lightly whipped cream
Fresh Strawberry Sauce (see below)

Place the gelatin and 2 1/2 tablespoons cold water in a cup and let it swell for a few minutes. Place the cup carefully in a saucepan of simmering water and leave it until the gelatin has dissolved.

Bring the water in the bottom of a double boiler to a boil. Break up the white chocolate and put it in the top of the double boiler. Turn off the heat. Stir the chocolate until it dissolves completely.

Remove the top pan from the double boiler and add the egg yolks. Stir with a wooden spoon—the mixture may suddenly block at this stage, but if you stir like mad it will be fine.

Put a little of the chocolate mixture into the gelatin, stir well, and then mix this carefully back into the rest of the chocolate. Fold in the lightly whipped cream immediately. Pour into a serving dish, cover, and refrigerate for at least 3 hours before serving. Alternatively, fill espresso cups, shot glasses, or chocolate boxes (see above). Cover and let it set in the fridge.

Fresh Strawberry Sauce

1 pound fresh strawberries
2/3 cup confectioners' sugar
lemon juice, to taste

Clean and hull the strawberries, place in the bowl of a blender along with the sugar, and whizz to a puree. Strain, taste, and add lemon juice as necessary. Cover and store in the fridge. It will keep for a day or two.

White Chocolate Mousse with Dark Chocolate Sauce

2 ounces dark chocolate (about 1/3 cup
  broken up)
1 square (1 ounce) unsweetened chocolate
About 3/4 cup Stock Syrup (see recipe
  on p.252)
1/2 teaspoon rum or vanilla extract (optional)

Follow the recipe for White Chocolate Mousse (see recipe above) and, after folding in the whipped cream, pour the mixture into shot glasses. When set, pour some Dark Chocolate Sauce over the top—divine.

To make the sauce, melt the chocolate in a double boiler over simmering water or in a low heat oven. Gradually stir in the syrup. Flavor with rum or vanilla extract.

Boozy Chocolate Mousse

SERVES 8   (P: 20 mins. + TIME TO SET)

1$^1/4$ cups cream
7 ounces good-quality chocolate, chopped
   (about 1–1$^1/4$ cups)
2 cage-free, organic large egg yolks
$^1/4$ cup brandy or 2$^1/2$ tablespoons
   Jamaica rum
2 tablespoons unsalted butter

For serving: light cream

In a heavy saucepan, heat the cream until it shivers—almost boiling. Remove from the heat and leave it for about 1 minute. Add the chocolate and whisk until fully smooth. Beat in the egg yolks and brandy or rum. Finally add the butter and whisk until smooth and silky.

Pour into individual serving bowls, espresso cups, or chocolate boxes (see left). Cover well and let set for 1–3 hours, depending upon the size of the serving containers, in the fridge. Serve with a pitcher of light cream.

Variations
You can use orange zest and orange liqueur instead of brandy.
For a lighter mousse, fold in 2 stiffly beaten egg whites before pouring into containers.

Chocolate and Peanut Butter Pie

SERVES 8   (P: 45 mins. + 5 HOURS TO SET)

This is an all-American flavor and it's always a wow for a party.

$^1/2$ cup (1 stick) unsalted butter
4 ounces good-quality dark chocolate,
   chopped (about $^2/3$ cup)
2$^1/2$ tablespoons strong coffee (preferably
   espresso)
1 x 10-inch Sweet Pastry Dough,
   (see p.247), baked blind
$^1/2$ cup cream cheese
$^2/3$ cup confectioners' sugar
1 cup smooth peanut butter
$^1/3$ cup milk
1$^1/2$ cups whipping cream

Melt the butter and chocolate together in the top of a double boiler over hot, but not simmering water, or melt in a microwave. Whisk in the coffee and let it set for a while. When the chocolate is beginning to set, pour the chocolate mixture into the blind-baked pie shell and refrigerate while you make the rest of the filling.

Put the cream cheese, confectioners' sugar, peanut butter, and milk into a food processor and whizz for a few seconds or until smooth. Whip the cream until soft peaks form. Tip the peanut butter mixture into a mixing bowl and fold the cream into the mixture. Pour into the pie shell, smooth the top, and let it set completely in a cool place, about 4–5 hours.

Chocolate Truffle Tree

MAKES 30   (P: 30 mins. + 5 HOURS TO SET)

A really indulgent centerpiece for a dinner party. Produce this at the end of the meal, accompanied by strong espresso coffee.

1 styrofoam or oasis cone
30–90 chocolate truffles (see below)
   depending upon the size of the truffle tree
30–90 toothpicks
gold or silver foil

For the chocolate truffles:
12 ounces good-quality dark chocolate,
   chopped (about 2 cups)
$^1/3$ cup granulated sugar
1 cup plus 2 tablespoons (2$^1/4$ sticks)
   unsalted butter
3 cage-free, organic egg yolks

For the coatings:
white chocolate and coconut
white chocolate and flaked, toasted, roughly
   chopped, skin-on almonds
dark chocolate
cocoa powder
very fine praline powder
chopped pistachio nuts

To make the truffles, put the chocolate, sugar, and butter into a heavy saucepan, add 1 tablespoon cold water, and melt on the lowest possible heat. Cool slightly and whisk in the egg yolks. Leave in a cool place to set and solidify for 4–5 hours.

When solidified, shape the truffles into balls (larger than a hazelnut, smaller than a walnut) and roll in whichever coatings you choose. Let them set.

Cover the cone neatly with aluminum foil and place on a glass or china cake stand. You might like to use a golden doiley and place the foil-covered cone in the center.

Use toothpicks to attach the truffles to the mold. Build up in layers with one single truffle on top. It's fun to stick a few long sparklers into the top and light them just as you bring the truffle tree to the table.

Black Currant Fool

SERVES 10   (P: 30 mins. + CHILLING TIME)

12 ounces fresh or frozen black currants
  (about 3¹/₄–3³/₄ cups)
1³/₄ cups Stock Syrup (see below)
1³/₄ cups lightly whipped cream
cream, for drizzling

For serving: shortbread cookies

Cover the black currants with the Stock Syrup. Bring to a boil and cook for about 4–5 minutes, or until the fruit bursts. Blend the fruit and syrup mixture in a blender, then strain or puree it, measure it, and let cool. Set a little puree aside for garnishing.

When the puree has cooled, add up to an equal volume of the whipped cream, according to taste. The resulting black currant fool should not be very stiff, more like the texture of lightly whipped cream. If it is too stiff, stir in a little milk rather than more cream. Taste; it may need a little more sugar. Serve chilled, with shortbread cookies.

Alternatively, spoon ¹/₄ cup of the black currant fool into the bottom of each of 10 sundae glasses, then a layer of lightly whipped cream, follow with another layer of black currant fool, and top with a little cream. Drizzle a little thin black currant puree over the top and chill.

Stock Syrup

2¹/₃ cups granulated sugar
2¹/₂ cups water

To make the stock syrup, dissolve the sugar in the water over a low heat, stirring often, and bring to a boil. Boil for 2 minutes, then let the syrup cool. Store in the fridge until needed—it will keep for weeks.

Black Currant Coulis

8 ounces black currants (about 2¹/₄ cups)
1 cup Stock Syrup (see left)
¹/₂–²/₃ cup water

Put the black currants into a saucepan, add 1 cup of the syrup, bring to a boil, and cook for 3–5 minutes until the black currants burst. Blend in a blender and strain through a fine mesh nylon strainer. Let it cool, then add ¹/₂–¹/₃ cup water.

Frosted Black Currant Parfait with Black Currant Coulis

This is a really swanky name for a dessert I discovered by accident when I froze some leftover black currant fool. I serve this parfait regularly at dinner parties. It is so easy.

Pour the Black currant Fool (see above) into a loaf pan lined with plastic wrap. Cover and freeze. Serve cut in slices with Black currant Coulis (see above) drizzled over the top (see photograph opposite).

Olive Oil Ice Cream with Blood Orange Segments

SERVES 6–8   (P: 15 mins. + FREEZING TIME)

Jeannie Chesterton gave me this recipe when we spent a few blissful days at her tiny guest house, Finca Buenvino, in the middle of the chestnut forests near Aracena in Andalucia.

1 cup sugar
¹/₂ cup water
4 cage-free, organic eggs
scant cup pale light extra virgin olive oil
pinch of salt
1 cup milk

For serving: 7 ounces blood orange segments (about 1 medium orange)
sea salt flakes, such as Maldon Sea Salt

Pour the sugar and the water into a saucepan, place over a low heat, and stir to dissolve the sugar before the water comes to a boil. Continue to boil for about 5 minutes or until the syrup reaches the thread stage (see p.270), then remove from the heat and let cool.

Whizz the eggs in a food processor and add the oil gradually while the machine is still running. Next add the cooled syrup in a very thin stream. Finally, add the salt and the milk. This ice cream is best frozen in a sorbetière; otherwise, just freeze in a covered plastic box.

Serve with blood orange segments and a few sea salt flakes.

Brioche with Sugared Strawberries and Mascarpone

SERVES 8   (P: 15 mins.)

A delicious dessert but also divine for brunch.

1 loaf of brioche
1–1¹/₂ pounds fresh organic strawberries
granulated sugar, to taste
freshly squeezed lemon juice, to taste
1 cup mascarpone or crème fraîche
a little milk

For garnishing:
sprig of mint (optional)
confectioners' sugar (optional)

Slice the brioche into generous ¹/₂-inch slices. Clean and hull the strawberries and slice lengthwise into a shallow bowl. Sprinkle with sugar and squeeze some lemon juice over them. Toss gently, then taste—they should be quite sweet, so add extra sugar as needed.

Whip the mascarpone or crème fraîche, adding a little milk to soften if necessary. Taste, and add a little sugar if it seems too tart. Keep refrigerated until ready to serve.

Just before serving, put the plates in the oven to heat and toast the brioche slices. Put a slice of toasted brioche on each plate and pile some sugared strawberries on top. Top with a spoonful of mascarpone or crème fraîche. Garnish with a sprig of fresh mint and a shake of confectioners' sugar—these are not essential but they make the dish look more elegant.

The brioche may be cut in triangles and arranged in an upright position to give a little more height. Individual brioches may also be used—they look and taste delicious.

Crème Brulée

SERVES 4 (P: 15 mins. + OVERNIGHT TO CHILL)

The ultimate custard and a universally favorite pudding. I like to eat it with a compote of fruit—perhaps poached apricots with sweet geranium leaves.

2 cage-free, organic large egg yolks
2 teaspoons sugar
1^1/$_4$ cups heavy cream
^{1}/$_2$ vanilla bean (optional)

For the caramel topping:
^{1}/$_2$ cup sugar
^{1}/$_3$ cup water
^{1}/$_2$ cup whipped cream (optional)
  or ^{1}/$_2$ cup granulated sugar for blowtorch
  method

Start the recipe at least 12 hours in advance of serving.

Mix egg yolks with the sugar in a bowl. In a saucepan, heat the cream with the vanilla bean (if using) until it just shivers but do not let it boil. Pour it slowly onto the yolks, whisking all the time. Return to the saucepan and cook over medium heat, stirring until the custard is thick enough to coat the back of a spoon. It must not boil. Remove the vanilla bean, pour the custard into a serving dish, and chill overnight. Be careful not to break the skin or the caramel may sink when added later.

Next day make the caramel. In a small pan over medium heat, dissolve the sugar in the water. Bring to a boil and cook until it caramelizes to a chestnut-brown color. Remove from the heat and immediately spoon a thin layer of caramel over the top of the custard. (Alternatively, sprinkle the top of the custard with a layer of granulated sugar or raw sugar, spray with a film of cold water, then caramelize with a blowtorch).

Let it cool and pipe a line of whipped cream around the edge to seal the join where the caramel meets the side of the dish. Serve within 12 hours, or the caramel will melt.

To serve, crack the top by knocking sharply with the back of the serving spoon.

Note: Using 2 yolks only just sets the cream. Be sure to use large eggs and measure the cream slightly short of 1^1/$_4$ cups. The cream takes some time to thicken and usually does so just under boiling point. It the custard is not properly set, or if the skin that forms on top while cooking is accidentally broken, the caramel will sink to the bottom of the dish once it's added. If you notice either of these problems, freeze the pudding for 1–2 hours before spooning the hot caramel on top.

Bumble's Ginger Roulade

SERVES 8–10   (P: 30 mins./C: 15 mins.)

I spent a fun weekend at Strathgarry House in Scotland, teaching a cookery class with Bumble and her sisters, where she gave me this delightful recipe.

^{1}/$_2$ cup (1 stick) butter
^{2}/$_3$ cup golden syrup or corn syrup
^{1}/$_4$ cup granulated sugar
^{2}/$_3$ cup hot water
4 ounces all-purpose flour (about ^{3}/$_4$–1 cup)
1 teaspoon baking powder
1 teaspoon ground ginger
1 cage-free, organic egg
confectioners' sugar
1^1/$_4$ cups lightly whipped cream
2 ounces crystallized ginger, chopped,
  (about ^{1}/$_4$ cup) (optional)

large jelly roll pan—10 x 15 inches
baking paper

Preheat the oven to 350°F. Line the jelly roll pan with baking paper.

Put the butter, golden syrup, and sugar with the hot water in a saucepan and warm over a low heat until the ingredients begin to melt.

Mix the flour, baking powder, and ginger together in a bowl. When the liquids have cooled, stir in the dry ingredients. Separate the egg and add the yolk to the saucepan.

Beat the egg white until it forms stiff peaks and fold gently into the mixture. Pour into the lined jelly roll pan and bake for 12–15 minutes. Remove from the oven, cover with a damp cloth, and let cool.

Meanwhile, dredge a sheet of waxed paper with confectioners' sugar. Turn out the cooled roulade onto the waxed paper sheet, then fill with lightly whipped cream and crystallized ginger (if using) and roll up. Transfer to a serving plate, and decorate with rosettes of whipped cream and crystallized ginger.

Top Tip: Bumble discovered quite by accident that this ginger roulade freezes really well. You can pull it out when needed, cut it into thick slices, put it into a gratin dish, sprinkle with sugar, and heat it through in a very hot oven (450°F) for 8–10 minutes. Apparently it is delicious this way.

Fluffy Lemon Mousse with Crystallized Lemon Peel

SERVES 6–8   (P: 45 mins.)

3 cage-free, organic large eggs
1 cup sugar
juice and finely grated zest of 3 lemons,
    unwaxed
1¼ cups heavy cream
1 tablespoon powdered gelatin
¼ cup cold water

For the decoration:
⅔ cup whipped cream (optional)
tiny sprigs of lemon balm or sweet
    geranium leaves
Crystallized Lemon Peel (see recipe below) or
    funky sprinkles

Separate the eggs. Put the yolks into a mixing bowl and add the sugar and lemon zest. Using an electric beater if possible, beat until thick and fluffy. Strain and heat the lemon juice until warmed through, add to the egg mixture and continue to beat until the mousse reaches the "ribbon" stage (if you lift the beaters out of the bowl and trace a figure of 8 on top, it should hold its shape for 30 seconds)—this will take about 15 minutes.

Lightly whip the cream and fold it into the egg mixture. Put the gelatin and the water into a small bowl and let the gelatin swell for 5 minutes. Place the bowl into a saucepan of simmering water until the gelatin has dissolved completely. Add some of the lemon mixture to the gelatin and then carefully fold both mixtures together. Set the soufflé mixture on ice or chill in the fridge. Check it regularly.

Just as the mixture begins to thicken around the edge of the bowl, beat the egg whites in a clean bowl and using clean beaters until they form stiff peaks and fold gently into the soufflé base. Pour into individual square, oval, or round bowls, glasses, or espresso cups.

Decorate the top with tiny sprigs of lemon balm or sweet geranium leaves and Crystallized Lemon Peel (see below) or funky sprinkles.

Crystallized Lemon Peel

We always try to have crystallized lemon, orange, and lime peel in a jar to decorate tarts, scatter on mousses, or just to nibble.

2 unwaxed lemons
1 cup cold water
Stock Syrup (see p.252)
superfine sugar

Peel the lemons very thinly with a swivel-top peeler, taking care not to include any white pith. Cut the strips into fine juliennes. Put into a saucepan with the cold water and simmer for 5 minutes. Drain, refresh in cold water, cover with fresh water, drain, and refresh again.

Put the julienne strips of peel into a saucepan, add the Stock Syrup, and heat gently until the lemon juliennes look translucent. Remove with a slotted spoon and let cool on baking paper or foil or a cake rack. When cold, toss them in the sugar and let dry in a cool, airy place.

The dried crystallized peel can be stored in a jar or airtight tin for weeks, and perhaps months.

Fresh Apricot Cobbler

SERVES 6–8   (P: 30 mins./C: 45 mins.)

Cobblers, which are similar to crumbles, always inspire cries of nostalgia. They are so easy to make—use whatever fruit you have in season.

1½ pounds fresh apricots, or peaches or
    nectarines, or a mixture, pitted and cut
    into wedges
scant ½ cup granulated sugar
4 teaspoons white flour or cornstarch
juice of ½ lemon
grated zest of ½ lemon (optional)

For the cobbler topping:
4 ounces white flour (about ¾–1 cup)
¾ teaspoon baking powder
¼ teaspoon baking soda
1 tablespoon granulated sugar
2 tablespoons butter, cut into cubes
½ cup buttermilk (if unavailable, use
    regular milk)
1 tablespoon granulated sugar, for sprinkling

2½-pint pie dish

Preheat the oven to 400°F.

Put the sliced fruit in a bowl, add the sugar and flour, a tablespoon of lemon juice, and the grated zest, if using, toss well, and transfer to a pie dish.

To make the topping, sift the flour, baking powder, and baking soda into a bowl and add the tablespoon of sugar. Rub in the butter and mix gently with the buttermilk until it just comes together.

Drop tablespoons of the topping over the filling. It doesn't matter if there are spaces, the dough will expand as it cooks. Sprinkle with the remaining tablespoon of sugar. Bake for 30–45 minutes or until puffed and golden. Serve warm with crème fraîche or lightly whipped cream.

Normandy Pear or Apple Tart

SERVES 8–10   (**P:** 2 HOURS/**C:** 45 mins.)

**This is certainly one of the most impressive
of French tarts. It is wonderful served warm
but is also very good cold and keeps for
several days. Splash in a little kirsch if you
are using pears, or calvados or apple brandy
if you are using dessert apples.**

4–5 ripe Poached Pears or Apples (see below)

For the pie dough:
7 ounces all-purpose flour (about 1¹/₂ cups)
pinch of salt
¹/₂ cup (1 stick) cold butter
1 cage-free, organic egg yolk
3–4 tablespoons cold water

For the frangipane:
¹/₂ cup (1 stick) butter at room temperature
¹/₂ cup sugar
1 cage-free, organic egg, plus 1 egg yolk
4 ounces whole blanched almonds, ground
  (about 1¹/₄ cups), or a mix of ¹/₂
  ready-ground almonds and ¹/₂
  blanched and ground
3 tablespoons white flour
2¹/₂ tablespoons kirsch if using pears,
  or calvados if using apples
²/₃ cup Apricot Glaze (see below)

For serving: lightly whipped cream

9-inch diameter flan ring, or
  removable-bottomed fluted tart pan

First make the pie dough. Sift the flour and salt into a bowl, cut the butter into cubes, and rub
into the flour using your fingertips. Keep everything as cool as possible; if the butter is
allowed to melt, the finished pie crust may be tough. When the mixture resembles coarse
bread crumbs, stop. Stir in the egg yolk using a fork or knife (whichever you feel more
comfortable using), add just enough cold water to bring the dough together, then collect the
dough into a ball with your hands. This way you can judge more accurately if you need a few
more drops of liquid. Although slightly damp dough is easier to handle and roll out, the
resulting crust can be tough and may well shrink out of shape as the water evaporates in the
oven. A drier and more difficult-to-handle pastry dough will give a crisper, "shorter" crust.
Cover the pie dough with plastic wrap and let it rest in the fridge for at least 15 minutes,
preferably 30 minutes. This will make the dough much less elastic and easier to roll.

Preheat the oven to 350°F.

Roll out the dough. Line the tart pan with it, prick lightly with a fork, flute the edges, and chill
again until firm. Bake blind for 15–20 minutes. Remove from the oven and increase the heat
to 400°F.

To make the frangipane, cream the butter, beat in the sugar, and continue beating until the
mixture is light and soft. Gradually add the egg and yolk, beating well after each addition. Stir
in the ground almonds and flour and then add the kirsch or calvados. Pour the frangipane
into the pie shell, spreading it evenly.

Drain the pears or apples well and cut them crosswise into very thin slices, then lift the sliced
fruit halves intact and arrange them around the tart on the frangipane, pointed ends towards
the center. Arrange a final half pear or apple in the center.

Bake the tart for 10–15 minutes until the crust is beginning to brown. Reduce the oven
temperature to 350F° and continue baking for 15–20 minutes or until the fruit is tender and
the frangipane is set in the center and nicely golden.

Meanwhile make the Apricot Glaze (see recipe below). When the tart is fully cooked, paint
generously with the glaze, remove from the tart pan, and serve warm or cold with a bowl of
lightly whipped cream.

Poached Pears or Apples

1 cup sugar
2¹/₂ cups water
2 strips of lemon zest and the
  juice of ¹/₂ lemon
6 pears or apples

Bring the sugar and water to a boil with the strips of lemon zest in a non-reactive saucepan.
Meanwhile peel the fruit thinly, cut in half and core carefully with a melon baller or a
teaspoon, keeping a good shape. Put the fruit halves into the syrup, cut side uppermost, add
the lemon juice, and cover with a paper lid and then the pan lid. Bring to a boil and simmer
until the fruit are just soft—the tip of a knife or skewer should go through without resistance.
Remove from the heat and cool before using.

Apricot Glaze

**Apricot glaze is invaluable to have ready
made up in your fridge. It is used to glaze
tarts that contain green, orange, or white
fruit, e.g., kiwi fruit, peaches and oranges,
apples and pears.**

In a small saucepan (not aluminum), melt 12 ounces (about 1¹/₄ cups) apricot jam with the
juice of ¹/₄ lemon and just enough water to make a glaze that can be poured. Push the hot
jam through a nylon mesh strainer and store in an airtight jar. Reheat the glaze to melt it
before using. The quantities given above make a generous 1¹/₄-cup glaze.

Frosted Lemon and Rosemary Squares with Crème Fraîche

MAKES 24   (**P:** 3 mins./**C:** 25 mins.)

1 cup plus 2 tablespoons (2¼ sticks)
  butter, softened, plus extra for greasing
1¼ cups sugar
3 cage-free, organic eggs
9 ounces self-rising flour (about 1 scant cup)

For the glaze:
grated zest and juice of 2 unwaxed lemons
³/₄ cup superfine sugar
2¹/₂ tablespoons chopped fresh rosemary

For garnishing:
crème fraîche and sprigs of rosemary

jelly roll pan, 12 x 7 inches

Preheat the oven to 350°F. Grease the jelly roll pan well.

Put the butter into a food processor, add the sugar, eggs, and flour, and whizz for a few seconds to amalgamate. Spread evenly in the jelly roll pan. Bake for 20–25 minutes, or until golden brown and well risen.

Meanwhile, make the glaze. Mix the grated lemon zest and juice with the superfine sugar and chopped rosemary. As soon as the cake is cooked, pour the glaze over the top and let cool.

Cut the cake into squares and garnish each square with a spoonful of crème fraîche and a sprig of rosemary before serving. (See photograph on p.263.)

Frosted Tangerines

SERVES 10–12
              (**P:** 1 HOUR + 3 HOURS TO CHILL)

This clean, fresh ice tastes like a superior Popsicle. To cut the work in half, pour it into Popsicle molds. Clementines, mandarins, and satsumas may be substituted for tangerines in this recipe. Citrus fruit are at their best and most varied in the winter, when they are in season.

For the syrup:
1¹/₄ cups sugar
juice of ¹/₄ lemon
²/₃ cup water

20–28 tangerines
finely grated zest and juice of ¹/₂ lemon
confectioners' sugar (optional)

For garnishing:
vine leaves or bay leaves

First make the syrup. Put the sugar, lemon juice, and water into a saucepan over low heat and stir until the sugar dissolves. Bring to a boil, then boil for 2–3 minutes. Remove from the heat and let cool.

Meanwhile, grate the zest from 10 of the tangerines, then cut each of the ten in half and squeeze out the juice.

Cut the top off each of the remaining tangerines to make a lid for each one. With a small spoon, scoop the segments out of the main part of the fruit. Press the segments through a nylon mesh strainer into a measuring cup (alternatively, you could blend the pulp and then strain it). You should end up with 25fl.oz. (just over 3 cups) of juice. Put the tangerine shells in the fridge or freezer to chill. Add the grated lemon zest to the tangerine juice, and add the lemon juice and the syrup to taste—add confectioners' sugar or extra lemon juice if more sweetness or sharpness is required. The juice should taste sweeter than you would like it to be, because it will lose some of its sweetness when it freezes. Freeze until firm in one of the ways suggested below.

Finally, fill the chilled tangerine shells with scoops of the frozen sherbet. Replace the lids and store the frosted tangerines in the freezer. If you do not intend to serve them on the day you make them, cover them with plastic wrap. Serve the frosted tangerines on a white plate decorated with vine leaves or bay leaves, or on colorful plates for a children's party.

Make the sherbet in one of the following ways
1 Pour into the drum of an ice cream maker or sorbetière and freeze for 20–25 minutes. Scoop into the chilled tangerine shells and serve immediately, or store in a covered bowl in the freezer until needed.

2 Pour the juice into a stainless steel or plastic container and put into the freezer. After 4–5 hours, when the juice is semi-frozen, remove from the freezer and beat until smooth, then return to the freezer. Beat again when almost frozen and fold in one stiffly beaten egg white. Keep in the freezer until needed.

Californian Three-stone Pie

SERVES 8–12   (**P:** 1¼ HOURS/**C:** 1 HOUR)

This pastry dough is made by the creaming method, so people who are convinced that they suffer from "hot hands" don't have to worry about rubbing in the butter.

For the break-all-the-rules pastry dough:
1½ cups (3 sticks) butter at room temperature
⅓ cup sugar
3 cage-free, organic eggs
18 ounces white flour, preferably
  unbleached (about 3¾–4 cups)

For the filling:
2¼ pounds apricots, peaches, and nectarines
1 cup sugar
¼ cup all-purpose flour or cornstarch
egg wash

For serving:
lightly whipped cream or crème fraîche
superfine sugar

13 x 9 inch baking dish

Preheat the oven to 350°F.

Cream the butter and sugar together by hand or in a stand mixer (do not overcream). Add the eggs and beat for a minute or two. Reduce the speed to the lowest setting and mix in the flour. Turn out onto a piece of floured waxed paper, flatten into a circle, wrap, and chill. This dough needs to be chilled for at least 1 hour otherwise it is difficult to handle.

Remove the pits and slice the fruit into a bowl, sprinkle with the sugar and flour, and toss well.

Roll out the dough to a thickness of just over ⅛-inch, and use about two thirds of it to line a suitable baking dish. Spoon the sugared fruit into the pie shell. Cover with a lid of pastry dough rolled out to the same thickness and seal the edges by pressing together. Decorate with peach shapes and leaves cut out from the pie dough trimmings. Brush with egg wash and bake until the fruit is tender and juicy and starts to ooze through, about 45–60 minutes.

Sprinkle lightly with superfine sugar and serve with lightly whipped cream or crème fraîche.

Bananas in Lime Syrup

SERVES 4
(**P:** 15 mins./**C:** 5 mins. + 1 HOUR TO MACERATE)

This is my number one standby dessert when there is nothing in the house and all else fails. It is so delicious and refreshing that it's a must in anybody's easy entertaining repertoire.

½ cup sugar
½ cup water
4 bananas
juice and zest of 1 lime

Put the sugar and water into a saucepan and stir over a gentle heat until the sugar dissolves. Bring to a boil, simmer for 2 minutes, and let cool.

Peel the bananas and cut into slices. Put the slices into a bowl and cover with the cold syrup. Add the lime zest and juice to the syrup and let macerate for at least 1 hour. Serve chilled.

Mangoes in Lime Syrup

Use 2 ripe mangoes instead of bananas in the above recipe. Peel the mango, slice quite thinly down to the pit and continue as above.

Mango, Banana, and Passion Fruit in Lime Syrup

Add the juice and seeds of 1 passion fruit to 1 ripe mango and 2 bananas and continue as above.

time for tea

Tea time is redolent of a more leisurely age, of Edwardian tea gowns, grand hotels, and elegant gardens. For some, it was a time for planning social events and gossiping over a pot of imported tea and dainty sandwiches and cakes. For others, it was seen as an essential snack, needed to get them through to dinner.

Either way, it is a meal we should find more time for. Invite friends and family over for a lazy afternoon, to catch up on the week's happenings over a fragrant pot of tea or coffee. It is also a great opportunity to entertain people with children as it is the one meal where kids can join in and play around you.

Spend a couple of hours baking a cake or cookies—ideally one centerpiece cake, for example a chocolate meringue layer cake (see p.247), as well as some savory coffee walnut cookies (see p.274) or lemon and rosemary squares (see p.258). Some sandwiches are always welcome, though I leave it up to you whether to trim the crusts. Why not try a fruit bread or Barm Brack, which can be made a day in advance and stored in an air-tight container? Remember the old tradition of always having something in the tin in case someone drops in?

To drink, offer some homemade lemonade and freshly brewed coffee and tea (leaves give a much better flavor than tea bags). Green tea is now often served for tea and it is a good idea to provide some caffeine-free alternatives such as fruit and herbal teas. They should all be served in elegant china cups and saucers.

coffee and cake

This is a time for pretty elegance, not modern minimalism. Indulge your girly side and flood it with warm pinks, patterns, and pastels. Use swathes of beautiful fabric as a tablecloth and don't worry about matching color schemes or clashing patterns. Choose bright plates, striped place mats, and frilly glass cake stands. Pile chairs with tasseled cushions and bring out exotic trinkets from trips abroad—bangles from India, beads from Morocco. Ask your guests to dress for the occasion—no jeans or sneakers—and just by doing that, you will create a special afternoon.

For the food, presentation is everything. A tea set or coffee set is essential (no mugs please), but it doesn't have to match. Nowadays you can buy individual pieces, old and new, and they also make fantastic presents, so hint madly near your birthday. A cake stand will show your efforts in the best light, but you could also buy squares of white lace to give your everyday plates a touch of glamour.

Use herbs and flowers to adorn the cakes, and petals in tea cups. Then lean back, sip your tea, and while away the time.

Tiramisu or Frosted Tiramisu with Irish Coffee Sauce

SERVES 8   (P: 1 HOUR)

1 cup strong espresso coffee
   (if your freshly made coffee is not strong
   enough, add 1 teaspoon instant coffee)
2¹/₂ tablespoons brandy
2¹/₂ tablespoons Jamaica rum
3 ounces good-quality dark chocolate
   (about ¹/₂ cup)
3 cage-free, organic eggs, separated
¹/₃ cup sugar
1 cup mascarpone cheese
38–40 ladyfingers
unsweetened cocoa powder, for dredging

For serving: Irish Coffee Sauce (optional—see
   below)

8¹/₂ x 4¹/₂-inch loaf pan, lined
   with plastic wrap

Mix the coffee with the brandy and rum. Roughly grate the chocolate (we do it in the food processor, using the pulse button). Beat the egg yolks with the sugar until the mixture reaches the "ribbon" stage (if you lift the beaters out of the bowl and trace a figure of 8 on top, it should hold its shape for 30 seconds) and is light and fluffy, then fold in the mascarpone cheese a tablespoon at a time.

Using clean beaters, beat the egg whites stiffly and fold gently into the cheese mixture. Now assemble the tiramisu. Dip each end of the cookies one at a time into the coffee mixture and arrange half of them side by side in the bottom of the loaf pan. Spread half the mascarpone mixture gently over the cookies, sprinkle half the grated chocolate over the top, then another layer of soaked cookies and finally the rest of the mascarpone.

Cover the loaf pan carefully with plastic wrap or better still slide it into a plastic bag and twist the end. Refrigerate. Just before serving, scatter the remaining chocolate over the top and dredge with unsweetened cocoa powder. Serve with Irish Coffee Sauce, if you like.

Frosted Tiramisu with Irish Coffee Sauce
Freeze for at least 6 hours. Cut the frosted tiramisu into thick slices and serve with Irish Coffee Sauce, if you like.

Teeny Weeny Tiramisu
Make the tiramisu in little glasses—they are ready to be eaten within 1 hour.

Irish Coffee Sauce

**This sauce keeps indefinitely so make up a
batch for ice cream, crêpes, mousses.**

1 cup sugar
¹/₃ cup water
1 cup strong coffee
1 tablespoon Irish whiskey

Put the sugar and water in a heavy saucepan and heat. Stir until the sugar dissolves and the water comes to a boil. Remove the spoon and do not stir again until the syrup turns a pale golden caramel. Draw the saucepan off the heat, add the hot coffee (beware it may froth up), and return to the heat to dissolve the caramel in the coffee. Let it cool before adding the whiskey.

A Great Lemon Meringue Pie

SERVES 6   (P: 1¹/₂ HOURS/C: 1¹/₂ HOURS)

This is real retro food and this version always gets a rousing response (see photograph on p.105).

For the pastry dough:
4 ounces white flour (about ³/₄–1 cup)
¹/₄–¹/₃ cup (¹/₂–³/₄ stick) butter
1 cage-free, organic egg yolk
1 cage-free, organic egg white, lightly beaten

For the lemon curd:
¹/₄ cup (¹/₂ stick) butter
¹/₂ cup sugar
finely grated zest and juice of 2 large
   unwaxed lemons
2 cage-free, organic eggs, plus 1 egg yolk,
   well beaten

For the meringue:
2 cage-free, organic egg whites
¹/₂ cup sugar

8-inch pie pan (or 8-inch flan ring on
   a cookie sheet)

First make the pastry dough as per the method for Normandy Pear or Apple Tart (see p.257).

Use the dough to line the pie pan and chill again for 15–20 minutes. Meanwhile preheat the oven to 350°F. Line the chilled pie shell with baking paper or foil and fill it with dried beans or baking beans. Bake for 25 minutes or until the pie shell is fully cooked. Remove the paper and beans, paint the pie shell with a little lightly beaten egg white, and put it back in the oven to seal for about 2–3 minutes.

Now make the lemon curd. Melt the butter in a saucepan over a very low heat, add the sugar, lemon juice, and zest, then stir in the eggs. Stir over a very low heat until the mixture coats the back of a spoon. Take the saucepan off the heat and pour the mixture into a bowl. It will thicken more as it cools. Fill the pie shell with the lemon curd mixture.

Now make the meringue: first, turn down the oven temperature to a cool 250°F. Beat the egg whites in a perfectly clean, dry bowl until they begin to get fluffy, then add half the sugar and continue to beat until the egg whites form stiff peaks. Fold in the remaining sugar and then either pipe or spread the beaten egg whites over the lemon mixture with a spoon. Note: do not beat the egg whites until you are ready to use them, since if they sit around, they lose volume. Bake the lemon meringue pie for about 1 hour until the meringue is crisp on the outside. Serve warm or cold. Alternatively cook in an oven preheated to 400°F for just 7 minutes—this will result in a meringue that is slightly colored, crisp on the outside, and soft underneath. Serve warm or cold.

Lemon Petit Fours
Preheat the oven to 475°F. Fill tiny petit four pastry shells with a spoonful of lemon curd and pipe a rosette of meringue on top. Bake the petits fours for 60 seconds.

Mile-high lemon Meringue Pie
Double the quantity of meringue in the recipe and pile it into a cone or pyramid on top of the lemon curd in the pie.

Sticky Toffee Pudding with Butterscotch and Pecan Nut Sauce

SERVES 6–8   (P: 1 HOUR/C: 1¼ HOURS)

8 ounces chopped dates (about 1¹/₂ cups)
1¹/₄ cups hot tea
oil, for greasing
¹/₂ cup (1 stick) unsalted butter
³/₄ cup sugar
3 cage-free, organic eggs
8 ounces self-rising flour (about
   1²/₃ cups), sifted
1 teaspoon baking soda, sifted
1 teaspoon vanilla extract
1 teaspoon espresso coffee powder

For the butterscotch pecan sauce:
¹/₂ cup (1 stick) butter
³/₄ cup dark soft brown Barbados sugar
¹/₂ cup granulated sugar
10 ounces golden syrup (about ³/₄–1 cup),
   if unavailable, use corn syrup
1 cup heavy cream
¹/₂ teaspoon vanilla extract
¹/₂ cup chopped pecans

Preheat the oven to 350°F.

Soak the dates in the tea for 15 minutes. Brush an 8-inch springform cake pan with oil and place oiled baking parchment on the bottom.

Cream together the butter and sugar until light and fluffy. Beat in the eggs, one at a time, and then fold in the flour. Add the baking soda, vanilla, and coffee to the dates and tea and stir this into the batter. Turn into the pan and bake for 1–1¹/₂ hours or until a skewer inserted in the center comes out clean.

To make the butterscotch pecan sauce, put the butter, sugars, and golden syrup into a heavy saucepan and melt gently over a low heat. Simmer for about 5 minutes. Remove from the heat and gradually stir in the cream, the vanilla, and the pecans. Return to the heat and stir for 2–3 minutes until all the sugar is dissolved and the sauce is absolutely smooth.

Pour some hot sauce onto a serving plate, spoon the sticky toffee pudding on top, and pour a generous quantity of the sauce over the pudding. Serve with lightly whipped cream. Put the remaining sauce in a bowl, and pass it around for extra helpings.

Sticky Toffee Pudding reheats very well.

Meringue Roulade with Pomegranate Seeds and Rose Water

SERVES 6–8   (**P:** 45 mins./**C:** 30 mins.)

sunflower oil, for greasing
4 cage-free, organic egg whites
1 cup sugar
1¹/₄ cups whipped cream, plus
  ²/₃ cup for rosettes

For the filling:
1–2 pomegranates
1–2 teaspoons rose water

For garnishing:
pomegranate seeds
rose petals if available (ensure before picking
  that the rose hasn't been sprayed)

For Christmas:
sprigs of holly with berries

jelly roll pan 12 x 7 inches

Preheat the oven to 350°F. Line the jelly roll pan with aluminum foil, and brush the foil lightly with oil.

Put the egg whites in a spotlessly clean food mixer bowl. Break them up with the beaters, then add all the sugar at once. Beat at full speed for 4–5 minutes, or until the egg whites hold a stiff peak when the beaters are lifted.

Spread the meringue gently over the pan with a palette knife or spatula. Bake for 15–20 minutes. When cooked, the meringue ought to be quite thick and bouncy, crisp on the outside but still soft in the center. Let it cool.

Meanwhile, cut the pomegranates in half around their "equator" and flick the seeds out into a bowl. Sprinkle with a few drops of rose water. Taste, and add more rose water if needed. Keep some seeds on one side to decorate the roulade.

To assemble, put a sheet of aluminum foil on the counter and turn the meringue out onto it. Remove the oiled foil. Spread the 1¹/₄ cups whipped cream and the pomegranate seeds over the meringue. Roll up the meringue from the long side and carefully ease it onto a serving plate. Pipe 6–8 rosettes of cream along the top of the roulade, and decorate with the reserved pomegranate seeds and rose petals, if available. An alternative for Christmas is to surround the roulade with berried holly and dredge it with confectioners' sugar. Serve the roulade cut into slices about an inch thick.

Yogurt and Cardamom Cream with Apricots and Saffron Syrup

SERVES 8–10
    (**P:** 30 mins. + 4–5 HOURS TO CHILL)

1 cup milk
1 cup heavy cream
1 cup sugar
¹/₂ teaspoon ground cardamom seeds
3 rounded teaspoons powdered gelatin
¹/₃ cup cold water
2 cups yogurt

Poached Apricots in Saffron Syrup (see below)

Put the milk, cream, and sugar into a stainless steel saucepan and add the ground cardamom. Stir over a low heat until the sugar has dissolved and the mixture is warm to the touch. Remove from the heat and let it infuse while you dissolve the gelatin.

Put the gelatin into a small bowl with the cold water. Let the gelatin swell for 4–5 minutes. Put the bowl into a saucepan of simmering water until the gelatin has melted and is completely clear.

Add a little of the infused milk mixture to the gelatin and stir well, then mix this into the rest of the milk. Whisk the yogurt lightly until smooth and creamy and stir it into the milk mixture.

Pour into a bowl or 8–10 individual molds or small glasses. Let it set in a refrigerator for several hours. Serve with Apricot and Saffron Syrup. Yogurt and Cardamom Cream is also great with sugared strawberries or Gooseberry and Elderflower Compote (see p.229).

Poached Apricots in Saffron Syrup

SERVES 8   (**P:** 5 mins./**C:** 10 mins.)

2 cups sugar (reduce the quantity of
  sugar if the apricots are very sweet)
2¹/₄ cups cold water
¹/₂–1 teaspoon saffron strands
2 pounds fresh apricots
juice of 2 lemons

Put the sugar and water into a saucepan, add the saffron, and bring to a boil. Add the apricots whole or, if you prefer, cut them in half and remove the pits. Cover the saucepan and simmer until the apricots are soft. Add the lemon juice, turn into a bowl, and chill before serving.

Almond Meringue with Kumquats

SERVES 6   (**P:** 45 mins./**C:** 45 mins.)

This meringue may break a few of the rules of dieting, but it is one of our best and favorite desserts. We fill it with any suitable fruit in season—strawberries, raspberries, loganberries, boysenberries, tayberries, raspberries, peaches—and combinations such as nectarine, mango and passion fruit, green gooseberry and elderflower, or rhubarb and strawberry… This recipe uses egg whites, so save the yolks for homemade Mayonnaise, (see p.296).

For the meringue:
1/4 cup whole almonds
1 cup confectioners' sugar
2 cage-free, organic egg whites

For the filling:
1 1/4 cups whipped cream
8 ounces Kumquat Compote (see below), about 1 cup

For garnishing:
whipped cream
wafers of chocolate (optional—see p.274)

baking paper or prepared baking sheet

Preheat the oven to 300°F.

Drop the almonds into boiling water and return to a boil for a minute or two to blanch them. When cool enough to handle, skin the almonds, then grind them or chop them up. They should not be ground to a fine powder but should be left slightly coarse and gritty.

Mark two 7 1/2-inch diameter circles on baking paper or a prepared baking sheet.

In a bowl that is free from any grease and is dry and spotlessly clean, mix the confectioners' sugar with the egg whites and beat until the mixture forms stiff, dry peaks. Fold in the ground almonds. Divide the mixture between the two circles and spread it evenly with a palette knife or spatula. Bake the meringues immediately for 45 minutes or until set crisp and just brown on top. Let them cool.

To assemble, sandwich the meringues together with the whipped cream and drained Kumquat Compote. Chill for some hours before serving. Decorate with piped rosettes of whipped cream and wafers of chocolate.

For a celebration, mold the meringue into a star or heart shape, or the numerals "2" and "1" for a 21st-birthday party, for instance.

This recipe can be multiplied easily, but don't beat more than 4 egg whites at a time otherwise you will lose volume.

Kumquat Compote

8 ounces kumquats
2/3 cup water
2/3 cup sugar

Cut each kumquat into 4 slices and remove the seeds. Put the kumquats in a saucepan with the water and sugar and let them cook very gently, uncovered, for 30 minutes. Let cool and drain off the excess juice before using as a filling for the meringue.

Top Tip: Kumquat Frizzle
Use the kumquat syrup—the excess juice from the Kumquat Compote—to make a Kumquat Frizzle. Put 1 tablespoon of the syrup into a champagne flute. Top with Prosecco or another sparkling wine.

Affrogata

Put a scoop of Homemade Vanilla Ice Cream (see p.270) into an espresso cup, top with a shot of espresso, and serve immediately. Yummeee!

Adorable Baby Banoffis

MAKES 8–12   (**P:** 15 mins./**C:** 3 HOURS)

Have a few jars of toffee ready in your cupboard so you can make this yummy dessert in minutes.

1 x 14-ounce can condensed milk
16–24 squares of graham crackers
3 bananas
freshly squeezed juice of 1 lemon
1 cup whipped cream
toasted slivered almonds
chocolate curls made from about 6 ounces
   chocolate (about 1 cup)

8–12 individual glasses or bowls

To make the toffee, put the unopened can of condensed milk into a saucepan and cover with hot water. Bring to a boil, cover, and simmer for 3 hours by which time the condensed milk will have turned into a thick unctuous toffee.

Break 2 to 3 graham crackers into each glass or bowl. Peel and slice the bananas, toss them in the lemon juice, and add to the bowls. Top each with a little toffee. Put a blob of lightly whipped cream on top. Sprinkle with the almonds, and decorate with a few chocolate curls.

Bread and Butter Pudding

SERVES 6–8   (**P:** 30 mins. + 1 HOUR
         OR OVERNIGHT TO CHILL/**C:** 1 HOUR)

This irresistible pudding is a must for an easy-entertaining repertoire. This version will reheat perfectly. Note that cinnamon or apple pie spice may be used instead of nutmeg to give an exotic flavor. It is also great served in a cappucino cup.

$^1/_4$ cup ($^1/_2$ stick) butter, softened, plus extra
   for greasing
12 slices good-quality white bread,
   crusts removed
$^1/_2$ teaspoon grated nutmeg
7 ounces plump raisins or golden raisins
   (about $1^1/_3$–$1^1/_2$ cups)
2 cups heavy cream
1 cup milk
4 cage-free, organic large eggs, lightly beaten
1 teaspoon vanilla extract
$^3/_4$ cup sugar
pinch of salt
1 tablespoon granulated sugar, for sprinkling

For serving:
lightly whipped cream or crème fraîche

1 x 8-inch square ovenproof pottery or
   china dish
1 pan large enough for the 8-inch dish to sit in

Butter the ovenproof dish.

Butter the bread and arrange 4 slices, buttered side down, in 1 layer in the dish. Sprinkle the bread with half the grated nutmeg and half the raisins and arrange another layer of bread, buttered side down, over the raisins. Sprinkle the remaining nutmeg and raisins on top. Cover the raisins with the remaining bread, buttered side down.

In a bowl whisk together the cream, milk, eggs, vanilla extract, sugar, and a pinch of salt. Pour the mixture through a fine mesh strainer over the bread in the dish. Sprinkle the granulated sugar over the top and let the mixture stand, covered loosely, at room temperature for at least 1 hour, or chill overnight.

Preheat the oven to 350°F.

Place the pudding in a water bath (a larger pan filled with hot water)—the water should come halfway up the sides of the baking dish. Place in the oven and bake for about 1 hour, or until the top is crisp and golden. Serve warm with some lightly whipped cream or crème fraîche.

Delicious Bread and Butter Puddings can be made using:
Barm Brack (see p.182) as a base. Add apple pie spice or cinnamon.
Panettone as a base—proceed as in recipe above.
Brioche as a base—proceed as in recipe above, or use apricot jam and lace with apricot brandy.
Rhubarb, gooseberry, and elderflower compote or spiced apple puree.
Cheese, to make a savory bread and butter pudding.
Marmalade—spread the slices of buttered bread generously with marmalade. Include or omit the raisins or golden raisins, as you choose.

Homemade Vanilla Ice cream

SERVES 12–16

    (P: 30 mins. + 5–6 HOURS FREEZING TIME)

This is my favorite homemade ice cream, very rich and very delicious. It is made with an egg mousse base, with lightly whipped cream and flavorings added. Ice creams made in this way have a smooth texture, and do not need additional beating during the freezing period or a sorbetière. They should not be served frozen hard, so remove from the freezer at least 10 minutes before serving. Only the egg yolks are used in the egg mousse base, so save the whites to make the meringues on pp.266–267.

4 cage-free, organic egg yolks

$^1/_2$ cup sugar

1 cup water

1 teaspoon vanilla extract

2$^1/_2$ pints lightly whipped cream

Put the egg yolks in a bowl and beat until light and fluffy.

Combine the sugar and water in a small heavy saucepan, stir over a low heat until the sugar is completely dissolved, then remove the spoon and boil the syrup until it reaches the "thread" stage, i.e., it will look thick and syrupy, and when a metal spoon is dipped in, the last drops of syrup will form thin threads.

Pour this boiling syrup in a steady stream onto the egg yolks, beating all the time. Add the vanilla extract and continue to beat until it becomes a thick, creamy white mousse. Fold the lightly whipped cream into the mousse, pour into a bowl, cover, and freeze.

Here are some ideas for serving the ice cream:

Ice Cream Sandwich

Individual sandwiches of ice cream between two chocolate chip and hazelnut cookies.

Toffee Ripple Ice Cream

Swirl toffee sauce through softened frozen ice cream.

Ice Cream Parfait with coffee, chocolate, and praline; strawberry, vanilla, and black currant; or mango, passion fruit, and vanilla. Line a loaf pan with plastic wrap and fill it with 3 various ice creams in layers. Serve the parfait in slices with a complementary sauce. Alternatively, fill the lined loaf pan with three alternate layers of vanilla ice cream and crushed praline powder. Serve cut into slices, sprinkled with extra crushed praline and perhaps a toffee sauce

Vanilla Ice Cream on a Stick

Spoon the ice cream into plastic Popsicle molds, cover and pop into the freezer. When the ice cream is partially frozen, insert ice cream sticks into the center of each one. Remove from the molds just before serving. To chocolate-coat them, dip the unmolded ice creams into cool melted chocolate and enjoy!

Sweet Geranium Cake with Blackberries

SERVES 8–10   (P: 30 mins./C: 1 HOUR)

1$^1/_2$ cups (3 sticks) butter, softened, plus extra for greasing

1$^3/_4$ cups sugar

4 cage-free, organic eggs

12 ounces self-rising flour (about 2$^2/_3$ cups)

For the sweet geranium syrup:

$^1/_4$ cup sugar

$^2/_3$ cup water

4–6 sweet geranium leaves (Pelargonium graveolens)

zest and juice of 1 unwaxed lemon

For serving:

2 pounds fresh blackberries

a little confectioners' sugar

lightly whipped cream

rose petals (optional)

Preheat the oven to 350°F. Grease a 9-inch round cake pan.

Put the butter into the bowl of a food processor and add the sugar, eggs, and flour. Whizz for a few seconds to amalgamate. Spread evenly in the cake pan. Bake for about 1 hour or until golden brown and well risen.

Meanwhile make the syrup. Put the sugar, water, and geranium leaves into a saucepan over a medium heat. Stir until the sugar dissolves, bring to a boil, and simmer for 2–3 minutes. Remove from the heat and add the lemon zest and juice. Set aside to cool, then strain.

As soon as the cake is baked, prick the surface, pour all the syrup over the top, and let it cool.

Remove the cake from the pan and serve with the blackberries, dusted with a little confectioners' sugar, and lightly whipped cream. A few rose petals scattered over the top look divine.

A slice of cake on its own with a cup of tea is also delicious.

Irish Rhubarb Tart

SERVES 8–12   (**P:** 45 mins./**C:** 1 HOUR)

This makes such a terrific pie crust. If I'm in a mad rush I make it in a food processor. It's easier to handle if chilled before rolling out, but works fine even if you use it right away and have to patch it up a bit. It's fun to trace a funny face or print a message on the tart.

For the pastry dough:
1 cup (2 sticks) butter, softened
1/4 cup sugar
2 cage-free, organic eggs, plus 1 egg beaten
   with a little milk, for glazing
12 ounces all-purpose white flour
   (about 2²/3 cups)

For the filling:
1 pound red rhubarb
3/4 cup sugar

For serving:
superfine sugar
lightly whipped cream
dark brown soft sugar

1 x 9-inch pie pan with 1¹/2-inch sides

First make the pastry dough. In a stand mixer, cream the butter and sugar together. Add the eggs and beat for several minutes.

Reduce the speed and add the flour a little at a time, to form a stiff dough. Turn out onto a floured counter and flatten into a circle. Transfer to a plate, cover with plastic wrap, and chill for at least 1 hour; this makes the dough much easier to handle.

Preheat the oven to 350°F. Roll out half the dough to about 1/8-inch thick and line a pie pan.

Cut the rhubarb into 1/2-inch slices. Put them into the pie shell and sprinkle with the sugar. Roll out the remaining dough. Cover the rhubarb with it and trim and seal the edges. Use the pastry dough trimmings to make pastry leaves and decorate the pie. Brush with egg wash and bake for 45–60 minutes until the tart is golden and the rhubarb is soft.

Sprinkle lightly with superfine sugar and serve with lightly whipped cream and dark brown sugar.

Note: This tart can also be filled with apples; gooseberries and elderflower; damson or other plums; blackberries and apples; peaches and raspberries; rhubarb and strawberries.

Dutch Apple Cake with Cinnamon Sugar

SERVES 8 (P: 45 mins./C: 35 mins.)

2 cage-free, organic large eggs

1 cup sugar

1/2 cup (1 stick) butter, plus extra for greasing

2/3 cup creamy milk

6 1/2 ounces all-purpose flour
  (about 1 1/3–1 1/2 cups), plus extra for sprinkling

1 tablespoon baking powder

3–4 large cooking apples

2 tablespoons sugar

lightly whipped cream, for serving

For the cinnamon sugar:

2 tablespoons sugar

1 teaspoon ground cinnamon

Preheat the oven to 400°F. Grease and flour a 13 x 9-inch roasting pan or lasagne dish.

Beat the eggs and the sugar together in a bowl until the mixture is really thick and fluffy.

Put the butter and milk in a saucepan, bring to a boil, and stir, still boiling, into the egg and sugar mixture. Sift the flour and baking powder and fold into the batter carefully, so that there are no lumps of flour. Pour the batter into the roasting pan or lasagne dish.

Peel and core the apples, cut them into thin slices and arrange them, overlapping each other, on top of the batter. Sprinkle with the remaining sugar. Bake for 10 minutes, then reduce the heat to 350°F and continue baking for 20–25 minutes or until the apple cake is well risen and golden brown. Mix the cinnamon and sugar and sprinkle on top. Cut into slices and serve with lightly whipped cream.

Pear and Chocolate Chip Crumble

SERVES 6–8   (**P**: 30 mins./**C**: 45 mins.)

Crumbles are year-round comfort food—vary the fruit according to the season.

1¹/₂ pounds pears
2 tablespoons sugar
¹/₃ cup best quality chocolate chips
1 teaspoon fresh ginger root, peeled
   and grated (optional)

For the crumble topping:
¹/₄ cup (¹/₂ stick) cold butter
4 ounces flour (about ³/₄–1 cup)
¹/₄ cup sugar
3 tablespoons chopped almonds or hazelnuts
   (optional)

1¹/₂-quart capacity ovenproof dish

Preheat the oven to 350°F.

Peel the pears, cut into quarters, remove the core, and cut into large chunks. Turn into an ovenproof dish, add the chocolate chips and ginger, (if using), and sprinkle with the sugar.

Rub the butter into the flour just until the mixture resembles really coarse bread crumbs. Add the sugar and chopped nuts if using. Sprinkle this mixture over the pears. Bake for 40–45 minutes or until the topping is cooked and golden. Serve with whipped cream.

Bramley Apple Crumble
Substitute 1¹/₂ pounds Bramley Seedling apples (or other cooking apples) for the pears, omit the chocolate. A good addition to the crumble topping is ¹/₂ teaspoon of ground cinnamon.

Blackberry and Apple Crumble
Use three parts apple to one part fresh or frozen blackberries and proceed as with the Bramley Apple Crumble.

Rhubarb Crumble
Partially stew 1¹/₂ pounds rhubarb with 1 cup sugar until half cooked and proceed as with the basic recipe.

Rhubarb and Strawberry Crumble
Partially stew 1 pound rhubarb with 1 cup sugar, stir in 2 cups strawberries, and proceed as with Rhubarb Crumble.

Plum or Apricot
Partially stew 1¹/₂ pounds plums or apricots and ¹/₃ cup sugar and proceed as with the basic recipe.

Variations on the Crumble Topping:
1 ¹/₄ cup rolled oats can be added to the topping instead of chopped nuts.
2 1 teaspoon ground cinnamon or apple pie spice is also a delicious addition.

Coffee and Walnut Cookies

MAKES 9–10   (P: 30 mins./C: 10 mins.)

For the cookie dough:
6 ounces all-purpose white flour
  (about 1¹/₃ cups), plus extra for dusting
¹/₃ cup (³/₄ stick) butter, cut into small cubes
¹/₄ cup sugar
1 cage-free, organic egg

For the coffee cream filling:
2 tablespoons butter, softened
¹/₃ cup confectioners' sugar, sifted
1 teaspoon coffee essence

For the coffee frosting:
²/₃ cup confectioners' sugar, sifted
scant ¹/₂ tablespoon coffee essence

For garnishing:
fresh walnut halves

Preheat the oven to 350°F.

First make the cookies. Sift the flour into a bowl. Rub in the butter, then add the sugar and mix well. Beat the egg, then mix into the dry ingredients to form a stiff dough. Turn out onto a floured board and roll out to a scant ¹/₈-inch thickness. Cut into 3¹/₄-inch circles. Bake for about 8 minutes until golden brown. Transfer the cookies to a wire rack and leave until cold.

Meanwhile, make the coffee cream filling. Cream the butter and add the sifted confectioners' sugar and the coffee essence. Continue to beat until light and fluffy, then set aside.

Next make the frosting. Sift the confectioners' sugar into a bowl. Add the coffee essence and about 1 tablespoon boiling water—just enough to mix to the consistency of a very thick cream. Beat until smooth and glossy.

When the cookies are cold, sandwich them together with the coffee cream filling and spread a little thick coffee frosting on top. Decorate each cookie with half a walnut. Great for a picnic.

Summerberry Tart with Rose Water Cream

SERVES 8–12   (P: 1 HOUR/C: 15 mins.)

1 x 10-inch Sweet Pastry Dough (see p.246)
red currant jelly, for glazing, heated
  gently to soften
1 pound mixed summer fruit, such as
  raspberries, loganberries, blueberries,
  small strawberries, black currants

For the rose water cream:
1¹/₄ cups lightly whipped cream
1 tablespoon confectioners' sugar
1–2 teaspoons rose water

Brush the bottom of the blind-baked pie shell with red currant jelly. Arrange the fruit in the pie shell in concentric circles, or for a more haphazard look, just scatter them into the shell. Brush generously with more red currant jelly.

In a bowl, mix together the lightly whipped cream with the confectioners' sugar and rose water. Taste and adjust the flavorings if needed. Serve with the Summerberry Tart.

Summerberry Tart with Cassis Cream
Substitute crème de cassis (black currant liqueur) for rose water in the above recipe.

don't forget dessert

Cakes, tarts, fools, and ice cream—it should not be a problem to find something to match your menu. Give your guests a sneak preview so that they leave room for dessert, no matter how tempting the previous courses. Always serve dessert at the table—it is often the best-looking of all courses, so show it off before you hack it to pieces.

This is a good opportunity to move from the table to more comfortable chairs, or to move guests around if you remain at the table. Giving your guests someone new to talk to can often give your dinner party a new lease of life. As the last course, dessert is also the most relaxed—let your guests linger over it. What's more—you can relax, too—all that is left is coffee and cheese.

Time for tea (see pp.260–263)
Sweet Geranium Cake with Blackberries (see p.270)
Chocolate Meringue Layer Cake (see p.247)
Frosted Lemon and Rosemary Squares (see (p.258)
Coffee and Walnut Cookies (see p.274)
Lana Pringle's Barm Brack (see p.182)

A savory tea
Wraps (see p.188)
Witches' Bread with Chocolate and Raisins (see p.182)
Mary Risley's Chocolate and Raspberry Truffles (see p.258)
Bumbles Ginger Roulade (see p.255)

What to drink
Tea is about teatime food but it's also about tea, the beverage, the cup that cheers and all that: Earl Grey, lapsang souchong, keemun, even green tea or rooibus, the South African red bush tea. If you must have alcohol—and this may suggest a little problem!—what about Pimm's No. 1 with lots of chilled 7-Up, a slice of lemon, and sprigs of mint and borage? It's light in alcohol and very refreshing, especially in summer.

the cheese course

We've now got so many delicious aged locally-made cheeses to choose from in these islands that the selection is mind-boggling. To round off a meal, serve one cheese in perfect condition with a few homemade crackers and crusty bread or a piece of Membrillo, plump dates, filberts… Better still, what could be easier than a cheese supper? Choose a selection of gorgeous cheeses. Lay them out on a bed of fresh fig or vine leaves or on timber boards or a flat basket. Provide lots of really good bread and crackers. Open a bottle of wine and enjoy.

Parmesan and Gruyère Cheese Soufflé

SERVES 8–10   (**P:** 20 mins./**C:** 25 mins.)

Guests are always wildly impressed by a well-risen soufflé and believe me it's not rocket science so don't imagine for one moment that you can't do it. A soufflé is simply a well-flavored sauce enriched with egg yolks and lightened with stiffly beaten egg. Soufflés are much more good humored than you think and can even be frozen when they are ready for the oven. The French do infinite variations on the theme, both sweet and savory. I love to make this recipe with some fresh Irish or local aged cheese, e.g., Desmond or Gabriel or a mature Coolea.

For the molds:
melted butter
¼ cup grated Parmesan cheese, optional

For the soufflé:
3 tablespoons butter
2½ tablespoons flour
1¼ cups milk
4 cage-free, organic eggs
½ cup finely grated Gruyère cheese
1 cup grated Parmesan
salt and freshly ground pepper
pinch of cayenne pepper
freshly grated nutmeg

8 individual soufflé dishes, 2½ x 1½ inches
  high or 1 large dish 6 x 2½ inches high

First prepare the soufflé dish or dishes: brush evenly with melted butter and if you like, sprinkle with a little freshly grated Parmesan.

Preheat the oven to 400ºF and warm a baking sheet. Melt the butter in a heavy saucepan, stir in the flour, and cook over a gentle heat for 1–2 minutes. Take off the heat and whisk in the milk, return to the heat, whisk as it comes to a boil, cover, and simmer gently for 3–4 minutes. Remove from the heat.

Separate the eggs and put the whites into a large copper, glass, or stainless steel bowl, making sure it is spotlessly clean and dry. Whisk the yolks one by one into the white sauce, add both cheeses, season with salt, pepper, cayenne, and a little freshly grated nutmeg. It should taste hugely seasoned at this point because the egg whites will dull the seasoning. Stir over a gentle heat for just a few seconds until the cheese melts. Remove from the heat (this can be made ahead up to this point).

Using clean beaters, beat the egg whites with a little pinch of salt, slowly at first and then faster until they are light and voluminous and hold a stiff peak when you lift up the beaters. Stir a few tablespoons into the cheese mixture to lighten it and then carefully fold in the rest with a spatula or tablespoon. Fill the mixture into the prepared soufflé dish or dishes (if you fill them three-quarters full you will get about 10 but if you smooth the tops you will have about 8). Bake in the oven for 8–9 minutes for the individual soufflés or 20–25 minutes for a large one. For the large one, you will need to reduce the temperature to 350ºF after 15 minutes, and putting it in a water bath (baking tray of hot water) to bake is a good idea. Serve immediately.

Top Tip: If you fill the soufflé dishes to the top, smooth off with a palette knife or spatula, then run a washed thumb around the edge of the dishes before they go into the oven to help to get the "top hat" effect when the soufflé is well risen.

Individual frozen soufflés can be baked from frozen but they will take a few minutes longer to cook.

Cheese Soufflés with Salad Greens:
Just before the soufflés are cooked, toss a mixture of salad greens in a bowl and divide between the plates. Carefully turn the soufflés out onto the greens and serve immediately.

Ardsallagh Goat Cheese with Lavender Honey and Figs

SERVES 4   (**P:** 10 mins.)

4 fresh fig or vine leaves
round of Ardsallagh goat cheese, or similar
  fresh soft goat cheese
2½ tablespoons lavender honey (see right)
4 fresh figs

For garnishing:
sprigs of lavender (optional)
fresh fig or vine leaves

Place a fig or vine leaf on each plate and place one small or a quarter of a larger cheese on each one. Drizzle with lavender honey.

Serve with fresh figs. Cut each fig into quarters, almost to the base, then pinch so the fig opens to resemble a flower. Decorate with a few sprigs of lavender (if using) and fresh fig or vine leaves.

Lavender Honey
Put 2–3 teaspoons of dried lavender flowers into a pot of good honey. Let it infuse for at least a week.

Raclette

A raclette party is so easy and such fun—just provide cheese, boiled potatoes, and pickles. Guests do their own cooking and there is a minimum of washing up. If you do a great deal of impromptu entertaining, a raclette stove is really worth having.

raclette cheese, about 6 ounces per person
freshly boiled potatoes, 3–4 per person
lettuce, such as Bibb lettuce, cut in half
  lengthwise, or a good green salad
cornichons or slices of dill pickle, 3–4 per person
radishes
tiny scallions (optional)
sea salt (or Kosher salt) and freshly
  ground black pepper

Put the raclette stove in the center of the table and turn on the heat. Cut the cheese into slices a scant 1/4-inch thick, and put a slice on each little pan.

While the cheese is melting, serve onto each person's heated plate freshly boiled potatoes and 3–4 leaves of crisp lettuce, such as Bibb lettuce, or a green salad. As soon as the cheese melts, each guest spoons it over the potato and puts another piece on the pan to melt.

Season with salt and pepper, and serve with pickles and radishes, and maybe a few tiny scallions as an accompaniment.

Ballymaloe Cheese Fondue

SERVES 2   (P: 10 mins./C: 5 mins.)

A fondue is such a retro dish and it can be great fun. When you sit at the table, choose your seat carefully, because if you drop your piece of bread into the fondue, you must kiss the person on your right (this could be your big chance!). My mother-in-law, Myrtle Allen, devised this recipe using Irish cheddar cheese. The fondue is a meal in itself, but even so it can be made in minutes. A fondue set is obviously an advantage if you own one, but if not, it is not essential. The quantities given here are perfect for a romantic supper for two. Each diner will need a fondue fork and an ordinary fork.

2 1/2 tablespoons white wine
2 small garlic cloves, crushed
2 teaspoons of a good relish or
  tomato chutney
2 teaspoons chopped parsley
6 ounces aged cheddar cheese, grated
  (about 1 3/4 cups)

For serving:
crusty white French bread, or other white bread

Put the white wine into a fondue pot or a small saucepan. Add the crushed garlic, tomato relish or chutney, chopped parsley, and cheese, and stir.

Just before serving, place over a low heat until the cheese melts and begins to bubble. Put the pot on the fondue stove and serve immediately.

Provide each diner with fresh, crusty French bread. Alternatively, the fondue may be served with cubes of ordinary white bread crisped up in a hot oven.

Camembert with Caramel and Walnuts

SERVES 6–8   (P: 5 mins./C: 15 mins.)

A complete sacrilege in some cheese lovers' opinion, but a fun way to use a less-than-totally gorgeous Camembert.

1 ripe Camembert cheese
7 whole walnuts, shelled
1/2 cup granulated sugar

For serving:
watercress leaves and crusty bread

Unwrap the Camembert, place on a serving plate, and arrange the walnuts on top.

Put the sugar into a heavy stainless steel saucepan over medium heat, and stir until the sugar dissolves and starts to caramelize. It will look lumpy and peculiar at first but will eventually melt. When the syrup turns to a chestnut-colored caramel, spoon it evenly over the top of the cheese and walnuts—it will solidify into a shiny crust.

To serve, crack the caramel with a knife and serve the cheese in slices, with some peppery watercress leaves and lots of crusty bread.

Saganaki (Greek Fried Cheese)

SERVES 6–8 (**P:** 5 mins./**C:** 5 mins.)

This is a meal made in minutes. Fried cheese cooked in a little round aluminum frying pan is called a saganaki. Greek kasseri cheese is traditionally used, but it can be made with various hard cheeses, including halloumi, kefalotiri Greek and Cypriot cheeses, and even French Gruyère. It must be served piping hot—Greek waiters occasionally run to get it to the customer while it is still bubbling.

8 ounces hard Greek or Cypriot cheese, such as kefalotiri or halloumi
butter or extra virgin olive oil, for frying
lemon juice, for sprinkling
cracked black peppercorns

For serving:
crusty white bread
green salad

Cut the cheese into slices about ¹/₂-inch thick. Melt a little butter or olive oil in a small frying pan, put in a few cheese slices in a single layer, reduce the heat, and let the cheese cook for 1 or 2 minutes until it begins to bubble. It should not brown. Sprinkle with a few drops of lemon juice and some freshly cracked pepper, rush it to the table, and eat with crusty white bread. Follow with a good green salad.

Melted Cooleeney Cheese in a Box

SERVES 6–8 (**P:** 5 mins./**C:** 20 mins.)

Cooleeney cheese is a delectable Camembert type of farmhouse cheese made by Breda Maher from the milk of her Fresian cows.

1 Cooleeney cheese, slightly underripe, or Brie, Camembert, or any farmhouse cheese sold in a wooden box
crusty white bread, or homemade Potato Chips (see recipe below)

Preheat the oven to 350°F.

Remove the labels from the box and the wrapper from the cheese. Ensure that the box is stapled, or it may fall apart in the oven. Put the cheese back in the box and bake in the oven for about 20 minutes, by which time it should be soft and molten in the center.

Cut a cross in the center of the cheese and serve immediately, with crusty white bread, or homemade potato chips.

Potato Chips

YOU WILL NEED 3–4 CHIPS PER PORTION.

2 very large potatoes
olive oil, for deep frying
salt

Scrub the potatoes and slice them as thinly as possible, preferably with a mandoline grater, to make long, thin slices. Deep-fry the potato slices until crisp and drain on paper towels. These can be cooked ahead of serving time and kept in a warm place. Sprinkle with salt.

Melted Gubbeen Cheese with Winter Herbs

SERVES 6–8 (**P:** 5 mins./**C:** 30 mins.)

Farmhouse cheese-maker Giana Ferguson gave me this little gem of a recipe for her washed salt rind cheese, which she makes on the family farm near Schull, in West Cork.

1 baby Gubbeen (or any washed rind cheese), 1 pound in weight, 4¹/₂-inch diameter
2 teaspoons chopped fresh thyme
1 large or 2 small garlic cloves, finely chopped
freshly ground black pepper

For serving: crusty bread, green salad

Preheat the oven to 350ºF. Cut a piece of aluminum foil about 12 inches square.

Split the baby Gubbeen cheese in half around its "equator." Put the bottom half on the center of the foil, generously sprinkle the cut surface with the thyme, garlic, and lots of black pepper. Top with the other half of the cheese. Gather up the edges of the foil, but leave a little vent for the steam to escape. Bake for 20–30 minutes or until soft and melting.

Open the package. Lift off the rind and eat the soft, herby, melting cheese with lots of crusty bread or boiled potatoes and a green salad. Exquisite!

Note: Cooleeney Irish cheese may also be used for this recipe. It will be perfect after baking for about 10 minutes.

Soft Yogurt Cheese (Labne)

This is so easy and wonderfully impressive. Use whole-milk yogurt to make a creamier cheese. Labne is a traditional yogurt cheese from Lebanon.

Line a strainer or colander with a double thickness of clean cheesecloth and place it over a bowl. Pour in the yogurt. Tie the four corners of the cloth to make a loose bundle. Suspend the bag of yogurt over a bowl and let it drip for 8 hours.

Remove the cheesecloth. Refrigerate in a covered plastic container. It will keep for 4–5 days in the fridge.

Soft Yogurt Cheese with Chives and Parsley

SERVES 4–6 (**P:** 10 mins. + 8 HOURS TO DRIP)

Dry the chives and parsley thoroughly before chopping.

2 cups plain, whole-milk yogurt
1/4–1/3 cup heavy cream (optional)
1/2 teaspoon very finely sliced chives
1 teaspoon finely chopped parsley
salt and sugar to taste

Follow the instructions for making Soft Yogurt Cheese (see recipe above) using 2 cups of plain, whole-milk yogurt, and let it drip for 8 hours.

In a stainless steel or glass bowl, mix the yogurt cheese with the remaining ingredients. Mix well and adjust the seasoning to taste. Cover and refrigerate for at least 1 hour. If some liquid accumulates, just discard it before you serve.

Lemon balm or chervil may also be used, and a little garlic if you like. Alternatively, add chopped mint, dill, or marjoram, and a drizzle of extra virgin olive oil; a little sea salt and some paprika is also good. Nasturtium flowers are another good addition.

Soft Yogurt Cheese with Fresh Berries

SERVES 4–6 (**P:** 10 mins./**C:** 8 HOURS)

2 cups plain whole-milk yogurt
1/2 cup heavy cream
3–4 tablespoons sugar
fresh summer berries
Fresh Strawberry Sauce (see p.250)

Follow the recipe above for Soft Yogurt Cheese. Add the cream and sugar to taste and serve with fresh summer berries and Fresh Strawberry Sauce.

Plate of Irish Goat's and Sheep's Milk Cheeses with Figs

Irish goat's milk cheeses include:
Croghan, Mine Gabhar, Ardsallagh, St. Tola, Clonmore, Corleggy, Corbetstown, Oísin, or Boilie.

Irish sheep's milk cheeses include:
Cratloe Hills, Knockalara, Crozier blue.

(If you cannot find Irish cheese, use a sheep's milk or goat's milk cheese of your choice.)

For serving:
fresh fig or vine leaves
fresh figs, 1 per person
crusty bread

Lay fresh fig leaves on a wooden board, wicker tray, or individual plates. Arrange a selection of fresh Irish goat's and sheep's milk cheeses on top. Serve with plump fresh figs—allow 1 per person—and lots of good, crusty bread.

Goat Cheese in Grappa with Crusty Bread

SERVES 4–6
   (P: 10 mins. + 24 HOURS TO MARINATE)

The lovely Australian cook Maggie Beer gave us this recipe, when she taught at the school. She says that "the strength of the grappa gives a wonderful balance to the creaminess of the goat cheese in this dish, and although you could substitute brandy, the 'kick' of the grappa is hard to beat."

12 ounces fresh soft goat cheese (we use
   Ardsallagh, our local goat cheese)

For the marinade:
2^1/2 tablespoons grappa, or brandy
^{1}/4 cup extra virgin olive oil
1 large garlic clove, finely sliced
2^1/2 tablespoons roughly chopped
   flat-leaf parsley
freshly ground black pepper

For serving:
arugula salad, dressed with extra virgin olive oil
   and balsamic vinegar
bread slices, brushed with extra virgin olive oil
   and toasted in the oven

Make the marinade by mixing all the ingredients together in a bowl.

Pour a little of the marinade into a shallow pottery dish. Lay the goat cheese on top and spoon the remaining marinade over it. Cover with plastic wrap and refrigerate for 24 hours, turning the cheese over once or twice.

About an hour before serving, let the cheese warm to room temperature. Serve with an arugula salad; slabs of bread, brushed with olive oil and toasted in the oven, are a must!

Manchego with Membrillo and Sardinian Parchment Bread

Serve triangles of aged Manchego cheese with quince cheese or jam and Sardinian parchment bread or another crusty white bread.

Some Good Things to Serve with Cheese

A cheese plate with complimentary nuts, dried fruit, relishes, perhaps a little salad, and some crackers or flavored breads makes such a yummy end to a meal.

Nuts
Fresh walnuts, pecans, almonds, hazelnuts, filberts, macadamia nuts, Brazil nuts

Dried Fruit
Plump dried Turkish figs, dried peaches, pears, Medjool dates

Relishes
Beet and ginger, tomato relish, jalapeño, pimiento

Honey
Particularly good with blue cheese

drinks

Tom Doorley has given some excellent advice on wine matching, but here are some lovely aperitifs and out-of-the-ordinary soft drinks. I do also recommend my mulled apple juice, elderflower champagne, and sweet lassis. For a really special touch, fill ice cubes with seasonal berries and fresh herbs.

Elderflower Champagne

MAKES ABOUT 5½ QUARTS

(P: 10 mins. + 24 HOURS + 2 WEEKS)

This magical, non-alcoholic recipe transforms perfectly ordinary ingredients into a delicious sparkling drink. My family make it religiously every year and then share the bubbly with their friends.

1 unwaxed, organic lemon
2 heads of elderflowers in full bloom
2¾ cups sugar
2½ tablespoons white wine vinegar
5 quarts water

With a swivel-top peeler, remove the zest from the lemon and reserve, then extract the juice from the lemon. Put the elderflowers into a bowl and add the lemon zest and juice, sugar, vinegar, and water. Cover and leave in a cool place for 24 hours.

Stir the liquid and strain it into a bowl or pitcher, then funnel into screw-top bottles and seal tightly. Lay them on their sides in a cool place. After 2 weeks, the elderflower champagne should be sparkling and ready to drink.

Elderflower Syrup

MAKES ABOUT 3 CUPS

(P: 10 mins. + 24 HOURS)

Great for elderflower lemonade, or add a dash in a flute of champagne or a gin and tonic. It also adds magical flavor to fruit dishes, such as fruit salad.

¾ cup sugar
2½ cups water
6 heads of elderflowers in full bloom
zest and juice of 2 unwaxed, organic lemons

Put the sugar and water into a saucepan over medium heat. Stir until the sugar dissolves, add the elderflowers, bring to a boil, and boil for 5 minutes. Remove from the heat and add the lemon zest and juice. Cover and set aside to cool. Let it infuse in a cool, dry place for 24 hours.

Strain and bottle in gin or vodka bottles. Seal well. Dilute as desired.

Rosemary Syrup

MAKES ABOUT 3 CUPS

Use as the basis of lemonades or fruit compotes.

2⅓ cups sugar
2½ cups water
2 rosemary sprigs

Put the sugar and water into a saucepan, add the sprigs of rosemary. Bring slowly to a boil, let it cool, strain, and store in a fridge. It will keep for weeks.

Good Things to have with Champagne, Sparkling Wine, or Prosecco

Add a teaspoon of one of these per glass:
Elderflower Syrup (see above)
Sloe Gin (see p.290)
Fraise des bois
Crème de mure
Framboise
Crème de cassis
Peach brandy
Crème d'abricots

Or drop a fresh strawberry, a few blackberries, raspberries, or black currants, or a slice of peach or apricot into each glass.

Maybe float a sprig of mint, lemon balm, lemon verbena, or sweet cicely on top to really guild the lily.

Herb flowers, violas, or violets also look darling floating in a glass of bubbly.

Mimosa

Half-fill a champagne flute with some fresh orange juice. Top up with champagne, sparkling wine, or prosecco. Ruby grapefruit juice also makes a mouth-watering drink.

Granita Fizz

Drop an ice cube of your favorite granita or sherbet into a glass and top up with sparkling wine, champagne, or prosecco.

Prosecco with Violet Syrup

Pour a little violet syrup into a glass, top up with prosecco or sparkling wine. Float a few fresh violets on top of each glass if available. Enjoy.

Homemade Lemonades

We always keep some chilled Stock Syrup in the fridge, to make a variety of lemonades. They contain no preservatives so they should be drunk within a few hours of being made.

Orange and Lemonade

juice of 2 oranges
juice of 4 lemons
2 cups Stock Syrup
about 1¹/₂ quarts water
ice cubes
sprigs of mint or lemon balm, for garnishing

In a large pitcher, mix together the citrus juices, the stock syrup, and water to taste. Add ice, garnish with sprigs of mint or lemon balm, and serve.

Limeade

juice of 5 limes
3 cups water
1¹/₄ cups Stock Syrup
ice cubes
sprigs of fresh mint or lemon balm, to garnish

Make and serve as above.

Ruby Grapefruit Lemonade

juice of 2 lemons
juice of 4 ruby grapefruit
2 cups Stock Syrup
water or sparkling water, to taste
Mint Ice Cubes (see below)

Mix together the citrus juices and the syrup, and add water or sparkling water to taste. Serve chilled, with mint ice cubes.

Rosemary Lemonade

A delicious thirst-quenching lemonade with a grown-up flavor!

juice of 3 lemons
1 cup Rosemary Syrup (see p.286)
3 cups water

Mix all the ingredients together. Taste and add more rosemary syrup if needed.

Elderflower Lemonade

Add 1 part Elderflower Syrup (see p.286) to 6 parts water and ice.

Ice Cubes with Mint, Herbs, Lemon Verbena, Flowers, and Berries

Fill ice cube trays with:
1. Sugared cranberries
2. Red currants and mint leaves
3. Lemon segments
4. Pomegranate seeds
5. Star anise
Cover with water and freeze

Summer Parties

Take empty ice cube trays and in each section put mint leaves, lemon balm leaves, sweet geranium leaves, or sweet cicely leaves. Cover with water and freeze.
1. Raspberries and mint
2. Wild strawberries
3. Violas or violets, rose petals or marigold petals

Christmas Drinks

Pop Kumquats in Brandy into a glass, top up with champagne or Sloe Gin (see p.290).

Funky tip: Soak lemon segments in elderflower syrup, freeze into ice cubes, and use in gin and tonics.

Sherbet Cubes

Use your favorite sherbet to make ice cubes and drop them into sparkling wine or prosecco. Strawberry sherbet, elderberry, rhubarb, black currant...all are delicious.

Blackberry Ice Cubes

Pop a juicy blackberry into each section of an ice cube tray, and add a tiny sweet geranium or mint leaf. Fill with cold water and freeze. Pop into a glass of dry white wine or lemonade.

Lassi

SERVES 1   (P: 5 mins.)

In India we came across many different types of lassi (a yogurt drink), some sweet and some salty. They are drunk with meals or as a refreshing beverage on a hot afternoon. In India the yogurt is rich and wonderful, so don't dream of using low-fat yogurt—use the best you can find, or make your own (see p.33).

Salty Lassi

SERVES 1   (P: 5 mins.)

1/4 cup best-quality plain yogurt
3/4 cup water and ice mixed
tiny pinch of salt
mint leaves (optional)

Whizz all the ingredients together in a blender for a few seconds. Serve in a chilled glass, scatter with a few mint leaves if you like, and serve immediately.

Sweet Lassi

SERVES 1   (P: 5 mins.)

1/4 cup best-quality plain yogurt
3/4 cup water and ice mixed
1/4–1 tablespoon sugar
1/8–1/4 teaspoon rose water or kewra (Indian essence)
rose petals for decorating (optional)

Whizz all the ingredients together in a blender. Pour into a chilled glass, scatter with rose petals if you like, and serve immediately.

Sharbat

SERVES 2–4   (P: 10 mins.)

This is an apple-milk drink and one of the many cooling summer drinks from Morocco.

2 red dessert apples
2 1/2 tablespoons granulated sugar
2 scant teaspoons rose water or orange-flower water

Laxmi's Lassi

SERVES 1   (P: 5 mins.)

Laxmi Nair, whose family owns the gorgeous Leela Palace Hotel in Mumbai, gave me this recipe.

1/3 cup best-quality plain yogurt
3/4 cup water and ice mixed
1/2 green chile, seeded and chopped
2 fresh curry leaves
4 mint leaves
pinch of salt

Whizz all the ingredients together in a blender for a few seconds. Pour into a chilled glass and serve immediately.

Leela Palace's Lassi

SERVES 1   (P: 25 mins.)

tiny pinch of saffron strands
1 cup best-quality plain yogurt
1 1/2 tablespoons roughly chopped pistachio nuts
1 teaspoon sugar
1 teaspoon chopped mint
2 cups milk
shaved ice (optional)

Put the saffron strands in a tiny bowl, pour in 1 tablespoon of water, and soak for 10–15 minutes. Put the remaining ingredients in a blender and whizz. Pour into a tall glass, drizzle the saffron over the top, and serve.

Peel, core, and cut up the apples. Put them into a blender, along with the sugar, rose water or orange-flower water, and milk. Whizz at high speed for 15 seconds. Serve, with some shaved ice if you like, in small glasses.

Fresh Herb Tisanes

From spring onwards, when the herb garden is full of abundance, we make lots of tisanes and herb teas. All you need to do is pop a few leaves into a teapot and pour on the boiling water—infinitely more delicious than the dried herb tea bags.

A Paris restaurant I dined in recently served herb infusions in the most delightful way. The waiter came to the table with several china bowls of fresh herbs on a silver salver. With tiny silver tongs he put the guest's chosen herb into a little china teapot, poured on boiling water, and served it with a flourish. Exquisite.

choice of herb, e.g., lemon verbena, rosemary, sweet geranium, lemon balm, spearmint, peppermint
water

Bring fresh cold water to a boil, scald a china tea pot, and discard the water.

Take a handful of fresh herb leaves and crush them gently. The quantity will depend upon the strength of the herb and how intense an infusion you enjoy. Put them into the scalded teapot. Pour the boiling water over the leaves, cover the teapot, and let them infuse for 3–4 minutes.

Serve immediately in china teacups.

Mulled Red Wine

SERVES 8   (**P:** 5 mins./**C:** 30 mins.)

Just before the festive season, we make up lots of little packages with the sugar, spices, and thinly pared lemon rind, so when guests arrive, it's just a question of opening a bottle of wine and warming it in a stainless steel saucepan with the spices. Leftover mulled wine keeps for a few days and reheats perfectly.

about 1/2 cup sugar (or a smidge under)
1 bottle of good red wine
thinly pared zest of 1 lemon
1 small piece of cinnamon stick
1 blade of mace
1 whole clove

Put the sugar into a stainless steel or cast-iron saucepan, pour in the wine, and add the lemon zest, cinnamon, mace, and clove. Heat over a gentle heat, stirring often to ensure the sugar is fully dissolved. Serve hot but not scalding, otherwise your guests will have difficulty holding their glasses.

Mulled White Wine

SERVES 8   (**P:** 5 mins./**C:** 30 mins.)

1/2 cup sugar
1 1/2 liters (about 6 cups) chardonnay or
   other white wine
3 cinnamon sticks
6 whole cloves
4 star anise
2–3 sprigs of thyme
1 thinly pared zest of orange

Put the sugar into a stainless steel or cast-iron saucepan, pour in the wine, and add all the other ingredients. Heat over a gentle heat, stirring often to ensure the sugar is fully dissolved. Let it infuse for 10 minutes. Serve warm.

Sloe Gin

Sloes are very tart little purple berries that grow on prickly bushes, often draped over the top of stone walls. They are in season in September and October. It's great fun to organize a sloe-picking expedition and have a sloe-gin-making party. Sloe gin makes a terrific Christmas present.

1 1/2 pounds sloes
1 3/4 cups white granulated sugar
1 1/4 liters (about 5 cups) gin

darning needles, for pricking
sterilized glass jars and bottles

Wash and dry the sloes, prick in several places (we use a clean darning needle). Put them into sterilized glass jars and cover with the sugar and gin. Seal the jars tightly and set aside in a cool, dry place.

Shake every couple of days to start with, and then every now and then for 3–4 months, by which time it will be ready to strain and funnel into bottles.

Sloe gin will improve on keeping so try to resist drinking it for another few months.

Damson gin can be made in the same way using damson plums.

Classic Margarita

SERVES 2   (**P:** 5 mins.)

One sip of margarita and I'm transported to my beloved Mexico. I close my eyes and see the swirling colors and hear the lively music. Kosher salt, unlike table salt, has no additives. This will help keep the liquid from clouding.

Kosher salt
1/2 lime, plus 2 1/2 tablespoons lime juice
1/2 cup white tequila
2 1/2 tablespoons orange liqueur,
   such as Cointreau or Triple Sec
6 ice cubes

2 cocktail glasses

Pour some Kosher salt into a saucer or small plate. Rub the rims of the two cocktail glasses with the lime, then dip the rims of the glass into the salt and spin to frost.

Put the tequila, orange liqueur, lime juice, and ice cubes into a pitcher or cocktail shaker and mix well. When thoroughly chilled, strain and divide between the two glasses. Serve immediately.

Granita Cocktail

To a glass of prosecco or sparkling wine, add a scoop of your favorite granita or sherbet. Try watermelon, strawberry, lemon verbena… Sublime!

Mojito

MAKES 1   (P: 10 mins.)

4 teaspoons granulated sugar
3–4 fresh mint leaves
freshly squeezed juice of 1 lime
2 ice cubes, crushed
1 ounce (2 tablespoons) white rum
splash of club soda

Put the sugar and fresh mint leaves in a chilled glass, muddle or crush with a wooden pestle or the thick handle of a wooden spoon. Add the freshly squeezed lime juice and rum, then add the ice, stir, and top up with club soda. Add a straw and enjoy!

Banana Daiquiri

SERVES 2   (P: 5 mins.)

1/2 cup light rum, such as Havana Club
1 ounce (2 tablespoons) orange liqueur,
  such as Cointreau
2 ripe bananas, cut up
1/4 cup lime juice
2 cups ice

Whizz all the ingredients in a blender. Pour into chilled glasses and enjoy!

Watermelon Juice

SERVES 8–12   (P: 20 mins.)

1 cup water
2/3–3/4 cup sugar
1 large watermelon
zest and juice of 4 limes
ice cubes
sprigs of mint, for the garnish

Put the water and sugar in a saucepan and bring to a boil. When the sugar has dissolved, remove the pan from the heat.

Cut the watermelon flesh into 2-inch chunks and pick out the seeds. Working in batches, put the chunks into a food processor and puree. Stir the sugar syrup,

Mulled Apple Juice

SERVES 8   (P: 5 mins./C: 10 mins.)

3 cups pure apple juice
3 cups bottled water
1 orange, preferably unwaxed
12 whole cloves

3 small cinnamon sticks
6 allspice berries or pimento berries
1/2 teaspoon grated nutmeg
1/3 cup sugar

Caipirinha

MAKES 1   (P: 10 mins.)

Brazil's national cocktail and so hip.

1 lime, well washed
2 teaspoons granulated sugar
1/4 cup Cachaca (Brazilian white rum)
  or white rum
crushed ice

Cut the lime in quarters. Pop into a tumbler. Sprinkle with sugar and crush with a wooden pestle until the juice comes out of the lime and the zest infuses the sugar. Add the Cachaca or white rum and some crushed ice. Stir and enjoy.

Pink Grapefruit and Pomegranate Cocktail

Mix freshly squeezed pink grapefruit juice with grenadine syrup. Sweeten to taste with Stock Syrup (see p.288) and dilute with spring or sparkling water. Add ice cubes and garnish with pomegranate seeds and mint leaves.

lime zest, and juice into the melon puree. Dilute with water to taste and add a few ice cubes and a sprig of fresh mint to each glass.

Watermelon Granita
Proceed as above but do not dilute with water at the end. Freeze the watermelon liquid in a sorbetière in the usual way.

Pour the apple juice and water into a stainless steel saucepan. Wash the orange well in warm water, and peel the rind thinly. Add to the pan, along with the rest of the spices and the sugar. Heat gently. Adjust the spicing or sugar if needed, and serve hot.

basics

Guacamole

1 ripe avocado
1–2¹/₂ tablespoons freshly squeezed lime juice
4 teaspoons extra virgin olive oil
1¹/₂ tablespoons freshly chopped cilantro or
  flat-leaf parsley
sea salt (or Kosher salt) and freshly
  ground pepper

Scoop out the flesh from the avocado.
Mash with a fork or in a mortar and pestle,
add the lime juice, olive oil, cilantro, and salt
and freshly ground pepper to taste. Serve
immediately. Otherwise, cover the surface of
the guacamole with a sheet of plastic to
exclude the air. Keep cool until needed. A
little finely chopped chile or tomato may be
added to the guacamole.

Tomato and Cilantro Salsa

**This sauce is ever present on Mexican tables
to serve with all sorts of dishes. Salsas of all
kinds, both fresh and cooked, have now
become a favorite accompaniment to
everything from panbroiled meat to a piece
of sizzling fish.**

6 very ripe tomatoes, chopped
2¹/₂ tablespoons finely chopped red onion
1 garlic clove, crushed
¹/₂–1 chile, seeded and finely chopped
2¹/₂ tablespoons chopped fresh cilantro
freshly squeezed lime juice – about 1 lime
salt, freshly ground pepper, and sugar

Mix all the ingredients together. Season with
salt, freshly ground pepper, and sugar. Taste,
and adjust the seasoning if necessary.

Tomato and Red Onion Salsa

4 very ripe but firm tomatoes, cut into
  small pieces
1 small red onion, cut in half and thinly sliced

¹/₂–1 green chile
4 teaspoons lime juice
4 teaspoons extra virgin olive oil
1–2¹/₂ tablespoons chopped cilantro
salt, freshly ground pepper, and sugar to taste

Mix all the ingredients gently in a bowl. Taste,
and adjust the seasoning if needed.

Mango Salsa

2 ripe mangoes, cut into ¹/₄-inch pieces
2¹/₂ tablespoons Sweet Chile Sauce (see p.296)
2¹/₂ tablespoons lime or lemon juice
2¹/₂ tablespoons chopped cilantro

Mix all the ingredients together in a bowl.
Taste, and adjust seasoning if needed. Cover
and chill until ready to use—it's best fresh, so
eat it within a day.

Banana and Cardamom Raita

**This is delicious served with spicy vegetable
stews, mild Madras curry, or panbroiled
chicken breast. Perhaps surprisingly, it keeps
for days in the fridge and we've also enjoyed
it as a pudding.**

¹/₂ cup raisins and/or golden raisins
¹/₄ cup almonds, blanched and slivered
1 cup plain yogurt
¹/₂ cup cream
¹/₂ cup sour cream
1 tablespoon pure honey, plus extra to taste
4–6 cardamom pods
3 firm ripe bananas
pinch of salt

Pour boiling water over the raisins and let soak
for 10 minutes, then drain.

Meanwhile, dry-toast the almonds in a frying
pan until golden.

Mix the yogurt with the creams, add the

honey, taste, and add more honey if
needed. Add the raisins and almonds,
reserving a few almonds for the garnish.

Remove the seeds from the cardamom
pods, crush using a mortar and pestle, and
stir into the yogurt mixture.

Slice the bananas, season with a pinch of
salt, and add to the yogurt. Stir thoroughly,
turn into a serving bowl, and chill for an
hour if possible before serving. When ready,
scatter with the reserved almonds.

Tomato Puree

**Tomato Puree is one of the very best ways of
preserving the flavor of ripe, summer
tomatoes for winter. We make lots of
homemade tomato puree at the end of the
summer when the tomatoes are really ripe—
it's great to have in the freezer for tomato
soup, stews, casseroles, etc.**

2 pounds very ripe tomatoes
1 small onion, chopped
1 teaspoon sugar
a good pinch of salt
a few grindings of black pepper

Cut the tomatoes into quarters, put into a
stainless steel pot with the onion, sugar, salt,
and freshly ground pepper.

Cook over a gentle heat until the tomatoes
are soft (no water needed). Put through the
fine blade of a mouli-legume (food mill) or
a nylon mesh strainer. Let cool until cold,
then refrigerate or freeze.

Homemade Veg Broth

Basically you can make a vegetable broth from whatever vegetables you have available but try not to use too much of any one vegetable unless you particularly want that flavor to predominate.

1 small white turnip
2 onions, peeled and roughly sliced
green parts of 2–3 leeks
3 celery stalks, washed and roughly chopped
3 large carrots, scrubbed and roughly chopped
1/2 fennel bulb, roughly chopped
4 ounces mushrooms or mushroom stalks
  (about 1 cup)
4–6 parsley stalks
bouquet garni (parsley, thyme, and a bay
  leaf tied together)
few peppercorns
2 1/2 quarts cold water

Put all the ingredients into a large pot, add the cold water, bring to a boil, then reduce the heat, cover, and simmer for 1–2 hours. Strain through a fine mesh strainer. Keeps for a week in the fridge or may be frozen.

Homemade Chicken Broth

Keep your carcasses, giblets, and vegetable trimmings and use them for your stockpot. Nowadays some supermarkets and poulterers are happy to give you chicken carcasses and often giblets as well just for the asking because there is so little demand.

2–3 raw or cooked chicken carcasses or a
  mixture of both
giblets from the chicken, i.e., neck, heart,
  gizzard (save the liver for another dish)
1 onion, sliced
1 leek, split in two
1 outside stalk of celery (not the heart, use the
  coarser outside stalks) or 1 lovage leaf
1 carrot, sliced
a few parsley stalks
sprig of thyme
6 peppercorns
3 3/4 quarts cold water

Chop up the carcasses as much as possible. Put all the ingredients into a very large pot and cover with the cold water. Bring to a

boil and skim the fat off the top with a tablespoon. Simmer for 3–5 hours. Strain and remove any remaining fat. If you need a stronger flavor, boil down the liquid in an open pan to reduce the volume by one-third or one-half. Do not add salt.

Note: broth will keep for several days in the refrigerator. Broth also freezes perfectly. For a cheap freezer container, use large yogurt cartons. To defrost, sit the carton in a pitcher of hot water to loosen it, then let it slide out into a pot.

The above recipe is just a guideline. If you have just one carcass and don't feel like making just a small quantity of broth, why not freeze the carcass and save it up until you have 6 or 7 carcasses plus giblets, then you can make a really good sized pot of broth and get the best value for your fuel.

There are some vegetables which should not be put in the stock, e.g., potatoes because they soak up flavor and make the stock cloudy; parsnips—too strong, beets—they are too strong also and the dye would produce a red stock—great for beet soup. Cabbage or other brassicas give an off-taste when cooked for a long time. A little white turnip is sometimes an asset, but it is very easy to overdo it. I also ban bay leaf in my chicken broths because I find that the flavor of bay can predominate easily and add a sameness to soups made from the broth later on.

Basic Fish Stock

MAKES ABOUT 2 QUARTS

Fish stock takes only 20 minutes to make. If you can get lots of fresh fish bones from your fishmarket it's well worth making two or three times the recipe, because it freezes well.

2 1/4 pounds fish bones, preferably sole, turbot,
  or flounder or other white fish
1–2 teaspoons butter
3 1/2 ounces onions, finely sliced (about 1 cup)
1/2–1 cup dry white wine
4 peppercorns
bouquet garni containing a sprig of thyme,
  4–5 parsley stalks, small piece of celery, and
  a tiny scrap of bay leaf

Wash the fish bones thoroughly under cold running water until no trace of blood remains, and chop into pieces. In a large stainless steel pot, melt the butter, add the onions, toss and sweat over a gentle heat until soft but not colored. Add the bones to the pot, stir, and cook very briefly with the onions. Add the dry white wine and boil until nearly all the wine has evaporated. Cover with cold water and add the peppercorns and the bouquet garni. Bring to a boil and simmer for 20 minutes, skimming often. Strain. Let cool, degrease if necessary, and refrigerate.

Hollandaise Sauce

2 cage-free, organic egg yolks
1/2 cup (1 stick) butter, cut into pieces
1 teaspoon freshly squeezed lemon juice

Put the egg yolks in a heavy stainless steel saucepan over a low heat, or in a bowl over hot water. Add 2 teaspoons of cold water and whisk thoroughly. Add the butter one piece at a time, whisking all the while. As soon as one piece melts, add the next. The mixture will gradually thicken, but if it shows signs of becoming too thick or of scrambling, remove from the heat immediately and add a little cold water if necessary. Do not leave the pan or stop whisking until the sauce thickens to coating consistency. Remove from the heat and add the lemon juice to taste.

Note: A low heat is crucial when making hollandaise sauce in a saucepan directly over the heat: it should be possible to put your hand on the side of the pan at any stage—if it feels too hot for your hand, it is also too hot for the sauce. However, if the sauce is very slow to thicken it may be because you are being excessively cautious and the heat is too low. Increase the heat slightly and continue to whisk until the sauce thickens to coating consistency.

Top Tip: If you are making hollandaise sauce for the first time, keep a bowl of cold water close by so you can plunge the bottom of the saucepan into it if it becomes too hot and the sauce becomes too thick or scrambles.

Béarnaise Sauce

SERVES 6–8

Substitute mint for French tarragon and the name changes to sauce paloise; delicious with roast or panbroiled lamb. If you do not have tarragon vinegar at hand, use a wine vinegar and add some extra chopped tarragon.

¹/₃ cup tarragon vinegar
¹/₃ cup dry white wine
2 teaspoons finely chopped shallots
  (if unavailable, use mild onion)
pinch of freshly ground pepper
2 cage-free, organic egg yolks
¹/₂–³/₄ cup (1–1¹/₂ sticks) butter,
  salted or unsalted, depending upon
  what it is being served with
4 teaspoons freshly chopped French
  tarragon leaves

Boil the first 4 ingredients together in a shallow, heavy stainless steel saucepan until completely reduced and the pan is almost dry but the shallots are not browned. Add 1 tablespoon of cold water immediately. Pull the pan off the heat and let it cool for 1–2 minutes.

Whisk in the egg yolks and add the butter bit by bit over a very low heat, whisking all the time. As soon as one piece melts, add the next piece; it will gradually thicken. If it shows signs of becoming too thick or scrambling, remove from the heat immediately and add a little cold water. Do not leave the pan or stop whisking until the sauce is made. Finally add the freshly chopped French tarragon and taste for seasoning.

Sweet Chile Sauce

3 large red chiles, finely chopped (seeds
  and all)
1 garlic clove, crushed
³/₄ cup granulated sugar
¹/₂ cup rice vinegar
1 teaspoon salt

Put all the ingredients into a little saucepan over a low heat. Stir to dissolve the sugar. Bring to a boil and continue to cook, stirring from time to time, for 5–6 minutes or until the mixture thickens to a syrupy texture. Cool and pour into a jam jar or bottle.

Onion Sauce (Sauce Soubise)

SERVES 8–10

Great with roast lamb or panbroiled lamb chops. Onion sauce is a sort of "forgotten flavor" which makes a delicious change from the more usual mint jelly.

¹/₄ cup (¹/₂ stick) butter
3 onions, about 1 pound in weight, thinly
  sliced or finely chopped
¹/₂ teaspoon salt
¹/₄ teaspoon freshly ground pepper
2 teaspoons flour
1¹/₄ cups milk, or 1 cup milk
  and ¹/₄ cup cream

Melt the butter over a gentle heat, add the onions, and cook in a covered saucepan over a low heat until really soft but not colored. Season with salt and freshly ground pepper. Stir in the flour, add the milk, and simmer gently for another 5 minutes.

This sauce keeps for 3–4 days covered in the fridge and may, of course, be reheated.

Onion and Mint Sauce
Add 3–4 tablespoons freshly chopped mint to the Onion Sauce before serving.

Mayonnaise and Variations

Mayonnaise takes less than 5 minutes to make by hand, faster than in a food processor. All the ingredients should be at room temperature if possible. As ever, the quality of the eggs matters. Fresh cage-free eggs will create a better, more stable emulsion.

2 cage-free, organic egg yolks
¹/₄ teaspoon Dijon mustard or pinch of
  English mustard
¹/₄ teaspoon salt
2 teaspoons white wine vinegar
1 cup oil (sunflower, arachide, or olive
  oil or a mixture). We use ³/₄ cup
  arachide oil and ¹/₄ cup olive oil;
  alternatively use 7:1 sunflower oil to olive oil

Put the egg yolks into a medium-size bowl with the mustard, salt, and the white wine vinegar (keep the whites to make meringues). Put the oil into a measuring cup with a good pouring spout. Take a whisk in one hand and the oil in the other and drip the oil onto the egg yolks, drop by drop, whisking at the same time. Within a minute you will notice that the mixture is beginning to thicken. When this happens you can add the oil a little faster, but don't get too cheeky or it will suddenly curdle because the egg yolks can only absorb the oil at a certain pace. Taste, and add a little more seasoning and vinegar if necessary.

If the mayonnaise curdles it will suddenly become quite thin, and if left sitting the oil will start to float to the top of the sauce. Should this happen, you can quite easily rectify the situation by putting another egg yolk or 1–2 tablespoons of boiling water into a clean bowl, then whisk in the curdled mayonnaise, half a teaspoon at a time until it re-emulsifies.

Food processor method
Mayonnaise may be made in a food processor, however 4 egg yolks are the minimum because even in the smallest capacity bowl the blades are unable to pick up two egg yolks. Even in the food processor, the oil must be added slowly at first to establish the emulsion, thereafter the oil may be added in a steady stream.

If the oil is added too slowly the heat generated by the blades whizzing around can curdle the mayonnaise, so try not to be too cautious.

White wine vinegar is the classic seasoning but lemon and lime juice is sometimes used. It keeps for a minimum of 5–7 days, covered in a fridge. Bring back to room temperature before stirring into other recipes otherwise it may curdle.

Which oil?
Many mayonnaise recipes call for olive oil, however, if extra virgin olive oil is used the sauce will be too strong for most tastes. We use 7 parts sunflower or peanut oil and 1 part extra virgin olive oil or 6 to 2 for a more distinct olive flavor.

Aioli or Garlic Mayonnaise
Ingredients as above, plus:
1–4 garlic cloves, depending upon size
2 teaspoons chopped parsley

Crush the garlic and add to the egg yolks just as you start to make the mayonnaise. Finally add the chopped parsley and taste for seasoning.

Cilantro Mayonnaise

Add 1–2½ tablespoons of chopped cilantro to the basic Mayonnaise recipe.

Basil Mayonnaise

Pour boiling water over a good handful of basil leaves, count to 3, drain immediately, and refresh in cold water. Chop, and add to the egg yolks and continue to make the Mayonnaise in the usual way.

Tomato and Basil Mayonnaise

Add 1–2½ tablespoons of aromatic Tomato Puree (see p.294) to the Basil Mayonnaise.

Chili Basil Mayonnaise

Add a good pinch of chili powder to the egg yolks when making Garlic Mayonnaise, omit the parsley, and add the basil instead. Great with salads and sandwiches.

Spicy Mayonnaise

Add 1–2 teaspoons Ballymaloe Tomato Relish or a good tomato chutney to the basic Mayonnaise. Add ½–1 teaspoon chili sauce to taste.

Wasabi Mayonnaise

Add 1–2½ tablespoons wasabi paste to the eggs instead of mustard.

Roasted Red Pepper Mayonnaise

Add 1–2 roasted red peppers (see p.298), seeded and peeled (do not wash). Puree the red pepper flesh, and add the puree and juices to the Mayonnaise. Taste, and correct the seasoning.

Whole-grain Mustard Mayonnaise

Add 1–2½ tablespoons whole-grain mustard to the basic Mayonnaise.

Lemon Mayonnaise

Use lemon juice instead of vinegar in the basic Mayonnaise.

Fennel Mayonnaise

Rick Stein introduced me to this delicious sauce. Add 1 tablespoon Pernod and 2½ tablespoons of finely chopped fennel bulb to the basic mayonnaise recipe.

Dill Mayonnaise

Add 3–4 tablespoons of freshly chopped dill to the basic Mayonnaise recipe.

Asian Mayonnaise

Add 2 teaspoons of Wasabi paste, 2½ tablespoons of Sweet Chile Sauce (see p.296), ¼ cup of freshly chopped cilantro, and the juice of ½ a lime to the basic Mayonnaise recipe.

Tapenade Mayonnaise

Add ¼–⅓ cup of Tapenade (see p.75) to the basic Mayonnaise recipe.

Croûtons

SERVES 4

Sprinkle over salads or serve with soups.

1 slice of slightly stale bread, ¼-inch thick
sunflower or olive oil

First cut the crusts off the bread, next cut the bread into ¼-inch strips and then into exact cubes.

Heat the sunflower or olive oil in a frying pan—the oil should be at least ¾-inch deep and almost smoking.

Add the croûtons to the hot oil. Stir once or twice, they will color almost immediately. Put a metal strainer over a pyrex or stainless steel bowl. When the croûtons are golden brown, pour the oil and croûtons into the strainer. Drain the croûtons on paper towels.

Note: Croûtons may be made several hours or even a day ahead. The oil may be flavored with sprigs of rosemary, thyme, or onion.

Croûtons may be stamped out into various shapes: hearts, stars, clubs, diamonds, etc…

Pesto

MAKES 2 JARS

If you any have difficulty getting basil, use parsley, a mixture of parsley and mint, or parsley and cilantro—different but still delicious. Pesto keeps for weeks, covered with a layer of olive oil in a jar.

4 ounces fresh basil leaves (about 8 cups)
⅔ cup extra virgin olive oil
¼ cup fresh pine nuts (taste when you buy to ensure they are not rancid)
2 large garlic cloves, peeled and crushed
2 ounces Parmesan cheese, freshly grated (about 1 cup)
salt to taste

Whizz the basil with the olive oil, pine nuts, and garlic in a food processor or pound in a mortar and pestle. Scoop into a bowl and fold in the Parmesan. Taste, and season. Pour into sterilized jars. Cover with a layer of olive oil. Screw on the lid and store in the fridge.

Pesto also freezes well but for best results, don't add the Parmesan until defrosted.

Top Tip: Each time you use some pesto, clean the top and sides of the jar and make sure the pesto is covered with a layer of extra-virgin olive oil before replacing in the fridge. Otherwise the pesto will darken and go moldy where it is exposed to the air.

Dill Tzatziki

This delicious cucumber and yogurt mixture is a Greek specialty, literally made in minutes, and is served with grilled fish or meat or as an accompanying salad.

1 crisp cucumber, peeled and cut into ⅛–¼-inch pieces
1–2 garlic cloves, crushed
dash of lemon juice
2 cups Greek yogurt or best-quality plain yogurt (not low-fat)
⅓ cup cream (optional)
2½ heaped tablespoons chopped dill
salt, freshly ground pepper, and sugar to taste

If you have time, put the chopped cucumber into a strainer, sprinkle with salt, and let it drain for about 15 minutes. This drains out extra moisture. Put into a bowl and mix with the crushed garlic, a dash of lemon juice, the yogurt, and cream if you like a really creamy texture. Stir in the dill, taste, and season with the salt, pepper, and sugar.

Roast Peppers

There are three ways to roast peppers:
1. Preheat the broiler, or better still, use a charcoal grill or barbecue. Broil the peppers on all sides, allowing them to become quite charred.
2. Preheat the oven to 475°F. Place the peppers on a baking tray and bake for 20–30 minutes until the skin blisters and the flesh is soft.
3. Put a wire rack over a mild gas jet, then roast the pepper on all sides until charred.

When the peppers are roasted, put them into a bowl and cover tightly with plastic wrap for a few minutes to make them much easier to peel. Pull the skin off the peppers and remove the stalks and seeds. Do not wash the peppers or you will lose the precious sweet juices. Divide each pepper into 2 or 3 pieces along the natural division. They will keep for 1–2 days in the fridge.

Onion Marmalade

MAKES 2 CUPS

This is especially delicious with pâtés and terrines of meat, game, poultry, and goat cheese. It will keep for months.

1/4 cup (1/2 stick) butter
1 1/2 pounds onions, thinly sliced
2/3 cup sugar
1 teaspoon salt
1/2 teaspoon freshly ground black pepper
1/2 cup sherry vinegar
1 cup full-bodied red wine
2 1/2 tablespoons crème de cassis

Melt the butter in a saucepan until it becomes a deep nut brown color. Toss in the onions and sugar, add the salt and pepper, and stir well. Cover the saucepan and cook for 30 minutes over a gentle heat, stirring from time to time with a wooden spatula.

Add the sherry vinegar, red wine, and crème de cassis. Cook for another 30 minutes uncovered, stirring regularly.

Core the tomatoes and cut a cross into the bottom of each one. Put the tomatoes in a deep bowl and pour boiling water over them, then count to ten and drain gently. Peel off the skins.

Chop roughly then transfer to a stainless steel saucepan and add the sugar. Grate the zest of the orange and lemon, then juice the citrus fruit. Add the zest and juice to the pan.

Warm a heavy frying pan over a medium heat. Put the star anise, cardamom pods, coriander seeds, juniper berries, cloves, and peppercorns into the pan, and stir for 2–3 minutes until fragrant. Turn into a mortar and grind with a pestle. Discard the cardamom husks, then add the ground spices to the tomatoes. Split the vanilla bean and add it to the saucepan.

Cook the mixture over a low heat for about 30 minutes, until all the tomatoes have softened. When the jam thickens slightly, pour into small clean jars. Cover and seal.

Let the jam mellow for a few days before using. It will keep in a cool, dark place for several months but store it in the fridge after opening.

Pickled Lemons

This is a brilliant unorthodox method which Claudia Roden showed us a few years ago when she taught a class with Diana Kennedy at the Cookery School

8 lemons
8 tablespoons salt
Sunflower or arachide oil

With a good sharp knife make 8 fine superficial, not deep incisions into the lemon skin from one end of the lemon to the other. Put the lemons into a large stainless steel saucepan and cover with salted water. Put a plate or smaller lid on top of them to keep them down, otherwise they float. Cover and boil for 25-30 minutes or until the peels are very soft. When cool enough to handle, scoop out the flesh, pack the skins into a glass jar and cover with oil.

Polenta

SERVES 6–8

Cornmeal or polenta can be served the moment it's ready, while it's still soft and flowing, or it can be poured into a dish and allowed to get cold. When cold, it can be sliced and charbroiled, panbroiled, or fried, and served with all sorts of toppings. It can even be cut into thin slices and layered with a sauce, just like lasagne. When cooking and stirring polenta I use a whisk at the beginning, but as soon as it comes to a boil I change to a flat-bottomed wooden spoon.

2 quarts water
2 level teaspoons sea salt (or Kosher salt)
1 1/2 cups coarse polenta flour (coarse cornmeal)—if using quick-cook polenta, follow the instructions on the package

Pour the water into a deep heavy pot and bring to a boil. Add the salt, then very thinly and gradually sprinkle in the polenta, whisking all the time—this should take you 3–4 minutes. Bring to a boil, stirring continuously, and when it starts to bubble and "erupt" like a volcano, reduce the heat down to the absolute minimum—use a heat diffuser mat if you have one. Simmer, stirring regularly, for about 40 minutes.* The polenta is cooked when it is very thick but not solid, and comes away from the sides of the pot as you stir.

* If, after the polenta has come to a boil, you reduce the heat to medium and stir continuously, the cooking time can be reduced to about 20 minutes, but polenta is more digestible if cooked more slowly over a longer period.

Soft, Wet, or Creamy Polenta

Wonderful with game birds or juicy meat or vegetable stews. It can also be served with a rich tomato sauce and spicy sausages.

polenta as cooked in previous recipe
1/2 cup (1 stick) butter
3 ounces Parmesan cheese, grated (about 1 1/2 cups)

sea salt (or Kosher salt) and freshly
  ground pepper
fresh sage leaves, fried briefly

As soon as the polenta is cooked, add the
butter, Parmesan, and some pepper. Taste,
and add a little salt if needed. The polenta
should be soft and flowing; if it is a little too
stiff, add a few tablespoons boiling water.
Serve immediately. A few fried sage leaves
are a delicious addition.

Polenta with Fresh Herbs
Add 1/4–1/3 cup of freshly chopped herbs,
such as parsley, chives, thyme leaves, sage,
and rosemary into the polenta when it is
cooked.

Charbroiled Polenta

**Cold polenta can be cut into squares,
diamonds, or slices and stored, covered, in
the fridge for several days. Grilled or fried, it
makes the most delicious snacks or
accompaniment to meat or fish dishes, or
you can make a sophisticated appetizer for a
dinner party in just a few minutes.**

Make the polenta in the usual way (see
opposite).

Sprinkle water over a dish—I use a lasagne
dish (9 x 7 inches), which is just perfect for
this quantity, but a jelly roll pan is also good.
Pour in the cooked polenta and let it cool.
When cold, cut it into slices 1/2–3/4-inch
thick. The slices can be reheated
immediately, or covered and stored in the
fridge until needed.

To reheat, charbroil, panbroil, or pan-fry the
slices. If grilling, put the slices directly on the
bars of the grill at the highest heat, without
oil, and cook until hot through and grill-
marked on each side. If the polenta is to be
sautéed, use a little olive oil or butter.

foods to keep on hand

**Busy people who want to be able to whizz
up quick and easy meals in minutes will
need to make sure that their fridge and
cupboards are always well stocked. The
following are some suggestions for items
that we find invaluable.**

To keep in stock
Aged cheddar cheese
Ballymaloe Cucumber Pickle
Ballymaloe Tomato Relish
Butter
Canned beans, chickpeas
Carrots
Chicken broth/cube
Crackers or Carrs Water Biscuits
Dried fruit, especially apricots
Eggs, cage-free and organic if possible
English mustard powder
Extra virgin olive oil
Fish: sardines, tuna fish, anchovies
Flour, e.g., all-purpose, self rising,
  brown bread flour, white bread flour,
  coarse whole-wheat
French mustard
Garlic
Good-quality dark chocolate
Grains, e.g., couscous, bulgar, quinoa
Harissa or chili sauce
Homemade jam
Honey
Marmalade
Nam pla (fish sauce)
Nuts, e.g., hazelnuts, walnuts, and almonds
Oatmeal
Olives

Onions
Oyster Sauce
Parmesan cheese
Pasta/noodles/macaroni/shells/penne, etc.
Peanut and sunflower oil
Pesto
Pita bread (in the freezer)
Plum sauce
Polenta or cornmeal
Potatoes
Red and white wine vinegar
Rice, e.g., basmati, Thai fragrant
Salami, chorizo
Salt: Maldon or Halen Mon sea salt,
  or Kosher salt
Sesame oil
Tortillas

Easy Entertaining Equipment
Fondue set
Paella cooker
Raclette set
Waffle iron

index

credits

The author and publisher would like to thank the following for their kind help with props and locations:
Red plastic bowls on pp.l04–105: **Guzzini,** London.
Red suede cushions on pp.102–103: **Alma Leather,** London.
Daisy curtains, metal trays with wooden handles on p.191: **Dotcomgiftshop.com**

Plastic tablecloth, lace glasses, paper doilys on party bags and under cupcakes on pp.190–195: **Lovely, Lovely at Selfridges,** London.
Green plastic 3-tier cake stand, pink metal jug, paper party bags on pp.190–195: **Urchin,** London.
Striped candles, star-shaped and heart-shaped sparklers on pp.192–195: **Talking**

Tables, London.
Striped "Happy" cushions on p.191: **Life at Nettlebed,** London.
Indian umbrella on p.261: **Source,** London
Cushions on p.261: **Life at Nettlebed,** London.
Flask on p.261: **Dotcomgiftshop.com**
Location on pp.46–49 through **Olive Locations,** London.